SOCIAL INSTITUTIONS AND INTERNATIONAL HUMAN RIGHTS LAW IMPLEMENTATION

Having articulated numerous human rights norms and standards in international treaties, the pressing challenge today is their realisation in States' parties around the world. Domestic implementation has proven a difficult task for national authorities as well as international supervisory bodies. This book examines the traditional State-Centric and legalistic approach to implementation, critiquing its limited efficacy in practice and failure to connect with local cultures. The book therefore explores the permissibility of other measures of implementation, and advocates more culturally sensitive approaches involving social institutions. Through an interdisciplinary case study of Islam in Indonesia, the book demonstrates the power of social institutions like religion to promote rights compliant positions and behaviours. Like the preamble of the 1948 Universal Declaration of Human Rights, the book reiterates the role not just of the State but indeed 'every organ of society' in realising rights.

Julie Fraser is a human rights lawyer with experience in both academia and practice. As an Assistant Professor with the Netherlands Institute of Human Rights (SIM) at Utrecht University, Julie has published, presented, and taught on topics including human rights law, women's rights, and transitional justice.

SOCIAL INSTITUTIONS AND INTERNATIONAL HUMAN RIGHTS LAW IMPLEMENTATION

Every Organ of Society

JULIE FRASER
Utrecht University

CAMBRIDGE
UNIVERSITY PRESS

University Printing House, Cambridge CB2 8BS, United Kingdom

One Liberty Plaza, 20th Floor, New York, NY 10006, USA

477 Williamstown Road, Port Melbourne, VIC 3207, Australia

314–321, 3rd Floor, Plot 3, Splendor Forum, Jasola District Centre, New Delhi – 110025, India

79 Anson Road, #06–04/06, Singapore 079906

Cambridge University Press is part of the University of Cambridge.

It furthers the University's mission by disseminating knowledge in the pursuit of education, learning, and research at the highest international levels of excellence.

www.cambridge.org
Information on this title: www.cambridge.org/9781108489577
DOI: 10.1017/9781108777711
© Julie Fraser 2020

This publication is in copyright. Subject to statutory exception and to the provisions of relevant collective licensing agreements, no reproduction of any part may take place without the written permission of Cambridge University Press.

First published 2020

A catalogue record for this publication is available from the British Library.

Library of Congress Cataloging-in-Publication Data
Names: Fraser, Julie, 1981– author.
Title: Social institutions and international human rights law implementation : every organ of society / Julie Fraser, Utrecht University.
Description: Cambridge, United Kingdom ; New York, NY, USA : Cambridge University Press, 2020. | Based on author's thesis (doctoral - Universiteit Utrecht, 2018) issued under title: "Every organ of society" : exploring the role of social institutions in the effective implementation of international human rights law. | Includes bibliographical references and index.
Identifiers: LCCN 2020009259 (print) | LCCN 2020009260 (ebook) | ISBN 9781108489577 (hardback) | ISBN 9781108777711 (epub)
Subjects: LCSH: Human rights–Social aspects. | International and municipal law. | Human rights and international law. | Human rights advocacy. | Civil rights (Islamic law)–Indonesia.
Classification: LCC K3240 .F727 2020 (print) | LCC K3240 (ebook) | DDC 341.4/8–dc23
LC record available at https://lccn.loc.gov/2020009259
LC ebook record available at https://lccn.loc.gov/2020009260

ISBN 978-1-108-48957-7 Hardback

Cambridge University Press has no responsibility for the persistence or accuracy of URLs for external or third-party internet websites referred to in this publication and does not guarantee that any content on such websites is, or will remain, accurate or appropriate.

To Elizabeth Reed, a.k.a. Gramses

CONTENTS

Foreword by An-Na'im   x
Acknowledgements   xviii

1 **Introduction: The Challenge of Human Rights Implementation**   1
  1.1 Introduction   1
  1.2 Countering Legalism, State-Centricity and Cultural Disconnect   7
  1.3 Terminology, Methodology and Case Study   14
     1.3.1 Why Islam, Indonesia and Women's Reproductive Rights?   16
     1.3.2 Structure of the Book   19

2 **Human Rights and Their Cultural Connection**   21
  2.1 Introduction   21
  2.2 Human Rights and Their History of Cultural Critiques   23
     2.2.1 Founding a Universal System of Human Rights: The UDHR   23
     2.2.2 Continued Cultural Challenges to Universality   29
     2.2.3 International Human Rights Today   35
  2.3 Culturally Sensitive Approaches to Human Rights Implementation   41
     2.3.1 Need and Scope for Cultural Sensitivity in Human Rights Implementation   42
     2.3.2 Reducing Reliance upon State Law   44
     2.3.3 Home-Grown Human Rights Solutions   48
     2.3.4 Utilising Culture's Dynamism and Contestation to Advance Human Rights   54
     2.3.5 Effectiveness of Culturally Sensitive Approaches to Implementation   58
  2.4 Conclusion: Human Rights and Their Cultural Connection   61

3 Domestic Implementation of International Human Rights Treaties: Legislative and Other Effective Measures 64

3.1 Introduction 64
3.2 UN Human Rights Treaties and State Discretion in Implementation Measures 66
    3.2.1 State Discretion in International Law 67
    3.2.2 Preference for Domestic Legal Incorporation 71
    3.2.3 Legalisation of Human Rights 76
    3.2.4 Other Measures for Implementing Human Rights 80
    3.2.5 Other Measures of Implementation: Permitted but Peripheral 87
3.3 UN Human Rights Treaty Bodies and Other Measures of Implementation 88
    3.3.1 UN Treaty Bodies' Reporting Guidelines 90
    3.3.2 UN Treaty Bodies' Concluding Observations 94
    3.3.3 UN Treaty Bodies and Other Measures: Always an Afterthought? 108
3.4 Conclusions: Legislative and Other Effective Implementation Measures 111

4 Domestic Implementation of International Human Rights Treaties: The Role of Public and Private Actors 114

4.1 Introduction 114
4.2 The State versus Everyone Else: Unhelpful Dichotomies in Human Rights 116
4.3 NSAs: Human Rights Responsibilities and (Indirect) Obligations 120
    4.3.1 NSAs' Obligations and Responsibilities under UN Declarations and Principles 121
    4.3.2 NSAs' Obligations and Responsibilities under UN Human Rights Treaties 125
    4.3.3 Hide and Seek: NSAs' Human Rights Responsibilities and Obligations 141
4.4 Privatising Human Rights Implementation and Shifting Obligations 143
    4.4.1 Privatisation of Healthcare and International Human Rights Law 145
    4.4.2 Privatising Health: Shifting State Obligations from Fulfilling to Protecting 148
    4.4.3 Privatising Health: Shifting NSAs' Obligations from National to International? 153
    4.4.4 Privatising Rights Implementation: A Delicate Balance 158
4.5 Conclusions: Public and Private Actors in Domestic Implementation 160

5 Role of Islamic Law and Institutions in Implementing Women's Right to Family Planning in Indonesia 164

- 5.1 Introduction 164
  - 5.1.1 Research Design and Structure 167
- 5.2 Right to Reproductive Health under International Law and in Indonesia 168
  - 5.2.1 Reproductive Health and the Right to Family Planning under International Law 170
  - 5.2.2 Reproductive Health and the Right to Family Planning in Indonesia 180
  - 5.2.3 Reproductive Rights in International Law and Indonesia: A Community Concern 202
- 5.3 Family Planning, Islamic Law and Institutions in Indonesia 205
  - 5.3.1 Abridged Introduction to Islamic Law 206
  - 5.3.2 Islamic Law and Institutions in Indonesia 210
  - 5.3.3 Role of Islamic Law and Institutions in Indonesia's Family Planning Programme 215
  - 5.3.4 Pursuing Reproductive and Other Women's Rights through Islam 225
  - 5.3.5 Family Planning in Indonesia: Islam As a Master Key? 246
- 5.4 Reproductive Rights, Islam, Indonesia and the UN Human Rights Treaty Bodies 250
  - 5.4.1 Indonesia's Use of Social Institutions: Compliant with International Law? 250
  - 5.4.2 UN Treaty Body Recommendations to Indonesia on Reproductive Rights 253
  - 5.4.3 UN Treaty Bodies and Social Institutions: A Missed Opportunity 261
- 5.5 Conclusions: Role of Islamic Law and Institutions in Implementing Women's Right to Family Planning in Indonesia 263

6 Conclusions: Social Institutions and the Future of Domestic Human Rights Implementation 268

- 6.1 Introduction 268
- 6.2 Connecting Rights to Communities: In Search of Better Narratives 270
- 6.3 All the Tools in the Toolbox: Rejecting Legalism in Implementation 276
- 6.4 Going beyond State-Centricity in Human Rights 281
- 6.5 Recommendations (or Where to Next?) 287

Select Bibliography 293
Index 312

FOREWORD

Reflections on the Mediation of the Universality of Human Rights

ABDULLAHI AHMED AN-NA'IM

I am delighted to offer this foreword to the outstanding book by Dr Julie Anne Fraser on the prospects of a sustainable practice of human rights around the world and specifically in the Muslim world. I am gratified to read her analysis and reflection on the dynamic evolution of cross-cultural perspectives on the multiple foundations of the universality of human rights. At a moral and intuitive level, the claim that human rights are due to every person by virtue of their humanity indicates that these rights should be protected for every person everywhere. While this proposition sounds reasonable and straightforward, questions of who is to protect the human rights of whom and how, and who is to evaluate the practice and how, remain intractable and problematic from an international law and international relations perspective. This book and this foreword address these issues.

The overarching legal and political difficulties for the international protection of human rights relate to the 'sovereignty and territorial integrity' of States, and were clear from the beginning of the Charter of the United Nations (UN) in 1945. Article 2.4 of the Charter provides: 'All Members [of the UN] shall refrain in their international relations from the threat or use of force against the territorial integrity or political independence of any state, or in any other manner inconsistent with the Purposes of the United Nations.' Article 2.7 emphasises that 'Nothing contained in the present Charter shall authorize the United Nations to intervene in matters which are essentially within the domestic jurisdiction of any state or shall require the Members to submit such matters to settlement under the present Charter; but this principle shall not prejudice the application of enforcement measures under Chapter VII.' These provisions indicate a broad outline of the protection of sovereignty and territorial integrity of States parties to the UN

Charter, in addition to the categorical principles of customary international law.[1]

In view of this very specific and limited authorisation of the use of force (i.e. either self-defence or as authorised by the Security Council under Chapter VII), there is no legal justification for unilateral extra-institutional (i.e. by one or a few states) action outside the UN's framework – such as the so-called humanitarian intervention into another State under the guise of protecting human rights. Whatever the justification claimed for the use of force, it must be established under international law and not some vague geopolitical reasoning or historical pretentions. It is reckless and irresponsible for the Permanent Members of the UN Security Council – especially the USA and Russia – to frequently violate the sovereignty and territorial integrity of many smaller and weaker States, often without bothering to offer any legal justification. This does not make the action lawful by the criteria of legality under international law. The legality of intervention must be the subject of a positive rule and doctrine, rather than simply assumed to be lawful by default.

Claims of the universality of the concept of human rights in general, or of specific human rights claims, are all inherently relative to the location and context of supporters and opponents alike. It is therefore what I call the 'overlapping consensus' of different cultural traditions and the practice of their respective communities that bestow the quality of being a human right. For example, as quoted by Hossein Houshmand in an article: 'An-Na'im says, "If international human rights standards are to be implemented in a manner consistent with their own rationale, the people (who are to implement these standards) must perceive the concept of human rights and its content as their own. To be committed to carrying out human rights standards, people must hold these standards as emanating from their worldview and values."'[2] The fact that Houshmand, an apparently Shi'i Muslim scholar from Iran, is quoting me, a Sunni Muslim scholar from Sudan, may indicate the possibilities for a global Muslim consensus on the process of identifying broad-based Muslim perspectives on the universality of human rights among Muslims.

---

[1] *The Republic of Nicaragua v. The United States of America* (1986) International Court of Justice Report 14.

[2] Abdullahi Ahmed An-Na'im, *Human Rights in Cross-Cultural Perspectives: A Quest for Consensus* (University of Pennsylvania Press 1992) p. 431, quoted by Hossein Houshmand, *Human Rights*, Volume 9, Numbers 1, 2, (Summer 2014, Winter 2015) 1-18, at p. 18. For a broader application of similar strategies see Andrew March, *Islam and Liberal Citizenship: The Search for an Overlapping Consensus* (Oxford University Press 2009).

For global humanity to be and to remain entitled to these rights, all human beings must be entitled to assert what they believe to be their entitlements as human rights from their own perspectives. For one community to presume to impose its view of human rights on other communities – or to deny the claim of others to assert their view in the same way – is an inherent contradiction to equal human dignity as the foundation of all human rights. This view is rooted in the claim of universality itself, which must be globally inclusive to support the concept and its normative contents. On the other hand, however, there is the inescapable paradox of normative relativity and local contextualisation of the practice of any doctrine of the universality of human rights. The apparent deadlock is that the universality of any human right can neither be imposed nor left to arbitrary unilateral choice. The hypocrisy and double standards of the present fiasco continue even when the text of human rights treaties is categorical and without exceptions, while the practice is driven by the expediency of propaganda and public relations.

Once such stark choices are laid out in such clear terms, human rights advocates will have to either abandon the pretense of rights' conformity with uniformity or as mediated through cultural transformation and political mobilisation. I propose mediation, across cultural perspectives, instead of unilateral imposition by one community upon another. Unilateral imposition of purported uniform human rights norms will not only fail in every instance but also undermine the broader principles and practice of respect for individual human dignity and collective social justice. A more realistic and sustainable approach is to follow and mediate human practice, instead of preempting uniformity by seeking to force different cultural norms and experiences into preconceived normative imperatives.

For instance, most international human rights treaties allow for exceptions and States tend to make their ratification of human rights treaties subject to 'reservations, declarations and understandings' to limit and adapt their obligations under the treaties to the values and socioeconomic context of their populations. The lack of coercive enforcement of human rights treaties also enables consensus to evolve among States which are parties to treaties and international organisations charged with supervising the implementation of the obligations created by the treaties over time and so forth. There are also possibilities for training and deliberations regarding some major human rights fields, such as the World Health Organization, Convention on the Rights of the Child and UNESCO, where State officials interact with relevant agencies and experts to inform and develop their national compliance with the human rights in questions. Still, there is a constant tension between national policies and political context on the one hand, and international human rights obligations on the other. That tension may also reflect lingering resentment of European colonialism and continued under-development.

There are many plausible theories for the colonial/imperial thrust of Europe into different regions of the world, but a dynamic mix of cultural and geopolitical relations probably constitute some of the most likely factors, especially in the relations of Europe with North Africa and Asia.[3] This dimension may be the most relevant here in view of Fraser's focus on Islam in Indonesia in Southeast Asia. Various parts of the region have been in close contact since ancient times, but the recent colonial and current neocolonial entanglements have been more transformative of traditional Muslim communities. As a result of these combinations of events and changing dynamics of relations, Muslim societies emerged as separate nations, with their respective States subject to the general principles governing the behaviour of States which are members of comprehensive international organisations. In reacting to their new environment, Muslim communities are reacting to what they know about the history, geopolitics, ethical assumptions, etc. of the present international order and how it works.

For instance, the League of Nations' Mandate for France and the United Kingdom in the East Mediterranean territories of the defeated Ottoman Empire enabled those European colonial powers to define and establish the nation-states of Iraq, Lebanon, Syria, Jordan and Israel. From the perspective of the Muslims of the region, those former Western colonial powers are implicated in the violent instability throughout that region by the end of the twentieth and beginning of the twenty-first centuries, denying the Palestinian right to self-determination, and the deadlock between Turkey, Syria and the Kurdish communities in the region. The UN human rights system emerged under the authority of the UN Charter, and international trade is now regulated by the World Trade Organization (from the GATT in 1947 to WTO since 1995). Again, these institutions are likely to be perceived by some Muslims as tools of Western imperialism and economic exploitation.

The point of the preceding reflections is that the international human rights paradigm should not be taken in isolation of the recent colonial

---

[3] See, for example, Edward W. Said, *Orientalism* (Vintage Books 1979); *Culture and Imperialism* (Vintage Publishing 1994).

and post-colonial histories of different regions of the world and their populations. Such histories are unlikely to be taken by local populations as separate or independent of other aspects of international factors and policy issues, like the universality of human rights. Indeed, how can human rights advocates expect or even assume that their activities are taken by post-colonial communities as innocent and independent of the colonial history and post-colonial relations with Western powers and their foreign policy agenda? Human rights attitudes and policies accepted by Western communities are likely to be seen elsewhere as the outcome of a brutal colonisation continuing into post-colonial hegemony, rather than mandated by their own traditional, cultural or religious factors. This does not mean that the cultural legitimacy of human rights is never contested or deemed irrelevant anywhere, but only says that such legitimacy and relevance must be founded on the experiences and values of the relevant communities of believers. Fraser well elaborates this view in her case study from Indonesia.

To reflect on the mediation of human rights in relation to Islam and Muslims, I would first note that I prefer the term 'Muslims' to include all persons and communities who self-identify as Muslims, over the term 'Islamic', which is an ambiguous and contested notion that is claimed by all sort of actors in relation to divergent and contradictory objectives. The question of whether Islam as a world religion is innocent or guilty is incoherent in this context because Islam in the abstract is not an entity that can be or act one way or the other. For instance, Boko Haram members in Northeast Nigeria claim their movement to be Islamic, while to the majority of Muslims in Nigeria and around the world, the views and actions of the members of Boko Haram are antithetical to Islam. We should also recall the chauvinistic and counter-chauvinistic historical and current agenda for attributing moral agency – or the lack of it – to Islam.

It is more productive to emphasise that it is always Muslims who believe, think, decide and act one way or the other in their own specific historical context, and not Islam as the religion of a quarter of humanity today, from West China, to Southeast Asia and West Africa. Locating the issues within the human agency of Muslims makes it possible for them to act or to refrain from acting in one way or another, while describing the issues as Islamic as such makes it beyond the ability of Muslims to change. As a Muslim, I can respond to the conflicting claims of Iran, Saudi Arabia and others, for instance, to be 'Islamic' by explaining why I disagree with such competing human interpretations of Islam and presenting my own alternative interpretation for a humane Islamic alternative to all of those perspectives. Yet, there is no coherent way to evaluate which position is more truly Islamic than the other. There is no specific form of political doctrine of Islam, except for general principles like respect for human dignity, justice and seeking consultative accountable government, which have always been believed to be practiced by a variety of monarchial, republican or despotic regimes.

Once the sources, methodologies and main Schools of Islamic Jurisprudence (*Madhahib*) that formulated the structure and content of what is now known as Sharia were established by the tenth century CE, those methodologies and principles enjoyed a great deal of stability for extended periods of time until recently. In the belief that those founding Schools have elaborated all that can and should be known about Sharia, the masses of Muslims found it safer to blindly follow (*taqlid*) one scholar or follow one *Madhahib*, instead of accepting responsibility for their own independent choice among competing views. To justify the practice of *taqlid* since the tenth century, Muslim scholars invented the fiction of 'closing of the gate of *Ijtihad*' although there was no gate to be closed and no one had the religious authority to close it even if it existed.

It may be understandable that Muslim scholars did that to enforce what they believed to be politically and socially necessary for stability and conformity, but the consequence has been a highly unacceptable degree of stagnation. While there may have been minor adjustments or variations among and within the *Madhahib*, that could only be done within the sources and methodologies of the established *fiqh*. Although it is widely acknowledged among Muslims that there is now a need for fresh *Ijtihad* to address the problematic aspects of traditional formulations of Sharia, Muslims at large have generally failed to produce a coherent and legitimate methodology for Islamic reform to deal with those aspects based on Quran and Sunna. The only exception in my view is *Ustadh* Mahmoud Mohamed Taha of Sudan, who was executed on 18 January 1985, following a sham trial for apostasy.[4]

Here lay the deep-rooted causes of the religious dimension of the ambivalence of Muslims regarding some major human rights issues, such as the rights of women and non-Muslims, and the freedom of religion and belief.[5] While failing to address the obvious problems, Muslim

---

[4] Abdullahi Ahmed An-Na'im, The Islamic Law of Apostasy and its Modern Applicability: A Case from The Sudan, *Religion* (1986) Vol. 16 pp. 197-223.
[5] See generally, Abdullahi Ahmed An-Na'im, *Toward an Islamic Reformation: Civil Liberties, Human Rights and International Law* (Syracuse University Press 1990).

discourse about Islam and human rights is totally apologetic: refusing to acknowledge the problems with traditional Sharia, yet claiming exaggerated credit for traditional Muslim scholars who upheld human rights even before the concept was known to other human societies. While prohibiting chattel slavery in their modern legal systems as totally abhorrent, Muslims today still fail to address the issue from the perspective of Sharia. The reason for this confusion is not only that the gate of *Ijtihad* is believed to be closed but also that even if it is wide open, *Ijtihad* is not permitted by traditional methodologies (*usul al-Fiqh*) to challenge any principles of Sharia that are founded on explicit or categorical texts of the Quran or Sunna. Scores of Muslim scholars since the nineteenth century have called for the opening of the gate of *Ijtihad*, yet none of them have so far actually practiced *Ijtihad* in order to provide Muslims with a coherent methodology that enables them to repudiate aggressive Jihad to propagate Islam or to end the institution of slavery from a Sharia perspective.

The only exception, to my knowledge, is *Ustadh* Mahmoud Mohamed Taha who proposed shifting the basis of Sharia from the Quran and Sunna of the latter Medina stage, to that of the earlier Mecca stage. As he explained in his book *The Second Message of Islam*,[6] Taha argued that Sharia principles founded on the Medina revelations, which was the first message of Islam, authorised aggressive Jihad to spread Islam and the subordination of women to men, and of non-Muslims to Muslims. Those principles, argued Taha, were transitional, while the universal principles of justice, equality and human dignity founded on the Mecca revelations, which he called 'the second message', did not include any of those principles. Fraser's study of Islam in Indonesia highlights these same principles of justice, equality and dignity. Taha argued that the postponed second message of Islam is now applicable because humanity at large is ready to live up to those standards through the tripartite principles of political and economic equality and social justice (democracy, socialism and social justice). He also emphasised the imperative requirements of self-determination and peaceful international relations under the rule of international law.

I believe that *Ustadh* Mahmoud's methodology is coherent and consistent with original Islamic principles and will be acceptable to Muslims

---

[6] The original edition of Taha's book was published in Arabic in 1967. The first English translation, as *The Second Message of Islam,* was published in 1987.

if presented to them in a peaceful and orderly manner. Competing methodologies should also be presented for debate. The question for this foreword is whether domestic and international conditions do, in fact, support the optimistic claim that humanity in the twenty-first century is ready for the second message of Islam.

ACKNOWLEDGEMENTS

This book is the product of over five years' work and the input of many people. It is based on my PhD research, which was funded by the Dutch Government and supervised by Prof. Dr Tom Zwart (Utrecht University) and Prof. Dr Yvonne Donders (University of Amsterdam). To them I am indebted. I also wish to acknowledge and thank the members of my PhD Defence Committee, Prof. Dr Abdullahi Ahmed An-Na`im (Emory University), Prof. Dr Eva Brems (Ghent University), Prof. Dr Antoine Buyse (Utrecht University), Dr Lucien van Liere (Utrecht University) and Prof. Dr Barbara Oomen (Utrecht University).

I am grateful for the input and camaraderie of all of my colleagues at the Netherlands Institute of Human Rights (SIM) and the Montaigne Centre for the Rule of Law and Administration of Justice at Utrecht University, including Dr Stacey Links, Dr Qiao Cong-rui and Dr Brianne McGonigle Leyh. I have benefited from the close and supportive academic community in the Netherlands, which included the members of the Netherlands Network of Human Rights Researchers and the focus area of Culture, Citizenship and Human Rights. I was also grateful to have participated in international networks with other scholars who kindly shared their expertise, including the Association of Human Rights Institutes, the Asian Law Institute and the Cross-Cultural Human Rights Centre.

Given that this book is based on field work and empirical research, I must acknowledge and thank the many people who assisted me. In particular, I am grateful for the guidance of Ms Pramila Patten, Ms Hilary Gbedemah and Prof. Dr Kees Flinterman. To all of my colleagues and interview participants in Indonesia, this book would simply not have been the same without you. Thank you for your time, your insights and your inspiration. I am lucky to have been able to go abroad for research, and acknowledge the privileges I enjoyed (but did not earn).

In my research I was supported by a number of women who helped me directly and indirectly, personally and professionally. I would like to acknowledge them, as well as all of the women in academia who blazed the trail before me. I am grateful also for the comments of peer reviewers, as well as the invaluable editorial and secretarial support I received. To everyone who read a chapter, debated a concept or simply listened to me thinking out loud – thank you. I shall pay the favour forwards.

Finally, to all my friends and family, I am grateful for your patience and positivity. The success is made meaningful when shared with you. For the lifetime of love and support that I have received from my biggest fans, Carol, Col and Shell, I can only say thank you. And to my love, David, thank you for holding my hand throughout.

1

Introduction: The Challenge of Human Rights Implementation

1.1 Introduction

The world's first ever gathering of women Muslim clerics (*ulama*) was held for three days in April 2017 at an Islamic Boarding School in Cirebon, West Java, Indonesia. Hundreds of participants, including both female and male *ulama*, academics, journalists and activists, attended the National Congress of Female Muslim Clerics, an event years in the making.[1] While most participants were Indonesian, foreign representatives were also present from countries including Saudi Arabia, Pakistan, India, Nigeria and Kenya. Addressing themes such as 'Amplifying Women Ulama's Voices, Asserting Values of Islam, Nationhood and Humanity', the Congress sought to recognise and celebrate female *ulama*, and to address pressing issues facing women such as sexual violence, religious extremism, child marriage and polygamy. While addressing these serious issues, the Congress was also an opportunity and space for women *ulama* to develop contacts, build networks and share experiences. The Congress included cultural and musical performances and even provided reproductive healthcare services to participants.

At the Congress, the *ulama* issued rare religious rulings (*fatwas*) against child marriage, sexual violence and environmental destruction. Simply issuing the *fatwas* was an historic act, as male *ulama* have typically monopolised this exercise. The Indonesian Ulama Council (*Majelis Ulama Indonesia* – MUI), one of the main bodies in Indonesia

---

[1] See the official website (in Bahasa Indonesia) of the Congress (Kongres Ulama Perempuan Indonesia) https://kupi-cirebon.net (accessed 14 November 2017). Select parts of this introduction were published as Julie Fraser, In Search of New Narratives: The Role of Cultural Norms and Actors in Addressing Human Rights Contestation, in Rosemarie Buikema, Antoine Buyse and Antonius Robben (eds.), *Cultures, Citizenship and Human Rights* (Routledge, 2019), pp. 175–95; Julie Fraser, Challenging State-Centricity and Legalism: Promoting the Role of Social Institutions in the Domestic Implementation of International Human Rights Law (2019) *The International Journal of Human Rights* 23:6, pp. 974–92.

that issues *fatwas*, is comprised almost entirely of men.[2] The Congress' *fatwas* are therefore an important symbol of the women *ulamas'* religious authority. The *fatwa* against child marriage is all the more noteworthy given that MUI and other Islamic institutions continue to support child marriage, which has long been legal under Indonesian State law despite being contrary to international human rights law.[3] Child marriage is widespread across Indonesia, which has one of the highest number of child brides worldwide, with one in seven girls married before they turn 18.[4] In their *fatwa*, the women *ulama* argued for the minimum age for legal marriage to be set at 18 years for girls, and urged the Government to raise the current age from 16. While the *fatwa* (like all *fatwas*) is not legally binding, it holds great authority in Indonesia, the country with the largest Muslim population in the world. At its conclusion, the Congress presented their recommendations to Indonesia's Minister of Religious Affairs, on behalf of the Government.

This remarkable Congress was an initiative of Indonesian Muslim women who sought to counter male authority in Islam and the dominant male interpretations of Islamic law. Their strategy is to achieve this by 'strengthening the expertise and knowledge of female ulama, networking among them, affirmation and appreciation of their work, as well as strengthening their cultural existence'.[5] In their deliberations and argumentation at the Congress that gave rise to the *fatwas*, the women *ulama* used classical Islamic texts, including the *Qur'an* and the *Hadith* (the Prophet's sayings or statements). However, they also relied upon the Indonesian 1945 Constitution and international law, including the *Universal Declaration on Human Rights* (UDHR).[6] This is a prime example of how international human rights can be used by diverse groups in diverse ways. It shows how various actors beyond the state

---

[2] Nor Ismah, Destabilising Male Domination: Building Community-Based Authority among Indonesian Female Ulama (2016) *Asian Studies Review* 40:4, p. 491.

[3] See Indonesian Marriage Law No. 1 of 1974, article 7.

[4] UN Human Rights Council, Report of the Special Rapporteur on the Right of Everyone to the Enjoyment of the Highest Attainable Standard of Physical and Mental Health on His Mission to Indonesia, A/HRC/38/36/Add.1 (5 April 2018), paras. 91–2.

[5] Kongres Ulama Perempuan Indonesia, Amplifying Women Ulama's Voices, Asserting Values of Islam, Nationhood and Humanity, https://kupi-cirebon.net/international-forum-women-ulama/ (accessed 15 November 2017).

[6] Universal Declaration of Human Rights (adopted 10 December 1948), UNGA Res. 217 A(III) (UDHR).

are involved in the promotion and protection of human rights, and how they legitimise human rights in context by reference to social institutions like religion.

In fact, the following year, in December 2018, the Indonesian Constitutional Court unanimously ruled that the current legal age of 16 years for girls to marry was unconstitutional.[7] The case had been brought by three wives who had been pushed into childhood marriages and forced to quit school. The Court held that child marriage violated the Constitution's protection of a girl's right to education and to a healthy life, and that the differences in ages for boys and girls was discriminatory. Importantly, the Court referred to the *Convention on the Elimination of All Forms of Discrimination against Women* (CEDAW)[8] and to bringing Indonesian law into line with its international obligations. This decision is all the more remarkable, given that the same Court only three years earlier had declined to overturn the marriage age for girls.[9] Intervening in this period was the women *ulama's fatwa* against child marriage. While it is unclear exactly how much of an influence it had on the Constitutional Court's decision-making, given the authority of *fatwas* within Muslim communities, it is hoped that it may also succeed in curbing the high prevalence of child marriages in practice.

As this example shows, while vitally important to have international human rights law and the minimum standards as espoused in the numerous and growing treaties, it is the way the law is operationalised that makes an impact on people's lives. Without action at the national level, international human rights treaties are empty promises or 'dead letters'.[10] As such, the heart of human rights protection lies not in the creation or existence of international treaties, but in their domestic implementation.[11] However, the mismatch between treaty ratification and implementation 'is one of the most glaring shortcomings of the

---

[7] Indonesian Constitutional Court, Decision Number 22/PUU-XV/2017 relating to applicants Endang Wasrinah, Maryanti and Rasminah (13 December 2018). The Court gave the Indonesian Government three years to amend the Marriage Act appropriately.

[8] See section 3.16 of the Constitutional Court's judgment ibid. *Convention on the Elimination of All Forms of Discrimination against Women* (adopted 18 December 1979, entered into force 3 September 1981), 1249 UNTS 13 (CEDAW).

[9] Indonesian Constitutional Court, Decision Number 30-74/PUU-XII/2014 (2015).

[10] Oona Hathaway, Why Do Countries Commit to Human Rights Treaties? (2007) *Journal of Conflict Resolution* 51:4, p. 592.

[11] Rhona K. M. Smith, *Textbook on International Human Rights* (Oxford University Press, 2012), p. 177.

international human rights system'.[12] Therefore, this book addresses the pressing contemporary challenge of human rights implementation, which has been highlighted by UN Secretaries-General, High Commissioners for Human Rights, States and scholars.[13] It is through domestic action, like the women's Congress in Indonesia, that international human rights obligations can be transformed into reality. This action can and must take various forms.[14] Having established the framework of international human rights law, 'the ball is now in the court of the States and other international players to ensure its effective realization and implementation'.[15] While there is a role for international actors, like the UN treaty bodies, states are primarily responsible for the domestic implementation of international human rights treaties. This is a result of the state being designated as the principal duty-bearer in the treaties, and is connected to issues of sovereignty and consent in international law.

By ratifying the treaties, states undertake to respect and ensure to everyone in their jurisdiction the rights protected therein.[16] They are obliged to take all necessary steps to give effect to the rights by enacting legislation or undertaking other measures in political, economic, social and cultural fields.[17] While the treaties set out the standards to be

[12] Ilias Bantekas and Lutz Oette, *International Human Rights Law and Practice* (Cambridge University Press, 2013), p. 88. See also Michael Freeman, Putting Law in Its Place: An Interdisciplinary Evaluation of National Amnesty Laws, in Saladin Meckled-García and Başak Çali (eds.), *The Legalization of Human Rights: Multidisciplinary Perspectives on Human Rights and Human Rights Law* (Routledge, 2006), p. 50.

[13] See, for example, Mary Robinson, From Rhetoric to Reality: Making Human Rights Work (2003) *European Human Rights Law Review* 2:1, pp. 1–8; Christof Heyns and Frans Viljoen, *The Impact of the United Nations Human Rights Treaties on the Domestic Level* (Kluwer Law International, 2002), p. 1; Jean-Philippe Thérien and Philippe Joly, 'All Human Rights for All': The United Nations and Human Rights in the Post-Cold War Era (2014) *Human Rights Quarterly* 36:2, pp. 380–1, citing UN Secretary-General, Report of the Secretary-General on the Work of the Organization, Delivered to the UN GA, A/62/1 (31 August 2007), para. 80; Office of the High Commissioner for Human Rights, Annual Report 2008: Activities and Results (30 April 2009) p. 5, www.ohchr.org/Documents/Press/OHCHR_Report_2008.pdf (accessed 14 November 2017).

[14] Ineke Boerefijn, International Human Rights in National Law, in Catarina Krause and Martin Scheinin (eds.), *International Protection of Human Rights: A Textbook* (Turku/Åbo: Åbo Akademi University, Institute for Human Rights 2009), p. 577.

[15] Smith (n. 11), p. 35.

[16] See, for example, *International Covenant on Civil and Political Rights* (adopted 16 December 1966, entered into force 23 March 1976), 999 UNTS 171 (ICCPR), art. 2(1); *Convention on the Rights of the Child* (adopted 20 November 1989, entered into force 2 September 1990), 1577 UNTS 3 (CRC), art. 2(1).

[17] See, for example, ICCPR, art. 2(2); CRC, art. 4; CEDAW, arts. 2 and 3.

achieved, they typically do not prescribe the methods by which to do so, as illustrated by the vague obligation to undertake 'other measures' of implementation.[18] As a general rule, states enjoy discretion as to how they implement a treaty in their domestic order – unless the treaty specifies implementing modalities.[19] This reflects the fact that the treaties uphold sovereignty and defer to the state to determine and implement the measures that will be most effective in context. While sovereignty has been deemed the 'Achilles heel' regarding the enforcement of the international human rights system,[20] it can be seen as better suited at the implementation stage. This is because implementation measures need to be contextualised in order to be effective, rather than simply one-size-fits-all. States are inherently well-placed to tailor implementation measures to suit their own national context.

This state discretion and tailoring of implementation measures are intrinsic parts of the system of international human rights law. While the human rights standards established in the treaties are to be enjoyed universally, the methods of state implementation do not need to be uniform.[21] Nor, in fact, should they be. The astounding diversity across the world's almost two hundred states rebuts any presumption of uniformity. The international system accommodates this diversity via multiple mechanisms, and this inclusiveness reaffirms the universal application of human rights. One of these mechanisms is state discretion in implementation, which can be used to accommodate diversity both between as well as within states.[22] For example, due to the cultural

---

[18] See, for example, ICCPR, art. 2(2); CRC, art. 4; CEDAW, art. 2.
[19] UN Human Rights Committee, General Comment No. 31, The Nature of the General Legal Obligations Imposed on States Parties to the Covenant, CCPR/C/21/Rev.1/Add.13 (29 March 2004), paras. 4, 13.
[20] Sarah Joseph and Joanna Kyriakakis, The United Nations and Human Rights, in Sarah Joseph and Adam McBeth (eds.), *Research Handbook on International Human Rights Law* (Edward Elgar, 2010), p. 1.
[21] Cees Flinterman, The Universal Declaration of Human Rights at 60 (2008) *Netherlands Quarterly of Human Rights* 26:4, p. 482; Eva Brems, Reconciling Universality and Diversity in International Human Rights: A Theoretical and Methodological Framework and Its Application in the Context of Islam (2004) *Human Rights Review* 5:3, p. 13.
[22] Yvonne Donders, Human Rights: Eye for Cultural Diversity, Inaugural Lecture delivered upon the appointment to the chair of Professor of International Human Rights and Cultural Diversity at the University of Amsterdam (29 June 2012), pp. 18–19. Other mechanisms to accommodate diversity in international human rights law include subsidiarity, limitation clauses, exhaustion of domestic remedies, and the margin of appreciation: David Kinley, Bendable Rules: The Development Implications of Human Rights

dimension[23] of almost all human rights, states must tailor their implementation measures to each context, with the result that measures may not be applicable let alone replicable elsewhere. According to the UN treaty bodies responsible for supervising states parties' implementation of the treaties, the controlling criteria for implementation measures is that rights are *effectively* protected – a duty of result not conduct.[24] It is the intention of the treaties, and therefore central to the work of the treaty bodies, that human rights are meaningfully enjoyed in practice, and not just protected in theory. Human rights make little sense if they only exist in the books.[25]

Despite broad treaty ratification and discretion in the system for the tailored domestic implementation, every state struggles to guarantee human rights to varying degrees. The gap therefore becomes apparent between the concept of rights and practice; between the norms and their implementation. There are various reasons for this gap, including limited political will and economic resources, as well as the disconnect between international human rights law and some cultural norms around the world. In the treaties, human rights are formulated as general and abstract principles as a compromise to ensure their universal application and to avoid bias towards any particular tradition. However, such framing does not directly or necessarily evoke the lived experiences and worldviews of many of their beneficiaries. In fact, in many places, human rights are perceived as foreign impositions separate from – or even at odds with – local cultural norms and values. On this basis, human rights are often rejected, sometimes explicitly in the name of culture. Since the drafting of the UDHR, this issue of cultural relativity has plagued debates on the universality of human rights. As this indicates, international human rights suffer from a legitimacy deficit in many communities, with 'battles for the universal recognition of human rights ... nowhere near won'.[26]

Pluralism, in Brian Tamanaha, Caroline Sage and Michael Woolcock (eds.), *Legal Pluralism and Development: Scholars and Practitioners in Dialogue* (Cambridge University Press, 2012), pp. 51–3.

[23] Donders, ibid., p. 17; Federico Lenzerini, *The Culturalization of Human Rights Law* (Oxford University Press, 2014), pp. 123, 152.

[24] Oscar Schachter, The Obligation of the Parties to Give Effect to the Covenant on Civil and Political Rights (1979) *The American Journal of International Law* 73:3, p. 462.

[25] Eva Brems, *Human Rights: Universality and Diversity* (Nijhoff, 2001), p. 311.

[26] Radhika Coomaraswamy, The Contemporary Challenges to International Human Rights, in Scott Sheeran and Sir Nigel Rodley (eds.), *Routledge Handbook of International Human Rights Law* (Routledge, 2013), p. 139.

Therefore, abstract international human rights norms need to be brought down-to-earth and made meaningful to the diverse communities in states parties. Human rights need to be (re)connected to the various foundations of rights in the world's traditions, including religion, custom and philosophy. If this can be achieved and local narratives of human rights embraced, people may come to support human rights 'as prerogatives that their own culture attributes to all members of the community'.[27] This task can be seen as part of the obligation on states parties to domestically implement human rights. And, as seen in the Indonesian example, social institutions like religion can also play an important role. In this way, rights can be effectively implemented by both public and private actors, tools, norms and resources – legislative and 'other measures'. After all, as proclaimed in the UDHR's preamble, 'every organ of society' is responsible for the 'universal and effective recognition and observance' of human rights. Involving locally embedded social institutions like religious groups and leaders can help ensure that rights are both communicated and implemented in culturally appropriate ways. This will not only facilitate their adoption in the community, but also demonstrate due respect to culture and counter some of the cultural relativist critiques of human rights. Such an approach is pragmatic, as it can be effective in securing rights, as well as principled in its respect for cultural diversity.[28]

1.2 Countering Legalism, State-Centricity and Cultural Disconnect

While states parties have broad discretion in the measures they can take to implement their international human rights treaty obligations, legislation is the primary measure emphasised by the UN treaties, treaty bodies and literature. Some treaty articles specifically require legislation, such as article 2(a) CEDAW, which obliges states 'to embody the principle of the equality of men and women in their national constitutions or other appropriate legislation'. In addition, the treaty bodies routinely recommend states parties to legally incorporate the treaties domestically, and much of the literature on implementation focuses almost entirely on legal

---

[27] Lenzerini (n. 23), p. 218.
[28] Julie Fraser and Henrike Prudon, Integrating Human Rights with Local Norms: Ebola, Burial Practices, and the Right to Health in West Africa (2017) *Intercultural Human Rights Law Review* 12, p. 72.

incorporation. Undoubtedly, legal incorporation can be a way to protect rights, formally enshrining them as state norms, making them binding nationally, and providing a framework for their domestic enforcement. While legislation may sometimes be sufficient to protect rights, it may also prove insufficient in practice. A survey of the Human Rights Committee's Concluding Observations revealed numerous gaps between states parties' constitutional guarantees and the reality of human rights violations.[29] Legislation may be ineffective for various reasons such as a lack of awareness of the law or its poor enforcement due to limited resources. While sometimes being impotent in these ways, legislation can also be counter-productive, particularly where it conflicts with local cultural norms.[30] As such, it is argued that the efficacy of legal incorporation (especially in isolation) has been oversold.

Noting the strong focus on and prioritisation of legal incorporation, some scholars have critiqued such legalism in the international human rights system on several grounds. The 'legalisation' of human rights refers to 'the practice of formulating human rights claims as legal claims and pursuing human rights objectives through legal mechanisms'.[31] The default focus on state law has had numerous implications for human rights, including overshadowing other implementation methods that may be similarly or even more effective in practice. For example, legalism has entrenched law as the primary disciplinary lens through which to analyse and understand human rights, to the exclusion or diminution of other relevant social sciences such as politics, sociology and anthropology.[32] Insights from these disciplines could enhance the understanding of human rights in context as well as their interrelationship with other

---

[29] Smith (n. 11), p. 49.

[30] For example, the Indonesian Government withdrew its legislative ban on medically performed female genital mutilation/cutting (FGM/C) due to backlash by Islamic leaders and *fatwas* against the prohibition. See UN CEDAW Committee, Consideration of reports submitted by States parties under article 18, Combined sixth and seventh periodic reports of States parties: Indonesia, CEDAW/C/IDN/6-7 (7 January 2011), paras. 132, 152; UN CEDAW Committee, Concluding Observations of the Committee on the Elimination of Discrimination against Women: Indonesia, CEDAW/C/IDN/CO/6-7 (7 August 2012), paras. 21–2; UN Human Rights Committee, Concluding Observations on the initial report of Indonesia, CCPR/C/IDN/CO/1 (21 August 2013), para. 12.

[31] Jack Donnelly, The Virtues of Legalization, in Saladin Meckled-García and Başak Çali (eds.), *The Legalization of Human Rights: Multidisciplinary Perspectives on Human Rights and Human Rights Law* (Routledge, 2006), p. 67.

[32] Koen de Feyter, Law Meets Sociology in Human Rights (June 2011) *Development and Society* 40:1, p. 51.

social forces.[33] This understanding could aid in determining the implementation methods most likely to be effective in practice in a given context. A central critique, therefore, of legalism in human rights is that a preoccupation with the law can lead to a disinclination to acknowledge the law's limitations. Viewing human rights problems only through a legal framework fails to consider solutions that may lie outside the law, or to recognise that the law may not be able to present a suitable remedy at all.

Due to this legalism, ample attention has been devoted to the formal role of the state and legal measures such as incorporation, with less attention directed to non-legislative or 'other measures' of implementation. As noted above, the treaties only vaguely refer to other measures without providing an elaboration thereof, and scholarship has not comprehensively elucidated what such measures may (or may not) entail. The variety and role of other measures have therefore been under-explored and under-exploited. As a result, there is not a clear understanding of the nature and scope of these other measures and their potential efficacy in practice, as the UN treaty bodies, state policymakers, academics and others continue to focus predominantly on state legislative measures. This is both a function and reinforcement of legalism in human rights, as well as state-centricity. A contribution of this book is therefore its examination and articulation of 'other measures' for domestically implementing human rights.

Another aspect of legalism in human rights is that it necessarily focuses on the state as the legislator and enforcer. Casting state law as *the* law recognises only the modern state model and marginalises other plural legal systems beneath and beyond the state that exist in virtually all countries in the world.[34] Numerous scholars have critiqued the state-centric nature of international human rights law, questioning its contemporary ability to effectively protect rights in context. This is largely due to the shifting role of the state due to phenomena including globalisation and privatisation. While state law and courts can be effective in implementing rights, a multiplicity of other actors and tools can also be effectively employed. As recognised in the UDHR and by the UN

---

[33] Denis Galligan and Deborah Sandler, Implementing Human Rights, in Simon Halliday and Patrick Schmidt (eds.), *Human Rights Brought Home: Socio-legal Perspectives on Human Rights in the National Context* (Hart Publishing, 2004), p. 25.

[34] William Twining, Legal Pluralism 101, in Brian Tamanaha, Caroline Sage and Michael Woolcock (eds.), *Legal Pluralism and Development: Scholars and Practitioners in Dialogue* (Cambridge University Press, 2012), p. 114; Brian Tamanaha, Understanding Legal Pluralism: Past to Present, Local to Global (2008) *Sydney Law Review* 30, p. 375.

treaty bodies, non-state actors (NSAs) play a crucial role in human rights implementation and even have international responsibilities.[35] However, the focus of international human rights law on the state as the primary addressee and state law as the primary tool has eclipsed the role of other actors and norms. These non-state norms and actors can be important – even crucial – assets in effective human rights implementation. Scholars have identified the need to make space in international human rights law to better account for the role of NSAs, creating counter-narratives and debunking myths of the state.[36]

Specifically, this book examines the role of informal social institutions (like kinship groups, religion and traditional healers) in other measures of human rights implementation. Social institutions are central in the development of complex social organisation and interaction, and – particularly important for human rights implementation – can efficiently guide and shape human behaviour. In this way, they can even be more potent than state law. As culturally embedded institutions, social institutions typically enjoy local legitimacy, which foreign norms like human rights often lack. Despite these benefits, the role of social institutions in human rights implementation is under-theorised. While the negative role of cultural norms and actors, and particularly religious ones, in abusing rights has been the subject of much scholarship (for example, regarding female genital mutilation/cutting (FGM/C), polygamy, denying women's franchise etc.), their positive role in implementing and protecting rights has received less attention. In fact, the international discourse around culture in human rights tends to essentialise and 'other' culture. As such, another contribution of this book is its analysis of the positive role of culture and social institutions in the domestic implementation of international human rights law from a legal and practical perspective.

In fact, some contend that, as originally conceived in the UDHR, human rights were never intended to be so legalistic or state-centric.[37]

---

[35] See further Chapter 4.
[36] Manisuli Ssenyonjo, Non-State Actors and Economic, Social, and Cultural Rights, in Mashood Baderin and Robert McCorquodale (eds.), *Economic, Social, and Cultural Rights in Action* (Oxford University Press, 2007), pp. 109, 134; Cedric Ryngaert, Non-State Actors: Carving out a Space in a State-Centred International Legal System (2016) *Netherlands International Law Review* 63, p. 185, citing Mariana Valverde, *Chronotopes of the Law: Jurisdiction, Scale and Governance* (Routledge, 2015).
[37] Mary Ann Glendon, *A World Made New* (Random House, 2002), p. 161; Abdullahi Ahmed An-Na`im, The Spirit of Laws Is Not Universal: Alternatives to the Enforcement Paradigm for Human Rights (2016) *Tilburg Law Review* 21, p. 274.

Rather than relying only on formal state norms and actors, scholars have suggested a more effective way to implement human rights may be for the state to employ culturally sensitive measures based on the local context. This is because '[h]uman rights are most secure when they are embedded in culture',[38] and scholars have long connected the poor cultural legitimacy of human rights with their violation.[39] When human rights are not accepted as societal norms, they are more difficult to protect in practice. For instance, a culturally insensitive law is likely to be un- or under-implemented and therefore unsuccessful in protecting rights. Numerous examples can be drawn from legislative measures to criminalise FGM/C that do not in fact reduce its practice.[40] As this demonstrates, embedded cultural norms and practices like FGM/C do not yield automatically to state legislative prohibitions.[41] As such, scholars have advocated home-grown and bottom-up contextual approaches to human rights implementation that protect the right in question while remaining culturally compatible.

One such example is the receptor approach, which advocates the state's use of local social institutions, like religion in Indonesia, to implement human rights.[42] Similarly, the established and trusted system of traditional healers in South Africa could be engaged, trained and equipped to ensure that HIV/AIDS patients have access to the necessary antiretroviral drugs, contributing to the right to health.[43] By relying where possible on locally embedded protections and remedies, the

---

[38] Michael Freeman, Universalism of Human Rights and Cultural Relativism, in Scott Sheeran and Sir Nigel Rodley (eds.), *Routledge Handbook of International Human Rights Law* (Routledge, 2013), p. 61.

[39] See, for example, Abdullahi Ahmed An-Na'im, Toward a Cross-Cultural Approach to Defining International Standards of Human Rights: The Meaning of Cruel, Inhuman, or Degrading Treatment or Punishment, in Abdullahi Ahmed An-Na'im (ed.), *Human Rights in Cross-Cultural Perspectives: A Quest for Consensus* (University of Pennsylvania Press, 1992), p. 19.

[40] FGM/C 'remains quite prevalent in many new African nations despite extensive national and international legislation against the practice': Bonny Ibhawoh, Between Culture and Constitution: Evaluating the Cultural Legitimacy of Human Rights in the African State (2000) *Human Rights Quarterly* 22, p. 849. For a specialised study on measures to eliminate FGM/C, see Annemarie Middelburg, *Empty Promises? Compliance with the Human Rights Framework in Relation to Female Genital Mutilation/Cutting in Senegal* (Middelburg, 2016).

[41] Donders (n. 22), p. 24; Ibhawoh (n. 40), p. 857.

[42] Tom Zwart, Using Local Culture to Further the Implementation of International Human Rights: The Receptor Approach (2012) *Human Rights Quarterly* 34, pp. 546–69.

[43] Ibid., p. 564.

receptor approach aims to respect culture while simultaneously enhancing human rights implementation. Other contextual or culturally sensitive approaches have been advocated by scholars including An-Na'im, Merry and Nyamu. They promote reliance upon local cultural norms and resources as well as the agency existing within communities to implement rights. Culturally sensitive approaches rely on the legitimacy enjoyed by these local norms and actors to promote human rights as consistent with their community's values. Central to this is the fact that culture is internally contested and not static but rather dynamic, continually evolving[44] – a fact frequently misunderstood in international human rights law. While staying within the framework of international law, these approaches eschew legalism and state-centricity in the domestic implementation of human rights and advocate a role for local cultural actors and norms like social institutions.

This book focuses on the role of locally embedded and culturally legitimate social institutions in implementing human rights through non-legislative methods. The purpose is to determine the compatibility of this approach with international human rights law, and also its potential to improve human rights implementation in context. On this basis, the book includes a case study, which both illustrates and tests the role of social institutions in the domestic implementation of human rights in practice. The study examines the role of Islamic norms and actors in implementing women's right to family planning in Indonesia. This case study is significant given the need for more multidisciplinary and empirical insights in international human rights law. Typically, human rights scholarship stops with formal legal measures and institutional descriptions based on judicial and secondary literature sources – and rarely examines the effectiveness of implementation.[45] This can be seen as a result of the legalistic approach to human rights. However, the examination of whether human rights measures are practical and effective cannot be determined solely on a legal basis.[46]

---

[44] Lenzerini (n. 23), pp. 238–9.
[45] Hans-Otto Sano and Hatla Thelle, The Need for Evidence-Based Human Rights Research, in Fons Coomans, Fred Grünfeld and Menno Kamminga (eds.), *Methods of Human Rights Research* (Intersentia, 2009), pp. 93–4; Patrick Schmidt and Simon Halliday, Introduction: Socio-legal Perspectives on Human Rights in the National Context, in Simon Halliday and Patrick Schmidt (eds.), *Human Rights Brought Home: Socio-legal Perspectives on Human Rights in the National Context* (Hart Publishing, 2004), pp. 3–4.
[46] de Feyter (n. 32), p. 63.

1.2 COUNTERING LEGALISM AND STATE-CENTRICITY

Finally, as frequently reiterated in contemporary times, this is a challenging period for human rights. Despite recently celebrating seven decades of the UDHR, five of the two International Covenants, four of CEDAW, and three of the CRC, human rights continue to be contested. Scholars and practitioners have been warning of the increasing threats to democratic values and human rights around the world, highlighted by the election of leaders like Trump and Duterte and the United Kingdom's Brexit vote. There are also challenges to international institutions, like the United States of America leaving the UN Human Rights Council, and Burundi and the Philippines withdrawing from the Rome Statute system. The former UN High Commissioner for Human Rights, Zeid Ra'ad al-Hussein, cautioned that 'the further away we get from those historical and dreadful experiences [of WWII], the more we tend to play fast and loose with the institutions created to prevent repetition'.[47] Scholars have commented on the challenges to and perceived decline of human rights. Hopgood warns of human rights' 'endtimes' due to the increasing contestation combined with the relative demise of the West and rise of the South.[48] He notes that these (re)emerging states are not secular, with religion playing a stronger role in influencing public attitudes. De Sousa Santos would agree, noting that 'theology's center of gravity has moved to the Global South'.[49] Hopgood argues that 'the foundations on which secular human rights were based are not available universally'.[50]

It is difficult to share Hopgood's perspective in this respect for several reasons. First, human rights have been contested internationally at least since the UDHR, and in many ways are characterised by their contestation. It is furthermore questionable whether secular foundations for human rights were ever available universally. It is also unclear why they should be, given the huge diversity of the world's some two hundred

---

[47] The Associated Press, UN Rights Chief Warns UN Could 'Collapse' without Change, *New York Times* (20 August 2018), www.nytimes.com/aponline/2018/08/20/world/europe/ap-eu-un-human-rights.html (accessed 27 August 2018).

[48] See Stephen Hopgood, *The Endtimes of Human Rights* (Cornell University Press, 2013); Stephen Hopgood, Human Rights on the Road to Nowhere, in Stephen Hopgood, Jack Synder and Leslie Vinjamuri (eds.), *Human Rights Futures* (Cambridge University Press, 2017), pp. 283–310.

[49] Boaventura de Sousa Santos, *If God Were a Human Rights Activist* (Standford Studies in Human Rights, 2015), p. 21.

[50] Stephen Hopgood, The Endtimes of Human Rights, in Doutje Lettinga and Lars van Troost (eds.), *Debating the Endtimes of Human Rights: Activism and Institutions in a Neo-Westphalian World* (Amnesty International, 2014), p. 17.

states and the foundationally relative nature of human rights.[51] While culture, including religion, has formed the basis of many critiques of human rights, it is also a source and promoter of rights. For example, many drafters of the UDHR viewed their own religious beliefs as a source of human rights. Indeed, religion 'has always been an inspiring source for the social groups and movements that have struggled against injustice and oppression throughout history'.[52] Religious organisations have also been providing human rights related services like education and healthcare for centuries. Therefore, a relative increase in religiosity is not necessarily detrimental to the cause of human rights. In fact, a move away from a solely Western, secular view of human rights towards a broader one that encompasses other philosophical or religious traditions is to be welcomed. These other perspectives have important contributions to make to the global emancipatory potential of human rights.[53]

Today's challenging times may not present us with the end of human rights, but rather an opportunity to take stock, re-imagine, and re-engage a wider variety of norms and actors on human rights. In addition to formal state institutions, social institutions like religion are also needed to participate in resolving human rights contestation and forging supporting narratives. Given the multiplicity of challenges facing human rights, it is necessary to have a plurality of actors and norms – including social institutions – working in support of rights.

1.3 Terminology, Methodology and Case Study

The book focuses on 'social institutions', a term stemming from social science, sociology in particular. Relatively rare in the legal discipline, the term could cause confusion in the context of public international law as it does not fit seamlessly into legal concepts and terminology. A sociological definition holds that social institutions are:

---

[51] Jack Donnelly, *Universal Human Rights in Theory and Practice* (3rd ed., Cornell University, 2013), p. 99.

[52] See, for example, de Sousa Santos (n. 49), p. 22; and Monica Duffy Toft, False Prophecies in the Service of Good Works, p. 50 and Steve Crawshaw, Neo-Westphalia, So What? p. 37, in Doutje Lettinga and Lars van Troost (eds.), *Debating the Endtimes of Human Rights: Activism and Institutions in a Neo-Westphalian World* (Amnesty International, 2014). Hopgood himself argues that the human rights movement coming out of Europe was largely based on Christianity.

[53] Fernanda Bragato, Human Rights and Eurocentrism: An Analysis from the Decolonial Studies Perspective (2013) *The Global Studies Journal* 5:3, p. 54.

a complex of positions, roles, norms and values lodged in particular types of social structures and organising relatively stable patterns of human activity with respect to fundamental problems in producing life-sustaining resources, in reproducing individuals, and in sustaining viable societal structures within a given environment.[54]

Giddens notes that social institutions 'are the more enduring features of social life' that shape human activity and usually reproduce themselves trans-generationally.[55] Social institutions are central in the development of complex social organisation and interaction, efficiently guiding behaviour and framing choice.[56] Examples of social institutions include the family and kinship groups, language, monarchies and religion. As seen from these examples, social institutions are of vital importance to human life. This definition of social institutions also includes norms or conventions (such as religious or customary law), the multiple existence of which within a given community creates situations of legal pluralism. Social institutions also comprise formal and informal organisations, such as sporting clubs, cultural/artistic collectives, as well as neighbourhood and women's associations.

As can be seen from these examples, some social institutions are also non-state actors, such as trade unions, religious organisations and sporting associations. However, not all non-state actors (as a large and ill-defined group) will be social institutions (for example, individuals or businesses). Some social institutions are themselves not actors (such as norms and conventions) but motivate, guide or enable actors. On this basis, social institutions are loosely categorised as non-state actors and norms for the purposes of the legal analysis in this book. This is necessary as international law strongly distinguishes between states and non-states, with no specific nuance of the latter. This categorisation is, however, not entirely satisfying and reflects the difficulty of multidisciplinary work where concepts do not necessarily align across disciplines. For example, language is a social institution but neither a norm or an actor *per se*.

---

[54] Jonathan Turner, *The Institutional Order: Economy, Kinship, Religion, Polity, Law, and Education in Evolutionary and Comparative Perspective* (Longman, 1997), p. 6.

[55] Anthony Giddens, *The Constitution of Society: Outline of the Theory of Structuration* (Polity Press, 1984), p. 24; Seumas Miller, Social Institutions, in Edward Zalta (ed.), *The Stanford Encyclopedia of Philosophy* (Winter 2014 Edition, 8 February 2011), https://plato.stanford.edu/archives/win2014/entries/social-institutions/ (accessed 14 November 2017).

[56] Seth Kaplan, *Human Rights in Thick and Thin Societies: The Universal Declaration and Bridging the Gap* (Cambridge University Press, 2018), pp. 10, 58.

As the book addresses the role of law in society it employs traditional doctrinal legal research combined with multidisciplinary insights and a qualitative methodology. The socio-legal methodology was desk research of primary sources and secondary literature, supplemented by practical research at a UN treaty body (the CEDAW Committee) in Geneva and field work in Indonesia. The field work entailed interviews with Indonesian academics, Islamic leaders and scholars, government and civil society representatives, as well as experts working in women's reproductive health. The author is grateful to all who participated. The purpose of the case study is to illustrate culturally sensitive approaches to human rights implementation via social institutions in practice. As such, the study is used to reflect upon these approaches, amending or qualifying them as necessary. The intention is for the case to be generalisable to the theoretical framework, but not (necessarily) generalisable to a wider population. In fact, the theory propounded specifically advocates tailoring human rights implementation to each context, denouncing a one-size-fits-all approach. The choice of case study is explained below.

1.3.1 Why Islam, Indonesia and Women's Reproductive Rights?

Islam was chosen as the focus social institution of the case study. Religion in general is an important social institution, and Islam is a highly influential one with 1.8 billion followers, comprising one-quarter of the world's population. Rather than being found in only certain areas or regions, Islam is present in many states around the world – particularly in Africa and Asia – and can be considered a global presence. Islam is the fastest growing religion, soon to overtake Christianity as the largest. In addition to this sheer growth in numbers, the influence of Islamic law on the national legislation and jurisprudence of Muslim majority states is also growing. Indeed, as noted above, religion is experiencing a sort of resurgence, especially in political and public life.[57] Within the last few decades it has become a global phenomenon for people to claim 'religion as a constitutive element of public life'.[58] Studies show that the world is becoming more religious, with the relative size of religiously unaffiliated

---

[57] Toft (n. 52), p. 48; Mohammad H. Fadel, Public Reason as a Strategy for Principled Reconciliation: The Case of Islamic Law and International Human Rights Law (2007) *Chicago Journal of International Law* 8:1, p. 1.

[58] De Sousa Santos (n. 49), p. 11.

1.3 TERMINOLOGY, METHODOLOGY AND CASE STUDY

people declining.[59] One scholar has claimed that the pertinent 'question of the twenty-first century may very well be religion, particularly Islam'.[60]

Like other religions, Islam has a strong normative system, the subject matter of which is wide-ranging and comprehensive, relating to an individual's relationship with God as well as with their family and wider community. As such, Islamic norms overlap greatly with human rights. While there is much agreement between Islam and human rights,[61] of all the cultural critiques of rights, Brems concluded that those based on Islam come the closest to rejecting the universality of rights.[62] For these reasons, Islam was selected as a significant and pressing social institution to study regarding its role in human rights implementation. Indonesia was selected as the state with the largest Muslim population in the world, of around 200 million, and also the world's fourth largest population. Despite this fact, many studies of Islam often ignore Indonesia, focusing only on the Middle East or North Africa. Indonesia also has a vibrant civil society, and strong Islamic institutions that boast huge combined memberships of over 100 million – the largest in the world. These institutions are independent of the state and their operations impact upon numerous human rights. Indonesia has ratified most of the international human rights treaties, served on the UN Human Rights Council, and is part of regional human rights mechanisms. Indonesia was also an advocate and keen participant in the 1990s Asian values debate regarding culture and human rights.

Rinaldo identifies Indonesia as 'a vital site for sociological investigations of social and political changes in Muslim societies, including the question of women's agency in religious contexts'.[63] According to

---

[59] Pew Research Centre, Michael Lipka and David Mcclendon, Why People with No Religion Are Projected to Decline as a Share of the World's Population (7 April 2017), www.pewresearch.org/fact-tank/2017/04/07/why-people-with-no-religion-are-projected-to-decline-as-a-share-of-the-worlds-population/ (accessed 27 August 2018); Pew Research Centre, The Future of World Religions: Population Growth Projections, 2010–2050 (2 April 2015), www.pewforum.org/2015/04/02/religious-projections-2010-2050/ (accessed 1 February 2019).

[60] Fadel (n. 57), p. 1.

[61] Abdullahi Ahmed An-Na'im, Why Should Muslims Abandon *Jihad*? Human Rights and the Future of International Law, in Richard Falk, Balakrishnan Rajagopal and Jacqueline Stevens (eds.), *International Law and the Third World: Reshaping Justice* (Routledge, 2008), p. 87.

[62] Brems (2001) (n. 25), pp. 288, 290.

[63] Rachel Rinaldo, Pious and Critical: Muslim Women Activists and the Question of Agency (2014) *Gender & Society* 28:6, p. 826.

Menchik, debates in Indonesia regarding modernity and the Islamic revival 'have been fought on the terrain of women's bodies'.[64] Women's rights are often the most contentious rights,[65] and are commonly invoked as the quintessential example of the conflict between human rights and culture – including at times Islam. CEDAW is simultaneously one of the most ratified *and* widely reserved of the UN treaties, with many of these reservations relating to culture.[66] Among women's rights, and as iterated *inter alia* in their reports to the UN treaty bodies, Indonesia has faced significant barriers in protecting women's reproductive rights and has one of the worst maternal mortality rates in the region.[67] The Government has therefore prioritised women's reproductive health, the related rights of which continue to be highly controversial across the world. Women's reproductive rights were therefore chosen for the study, also given their strong nexus with culture, which informs perspectives on sexuality, reproductive health, childbearing and rearing.

Given the broad scope of reproductive rights, which includes maternal mortality, nutrition and breastfeeding, sexually transmitted diseases, FGM/C, and child marriage, this research focuses on only one element: family planning. Family planning is a key aspect of reproductive rights, as the lack of effective means to control fertility and space births can endanger many aspects of women's health and even life. Family planning is an important issue on the global (health and development) agenda, given that the world population doubled in the last century, with further growth expected. This has important implications for *inter alia* the environment, economy, health and development. Family planning was also selected due to the focus given to it in Indonesia by local, national

---

[64] Jeremy Menchik, The Co-evolution of Sacred and Secular: Islamic Law and Family Planning in Indonesia (2014) *South East Asia Research* 22:3, p. 364.

[65] Scholars have noted the lack of consensus on women's rights and that this represents one of the most pressing challenges to the universality of human rights. See Freeman (n. 38), p. 50; Coomaraswamy (n. 26), pp. 132–3; UN General Assembly, Report of the Special Rapporteur in the Field of Cultural Rights, A/67/287 (10 August 2012), para. 64.

[66] Approximately 30 per cent of States Parties to CEDAW have entered reservations. For example, Malaysia, Bangladesh, Morocco and Saudi Arabia, *inter alia*, declared their accession to CEDAW provided that the provisions do not conflict with Islamic *Shari'a*. See Marijke De Pauw, Women's Rights: From Bad to Worse? Assessing the Evolution of Incompatible Reservations to the CEDAW Convention (2013) *Merkourios Utrecht Journal of International and European Law* 29:77, pp. 51–65.

[67] UN CEDAW Committee, Consideration of Reports: Indonesia 2011 (n. 30), para. 136.

and international organisations, and its long-term status as a government priority. Indonesia's national family planning programme is five decades old and has a strong history of engagement with Islamic law and institutions. The programme has long been viewed as an international success given its reduction of Indonesia's fertility rate by one-half, and is advocated as an example for other (Muslim) states.

1.3.2 Structure of the Book

Following this introductory chapter, the book addresses in Chapter 2 the foundations of international human rights law, the intrinsic relationship between culture and rights, and revisits the long-standing debate on universality and cultural relativism. The chapter situates the book within literature on culturally sensitive approaches to human rights implementation that advocate embedding rights in cultural patterns and social institutions to secure their acceptance, protection and enjoyment. The next two chapters focus on the legal framework for human rights implementation under international human rights law to determine the compatibility of culturally sensitive approaches. Chapter 3 analyses the legal obligations on states parties to implement the treaties, focusing on legislative and other measures. It surveys the treaties and treaty body documents to illustrate the broad scope for states to use 'other measures'. Chapter 4 takes this analysis further by exploring the role of social institutions in such other measures of human rights implementation. Using the example of the right to health, it analyses the legal situation of a state 'outsourcing' the provision of rights-related services to non-state actors like some social institutions.

Chapter 5 explores these concepts in a case study, examining the role of Islamic norms and institutions in implementing women's right to family planning in Indonesia. Based on field research, the chapter analyses culturally sensitive approaches to human rights implementation in practice and the role of social institutions. It details Indonesia's international obligations regarding reproductive rights, and how Islamic law and actors were integral in implementing the right to family planning. These theoretical and practical insights are then relied upon to critique the practice of the UN human rights treaty bodies in their supervision of Indonesia. Finally, the conclusions in Chapter 6 draw from the findings throughout the book and propose recommendations to the UN treaty bodies and states parties to better accommodate cultural diversity and promote effective human rights implementation. Chapter 6 reflects on the broader themes of the book, including the need for new/better narratives to connect human rights to local communities, and the need to look beyond the limits of the state. In this way, the book seeks to provide new insights into the relationship between culture and human rights, and proposes a way forward via social institutions serving as bridges between international norms and their local manifestations.

2

Human Rights and Their Cultural Connection

2.1 Introduction

Universal human rights apply to everyone around the globe based on the inherent dignity of being human. Rather than being justified on the basis of religion, nature or philosophy, it was agreed in the *Universal Declaration of Human Rights* (UDHR) that rights inhere from human dignity.[1] This was a significant achievement, and the UDHR continues to be a landmark instrument establishing the international system of human rights. Since 1948, numerous human rights documents, resolutions and treaties have been agreed around the world, elaborating upon and expanding the scope and understanding of human rights. Despite this proliferation, detractors continue to challenge aspects and even the whole system of international human rights. Many of these critiques are based on culture, including religion, and specifically question the universality of rights. Accusations of cultural relativism were raised during the drafting of the UDHR, and reached a pinnacle years later with the Asian values debates in the 1990s.[2] Other critiques from postcolonial, decolonial and Third World scholars challenge the pervasive Western influence in international human rights law.[3] As noted in the first chapter, the persistent disconnect between culture and human rights contributes to their poor adoption and implementation in practice.

As such, it is evident that in relation to human rights, cultural concerns cannot be ignored or marginalised. Nor it is clear why they should be.

---

[1] Universal Declaration of Human Rights (adopted 10 December 1948), UNGA Res. 217 A(III) (UDHR).
[2] See, for example, Executive Board, American Anthropological Association (AAA), Statement on Human Rights (1947) *American Anthropologist* 49, pp. 539-43; Karen Engle, Culture and Human Rights: The Asian Values Debate in Context (1999-2000) *New York University Journal of International Law and Politics* 32, pp. 291-334.
[3] See, for example, Makau Mutua, *Human Rights: A Political and Cultural Critique* (University of Pennsylvania Press, 2002).

Culture is a vital aspect of all human societies around the world and is therefore also recognised as a human right in itself.[4] It is a premise of this book that the nexus between culture and human rights is a fait accompli not to be neglected.[5] Despite this, cultural rights have received less attention and articulation than other rights, and in fact the relationship between culture and human rights is often misunderstood and treated with suspicion. Culture is commonly conceived of as an obstacle or barrier to human rights enjoyment, with so-called harmful traditional practices identified for elimination. The practices typically cited here include female genital mutilation or cutting (FGM/C), early marriage, female infanticide and dowry traditions.[6] While much scholarship addresses the detrimental role of culture vis-à-vis human rights, this book articulates how culture is crucial for human rights and can be an asset in their implementation. Therefore, it is necessary to explore the complex relationship between culture and human rights, and to understand the depth and relevance of the cultural critiques.

This chapter briefly introduces the foundations and development of the international human rights system and its pertinent cultural critiques. It begins by revisiting the drafting of the UDHR and the initial cautions raised in the name of culture, as well as those critiques since 1948. The intention is to set out the history and development of the debate on human rights and culture in order to illustrate its ongoing relevance today for human rights implementation. In the final section, the chapter introduces contextual or culturally sensitive approaches to human rights implementation as advocated by scholars including An-Na'im, Merry, Nyamu and Zwart. This section analyses and evaluates these approaches, identifying their commonalities, strengths and weaknesses. A central element of these approaches is their focus on social institutions, which, due to their cultural embeddedness and normative overlap, can be employed in human rights implementation.

---

[4] See UDHR, art. 27; *International Covenant on Economic, Social and Cultural Rights* (adopted 16 December 1966, entered into force 3 January 1976), 993 UNTS 3 (ICESCR), art. 15(1)(a).
[5] Federico Lenzerini, *The Culturalization of Human Rights Law* (Oxford University Press 2014), p. 120.
[6] See, for example, UN Committee on the Elimination of Discrimination against Women (CEDAW Committee) and the Committee on the Rights of the Child (CRC Committee), Joint General Recommendation No. 31 of the Committee on the Elimination of Discrimination against Women/General Comment No. 18 on the Committee on the Rights of the Child on Harmful Practices, CEDAW/C/GC31-CRC/C/GC/18 (14 November 2014).

2.2 Human Rights and Their History of Cultural Critiques

2.2.1 Founding a Universal System of Human Rights: The UDHR

The UDHR is generally heralded as a consensus of global opinion on human rights and the first example of 'a universal document transcending culture and traditions to prescribe a global standard'.[7] As such, it is remarkable. While in a positive sense the UDHR founded the international system of human rights, the Declaration has been characterised not as a source of rights but rather 'as the instrumental expression of pre-existing human rights deriving from human dignity'.[8] Despite it being debated in the drafting process, the UDHR refrains from noting a particular source of human rights or dignity, such as God or the divine.[9] It simply states in article 1 that '[a]ll human beings are born free and equal in dignity and rights', without further explanation or justification. In this way, the UDHR leaves open the issue of the foundation or source of human rights, leaving scope to support a range of views. In fact, there is no need (and potentially no possibility) for agreement on a single foundation of human rights, which enables everyone to have their own view, be it philosophical, ideological, religious or secular.[10] As such, rights are foundationally relative, in that they can have a number of different foundations.[11]

Despite its pre-eminence, the UDHR is not uncontentious and has its imperfections.[12] While some view the UDHR as the legitimate

---

[7] Rhona K. M. Smith, *Textbook on International Human Rights* (5th ed., Oxford University Press, 2012), pp. 37, 42.

[8] Adam McBeth, Every Organ of Society: The Responsibility of Non-State Actors for the Realization of Human Rights (2008–2009) *Journal of Public Law & Policy* 30:1, p. 83.

[9] Bas de Gaay Fortman, Article 1 UDHR: From Credo to Realisation, in Yves Haeck, Brianne McGonigle Leyh, Clara Burbano-Herrera and Diana Contreras-Garduno (eds.), *The Realisation of Human Rights: When Theory Meets Practice: Studies in Honour of Leo Zwaak* (Intersentia, 2013), pp. 42–3; Johannes Morsink, *The Universal Declaration of Human Rights: Origins, Drafting, and Intent* (Pennsylvania Studies in Human Rights, 1999), pp. 284–90.

[10] Abdullahi Ahmed An-Na'im, Islam and Human Rights, in John Witte Jr and M. Christian Green (eds.), *Religion and Human Rights: An Introduction* (Oxford University Press, 2012), p. 57; Eva Brems, Reconciling Universality and Diversity in International Human Rights Law, in András Sajó (ed.), *Human Rights with Modesty: The Problem of Universalism* (Nijhoff, 2004), p. 217.

[11] Jack Donnelly, *Universal Human Rights in Theory and Practice* (3rd ed., Cornell University, 2013), p. 99. This was the apparent purpose of the drafters of the UDHR. See Mary Ann Glendon, *A World Made New* (Random House, 2002), pp. 146–7.

[12] Even at the time of drafting the UDHR, Eleanor Roosevelt urged UN third committee members to not be distracted 'by a search for absolute perfection'. Glendon (n. 11), pp. 139–40.

foundation of international human rights, others question the way it was created and, as such, its claims on universality. For example, the UDHR was drafted at a time when a large number of states, particularly from the African and Asian continents, were not part of the United Nations due to colonialism and, therefore, did not participate in imagining and crafting the rights therein.[13] The UDHR was voted on by only forty-eight member states in the United Nations,[14] compared to today's membership of over 190 states. Evidently, there is a prima facie democratic deficit regarding the UDHR's universal legitimacy. In fact, it is commonly agreed that the Western-based view of human rights has been the primary influence on the system of rights established by the United Nations. Mutua argues that the UDHR was driven by the West, is largely a product of Western thinking, and that burdened with such biases it cannot reflect 'universal' rights.[15] He asserts that given the dominance of Western cultural and political norms, it was 'presumptuous' for the UDHR to refer to itself as the 'common standard of achievement for all peoples and all nations'.[16]

Nonetheless, some have defended the representative nature of the UDHR's drafting process and its status as reflecting universal norms. They claim that while much of the initiative for the UDHR came from Western intellectuals and civil society, Western governments were not in fact strong supporters of the draft Declaration.[17] This was particularly the case for the 'Great Powers' who had human rights records at odds with the new standards proclaimed: racial segregation in the USA; and

---

[13] In 1945 there were fifty-one original member states to the UN, and in 1948 there were fifty-eight states, compared to over 190 states today. The greatest influx of states was in the 1960s with several African states joining, and in the early 1990s following the collapse of the Soviet Union. See UN, Member States, Growth in United Nations Membership 1945–Present, www.un.org/en/sections/member-states/growth-united-nations-membership-1945-present/index.html (accessed 24 January 2018). See also Wiktor Osiatyński, The Historical Development of Human Rights, in Scott Sheeran and Sir Nigel Rodley (eds.), *Routledge Handbook of International Human Rights Law* (Routledge, 2013), p. 12.

[14] The UDHR was adopted in 1948 by forty-eight states voting for, none against, and eight abstentions (Byelorussian SSR, Czechoslovakia, Poland, Saudi Arabia, Ukrainian SSR, USSR, Union of South Africa, and Yugoslavia). Regarding these abstentions, see Morsink (n. 9), pp. 21–8.

[15] Mutua (n. 3), p. 11.

[16] UDHR preamble; Mutua (n. 3), pp. 46, 154.

[17] Osiatyński (n. 13), p. 10; Glendon (n. 11), p. 10; Michael Freeman, Universalism of Human Rights and Cultural Relativism, in Scott Sheeran and Sir Nigel Rodley (eds.), *Routledge Handbook of International Human Rights Law* (Routledge, 2013), p. 49.

colonialism in France and Britain.[18] Indeed, Europe has a long history of torture, religious hatred (including the Inquisition and Holocaust), as well as racial and gender inequality.[19] Britain sought to ensure that the UDHR would not apply to the colonies, despite pressure from the Soviet Union and its allies.[20] Donnelly goes so far as to claim that the UDHR did *not* reflect 'long-held Western ideas and practices'.[21] Rather, it is contended that Latin American states were the most ardent supporters of the UDHR, joined by some Islamic, Buddhist and independent African states.[22] After all, the Conference of American States adopted the *American Declaration on the Rights and Duties of Man* six months prior to the UDHR.[23]

Furthermore, several non-Western states were involved and influential in drafting the UDHR. In addition to Western states, the UDHR's Drafting Committee comprised representatives from Lebanon, the USSR, China and Chile. In 1948, the UN Commission on Human Rights tasked with negotiating the UDHR comprised eighteen members, including Egypt, India, Iran, Philippines, Panama, Uruguay, Belarus, Ukraine and Yugoslavia.[24] Morsink further notes the 'significant contributions' of other individuals including from Argentina, Bolivia, Brazil, Pakistan, Syria and Turkey.[25] Scholars are divided over the impact of such diverse representation. Some have noted the 'enormous' contributions of such members and that, in particular, P. C. Chang of China ensured the

---

[18] Osiatyński (n. 13), p. 10.
[19] Eva Brems, Reconciling Universality and Diversity in International Human Rights: A Theoretical and Methodological Framework and Its Application in the Context of Islam (April–June 2004) *Human Rights Review* 5:3, p. 12; Eva Brems, *Human Rights: Universality and Diversity* (Nijhoff, 2001), p. 298.
[20] Balakrishnan Rajagopal, Counter-Hegemonic International Law: Rethinking Human Rights and Development as Third World Strategy, in Richard Falk, Balakrishnan Rajagopal and Jacqueline Stevens (eds.), *International Law and the Third World: Reshaping Justice* (Routledge, 2008), p. 65; Glendon (n. 11), p. 149.
[21] Donnelly 2013 (n. 11), p. 91.
[22] Osiatyński (n. 13), p. 12; Glendon (n. 11), p. 15.
[23] American Declaration of the Rights and Duties of Man, OAS Res. XXX adopted by the Ninth International Conference of American States (1948) reprinted in Basic Documents Pertaining to Human Rights in the InterAmerican System, OEA/Ser. L V/II.82 Doc. 6 Rev. 1 at 17 (1992) (2 May 1948). Adopted by the Ninth International Conference of American States, Bogotá, Colombia.
[24] See UN, Commission on Human Rights Membership, www.ohchr.org/EN/HRBodies/CHR/Pages/Membership.aspx (accessed 24 January 2018).
[25] Morsink (n. 9), p. 32.

UDHR's universal representation.[26] Others refute this, noting that while the representatives of Lebanon and China certainly shaped the UDHR, they were both educated in the USA and 'were firmly rooted in the European intellectual traditions'.[27] Of note, not a single sub-Saharan African state or representative was involved in the drafting process, and on this basis 'it is difficult to escape the conclusion that the document which finally emerged was largely reflective of Western traditions and concepts of the individual, society and state'.[28]

Concerns about the UDHR's claim of universality were raised at the time of drafting by *inter alia* the American Anthropological Association (AAA). In a 1947 Statement to the United Nations, the AAA cautioned against universal rights that did not accommodate cultural particularities.[29] Cultural relativists criticise human rights' claim to universality by submitting that the validity of a cultural norm can only be determined within that cultural framework, and that any judgment or evaluation of a norm from an external perspective is problematic, if not entirely invalid.[30] Relativists submit that as culture can determine rights,[31] there can be no (or limited) cross-cultural universal human rights. As such, any system claiming to be 'universal' would in effect oppress some populations while elevating others.[32] This argument is compelling in its emphasis on dignity and respect for everyone, as well as tolerance for

---

[26] Lydia H. Liu, Shadows of Universalism: The Untold Story of Human Rights around 1948 (Summer 2014) *Critical Inquiry* 40, pp. 404, 406; Glendon (n. 11), pp. 47, 225.

[27] Mutua (n. 3), pp. 154–5. See also Lenzerini (n. 5), p. 103; Glendon (n. 11), pp. 225–6.

[28] Antony Anghie, International Human Rights Law and a Developing World Perspective, in Scott Sheeran and Sir Nigel Rodley (eds.), *Routledge Handbook of International Human Rights Law* (Routledge, 2013), p. 114.

[29] Executive Board, AAA, Statement on Human Rights (1947) *American Anthropologist* 49:4, pp. 539–43. Following this initial scepticism and a period of estrangement, the AAA now embraces human rights and adopted a new statement in 1999: AAA Committee for Human Rights, Declaration on Anthropology and Human Rights (Adopted by the AAA membership June 1999), http://humanrights.americananthro.org/1999-statement-on-human-rights/ (accessed 25 November 2017). For an analysis of the AAA's position, see generally Karen Engle, From Skepticism to Embrace: Human Rights and the American Anthropological Association from 1947–1999 (2001) *Human Rights Quarterly* 23, pp. 536–59; Mark Goodale, Anthropology and the Grounds of Human Rights, in Dinah Shelton (ed.), *The Oxford Handbook of International Human Rights Law* (Oxford University Press, 2013), ch. 6.

[30] Mutua (n. 3), p. 22. See also Alison Dundes Renteln, The Unanswered Challenge of Relativism and the Consequences for Human Rights (1985) *Human Rights Quarterly* 7:4, pp. 514–40.

[31] Freeman (n. 17), p. 51.

[32] Goodale (n. 29), p. 150.

2.2 HUMAN RIGHTS & CULTURAL CRITIQUES

customs different to one's own. Indeed, the AAA's Statement was written in opposition to the context of colonialism and the belief in the superiority of Western culture and biology.[33] However, cultural relativism has also been criticised for neutralising moral judgment and precluding action against injustice.[34]

Potentially in an effort to overcome these accusations of Western bias, scholars have endeavoured to chart the foundations of human dignity and rights around the world and throughout history.[35] Mary Robinson put out a call for such projects, noting: 'More thought and effort must be given to enriching the human rights discourse by explicit reference to other non-Western religious and cultural traditions'.[36] It was recognised that in order '[t]o enhance its legitimacy, the emerging universal human rights regime must draw upon the cultural peculiarities of each society'.[37] Lenzerini sets out in detail the origins and evidence of human rights in pre-colonial societies, analysing sources including Hammurabi's Code, the *Qur'an*, Confucian thought, the Iroquois Nations' Constitution, and Aztec and Incan texts. He concludes that already in ancient times, ideas of human rights existed outside the West.[38] Equally, Lauren surveyed the foundations of justice and human rights in early legal texts and thought

---

[33] Karen Engle, Culture and Human Rights: The Asian Values Debate in Context (1999-2000) *New York University Journal of International Law and Politics* 32, p. 308; Alison Dundes Renteln, Relativism and the Search for Human Rights (1988) *American Anthropologist* 90, p. 57.

[34] Abdullahi Ahmed An-Na'im, Toward a Cross-Cultural Approach to Defining International Standards of Human Rights: The Meaning of Cruel, Inhuman, or Degrading Treatment or Punishment, in Abdullahi Ahmed An-Na'im (ed.), *Human Rights in Cross-Cultural Perspectives: A Quest for Consensus* (University of Pennsylvania Press, 1992), p. 24. See also Sally Engle Merry, Human Rights Law and the Demonization of Culture (And Anthropology along the Way) (May 2003) *PoLAR* 26:1, pp. 56-8.

[35] At the time of drafting the UDHR, UN Educational, Scientific and Cultural Organization (UNESCO) undertook a survey into whether the principles underlying the draft Declaration were indeed reflected in cultural traditions around the world. See Glendon (n. 11), pp. 73-8; Mark Goodale, The Myth of Universality: The UNESCO 'Philosophers' Committee' and the Making of Human Rights (2018) *Law & Social Inquiry* 43:3, pp. 596-617.

[36] She went on to say: 'By tracing the linkages between constitutional values on the one hand and the concepts, ideas, and institutions which are central to Islam or the Hindu-Buddhist tradition or other traditions, the base of support for fundamental rights can be expanded and the claim to universality vindicated'. Mary Robinson, Human Rights at the Dawn of the 21st Century (1993) *Human Rights Quarterly* 15, p. 632.

[37] Bonny Ibhawoh, Cultural Relativism and Human Rights: Reconsidering the Africanist Discourse (2001) *Netherlands Quarterly of Human Rights* 19:1, p. 49.

[38] Lenzerini (n. 5), pp. 33, 46.

around the world,[39] finding the claim of a 'Western monopoly' over rights unsupportable.[40] He concluded that human rights have emerged over the years in various ways in various 'places, societies, religious and secular traditions'.[41] Afshari asserts that the myth of Western ownership of the UDHR model should be 'consigned to history'.[42]

In contrast, others have argued that most known human societies did *not* have conceptions of human rights, and that human dignity does not imply human rights.[43] Donnelly claims that while traditional African societies, Islam, Confucian and Hindu thought have concepts of dignity, they do not equate to human rights, which are inherent (not granted) and inalienable (not conditional) rights (not privileges or benefits).[44] Despite his detractors,[45] Donnelly concluded that 'most non-Western cultural and political traditions lack not only the practice of human rights but the very concept'.[46] While not conflating dignity with rights, historical conceptions of human dignity around the world remain relevant foundations of human rights as conceived of today. Reiterated in numerous international and regional human rights instruments, human dignity is 'one of the most pervasive and fundamental ideas in the entire corpus of international human rights law'.[47] Highlighting the connection between modern rights and traditional notions of dignity, Ibhawoh claims that

---

[39] Lauren's analysis includes the Law of Moses; the Charter of Cyrus; the teaching of Mohammed; the classic Sanskrit treaties; and the Edicts of Asoka. See generally Paul Gordon Lauren, The Foundations of Justice and Human Rights in Early Legal Texts and Thought, in Dinah Shelton (ed.), *The Oxford Handbook of International Human Rights Law* (Oxford University Press, 2013), pp. 164–8, 172–4, 181–9.

[40] Ibid., p. 178.

[41] Ibid., p. 163.

[42] Reza Afshari, Relativity in Universality: Jack Donnelly's Grand Theory in Need of Specific Illustrations (2015) *Human Rights Quarterly* 37:4, p. 857.

[43] Donnelly (2013) (n. 11), p. 78; Jack Donnelly, Human Rights and Human Dignity: An Analytic Critique of Non-Western Conceptions of Human Rights (1982) *The American Political Science Review* 76:2, pp. 303–16; Rhoda Howard, Dignity, Community, and Human Rights, in Abdullahi Ahmed An-Na'im (ed.), *Human Rights in Cross-Cultural Perspectives: A Quest for Consensus* (University of Pennsylvania Press, 1992), pp. 81–102.

[44] Donnelly (1982), ibid., pp. 303–16.

[45] In rejection of Donnelly's analysis, see Renteln (n. 30), pp. 525–9; Mutua (n. 3), pp. 79–81; Lenzerini (n. 5), pp. 42–4 and fn. 63.

[46] Donnelly (1982) (n. 43), p. 303. See also Howard (n. 43), pp. 81, 90–1. For a critique of these positions, see Ann-Belinda Preis, Human Rights as Cultural Practice: An Anthropological Critique (1996) *Human Rights Quarterly* 18, p. 293.

[47] Paolo Carozza, Human Dignity, in Dinah Shelton (ed.), *The Oxford Handbook on International Human Rights Law* (Oxford University Press, 2013), p. 345. See also Fortman (n. 9), pp. 49–50.

rights 'are in fact merely contextual reinterpretations of the age-long notions of defining human worth and value'.[48]

2.2.2 Continued Cultural Challenges to Universality

In the decades since the UDHR's adoption, challenges to the universality of human rights has not abated. While most critiques accept human rights but refute certain elements, aspects or interpretations, a few fully reject the conception and system of international human rights.[49] In general, the debate centres around whether human rights are universal in nature and application, or whether they are culturally relative as dependent upon the socio-cultural context and setting.[50] Particularly in the 1990s, the universal versus culturally relative debate was 'a battlefield of fierce, heated, and passionate debate'.[51] Key challenges have been presented by, *inter alia*, cultural relativists, advocates of 'Asian values', postcolonial and Third World Approaches to International Law (TWAIL) scholars, and on the basis of Islam. While advancing different interests, a commonality of the critiques is that they depart from the position that the modern human rights concept was developed by a dominant (Western) group and is therefore inadequate for their group as it excludes their perspectives.[52] As such, human rights cannot be universal as they are structured according to a model not shared by all cultures.[53] Like those levelled at the UDHR, these critiques persist and continue to shape human rights as the system develops. These critiques are therefore briefly set out below.

As noted above, cultural relativism 'is founded on the notion of communal autonomy and self-determination which holds that there is infinite cultural variability in human society and no absolutes'.[54] Given the global variety of moral codes and the lack of hierarchy, outside criticism of a given code should not apply.[55] Cultural relativists across the spectrum typically argue that human rights norms are not culturally,

---

[48] Ibhawoh (2001) (n. 37), p. 45.
[49] Eva Brems, Enemies or Allies? Feminism and Cultural Relativism as Dissident Voices in Human Rights Discourse (1997) *Human Rights Quarterly* 19, pp. 141, 143-4.
[50] Ibhawoh (2001) (n. 37), p. 43.
[51] Preis (n. 46), p. 288.
[52] Brems (1997) (n. 49), p. 154.
[53] Lenzerini (n. 5), p. 246.
[54] Ibhawoh (2001) (n. 37), p. 46.
[55] Ibid.

ideologically, or politically *universal*, but rather belie a Western, Judeo-Christian bias.[56] Part of this bias is the strict focus on the individual (over the family or community), prioritisation of civil and political rights (over economic, social, and cultural rights (ESC rights)), and the emphasis on rights (over duties). Scholars of the firm relativist persuasion argue that the Western conception of human rights is of limited value and even meaningless to the developing world.[57] Because of this propensity to label rights inapplicable or invalid, human rights supporters fear that recognising the legitimacy of cultural relativism 'will undermine the entire universal human rights movement'.[58] Therefore, the contest between relativists and universalists has been fought doggedly.

While the issue of culture and human rights was first raised in relation to the UDHR, the debate reached a pinnacle in the 1990s. At this time, some Asian states and scholars argued that human rights were incompatible with 'Asian values' – giving rise to the so-called Asian values debate.[59] Several states were strong proponents of such Asian values, including Singapore, Malaysia, Indonesia and China. For Mr Lee Kuan Yew, then Singapore's Prime Minister and one of the movement's leaders, one of the cultural differences between the West and Asia was the latter's belief 'that the individual exists in the context of his [sic] family'.[60] Asian values, it was claimed, held a preference for 'strong central government over pluralism, social harmony over dissent, development over civil liberties'.[61] The proponents of Asian values did not contest the system of human rights or, in principle, their universality, but rather challenged the dominant Western interpretation of rights that ignored legitimate cultural differences.[62] The 1993 *Bangkok Declaration* provided that 'while' universal, rights must be considered 'bearing in

---

[56] Preis (n. 46), p. 288.
[57] Ibid., p. 291, citing Adamantia Pollis and Peter Schwab, Human Rights: A Western Construct with Limited Applicability, in Adamantia Pollis and Peter Schwab (eds.), *Human Rights: Cultural and Ideological Perspectives* (Praeger, 1980), p. 8.
[58] Ibhawoh (2001) (n. 37), p. 47.
[59] Lenzerini (n. 5), p. 59. See also Bilahari Kausikan, Asia's Different Standard (Fall 1993) *Foreign Policy* 92, pp. 24–41.
[60] Engle (n. 33), p. 327, quoting Lee.
[61] Radhika Coomaraswamy, The Contemporary Challenges to International Human Rights, in Scott Sheeran and Sir Nigel Rodley (eds.), *Routledge Handbook of International Human Rights Law* (Routledge, 2013), p. 128.
[62] Lenzerini (n. 5), pp. 59–60; Brems (2001) (n. 19), pp. 88–9. See also Christina Cerna, East Asian Approaches to Human Rights (1995) *Buffalo Journal of International Law* 2, pp. 201–13.

mind the significance of national and regional particularities and various historical, cultural and religious backgrounds'.[63] This sentiment was reflected again in the 2012 *ASEAN Human Rights Declaration*,[64] which was criticised internationally on the basis *inter alia* that it undermines universalism, privileging relativism.[65]

The issues raised in the Asian values debate were mirrored to an extent by critics from across Africa, including many postcolonial and TWAIL scholars. While reiterating the accusation of Western bias within human rights, some of these critics go further in submitting that as a result of this bias the entire system of international law is illegitimate.[66] TWAIL scholars have dedicated enormous intellectual energy to identifying the various political, economic and cultural biases embedded in the project of international law.[67] Mutua places human rights in an historical continuum rooted in colonialism/imperialism, Christian proselytism and racism. From this perspective, 'whites pose as the saviors of a benighted and savage non-European world' that must be transformed according to universal (read European) human rights.[68] The perspective of Southern

---

[63] Bangkok Declaration on Human Rights, adopted by the Regional Meeting for Asia of the World Conference on Human Rights, Bangkok (29 March–2 April 1993), A/CONF.157/ASRM/8-A/CONF.157/PC/59, art. 8.

[64] Association of Southeast Asian Nations (ASEAN) Human Rights Declaration, 18 November 2012, www.asean.org/storage/images/ASEAN_RTK_2014/6_AHRD_Booklet.pdf (accessed 24 January 2018).

[65] See UN News Centre, UN Official Welcomes ASEAN Commitment to Human Rights, but Concerned over Declaration Wording (19 November 2012), www.un.org/apps/news/story.asp?NewsID=43536#.VK1r9SvF9nE (accessed 7 January 2015); European Union, Statement by High Representative Catherine Ashton on the adoption of the ASEAN Human Rights Declaration (22 November 2012), www.consilium.europa.eu/uedocs/cms_Data/docs/pressdata/EN/foraff/133682.pdf (accessed 7 January 2015); US Department of State, Press Statement, Victoria Nuland, ASEAN Declaration on Human Rights (20 November 2012), https://2009-2017.state.gov/r/pa/prs/ps/2012/11/200915.htm (accessed 24 January 2018). See also Catherine Renshaw, The ASEAN Human Rights Declaration 2012 (2013) *Human Rights Law Review* 13:3, pp. 557–79.

[66] See Makau Mutua, What Is TWAIL? (2000) *American Society of International Law Proceedings* p. 36, (vol. 94); Abdullahi Ahmed An-Na`im, Why Should Muslims Abandon Jihad? Human Rights and the Future of International Law? in Richard Falk, Balakrishnan Rajagopal and Jacqueline Stevens (eds.), *International Law and the Third World: Reshaping Justice* (Routledge, 2008), p. 83.

[67] See Luis Eslava and Sundhya Pahuja, Between Resistance and Reform: TWAIL and the Universality of International Law (2011) *Trade, Law and Development* 3:1, p. 117; Obiora Chinedu Okafor, Newness, Imperialism, and International Legal Reform in Our Time: A TWAIL Perspective (2005) *Osgoode Hall Law Journal* 43:1&2, p. 177.

[68] Mutua (n. 3), pp. 20, 155.

states is informed by the view of human rights as part of colonialism's 'civilising mission' that served to legitimise the West's intervention in the non-European world.[69] Given this imperial history and the complicity of international law and human rights with Western political agendas, Rajagopal asserts that the human rights discourse operates in a hegemonic mode.[70]

In this way, the Western experience of human rights masquerades as universal, necessarily excluding 'the experiences of other peoples and alternative visions of a just society'.[71] Therefore, international human rights do not appropriately address the needs or reflect the views of the Global South, and cannot do so without wholesale reconceptualisation.[72] Like the critics in the Asian values debate, some seek reform of human rights to remedy the bias, while other TWAIL scholars are more radical in rejecting the system. Anghie, a proponent of reform, acknowledges that the history of human rights as part of the colonial legacy has caused many from Southern states to be ambivalent about rights, 'even while recognising the enormous appeal and promise of the project'.[73] Any reconceptualisation of rights to make them genuinely universal would need to include, *inter alia*, group or people's rights and greater emphasis on duties, development and ESC rights. As is evident from the 1981 *African Charter on Human and Peoples' Rights*, individual rights alone do not reflect the African experience of humans as 'an integral member of a group animated by a spirit of solidarity'.[74] This reflects also the position articulated in the Asian values debate that the family – and not the individual – is the basis of society.

Of all the cultural critiques of human rights, Brems concludes that those based on Islam come closest to rejecting universality.[75] Islamic conceptions of human rights are also oriented towards the community

---

[69] Anghie (n. 28), p. 112. See also Abdullahi Ahmed An-Na`im, The Spirit of Laws Is Not Universal: Alternatives to the Enforcement Paradigm for Human Rights (2016) *Tilburg Law Review* 21, P. 256.
[70] Rajagopal (n. 20), p. 66.
[71] Anghie (n. 28), p. 110.
[72] Mutua (n. 3), p. 6.
[73] Anghie (n. 28), p. 112.
[74] B. Obinna Okere, The Protection of Human Rights in Africa and the African Charter on Human and Peoples' Rights: A Comparative Analysis with the European and American Systems (1984) *Human Rights Quarterly* 6, p. 148.
[75] Brems (2001) (n. 19), pp. 288, 290.

2.2 HUMAN RIGHTS & CULTURAL CRITIQUES

and duties; however, a central issue for Islam (and other religions) is that rights must yield priority to divine law.[76] This can be seen in the 1990 *Cairo Declaration on Human Rights in Islam*, which subjects all of the rights therein to *Shari'a*.[77] Similarly, Muslim majority states often enter so-called 'Islamic reservations' when ratifying international human rights treaties, particularly the *Convention on the Elimination of All Forms of Discrimination against Women* (CEDAW).[78] Such reservations typically note that the treaty is only binding in so far as it does not conflict with Islamic law. While many argue that such reservations undermine the object and purpose of the treaties, their precise impact upon the treaty and legal obligations therein remains unresolved.[79] Despite this, An-Na'im concludes that Islam is in fact generally consistent with human rights, 'except for some specific, albeit very serious, aspects of the rights of women and freedom of religion.[80] Of note, the more recent 2004 *Arab Charter on Human Rights* does not broadly subordinate rights to Islamic law, only mentioning *Shari'a* once.[81] Given that Muslims make up around one-quarter of the world's population, An-Na'im finds it improbable for

---

[76] Olivier Roy and Pasqual Annicchino, Human Rights between Religions, Cultures, and Universality, in Ana Filipa Vrdoljak (ed.), *The Cultural Dimension of Human Rights* (Oxford University Press, 2013), p. 17; Lenzerini (n. 5), p. 77; Brems (2001) (n. 19), pp. 286–9.

[77] Organization of the Islamic Conference, Cairo Declaration on Human Rights in Islam (Cairo, 5 August 1990), art. 24.

[78] See Mervat Rishmawi, The Revised Arab Charter on Human Rights: A Step Forward? (2005) *Human Rights Law Review* 5:2, p. 368; Brems (2001) (n. 19), pp. 267–84; Yvonne Donders, Human Rights: Eye for Cultural Diversity, Inaugural Lecture delivered upon the appointment to the chair of Professor of International Human Rights and Cultural Diversity at the University of Amsterdam (29 June 2012), p. 11.

[79] See generally Lenzerini (n. 5), pp. 90–100; Yvonne Donders, Cultural Pluralism in International Human Rights Law: The Role of Reservations, in Ana Filipa Vrdoljak (ed.), *The Cultural Dimension of Human Rights* (Oxford University Press, 2013), pp. 205–39; UN General Assembly, Report of the Special Rapporteur in the Field of Cultural Rights, Universality, Cultural Diversity and Cultural Rights, A/73/227 (25 July 2018), para. 52.

[80] An-Na'im (n. 66), p. 87.

[81] League of Arab States, *Arab Charter on Human Rights* (adopted May 2004, entered into force on 15 March 2008). Article 3(3) relates to the equality between men and women within the framework of positive discrimination established by *Shari'a*. Rishmawi notes that, while it still falls short, the Charter is a significant improvement in terms of compatibility with international standards over the earlier Cairo Declaration. Rishmawi (n. 78).

any conception of human rights to be considered universal 'if it is inconsistent with the religious beliefs of Muslims at large'.[82]

As seen from these brief descriptions, despite more than seventy years since the adoption of the UDHR, the universality of rights is still contested. While the international human rights system has developed greatly in this time, challenges continue to be made based on culture. Critics contest both the conception and content of human rights, as well as their application in diverse communities around the world. Some have suggested that these critiques may be disingenuous, accusing some leaders and elites of pursuing such arguments in order to discredit the West and/or to hide or rationalise their own rights violations.[83] Others more sympathetic to relativistic arguments warn against the wholesale incorporation of traditional, communal values, which are often patriarchal in nature.[84] While there are certainly pitfalls and problematic issues requiring thorough consideration, scholars have urged that cultural critiques be taken seriously.[85] These critiques highlight that the human rights project is not yet complete, and that the need exists 'to adopt a broader view of human rights incorporating diverse concepts, and moral experiences'.[86] Importantly, these critiques typically demonstrate an eagerness to contribute meaningfully to the debate and development of human rights, rather than a withdrawal from the international system. They should therefore not be seen as a threat to be rebuffed, but as contributions seeking to improve the universality of rights.

The once highly polarised universalist versus relativist debate is now less dichotomous, with consensus around 'a set of core human rights to which all humanity aspires'.[87] Scholars note that the 'field is now crowded in the middle', with most adopting the position that while rights are universal, some space must be granted for legitimate cultural variations.[88] In fact, it is common for international documents and human

---

[82] An-Na'im (n. 10), p. 56.
[83] Brems (1997) (n. 49), p. 142, fn. 32. See also Coomaraswamy (n. 61), p. 130; Ibhawoh (2001) (n. 37), p. 55.
[84] Ibhawoh (2001) (n .37), p. 56.
[85] Freeman (n. 17), p. 60; Brems (2004) (n. 10), pp. 223–4; Jack Donnelly, The Relative Universality of Human Rights (2007) Human Rights Quarterly 29:2, p. 301; Glendon (n. 11), pp. 224, 229.
[86] Ibhawoh (2001) (n. 37), p. 61.
[87] Bonny Ibhawoh, Between Culture and Constitution: Evaluating the Cultural Legitimacy of Human Rights in the African State (2000) Human Rights Quarterly 22, pp. 838, 843.
[88] Afshari (n. 42), p. 855; Ibhawoh (2001) (n. 37), pp. 49, 58.

rights advocates to emphasise 'the need for a culturally sensitive universalism'.[89] However, not all cultural practices must be accommodated, with some practices (like slavery, torture, etc.) not being justified on any grounds. Similarly, cultural critiques should be considered where they 'function as an expression and guarantee of local self-determination', but not when they serve 'as an excuse for arbitrary rule and despotism'.[90] While the debate has moved away from extreme positions, it remains unresolved and of ongoing relevancy today. The international human rights system still needs to be buttressed by cultural experiences around the world in order to be considered universally legitimate and acceptable.[91] The UDHR is the alpha, but not the omega, of international human rights.[92]

2.2.3 International Human Rights Today

Notwithstanding this ongoing debate and cultural critiques, the UDHR continues to enjoy widespread support and is even suggested to be customary international law.[93] In the decades since the UDHR's adoption, the international human rights system has grown rapidly with the universality of rights repeatedly reinforced. The two international human rights Covenants were adopted in 1966 by the United Nations, which had a significantly larger membership than in 1948 due to decolonisation. The influence of these new member states was not insignificant.[94] For example, despite its absence in the UDHR, both 1966 Covenants affirm the right of self-determination in their first article.[95] In fact, the first human rights treaty concluded was not these two Covenants, but rather the *Convention on the Elimination of All Forms of Racial Discrimination*

---

[89] Engle (n. 33), pp. 322–3. See generally Donnelly's 'weak relativism' and Brems' 'inclusive universality': Donnelly (n. 11); Brems (2001) (n. 19).
[90] Ibhawoh (2001) (n. 37), pp. 58–9.
[91] Ibhawoh (2000) (n. 87), p. 843; Brems (2004) (n. 10), p. 223.
[92] Koen de Feyter, Localizing Human Rights, Institute of Development Policy and Management, Discussion Paper (January 2006), p. 8.
[93] Ibid., p. 7; Glendon (n. 11), p. 178. Regarding the UDHR's qualification as customary international law, see Henry Steiner and Philip Alston, *International Human Rights in Context: Law, Politics, Morals* (2nd ed., Oxford University Press, 2000), pp. 228–9.
[94] Anghie (n. 28), p. 116.
[95] Schrijver notes that self-determination was included 'against the wishes of Western countries'. Nico Schrijver, Paving the Way towards ... One Worldwide Human Rights Treaty! (2011) *Netherlands Quarterly of Human Rights* 29:3, p. 258. See also Glendon (n. 11), p. 214.

in 1965.[96] In this way, Southern states were able to participate in legislating this new body of law and be influential. However, Mutua cautions against overstating their role, noting that 'the levers of power' at the United Nations have traditionally been beyond their reach.[97] While former colonial states joined and participated in the United Nations, they did so based on rules agreed in their absence. As such, the end of colonialism did not necessarily include the end of colonial relations.[98] Despite the United Nations' ongoing power imbalances, the membership of former colonial states remains influential.

Since the end of the Cold War, the discourse on human rights in the 1990s changed and grew in significance, with the United Nations having far greater leeway to advocate the universal application of rights around the world.[99] The 1993 World Conference on Human Rights, which saw an unprecedented level of participation and representation, reaffirmed in the Vienna Declaration that the universality of rights was 'beyond question'.[100] In addition to these international developments, regional and domestic instruments also reinforce international human rights. For example, the UDHR has been used as a model for some ninety constitutions, including nineteen constitutions of former colonial states, with specific references to the UDHR.[101] Several regions have also adopted human rights instruments that largely reflect international human rights, with the instruments from Europe, the Americas, Africa, the ASEAN

---

[96] *International Convention on the Elimination of All Forms of Racial Discrimination* (adopted 7 March 1966, entered into force 4 January 1969), 660 UNTS 195 (CERD).

[97] Mutua (n. 3), p. 19. See also Abdullahi Ahmed An-Na`im, Conclusion, in Abdullahi Ahmed An-Na`im (ed.), *Human Rights in Cross-Cultural Perspectives: A Quest for Consensus* (University of Pennsylvania Press, 1992), p. 428.

[98] Antony Anghie, The Evolution of International Law: Colonial and Postcolonial Realities, in Richard Falk, Balakrishnan Rajagopal and Jacqueline Stevens (eds.), *International Law and the Third World: Reshaping Justice* (Routledge, 2008), pp. 44–5. Koskenniemi suggests that the entry of former colonies into the UN had the effect of simply rendering the inequality 'slightly more invisible'. See Martti Koskenniemi, *Histories of International Law: Dealing with Eurocentrism* (Oratie, Utrecht University, 16 November 2011), p. 21.

[99] Jean-Philippe Thérien and Philippe Joly, 'All Human Rights for All': The United Nations and Human Rights in the Post-Cold War Era (2014) *Human Rights Quarterly* 36:2, pp. 385, 378–9.

[100] UN General Assembly, Vienna Declaration and Programme of Action, A/CONF.157/23 (12 July 1993), para. 1.

[101] Osiatyński (n. 13), p. 12; Glendon (n. 11), p. 228. Some scholars, however, refute this as a virtue, stating that the constitutions in Africa were largely written by Europeans on the eve of independence, rather than as a genuine expression of African values. See Mutua (n. 3), p. 119; Ibhawoh (2000) (n. 87), p. 845.

2.2 HUMAN RIGHTS & CULTURAL CRITIQUES

region, and the Arab Charter all referring to the UDHR in their preambles. Despite these affirmations, the proliferation and widespread ratification of international human rights treaties, it is important to recall that states ratify treaties for different reasons – and not necessarily due to wholesale agreement or a genuine intention to implement them.[102] As such, attempts to legitimise human rights treaties based on their ratification alone is problematic.[103]

Notwithstanding the continued pre-eminence of the UDHR, international human rights have proven to be dynamic and have evolved over the last seventy years. This evolution can be seen in the development of new rights, and new conceptions and applications of existing rights. For example, new instruments continue to be agreed, such as the *Convention for the Protection of All Persons from Enforced Disappearance* and the *Convention on the Rights of Persons with Disabilities* in 2006.[104] New rights are emerging, including the right to the Internet and the right to a healthy environment. Additionally, as demonstrated by the Declaration on the Rights of Indigenous Peoples, the international community is becoming more open to the concept of collective rights as typically advanced by the South.[105] As this shows, human rights law is flexible and can evolve to accommodate cultural variation in response to legitimate demands. As a relatively new system of law, international human rights law is still evolving, subject to negotiation and renegotiation over time.[106] Mutua urges recognition of the fact that the human rights movement is still young, which gives it more of an 'experimental status' than a 'final truth'.[107]

---

[102] States might ratify treaties to help strengthen a universal normative framework; to be considered a positive member of the international community; for trade links or economic benefits; or in response to international and/or domestic pressure. Christof Heyns and Frans Viljoen, The Impact of the United Nations Human Rights Treaties on the Domestic Level (2001) *Human Rights Quarterly* 23:3, pp. 491–4.

[103] Renteln (n. 30), p. 540.

[104] *Convention on the Rights of Persons with Disabilities* (adopted 13 December 2006, entered into force 3 May 2008), 2515 UNTS 3; *International Convention for the Protection of All Persons from Enforced Disappearance* (adopted on 20 December 2006, entered into force 23 December 2010), UN Doc. A/61/488.

[105] Lenzerini (n. 5), p. 110. UN General Assembly, Declaration on the Rights of Indigenous Peoples, A/RES/61/295 (2 October 2007).

[106] Barbara Oomen and Esther van den Berg, Human Rights Cities: Urban Actors as Pragmatic Idealistic Human Rights Users (2014) *Human Rights and International Legal Discourse* 8:2, p. 162.

[107] Mutua (n. 3), p. 4.

Just as human rights continue to evolve, so do cultures.[108] Commenting on culture's perennial evolution, Lenzerini recalls that current cultural identities have been progressively adapted over time in response to circumstances, contestation and cultural interactions.[109] Rather than a product, culture is a process continually undergoing change, with no well-defined boundaries and multiple influencers.[110] Anthropologists have elaborated a view of culture as 'unbounded, contested, and connected to relations of power ... marked by hybridity and creolization rather than uniformity or consistency'.[111] As such, a paradox of culture is the way in which it combines stability (or the perception of it) with persistent dynamism.[112] Given this fluidity, cultural practices at odds with human rights may diminish over time (or new ones may emerge). On this basis, it is particularly important not to reify or essentialise culture, which negates its dynamic nature.[113] It is therefore vital for culture to be appropriately understood within the context of human rights. Anthropological insights have assisted in this regard, but problems persist.

One of the ongoing problems is the way in which international law typically conceives of 'culture'. Numerous scholars have critiqued essentialised portrayals of culture in international human rights law as static and monolithic, rather than recognising its nuanced and dynamic nature.[114] For example, references to traditional African or Asian societies tend to present cultural notions, their informal institutions and practices as static, whereas culture is in fact 'eclectic, dynamic, and subject to significant alteration over time'.[115] Debates regarding culture

---

[108] While an agreed definition remains elusive, 'culture' generally encompasses the complex features characterising a society/social group, including its modes of life, value systems, traditions and beliefs. See, for example, the preamble of the UNESCO Universal Declaration on Cultural Diversity, adopted by the 31st Session of the General Conference of UNESCO in Paris (2 November 2001); UNESCO Mexico City Declaration on Cultural Policies, adopted at World Conference on Cultural Policies, Mexico City (26 July–6 August 1982). The latter also specifically includes human rights.
[109] Lenzerini (n. 5), pp. 238–9.
[110] Donders (n. 78), p. 6; Lenzerini (n. 5), pp. 220–1.
[111] Merry (2003) (n. 34), p. 67.
[112] An-Na'im (n. 34), p. 27.
[113] William Twining, Legal Pluralism 101, in Brian Tamanaha, Caroline Sage and Michael Woolcock (eds.), *Legal Pluralism and Development: Scholars and Practitioners in Dialogue* (Cambridge University Press, 2012), p. 114.
[114] Ibid., p. 118. See also UN General Assembly, Report of the Special Rapporteur in the Field of Cultural Rights, A/67/287 (10 August 2012), paras. 16–17.
[115] Ibhawoh (2000) (n. 87), p. 841.

frequently occur on an abstract or highly generalised level where culture is conceptualised as static and homogeneous, as a bounded entity that is defined by its specific traits.[116] Merry notes that human rights discourses tend to view culture as an ancient practice, something primitive or backward that obstructs progress.[117] Culture is juxtaposed to law and human rights, which are represented as modern culture-free zones – despite the fact that law and modernity themselves are cultural systems.[118] In this way, culture itself is othered. The ubiquity of culture is frequently under-appreciated as one's culture is so deeply embedded in their identity and consciousness.[119] As a result, even that which is acutely culturally coded can be mistaken for objective or neutral by someone within that culture.[120]

In line with this view on the inter-connectedness of culture and human rights, scholars and practitioners have increasingly recognised the cultural dimension of human rights.[121] In particular, the UN Committee on Economic, Social and Cultural Rights (ESCR Committee) has held that the rights to food, water, health, education and housing must be culturally appropriate.[122] The Committee held that appropriateness refers to

---

[116] Preis says that culture is seemingly 'implicitly defined as a homogenous, bounded unit, almost as if it were "a thing"'. Preis (n. 46), pp. 289, 294.

[117] Merry (2003) (n. 34), pp. 58, 60.

[118] Ibid., pp. 62, 70. The Special Rapporteur in the Field of Cultural Rights notes that: 'The universality of human rights is itself an important cultural project.' Report of the Special Rapporteur, A/73/227 (n. 79), para. 43.

[119] An-Na'im (n. 34), p. 23. The Special Rapporteur in the Field of Cultural Rights (n. 114) notes in para. 2 that: 'Culture permeates all human activities and institutions, including legal systems, in all societies across the world.' She elaborates ((n. 79), para. 56) that: 'all people and all peoples have culture, not merely certain categories or geographies of people'.

[120] Preis notes that 'the temptation to confuse our local culture with universal human nature has proven to be such a marvellous temptation'. Preis (n. 46), p. 314.

[121] Donders (n. 78), p. 17; Lenzerini (n. 5), pp. 123, 152. For example, the Committee against Torture noted that reparations and rehabilitation services for victims should take into account the victim's culture, and the CEDAW Committee recognised that health legislation, plans and policies should take account of religion, tradition and culture: UN Committee against Torture, General Comment No. 3, Implementation of Article 14 by States Parties, CAT/C/GC/3 (13 December 2012), paras. 15, 32; UN CEDAW Committee, General Recommendation No. 24: Article 12 of the Convention (women and health) (1999), para. 9.

[122] UN ESCR Committee, General Comment No. 12, The Right to Adequate Food (Article 11), E/C.12/1999/5 (12 May 1999), paras. 7, 8, 11, 39; UN ESCR Committee, General Comment No. 15, The Right to Water (Articles 11 and 12), E/C.12/2002/11 (20 January 2003), para. 12(c)(i); UN ESCR Committee, General Comment No. 13, The Right to Education (Article 13), E/C.12/1999/10 (8 December 1999), para. 6(c) and (d); UN

the realisation of rights in a way that is 'suitable to a given cultural modality or context, that is, respectful of the culture and cultural rights of individuals and communities'.[123] The right to food has clear cultural connections given the role of food preparation and consumption in religion, such as kosher and halal requirements. Similarly, the right to health has cultural implications stemming from religious and other beliefs about life and death, sickness and healing. In recognition of this, the ESCR Committee requires states parties to ensure that all health facilities, goods and services are 'culturally appropriate'.[124] This demonstrates a growing sophistication of ideas regarding the nexus between rights and culture, and illustrates the way in which culture can – and should – be accommodated in human rights implementation. Doing so better ensures that rights are meaningful to the contextualised individual, who can enjoy them in line with their own view of 'the good life'.[125]

Finally, it is important to recall that while there is great diversity in the world and between cultures and peoples, there are also marked commonalities. As those who have studied the global foundations of human rights would attest, there are overwhelming similarities in matters of human rights.[126] As illustrated by the regional human rights instruments addressing largely the same catalogue of rights, it is increasingly clear that rights are compatible with the world's leading religious and philosophical traditions. Dismissing human rights entirely as 'Western' is to ignore diverse global voices calling for such rights and to deny people seeking their protection international recognition and solidarity.[127] The foundations and content of human rights may remain contentious today, but this is not fatal to the system of rights as developed by the international community. The system continues to evolve and is not based upon one single foundation but many, relying upon 'good moral

---

ESCR Committee, General Comment No. 4, The Right to Adequate Housing (Article 11), E/1992/23 (1991), para. 8(g); UN ESCR Committee, General Comment No. 14, The Right to the Highest Attainable Standard of Health (Article 12), E/C.12/2000/4 (11 August 2000), para. 12(c).

[123] UN ESCR Committee, General Comment No. 21, Rights of Everyone to Take Part in Cultural Life, E/C.12/GC/21 (21 December 2009), para. 16(e).
[124] UN ESCR Committee, General Comment No. 14 (n. 122), para. 12(c).
[125] Donnelly (2007) (n. 85), p. 303.
[126] Even according to Mutua: 'Although different cultures may appear to be radically distinctive and irreconcilable, they possess ideals from which universally-shared norms can be excavated'. Mutua (n. 3), p. 74.
[127] Coomaraswamy (n. 61), p. 130.

arguments' regardless of their origin that can be endorsed by people and states around the world.[128]

2.3 Culturally Sensitive Approaches to Human Rights Implementation

The universal versus culturally relative debate highlighted the need for human rights to better recognise and accommodate cultural diversity. The cultural critiques demonstrate that more still needs to be done to ensure that human rights genuinely reflect their universal character. The international human rights system has several mechanisms by which it can be flexible and accommodate diversity – including implementation.[129] It is now accepted that the universality of rights does not mean their uniformity in all contexts, nor does it imply their uniform implementation.[130] The UN's Special Rapporteur on cultural rights contends: 'Universality is about human dignity, not about homogeneity.'[131] It is submitted that while human rights apply universally, their domestic implementation should be contextualised. Attention is increasingly being paid to local perspectives of human rights and to the variety of contexts and cultural norms relevant to human rights enjoyment. On this basis, scholars and practitioners have called for more culturally sensitive approaches to human rights, greater respect for cultural diversity and protection of cultural rights. Such calls advocate cultural sensitivity in the conceptualisation, interpretation, implementation and adjudication of rights.

This book addresses contextualised or culturally sensitive approaches to human rights implementation. While novel in some ways, these approaches share commonalities in seeking to accommodate and employ

---

[128] Freeman (n. 17), pp. 51–2. See also Brems (2004) (n. 10), p. 216; Brems (2001) (n. 19), p. 299; Lenzerini (n. 5), p. 238; Glendon (n. 11), p. 226.
[129] The mechanisms to accommodate diversity include limitation clauses, the exhaustion of domestic remedies, the subsidiarity principle and doctrines such as the margin of appreciation. David Kinley, Bendable Rules: The Development Implications of Human Rights Pluralism, in Brian Tamanaha, Caroline Sage and Michael Woolcock (eds.), *Legal Pluralism and Development: Scholars and Practitioners in Dialogue* (Cambridge University Press, 2012), pp. 51–3.
[130] Donders (n. 78), p. 9; Cees Flinterman, The Universal Declaration of Human Rights at 60 (2008) *Netherlands Quarterly of Human Rights* 26:4, p. 482; Brems (2004) (n. 19), p. 13. Glendon notes that the UDHR itself was never intended to produce uniform practices: Glendon (n. 11), p. 230.
[131] Report of the Special Rapporteur, A/73/227 (n. 79), para. 8.

culture and social institutions within methods of human rights implementation. These approaches all tend to: (1) stress the need for such a cultural approach to implementation; (2) promote non-legislative measures to implement rights; (3) promote home-grown solutions to human rights problems; and (4) rely on culture's dynamism and contestation to further human rights compliance. A central feature of the various approaches is the contention that for rights to be real and effective, they should be implemented in consideration of local cultural standards and community values. It is submitted that these culturally sensitive approaches to human rights are necessary from both a normative perspective (emphasising the value of diversity and cultural rights) as well as from a practical one (legitimacy and efficacy).[132] This section analyses and evaluates the culturally sensitive approaches to human rights implementation advocated in literature, identifying their commonalities, strengths and weaknesses.[133]

2.3.1 Need and Scope for Cultural Sensitivity in Human Rights Implementation

Now seven decades after the UDHR, the language of international human rights law is unknown to many people around the world, with large numbers viewing rights as foreign, unfamiliar, or even irrelevant.[134] Where there is some knowledge, there can also be misunderstanding regarding the nature and content of rights, generating suspicion, mistrust and opposition. As such, it is necessary to improve general awareness and understanding of international human rights law in communities around the world. Further, given that human rights are conceived of only generally at the international level, it is important to develop their substantive meaning in local contexts. Due to the predominant Western influence on human rights, there is a particular gap between international human rights law and the experience of people typically in Southern states. This gap is an obstacle to the effective implementation of human rights. It is therefore necessary to recast

---

[132] Julie Fraser and Henrike Prudon, Integrating Human Rights with Local Norms: Ebola, Burial Practices, and the Right to Health in West Africa (2017) *Intercultural Human Rights Law Review* 12, p. 72.
[133] Select parts of this analysis were published in ibid., pp. 84–94.
[134] Oomen and van den Berg (n. 106), p. 181; Brems (2001) (n. 19), p. 311.

2.3 CULTURALLY SENSITIVE APPROACHES

rights in a meaningful way for the target audience of rights-holders, as human rights are only readily adopted when they take a familiar form.[135] Advocates of culturally sensitive approaches stress the need to translate both the language of international human rights law and the content of rights into local terms to give them universal meaning and relevance.

Consensus is growing around the need to develop a decentred or polycentric understanding of human rights that takes a global perspective reflecting a plurality of voices.[136] Advocates of culturally sensitive approaches emphasise the users' perspective, localising and vernacularising human rights.[137] These approaches highlight the view of human rights on the ground in context and identify human rights needs as those defined by local communities.[138] The aim is to make human rights more real and practical; less theoretical and aspirational. These approaches acknowledge that rights make 'little sense unless they are alive among the people'.[139] Importantly, it is 'not at odds with maintaining human rights as a global language' to create such a decentred approach, as international human rights law has no expectation of absolute uniformity.[140] Human rights neither require nor encourage global homogenisation or for communities to sacrifice (many) valued local practices.[141] Universality is in fact enhanced or enriched by input from diverse societies.[142] As noted, international human rights law has numerous mechanisms for accommodating cultural diversity, and advocates of culturally sensitive approaches promote maximising these opportunities to tailor human rights to local contexts.

---

[135] Sally Engle Merry, Legal Transplants and Cultural Translation: Making Human Rights in the Vernacular, in Mark Goodale (ed.), *Human Rights: An Anthropological Reader* (Blackwell Publishing, 2009), p. 297.

[136] Ilias Bantekas and Lutz Oette, *International Human Rights Law and Practice* (Cambridge University Press, 2013), pp. 41–2.

[137] Eva Brems and Ellen Desmet, Studying Human Rights Law from the Perspective(s) of Its Users (2014) *Human Rights and International Legal Discourse* 8, p. 111; De Feyter (n. 92) Merry (2009) (n. 135).

[138] Koen de Feyter, Law Meets Sociology in Human Rights (June 2011) *Development and Society* 40:1, p. 60.

[139] Brems (2004) (n. 10), p. 223.

[140] Koen de Feyter, Treaty Interpretation and the Social Sciences, in Fons Coomans, Fred Grünfeld and Menno T. Kamminga (eds.), *Methods of Human Rights Research* (Intersentia, 2009), p. 225; de Feyter (2006) (n. 137), p. 9.

[141] Donnelly (n. 85), p. 303.

[142] De Feyter (2006) (n. 137), p. 9; Cees Flinterman (n. 130), p. 482.

One of these opportunties to accommodate cultural diversity is during the domestic implementation of international human rights law. Donnelly holds that human rights implementation measures 'are legitimately matters of considerable local variability'.[143] Rights should thus be implemented in different ways in different places and at different times in order to reflect 'the free choices of free people to incorporate an essential particularity into universal human rights'.[144] Brems calls such contextual sensitivity in the implementation of international human rights law a 'flexibility solution'.[145] According to her theory of inclusive universality, international human rights law can be adapted via flexibility and transformation to become more responsive to contextual differences.[146] Zwart's receptor approach applies specifically to the domestic implementation of international human rights law and focuses on tailoring measures to local communities' social institutions.[147] Despite this scope for contextualised implementation, it is not unlimited. The limits imposed by the treaties (as well as the supervisory treaty bodies) prevent states parties from implementing rights in ways that undermine their universal nature or result in unacceptable variances.[148]

2.3.2 Reducing Reliance upon State Law

It is common for those advocating culturally sensitive approaches to promote measures other than state law for implementing human rights. While legislative measures are sometimes required by by the treaties, in isolation such measures are often ineffective in securing the full realisation of human rights. For instance, if a culturally insensitive law is enacted, it is likely to be un- or under-implemented in practice and therefore unsuccessful in protecting rights. Legal anthropologists have acknowledged this, commenting that state legislative efforts can often be ineffective where they attempt to compete with a community's internal norms in a given social field.[149] As pre-existing local cultural

---

[143] Donnelly (2013) (n. 11), p. 100.
[144] Ibid., p. 105.
[145] Brems (2001) (n. 19), p. 331.
[146] Brems (2004) (n. 10), p. 226.
[147] Tom Zwart, Using Local Culture to Further the Implementation of International Human Rights: The Receptor Approach (2012) *Human Rights Quarterly* 34, pp. 546-69.
[148] See further Chapter 3.
[149] Erika George, Virginity Testing and South Africa's HIV/AIDS Crisis: Beyond Rights Universalism and Cultural Relativism toward Health Capabilities (2008) *California Law*

2.3 CULTURALLY SENSITIVE APPROACHES

norms enjoy familiarity and legitimacy, they are not particularly susceptible to displacement by external norms. Given that international human rights law originates per se outside the national system, it can lack the fuller legitimacy that would normally attach to internally generated standards and therefore garner relatively weak commitment.[150] Numerous examples of this can be drawn from legislative measures to prohibit 'harmful traditional practices' that do not in fact reduce their occurrence. Sometimes, state law is simply 'impotent'.[151] It must therefore be acknowledged that state law has its limitations, and that legal measures alone will not implement all human rights standards.[152]

While in the West a 'legal system' has predominately (or exclusively) been defined as state-sanctioned law, other definitions include forms of normative ordering such as cultural traditions, or social institutions like customary and religious law.[153] Acknowledging such legal pluralism involves challenging the assumption that the state is the only institution that shapes the social order.[154] These other plural non-state normative orders are often complex systems that enjoy strong legitimacy and vastly pre-date human rights norms. As such, these normative orders can be very influential and resilient, highlighting the intrinsic flaw in the idea that external technical fixes (like state legislation) can rapidly transform the ways in which people understand, structure and regulate their lives.[155] As Burundi noted in its state report to the CEDAW

Review 96, p. 1485; Sally Falk Moore, Law and Social Change: The Semi-Autonomous Social Field as an Appropriate Subject of Study (1973) *Law and Society Review* p. 723, (Issue 4); Sally Engle Merry, Legal Pluralism (1988) *Law and Society Review* 22, pp. 879–80; Brian Tamanaha, Understanding Legal Pluralism: Past to Present, Local to Global (2008) *Sydney Law Review* 30, p. 402.

[150] Denis Galligan and Deborah Sandler, Implementing Human Rights, in Simon Halliday and Patrick Schmidt (eds.), *Human Rights Brought Home: Socio-legal Perspectives on Human Rights in the National Context* (Hart Publishing, 2004), p. 27.

[151] Tamanaha (2008) (n. 149), pp. 385–6.

[152] Anthony Woodiwiss, The Law Cannot Be Enough: Human Rights and the Limits of Legalism, in Saladin Meckled-García and Başak Çali (eds.), *The Legalization of Human Rights: Multidisciplinary Perspectives on Human Rights and Human Rights Law* (Routledge, 2006), p. 34.

[153] Merry (n.149), p. 870. See Tamanaha's discussion of the debate regarding what is law (n. 149), pp. 390–6.

[154] Twining (n. 113), p. 116.

[155] Caroline Sage and Michael Woolcock, Introduction, in Brian Tamanaha, Caroline Sage and Michael Woolcock (eds.), *Legal Pluralism and Development: Scholars and Practitioners in Dialogue* (Cambridge University Press, 2012), p. 2.

Committee, traditional customs 'are deeply rooted in its people's souls and are a core part of their lives'.[156] As such, where human rights legislation conflicts with local norms, 'the implementation process will be stifled or skewed'.[157]

However, the existence and influence of plural normative orders provides opportunities for implementing human rights. For example, in a given setting, multiple options are likely to exist for community members to resolve their disputes, including religious, kinship-based or formal state mechanisms.[158] Given the options, individuals can to an extent forum shop and select the mechanism best suited to their claim. Sometimes state legal mechanisms may be preferable if they are better able to protect the relevant right or individual in question, other times they may not. For instance, the state legal system may be unattractive if it is viewed as corrupt, inefficient or hostile by community members, or if it is inaccessible due to its cost, location, complexity and/or lack of cultural sensitivity.[159] In contrast, claimants may find non-state mechanisms to be familiar, readily available, affordable, efficient and socially legitimate.[160] As such, culturally based informal dispute resolution mechanisms are often required to supplement or complement a state's mechanisms. Taking a practical approach, Nyamu argues for the use of informal systems due to the inaccessibility of many formal judicial institutions.[161] While practical factors

---

[156] UN CEDAW Committee, Consideration of reports by States parties under article 18 of the Convention on the Elimination of All Forms of Discrimination against Women, Fifth and sixth periodic reports of States parties due in 2013: Burundi, CEDAW/C/BDI/5-6 (24 June 2015), para. 35.

[157] Patrick Schmidt and Simon Halliday, Introduction: Socio-legal Perspectives on Human Rights in the National Context, in Simon Halliday and Patrick Schmidt (eds.), *Human Rights Brought Home: Socio-legal Perspectives on Human Rights in the National Context* (Hart Publishing, 2004), p. 12.

[158] Valeska David and Julie Fraser, A Legal Pluralist Approach to the Use of Cultural Perspectives in the Implementation and Adjudication of Human Rights Norms (2017) *Buffalo Human Rights Law Review* 23, p. 82.

[159] Sage and Woolcock (2012) (n. 155), pp. 1–2. Elin Henrysson and Sandra Joireman, On the Edge of the Law: Women's Property Rights and Dispute Resolution in Kisii, Kenya (2009) *Law and Society Review* 43:1, p. 49; Celestine Nyamu-Musembi, An Actor-Oriented Approach to Rights in Development (2005) *IDS Bulletin* 36:1, p. 46.

[160] Sage and Woolcock (n. 159), p. 2.

[161] Celestine Nyamu-Musembi, Are Local Norms and Practices Fences or Pathways? The Example of Women's Property Rights, in A. A. An-Na'im (ed.), *Cultural Transformation and Human Rights in Africa* (Zed Books Ltd, 2002), p. 143.

2.3 CULTURALLY SENSITIVE APPROACHES

may be persuasive for claimants, it can also be a deliberate choice to avoid state legal mechanisms.[162]

George and Zwart advocate measures other than state legislation, highlighting the opportunity that exists in local customs and social institutions. Zwart's receptor approach works from the premise that human rights may be best implemented through non-state law measures via social institutions such as customary law, women's associations and traditional medicine. Borrowing its name from the receptors in biomedicine, the receptor approach uses human rights 'receptors' within communities that provide a gateway through which treaty obligations can be analysed, understood, translated and delivered for the rights-holders' enjoyment.[163] Using ethnography, the receptor approach seeks to identify the social institutions in a given society that can be employed to implement human rights.[164] For example, the system of traditional medicine and healers in South Africa can be utilised to ensure that HIV/AIDS patients have access to the necessary anti-retrovirals, contributing to the right to health.[165] George provides a similar example, arguing that the (predominantly Zulu) practice of virginity testing in South Africa be used to fight HIV/AIDS.[166] Essentially an abstinence only mechanism, virginity testing has re-emerged as a traditional public health measure in response to the HIV/AIDS epidemic.[167]

While it is acknowledged that non-legislative measures can be effective in implementing human rights, disagreement exists as to what extent such measures should supplement or complement state legal measures. Donders advocates the need for both legislative and other measures, noting a role for state law but that other mechanisms are also important,

---

[162] David and Fraser (n. 158), p. 82. See also Deborah Isser, Understanding and Engaging Customary Justice Systems, in Deborah Isser (ed.), *Customary Justice and the Rule of Law in War-Torn Societies* (United States Institute of Peace, 2011), pp. 326, 330.
[163] Zwart (n. 147), p. 548.
[164] Ibid., p. 554.
[165] See, for example, Rachel King, UNAIDS, Collaboration with traditional healers in HIV/AIDS prevention and care in sub-Saharan Africa: a literature review (September 2000), http://data.unaids.org/publications/irc-pub01/jc299-tradheal_en.pdf (accessed 25 November 2017).
[166] George (n. 149), pp. 1454-7.
[167] Ibid., pp. 1450, 1458. Renteln also addresses the rise in virginity restoration surgery: The Human Rights Dimensions of Virginity Restoration Surgery, in Marie-Claire Foblets, Michele Graziadei and Alison Dundes Renteln (eds.), *Personal Autonomy in Plural Societies: A Principle and its Paradoxes* (Routledge, 2018) See further Chapter 14.

such as education, awareness raising and social development.[168] She advocates a multidimensional approach to implementation involving a variety of instruments and actors.[169] In contrast, Zwart elevates the role and utility of non-legislative measures and questions the need for legislative efforts in all cases.[170] While Nyamu agrees that primary efforts should be made to work with local customs and practices, she recognises the additional need to amend domestic legislation, constitutions and administrative institutions in order to implement structural reform in line with human rights.[171] It is submitted that the key consideration for a state in determining which implementation measures to adopt is their effectiveness. In practice, a smart mix of both state legislative and other measures may be necessary, with all implementation measures being tailored to the specific local context.

2.3.3 *Home-Grown Human Rights Solutions*

In connection with promoting non-legislative measures, advocates of culturally sensitive approaches to human rights implementation also commonly emphasise the need for home-grown solutions. Home-grown or bottom-up solutions to local human rights problems can be identified by taking the users' or an actor-oriented perspective.[172] Adopting the perspective of people in the context of their social reality 'changes not only the way we think about human rights, but the way we "do" human rights'.[173] Advocates of home-grown solutions highlight the agency and strength of individuals and communities as well as the variety of tools and resources at their disposal. Some East Asian human rights activists contend that their cultural traditions 'provide the resources for local justifications of ideas and practices' that are normally realised through a human rights regime in the West.[174] Similarly, Freeman notes that

---

[168] Yvonne Donders, Human Rights and Cultural Diversity: Too Hot to Handle? (2012) *Netherlands Quarterly of Human Rights* 30:4, p. 378.
[169] Ibid., p. 381.
[170] Zwart (n. 147), pp. 549–51.
[171] Celestine Nyamu, How Should Human Rights and Development Respond to Cultural Legitimization of Gender Hierarchy in Developing Countries? (2000) *Harvard International Law Journal* 41:2, p. 417.
[172] Brems and Desmet (n. 137); Nyamu-Musembi (n. 159).
[173] Nyamu-Musembi (n. 159), p. 45.
[174] Daniel Bell, The East Asian Challenge to Human Rights: Reflections on an East West Dialogue (1996) *Human Rights Quarterly* 18, pp. 643–4.

2.3 CULTURALLY SENSITIVE APPROACHES

culture can serve as a resource promoting human rights, with, for example, kinship networks delivering the right to food in place of the government.[175] Therefore, rather than the state imposing a domestic human rights regime top down, local cultural resources can be relied upon to support and meet human rights standards in context.

In the receptor approach, Zwart stresses home-grown solutions and promotes utilising local social institutions to implement international human rights standards. For example, women's associations among ethnic groups in Senegal support women in relation to a range of health issues including sexually transmitted diseases, publicly advocating for women's health, and countering male dominance.[176] The receptor approach opposes the introduction (imposition) of foreign notions (including state laws) into local contexts if suitable cultural resources already exist. Nyamu has also argued that it is possible to realise rights through local practice and custom rather than relying solely on national legislation or the international human rights system.[177] A benefit of taking such an approach is that home-grown solutions to human rights problems enjoy local legitimacy as they stem from and are embedded in a cultural community's norms. According to An-Na'im, people will be committed to implementing human rights standards if they consider them to emanate from their own values and worldview, and not be imposed by outsiders.[178] By relying to the extent possible on home-grown remedies, culturally sensitive approaches to human rights implementation aim to respect and uphold local culture while simultaneously enhancing human rights protection.

Home-grown solutions are particularly important when a community's cultural norms or practices need to be reformed and brought into line with human rights standards. This is because changes to cultural practices are most likely to succeed if they arise from within the cultural community, rather than being imposed upon it. Government interference in such situations can even at times invoke fierce local resistance.[179] The receptor approach addresses this in its theory of 'amplification'. According to the receptor approach, if there is a full match between the

---

[175] Freeman (n. 17), p. 61.
[176] Cheikh Niang, The Dimba of Senegal: A Support Group for Women (1994) *Reproductive Health Matters* 4:2, p. 42. See also Ibhawoh (2001) (n. 37), p. 51.
[177] Nyamu-Musembi (2002) (n. 161), p. 126.
[178] An-Na'im (n. 97), p. 431.
[179] Yüksel Sezgin, How to Integrate Universal Human Rights into Customary and Religious Legal Systems (2010) *Journal of Legal Pluralism and Unofficial Law* 60:5, pp. 11–12.

social institution and the human right, the state can be deemed to be meeting its international human rights obligations. If there is only a partial match (i.e. using the example above that some women are not part of these associations or their advocacy is unsuccessful) then amplification is required and the state has to extend/reform the social institution in order to meet its human rights obligations.[180] Zwart stresses the need for any such amplification to be home-grown, community-based reform. This is because reforms that remain in line with local cultural arrangements have a better chance of being embraced by the community.[181] Ibhawoh would agree, noting:

> change and integration must be done with local initiative and involvement in a way that does not compromise the cultural integrity of the people. Local people and cultural communities must feel a sense of ownership of the process of change and adaptation.[182]

Despite criticism of the practice of virginity testing in South Africa and the polarising debate around it,[183] George argues that such a culturally embedded practice may be successful in reducing HIV/AIDS infection rates where other Government measures have failed. She argues that those opposing the practice 'fail to appreciate the opportunities that culture may present for positive change'.[184] Exploring pragmatically how culture can be mobilised to better promote health, George advocates creative compromises or alternative solutions that sufficiently address the criticism, but retain the beneficial aspects of virginity testing.[185] For example, by adapting the practice to focus on education by having testers provide girls with information about sexual and reproductive health, 'the "problem" of cultural practices could then become an effective part of the solution'.[186] This approach is similar to Zwart's proposal for the amplification of social institutions that come close but fall short of completely protecting a given human right. Both of these approaches by Zwart and George rely upon culture's inherent dynamism, which enables

---

[180] Zwart (n. 147), p. 558.
[181] Ibid.
[182] Ibhawoh (2000) (n. 87), p. 856.
[183] The practice is opposed by, *inter alia*, feminists, AIDS activists and medical experts, who argue that the practice is unhygienic, scientifically unproven and violates the human rights of those tested. George (n. 149), pp. 1460-3, 1470-81.
[184] Ibid., p. 1481.
[185] Ibid., pp. 1491-2.
[186] Ibid., p. 1510.

2.3 CULTURALLY SENSITIVE APPROACHES

established cultural forms to be deployed in new situations and take on new meanings.[187]

There are many examples and iterations of innovative home-grown human rights solutions in cultures around the world. For instance, despite the customary norms of Kenya's Kisii tribe providing land inheritance on a patrilineal basis, community members found ways to ensure women's access to land. The Kisii invented a customary practice known as 'daughter-in-law marriage', which enables women to gain heirs and legitimise their presence on the land. According to this practice, a Kisii woman pays the bride price and 'marries' her fictional son to a single woman who already has children, rendering that woman her daughter-in-law and the children her grandchildren.[188] The elder woman – now the mother-in-law – can then gain access to land through these grandchildren. This is an example of how creatively custom can be applied, its flexibility and dynamism, and how variations of cultural practices more compliant with human rights can be developed.[189] Those promoting culturally sensitive approaches to human rights highlight that it is not necessary to completely abolish a cultural practice deemed harmful, but rather to amend those aspects deemed detrimental.[190] Scholars have identified examples of such home-grown adaptations to traditional burial practices in West Africa that were employed to ensure cultural norms were met, while reducing the transmission of Ebola and protecting the right to health.[191]

Given the emphasis on the local, it is perhaps neither necessary nor desirable for home-grown implementation measures to specifically use the language of international human rights law, which is still unfamiliar in many parts of the world. Anthropologists report that 'the less familiar the idea, the less likely it is to be adopted'.[192] For this reason, Merry

---

[187] Merry (2003) (n. 34), p. 69.
[188] Henrysson and Joireman (n. 159), pp. 44–5, fn. 6; N. Thomas Hakansson, The Detachability of Women: Gender and Kinship in Processes of Socioeconomic Change among the Gusii of Kenya (1994) *American Ethnologist* 21, p. 530.
[189] While daughter-in-law marriage ameliorates the position of some women without access to land, it cannot be seen as a complete remedy (i.e. some women may not be able to afford the bride price) and it fails to recognise women's equality and right to access land. See also David and Fraser (n. 158), pp. 88–9.
[190] Yvonne Donders, Exploring the Cultural Dimension of the Right to the Highest Attainable Standard of Health (2015) PER 18, p. 211.
[191] Fraser and Prudon (n. 132), pp. 106–9.
[192] Peggy Levitt and Sally Engle Merry, Vernacularization on the Ground: Local Uses of Global Women's Rights in Peru, China, India and the United States (2009) *Global Networks* 9:4, p. 452.

advocates vernacularisation, 'the process of appropriation and local adoption of globally generated ideas and strategies' – including human rights.[193] 'Vernacularisers' are people who 'convey ideas from one context to another, adapting and reframing them from the way they attach to a source context to one that resonates with the new location'.[194] A vernaculariser's success depends upon the framing – the different ways of presenting and packaging ideas that resonate with a particular audience.[195] For example, Islam can be an appropriate frame to use in places like Indonesia, whereby the practical application of human rights in Muslim communities is promoted as consistent with their Islamic beliefs.[196] Via vernacularisers, international human rights can be translated 'down' to relate to local systems, with local stories and experiences being translated back 'up' to the international level using the global language of human rights.[197] Renteln defends dispensing with the language of rights, stating:

> If rights do not exist in term or concept in other societies, then it makes little sense to expect them to make more compelling demands in terms of rights. That other societies do not utilise a rights framework does not mean *prima facie* lack of respect for what Westerners express as rights.[198]

However, as with other forms of translation, vernacularisation is not necessarily a straightforward matter of identifying an equivalent term, as when human rights are vernacularised they can also take on aspects of the social and ideological characteristics of the new context.[199] Once reframed and adapted to local ideas of justice and equality, human rights concepts may be used for quite different purposes.[200] Freeman identifies this double-edged sword, noting that translation carries with it both the positives of improving rights adoption and implementation, as well as the risk of distorting or diluting rights.[201] Another risk of vernacularisation is that if rights are 'translated so fully that they blend into existing power

---

[193] Ibid., p. 441.
[194] Vernacularisers are 'conversant with both sides of the exchange but able to move across borders of ideas and approaches'. Ibid., p. 449.
[195] Ibid., p. 452; Merry (2009) (n. 135), p. 266.
[196] An-Na'im (n. 10), p. 62. See further Chapter 5.
[197] Sally Engle Merry, Transnational Human Rights and Local Activism: Mapping the Middle (2006) *American Anthropologist* 108:1, p. 42.
[198] Renteln (n. 30), p. 517.
[199] Levitt and Merry (n. 192), p. 446.
[200] Ibid., p. 448.
[201] Freeman (n. 17), p. 57.

relationships completely, they lose their potential for social change'.[202] While human rights are more easily accepted when used in ways that readily link to local issues and strategies, they also manifest less of a threat to the status quo.[203] Cultural resonance may therefore be disadvantageous if it reduces the ability of human rights to create radical change.[204] To an extent, it is precisely the unfamiliarity of human rights that makes them more effective in breaking down old modes of thought.[205] Renteln caveats her above remarks by noting that claims *should* be presented as rights if it renders the demands made more powerful.[206] However, caution is warranted, as while rights claims may sometimes be more powerful, they can also elicit a backlash and rejection.

A result of using home-grown implementation measures is that solutions around the world for the same (or similar) human rights problem may be very different. What works in one location for one cultural community may not be applicable or even replicable in another. For examples, women's associations may be a prominent feature of some communities but barely present in others. As such, states will have to specially tailor human rights implementation measures for each context, identifying and working with the most appropriate and effective home-grown solutions. A further complication is the great diversity of cultures within states. While some states may be more homogeneous than others (such as smaller nation-states), most contemporary states are made up of disparate regions and people(s). For example, in one state there may be numerous normative ordering systems functioning simultaneously that the state must engage with and navigate to implement rights. Advocates of culturally sensitive approaches to human rights would applaud such an outcome, reiterating that universalism does not mean uniformity, and that the international system not only accommodates, but also welcomes such diversity. In fact, insisting on uniformity would be counter-productive, as plurality enables human rights challenges to be addressed more effectively via different responses.[207]

---

[202] Merry (2009) (n. 135), p. 266.
[203] Levitt and Merry (n. 192), pp. 457-8.
[204] Merry (2009) (n. 135), p. 267.
[205] Ibid.
[206] Renteln (n. 30), p. 517.
[207] De Feyter (n. 92), p. 11.

2.3.4 Utilising Culture's Dynamism and Contestation to Advance Human Rights

Notwithstanding dominant positions and impressions of uniformity and conformity, cultures are heterogeneous and contested. Proponents of culturally sensitive approaches to human rights implementation highlight culture's dynamism and contestation as opportunities for promoting rights. As set out above, cultures are continuously changing, and human rights can be influential or even instrumental in such change.[208] For example, where a cultural practice may be at odds with human rights, the culture may shift to adopt a more compliant practice or perspective. This can be facilitated by culture's heterogeneity and contestation, as multiple interpretations and practices can typically be found co-existing within one cultural community. While a community's dominant cultural position may be antagonistic towards a particular right, it may not be the only position available.[209] Cultural assertions often fail to reflect the full social reality, where variation is observable but not necessarily explicitly acknowledged.[210] Nyamu advocates utilising this diversity within a culture and its dynamism to tend towards human rights compliance, arguing that rights can be realised through local norms and practices based on culture's constant motion.[211] Promoting intra-cultural dialogue, An-Na'im encourages everyone to employ alternatives within their culture to bridge gaps between cultural norms and international human rights law.[212]

In this way, culture offers various options to its members, or at least is open to accommodating varying responses to its norms.[213] Therefore, perceptions of cultural legitimacy and validity may differ within a society,[214] with members adopting different interpretations of norms and practices, and attaching varied levels of importance thereto.[215] These varied practices offer a starting point to internally challenge custom and advocate interpretations in line with international human

---

[208] Donders (n. 168), p. 381.
[209] Abdullahi Ahmed An-Na'im, Introduction, in Abdullahi Ahmed An-Na'im (ed.), *Human Rights in Cross-Cultural Perspectives: A Quest for Consensus* (University of Pennsylvania Press, 1992), p. 4.
[210] Nyamu (2000) (n. 171), p. 405.
[211] Nyamu-Musembi (2002) (n. 161), pp. 127, 132.
[212] An-Na'im (1992) (n. 97), p. 431. Similarly, Ibhawoh advocates 'internal cross-paradigmatic dialogue': Ibhawoh (2000) (n. 87), p. 855.
[213] An-Na'im (1992) (n. 34), p. 27.
[214] Ibhawoh (2000) (n. 87), p. 842.
[215] Brems (2001) (n. 19), p. 319.

rights law.[216] Human rights advocates can use these openings to demonstrate that a certain dominant position is not absolute, with deviations both possible and permissible. Due to culture's dynamism, these alternative practices and views can contest the dominant position, potentially shifting to become the new norm. Therefore, the focus is not on eliminating or modifying detrimental cultural norms or practices, but on identifying and promoting alternative, co-existing positions in line with human rights. As co-existing views/practices already enjoy cultural legitimacy (albeit perhaps somewhat limited), they are more likely to be readily implemented by the community than new, external norms.[217]

Nyamu advocates a critical pragmatic approach, in which those seeking to shift dominant cultural positions generate empirical evidence of alternative practices.[218] Collecting and presenting evidence of the variety of local practices stands in strong opposition to rigid or absolutist statements of culture.[219] She gives the example of the Akamba in Kenya, where, despite prevailing notions that daughters are not entitled to inherit, cases can be found where fathers provide for their daughters' inheritance.[220] Similar occurrences have been documented in Bali, Indonesia, where, despite customary patrilineal inheritance, many within the community provide for women's inheritance.[221] Such examples illustrate the need to examine alternative positions and actual practices within a culture, rather than simply the normative pronouncements. This is particularly the case even when customary norms have been codified into formal law. Nyamu argues that '[l]ocal practices are varied, and people's day-to-day interactions are more revealing of the "living" cultural norms'.[222]

Key to this approach is that culture is not deterministic: people can be and are agents of cultural change.[223] Culture is not a 'thing' part of a

---

[216] Nyamu-Musembi (2002) (n. 161), p. 134.
[217] Fraser and Prudon (n. 132), p. 107.
[218] Nyamu (2000) (n. 171), p. 413.
[219] Ibid., see also pp. 417–18; Nyamu-Musembi (2005) (n. 159), p. 46.
[220] Nyamu-Musembi (2002) (n. 161), pp. 133–4; Nyamu (2000) (n. 171), pp. 414–15, fn. 146.
[221] Ingrid Westendorp, Personal Status Law and Women's Right to Equality in Law and in Practice: The Case of Land Rights of Balinese Hindu Women (2015) *Journal of Human Rights Practice* 7, p. 443. See also David and Fraser (n. 158), pp. 85–90.
[222] Nyamu-Musembi (2002) (n. 161), p. 132.
[223] Ibid., p. 134. The Special Rapporteur notes that 'Cultures are shared outcomes of critical reflection and continuous engagements of human beings in response to an ever-changing world.' UN General Assembly, Report of the Special Rapporteur in the Field of Cultural Rights, A/67/287 (10 August 2012), para. 4.

cultural community, but a process of that community. Cultural processes are not unidirectional radiating from the centre to the periphery – indeed, the periphery 'talks back'.[224] This envisages the participation of and input from a variety of actors in the cultural community based on their agency, rather than a top-down hierarchy where those below receive rather than inform culture. As such, it is vital to not only recognise culture's diversity and dynamism, but also the agency of cultural actors. However, participation in such processes may not be equal or representative. Culture both influences and creates power relations, which impact upon who may be included/influential in cultural determinations.[225] Dominant groups have more power to hold out interpretations of cultural norms and values supportive of their own interests as the only valid view – as 'true culture'.[226] Meanwhile, the views of an individual or group of vulnerable or disadvantaged individuals may be diminished/silenced.[227] In this way, rather than representing a community, cultural norms may only reflect and serve the narrow interests of a dominant few.[228]

Given the politics of culture, a central question to be considered is who within a community gets to influence, interpret and determine the culture, and if there are multiple determinations (contestation), which is authoritative?[229] In intra-community dialogues about cultural norms and practices, scholars emphasise the need for inclusivity with the ultimate goal being the full participation and consultation of all community members.[230] Nyamu highlights women's meaningful participation in the shaping and articulation of a community's culture, while An-Na'im stresses the involvement of disadvantaged individuals or groups in general.[231] The UN Special Rapporteur in the field of cultural rights states that women's cultural rights include 'the right to transform existing

---

[224] Preis (n. 46), p. 306.
[225] Nyamu (2000) (n. 171), p. 405.
[226] Ibhawoh (2000) (n. 87), pp. 842, 854.
[227] Donders (n. 78), p. 18. See also the Report of the Special Rapportuer 2012 (n. 114), para. 22.
[228] Nyamu (2000) (n. 171), p. 404.
[229] Donders (n. 168), p. 378.
[230] Radhika Coomaraswamy, Identity Within: Cultural Relativism, Minority Rights and the Empowerment of Women (2002) The George Washington International Law Review 34, p. 494.
[231] Nyamu-Musembi (2002) (n. 161), p. 141; An-Na'im (1992) (n. 34), p. 28. See also the Report of the Special Rapporteur 2012 (n. 114, paras. 28–9) who notes that women must be able to 'revise and (re)negotiate existing traditions, values or practices'.

cultural patterns and thinking'.[232] Securing this inclusive participation may already involve conflict with and adjustment to local community norms. When pursuing such changes, Nyamu encourages appealing to the general principles of justice and fairness within a community's value system, which frequently results in the flexible application of what previously appeared to be rigid rules.[233] Similarly, An-Na'im advises engaging in discourse about the cultures' values and the rationale behind those values, which may assist to soften an offending position.[234]

All of the approaches discussed converge on the point that cultural change needs to be initiated and pursued by those within a cultural community. Despite this focus on internal actors, they also envisage a role for outside actors, including human rights activists, civil society, academics, the government, or representatives of international organisations. However, interventions by outsiders should be measured as they may be ineffective or, worse, counter-productive. Condemnation of cultural practices as contrary to human rights by (Western) outsiders can be viewed as disrespectful, with their interferences potentially creating or reinforcing suspicions of rights as paternalistic or even imperialistic.[235] Given the history of colonialism, '[t]he spectre of the Enlightenment-gone-wrong in the colonies still exists'.[236] As such, scholars recommend outsiders refrain from directly campaigning in a community, instead supporting the local, internal, pro-human rights forces who, as insiders, best understand how to proceed in their community, what changes can be made, and in what time period.[237] This may involve, for example, the state financially supporting local NGOs and individuals working to promote rights within a community.[238] Outsiders could also support vulnerable individuals or groups to participate in the articulation of a community's norms. While outsiders may sensitively and respectfully support/influence internal dialogue, they must not undermine the process or the outcome.[239]

---

[232] Report of the Special Rapportuer 2012 (n. 114), para. 36; see also para. 71.
[233] Nyamu (2000) (n. 171), p. 413. See also David and Fraser (n. 158), pp. 89–90.
[234] An-Na'im (n. 209), p. 4.
[235] Brems (2004) (n. 10), p. 226; Brems (2001) (n. 19), p. 513.
[236] Coomaraswamy (2002) (n. 230), p. 513.
[237] Brems (2004) (n. 10), p. 229; Coomaraswamy (2013) (n. 61), p. 132; Coomaraswamy (2002) (n. 230), pp. 499, 513; George (n. 149), p. 1514.
[238] See Westendorp (n. 221), p. 446; Sezgin (n. 179), pp. 30–1.
[239] Nyamu (2000) (n. 171), p. 394; An-Na'im (1992) (n. 34), p. 37.

Finally, another way in which cultures change and evolve is via interactions with and influences from other cultures. An-Na`im advocates instigating cultural change within a community via cross-cultural dialogue.[240] Such cross-cultural dialogue is to supplement and inform a community's internal dialogue, with the aim of shifting cultural norms to be human rights compliant. Engaging in dialogue about human rights across cultures also works to improve the cultural legitimacy of rights and their universality.[241] Via such mechanisms, culturally sensitive approaches to human rights implementation seek to maintain cultural integrity and legitimacy alongside human rights enjoyment. This is crucial, not only for social cohesion and continuity, but also for the effective implementation of human rights standards.

2.3.5 Effectiveness of Culturally Sensitive Approaches to Implementation

As seen from the above analysis, much has been done on a theoretical level to articulate both the need for and issues associated with greater cultural sensitivity in the implementation of international human rights law. While there are no quick solutions and also disagreements, a general framework has been articulated that can guide human rights advocates on the ground. This framework includes translating abstract international human rights concepts to the local context; reducing the role and reliance upon state law as an implementation measure; employing home-grown solutions for human rights problems; and relying on culture's dynamism and contestation to promote human rights compliance. The compelling reason for adopting such an approach lies in its ability to more effectively implement rights and to further their universality by making them meaningful and relevant to diverse communities. This is key given that states parties are obliged by the international treaties they ratify to 'give effect' to the human rights therein.

One of the underlying causes of human rights violations is in fact their lack of or insufficient cultural legitimacy.[242] It is therefore crucial for human rights to be assimilated by a community so that they are considered natural components of everyday life.[243] Building human rights

---

[240] An-Na`im (n. 234), p. 4.
[241] Ibid., pp. 4–5.
[242] An-Na`im (1992) (n. 34), p. 19.
[243] Lenzerini (n. 5), p. 218.

2.3 CULTURALLY SENSITIVE APPROACHES

practices on local cultural traditions may be slow, but is more likely to yield long-term commitment to human rights norms due to community 'buy-in'.[244] As this suggests, human rights require strong allies or domestic constituencies in order to have an impact.[245] Dictating standards to a society is, in principle, unacceptable and, importantly for present purposes, unlikely to succeed in practice.[246] Simply put: 'A legitimate rule is more effective than a non-legitimate rule'.[247] Because of this linkage with effectiveness, anyone – indeed everyone – dedicated to realising international human rights law should be interested in culturally sensitive approaches to implementation. However, the approaches are not unproblematic and raise certain issues that warrant consideration.

First, relying upon culture's dynamism to reform local norms and practices to align with international human rights law can be time consuming and uncertain. While change achieved via this process is likely to be sustained, it necessarily involves a delay or failure to protect rights in the interim. For example, women's rights are often rejected on the basis of cultural arguments and it can be unacceptable to require or expect women to wait for the process of cultural change before they can enjoy their inalienable human rights. While this may be more suitable for rights subject to progressive realisation, it would constitute a violation of rights immediately enforceable like the right to life or freedom from discrimination. While this situation is wanting, alternative state implementation measures such as enacting legislation may also prove ineffective in protecting rights in a timely manner. Law reform processes can also be slow and amending a law makes no sense if the amendments are not supported by a corresponding change in people's mindset.[248] It is thus necessary to acknowledge the limitations of all forms of implementation measures to transform society and protect human rights. As gradual reform measures from within a community are ultimately more likely to be respected as compared to top-down state measures,[249] 'human rights obligations that require profound societal changes should be realized progressively within a reasonable timeframe'.[250]

---

[244] Coomaraswamy (n. 61), p. 133; Bell (n. 174), p. 657.
[245] Heyns and Viljoen (n. 102), p. 522.
[246] An-Na'im (1992) (n. 34), p. 37.
[247] Fred Grünfeld, The United Nations and Non-State Actors: Legitimacy and Compliance (1997) *SIM Special* 19, p. 19.
[248] Brems (2004) (n. 19), p. 18.
[249] Sezgin (n. 179), pp. 29–30.
[250] Brems (2004) (n. 19), p. 18.

Given that the process of cultural evolution can be 'painstakingly gradual and complex',[251] it is important that members of cultural communities are not locked into a local normative system in which rights are not (yet) realised.[252] To ensure effective human rights protections and access to remedies, it is necessary for the state to remain involved in human rights implementation and to provide a safety-net. For example, it is important for women to be able to forum shop and select the system (formal or informal) and the norms (state or non-state) – or a combination thereof – that best protects their rights. In this way, women have the ability to 'opt-out' of their local cultural/customary system if necessary or desirable.[253] This may also apply to minorities within certain communities or to other individuals asserting rights in conflict with cultural norms. As such, the state cannot defer entirely to local norms, but needs to provide safeguards, supervision, and remedies where rights are not protected – as is their obligation under international law.[254] When meeting these obligations, states should continue to recognise and engage with other relevant normative systems.[255]

Finally, another issue to be considered regarding culturally sensitive approaches to human rights implementation relates to the determination of cultural norms. Given the complexities involved as well as the risk of essentialising culture, states should avoid making or codifying determinations of a community's culture. Essentialising and codifying norms often renders them static and detatches them from dynamic social processes.[256] As noted above, the community itself is best placed to make determinations of its own cultural norms and practices. In this way, a cultural community will be responsible for and have ownership over any changes to those norms and practices. This is important also in order to preclude or defend against accusations of coercion, manipulation or

---

[251] Ibhawoh (2000) (n. 87), p. 856.
[252] David and Fraser (n. 158), p. 115.
[253] Yvonne Donders, Do Cultural Diversity and Human Rights Make a Good Match? (2010) *International Social Science Journal* 61:199, p. 18; Sezgin (n. 179), p. 29; Brems (2001) (n. 19), p. 324; Report of the Special Rapporteur, A/73/227 (n. 79), paras. 65–7.
[254] See further Chapter 4.
[255] David and Fraser (n. 158), p. 115.
[256] In the South African case of *Bhe*, the Constitutional Court ruled that customary law preventing women from inheriting had not kept pace with how people live in contemporary times: *Nonkululeko Letta Bhe and others v. Khayelitsha Magistrate and others* 2005 (1) BCLR 1 (CC) (South Africa). See discussion in George (n. 149), pp. 1496–9; Zwart (n. 147), pp. 559–60.

social engineering by outsiders who engage with a community advocating cultural change.

2.4 Conclusion: Human Rights and Their Cultural Connection

Since the promulgation of the UDHR, culture has been a central antagonist in the development of international human rights law. Some of the strongest, most persistent and persuasive criticism of the international human rights system is based on cultural arguments. Such criticism by relativists, postcolonial and TWAIL scholars highlighted the need for human rights to better accommodate cultural diversity in order to ensure its universal nature. They challenged not only the norms stated, but also the process by which they were agreed. Importantly, the critiques generally seek to inform and improve the international human rights system, rather than to dismiss or dismantle it. They thus serve as constructive criticism, identifying both perceived shortfalls as well as potential solutions. This debate over the last seven decades has helped broaden and nuance the international human rights system, heralding a retreat from the dichotomous positions of universalism and relativism. However, it remains a pressing challenge for contemporary human rights law to better accommodate cultural diversity and dispel its (perceived) Western bias. For, notwithstanding the rich cultural diversity in the world, there are also marked commonalities – specifically in matters of human rights. Conceptions of human dignity can be sourced from cultures around the world, with a multiplicity of foundations supporting human rights. This ability to subsume different foundations exemplifies the plurality and flexibility inherent in human rights.

In fact, human rights and culture have many characteristics in common, like dynamism and contestation, and are mutually constitutive. Culture is an essential element of human rights, necessarily influencing their structure, perceptions, enforcement and adjudication.[257] Human rights are implicitly bound up in culture.[258] Due to insights from different disciplines, it is now beginning to be acknowledged that almost all human rights have a cultural dimension, like the right to housing, food

---

[257] Lenzerini (n. 5), p. 213.
[258] Regarding the concept of human rights as cultural, see also Melville Herskovits, Statement on the Human Rights, Submitted to the UN Commission on Human Rights by the American Anthropological Association Executive Board (1947) *American Anthropology* 49:4, pp. 539–43.

and health. The understanding of culture and human rights from the perspective of international law has become more sophisticated, however much room for improvement remains. For example, human rights and culture continue to be pitted against one another. Culture is often portrayed at times in international legal discourse as some 'thing' static and ancient, as an obstacle to human rights in the modern state. These misconceptions contribute to the othering of culture as something practised by distant (read backward) communities, as well as the invisibilisation of other pervasive cultural norms. Endeavours to present human rights as neutral or decontextualised inevitably reflect the dominant culture, which is Western, white and male.[259] Examples of culture as a source of practices conflicting with human rights are well known. Less well-known and appreciated is culture's dynamism and utility in remedying these conflicts and supporting human rights.

While human rights are universal, it is an error to assume that this prescribes uniformity. International human rights law accommodates cultural diversity via several mechanisms, including domestic implementation. It is becoming generally accepted that human rights implementation should be contextualised and undertaken in a culturally sensitive manner. Scholars have articulated culturally sensitive approaches to human rights implementation, which are pragmatic in their effective implementation of rights in practice, and principled in respecting cultural diversity. These approaches rely upon actors and norms other than those of the state, drawing upon local cultural resources like social institutions. In this way they challenge a myopic focus on the state in human rights implementation, emphasising the need for more polycentric approaches. While the state is a central figure in international law and state law will continue to play an important role in human rights, there are other actors and norms that can effectively implement human rights. Specifically involving social institutions can increase support for human rights law, promoting its legitimacy and respect in diverse societies around the world. This in turn reinforces the universality of rights.

This chapter demonstrated culture's multifaceted impact upon human rights, identifying it as a key factor in human rights realisation and enjoyment. Culture can conflict with rights, creating at times a protracted stand-off between local communities and the national authorities and/or international community. Culture can also support human rights,

---

[259] Brems (2001) (n. 19), p. 316; Report of the Special Rapporteur 2012 (n. 114), para 34.

providing them with local legitimacy, sustained respect and enhanced observance. It is because of these make-or-break-type functions that culture and related social institutions are important for human rights implementation. This chapter concludes that states should employ culturally sensitive approaches when domestically implementing international human rights law, as a matter of pragmatism and out of respect for cultural diversity. What remains to be seen is whether such approaches are compatible with the framework of international law and the obligations on states parties to human rights treaties.

3

Domestic Implementation of International Human Rights Treaties: Legislative and Other Effective Measures

3.1 Introduction

International human rights treaties have proliferated since the Universal Declaration of Human Rights (UDHR),[1] attracting significant endorsement from states, with the *Convention on the Rights of the Child* (CRC) securing near universal ratification.[2] While state ratification is an essential step, such commitment does not *per se* lead to compliance. In fact, some have suggested that, on occasion, state human rights practice even worsens after treaty ratification.[3] Clearly, international human rights standards do not apply automatically once agreed or enacted, nor do they take effect quietly and effortlessly.[4] Only through persistent action on the national level can international human rights obligations be translated into reality.[5] Empirical studies indicate that not only has the compliance gap persisted, but in some cases it has even grown in the last thirty years.[6] As such, compliance remains an outstanding issue, with all

---

[1] Universal Declaration of Human Rights (adopted 10 December 1948), UNGA Res. 217 A(III) (UDHR).

[2] *Convention on the Rights of the Child* (adopted 20 November 1989, entered into force 2 September 1990), 1577 UNTS 3 (CRC). The USA is the only UN member state not to have ratified the CRC.

[3] Eric Neumayer, Do International Human Rights Treaties Improve Respect for Human Rights? (Dec. 2005) *Journal of Conflict Resolution* 49:6, p. 941; Oona Hathaway, Why Do Countries Commit to Human Rights Treaties? (August 2007) *Journal of Conflict Resolution* 51:4, p. 593.

[4] Denis Galligan and Deborah Sandler, Implementing Human Rights, in Simon Halliday and Patrick Schmidt (eds.), *Human Rights Brought Home: Socio-legal Perspectives on Human Rights in the National Context* (Hart Publishing, 2004), p. 24.

[5] UN General Assembly, In Larger Freedom: Towards Development Security and Human Rights for All, Report of the Secretary-General, Annex, Plan of Action Submitted by the UN High Commissioner for Human Rights, A/59/2005/Add. 3 (26 May 2005), para. 22.

[6] Xinyuan Dai, The 'Compliance Gap' and the Efficacy of International Human Rights Institutions, in Thomas Risse, Stephen Ropp and Kathryn Sikkink (eds.), *The Persistent Power of Human Rights: From Commitment to Compliance* (Cambridge University Press, 2013), p. 85. Hathaway notes that while the empirical evidence shows that democratic

states struggling to varying degrees to implement their human rights treaty obligations. Implementation is an arduous task that requires the involvement of all branches of government and levels of state institutions, as well as the complicity of private actors. Having advanced thus far with standard setting in the treaties, the challenge of human rights implementation is now most pressing.[7]

As established in Chapter 2, one cause of poor human rights implementation is their cultural disconnect or lack of legitimacy in many societies around the world. The national socio-cultural context is highly relevant for the design and success of implementation measures, and rights can be more effectively guaranteed by employing culturally sensitive approaches. These approaches specifically advocate shifting focus from state legislative measures of implementation to 'other measures' including the use of social institutions. Contemporary research supports the view that civil society can greatly impact human rights efficacy in context.[8] In fact, many have criticised the overly legalistic approach to human rights implementation, which prioritises legislation and legal remedies over all other measures. Given the challenge of implementation, it is necessary to look beyond state legislative measures and to explore the alternatives in detail. Therefore, this third chapter analyses culturally sensitive approaches to implementation according to the framework of international human rights law. This involves an examination of the international human rights obligations on states parties to give effect to the treaties, and the types of implementation measures required or permitted.

This chapter examines the UN treaties and the treaty bodies' documents to determine the extent to which obligations must be domestically implemented through law, or where states can employ other measures. Addressed here is the state's discretion in implementation and the observable preference within the treaty body system and scholarship for the domestic legal incorporation/codification of treaty norms. The

---

states tend to have better human rights records than non-democratic ones, they are still not above reproach. Hathaway (n. 3), p. 594.

[7] Jean-Philippe Thérien and Philippe Joly, 'All Human Rights for All': The United Nations and Human Rights in the Post-Cold War Era (2014) *Human Rights Quarterly* 36:2, pp. 380–1.

[8] Neumayer (n. 3), p. 941; Christof Heyns and Frans Viljoen, The Impact of the United Nations Human Rights Treaties on the Domestic Level (2001) *Human Rights Quarterly* 23:3, p. 522; Gregory Schaffer and Tom Ginsburg, The Empirical Turn in International Legal Scholarship (2012) *American Journal of International Law* 106, p. 44.

chapter focuses on what types of other measures are permitted, as well as those recommended to states parties by the treaty bodies in supervising domestic implementation. Attention is also paid to what (if any) role is foreseen for non-state actors or norms (like social institutions) in implementation. This chapter demonstrates that when assessing human rights implementation measures, the focus of the international system is not on the method employed by the state, but on its effectiveness in practice. On this basis, and subject to certain conditions, there is broad scope within international law for states to use a variety of measures (other than state law) to implement human rights.

3.2 UN Human Rights Treaties and State Discretion in Implementation Measures

States parties are obliged by human rights treaties to domestically implement the standards therein, and are subjected to the scrutiny of the UN treaty bodies. Under international law, and as applied by the treaty bodies, states enjoy broad discretion in the measures they may employ to domestically implement their obligations. For example, the word 'measure' in the *International Covenant on Civil and Political Rights* (ICCPR) was intended at the time of drafting to be 'understood in a broad sense, covering legislative acts, administrative and judicial decisions, as well as other *de facto* measures'.[9] The Committee on the Elimination of Discrimination against Women similarly held that the 'term "measure" encompasses a wide variety of legislative, executive, administrtive and other regultory instruments, policies and practices'.[10] This section analyses the discretion states enjoy, as well as its limitations, before exploring the range of implementation measures required and permitted by the treaties. This includes an analysis of the treaties and the General Comments by the treaty bodies relating to implementation. This section focuses first on legal measures of implementation, such as incorporation or codification, as well as the pertinent critiques of such legalistic approaches. The section then moves to assess what other, non-legislative measures of implementation states parties may employ under the treaties.

---

[9] Ineke Boerefijn, *The Reporting Procedure under the Covenant on Civil and Political Rights* (Intersentia, 1999), p. 178. *International Covenant on Civil and Political Rights* (adopted 16 December 1966, entered into force 23 March 1976), 999 UNTS 171 (ICCPR).

[10] CEDAW Committee, General Recommendation No. 25: Article 4, paragraph 1, of the Convention (Temporary Special Measures) (Thirtieth session 2004), para. 22.

3.2.1 State Discretion in International Law

International law is premised on state sovereignty and consent and, with exceptions like customary international law, states can only be bound by their agreement. As such, states are only obliged to comply with and domestically implement the treaty norms that they have ratified. Furthermore, based on principles of non-interference and subsidiarity, international law does not typically prescribe the format or method of national implementation.[11] As seen in the human rights treaties, states parties are not given concrete instructions as to *how* the various rights are to be implemented – just that they must be implemented. While states may reserve certain provisions with the effect that they are not bound by them, the UN Human Rights Committee (HRCee) has held that states may not reserve 'an entitlement not to take the necessary steps at the domestic level to give effect to the rights of the Covenant'.[12] Therefore, unless a treaty prescribes an implementation modality, states may determine how best to give effect to the provisions domestically. In this way, implementation is a matter of 'domestic primacy'[13] under international human rights law, and states enjoy broad (but not unlimited) discretion in the manner of implementation.

For example, the ICCPR provides in article 2(2) that 'each State Party undertakes to take the necessary steps ... to give effect to the rights' therein. The HRCee noted that this article 'generally leaves it to the States parties concerned to choose their method of implementation'.[14] The International Law Commission confirmed this, noting 'the obligation leaves the State at least an initial freedom of choice of the means to be

---

[11] Paolo Carozza, Subsidiarity as a Structural Principle of International Human Rights Law (2003) *American Journal of International Law* 97:1, pp. 57–8.

[12] UN Human Rights Committee (HRCee), General Comment No. 24: Issues relating to reservations made upon ratification or accession to the Covenant or the Optional Protocols thereto, or in relation to declarations under Article 41 of the Covenant, HRI/GEN/1/Rev.9 (Vol. 1) (1994), para. 9; UN HRCee, General Comment No. 31: The Nature of the General Legal Obligations Imposed on States Parties to the Covenant, CCPR/C/21/Rev.1/Add.13 (29 March 2004), para. 5.

[13] Douglas Donoho, Human Rights Enforcement in Twenty-First Century (2006–7) *Georgia Journal of International and Comparative Law* 35:1, p. 12.

[14] UN HRCee, General Comment No. 3: Article 2 Implementation at the National Level, UN Doc. HRI/GEN/1/Rev.1 at 4 (1981), para. 1. This General Comment was subsequently replaced by General Comment No. 31 (n. 12). See generally also Anja Seibert-Fohr, Domestic Implementation of the International Covenant on Civil and Political Rights Pursuant to Its Article 2 Para. 2, in J. A. Frowein and R. Wolfrum (eds.), *Max Planck Yearbook of United Nations Law* (vol. 5, Kluwer, 2001).

used to achieve the result required'.[15] Equally, the *International Covenant on Economic, Social, and Cultural Rights* (ICESCR) does not specify the means by which it is to be implemented, providing in article 2(1) that states are to 'take steps' to progressively realise rights 'by all appropriate means'.[16] The UN Committee on Economic, Social, and Cultural Rights (ESCR Committee) held that this undertaking for states parties to 'take steps' is not, in itself, 'qualified or limited by other considerations'.[17] The other UN Conventions, such as the CRC, also do not specify how they are to be implemented, frequently referring instead to the obligation on states parties simply to 'take measures'.[18] As this illustrates, it is a general rule of international law that states parties are free to determine how they implement their treaty obligations.[19]

In addition, given the often vague language of human rights treaties, states also have discretion to determine what the standards mean in practice and what constitutes adequate compliance.[20] The general or abstract terms of human rights treaties permit significant discretion regarding the nature of rights and their implementation in practice, allowing for local variation.[21] This is not an error or loophole to be remedied but rather reflects 'the compromise between the universalist claims of human rights and the imperatives of local culture'.[22] Kinley argues that human rights' bendability is neither a sign of weakness nor a dilution of their universal value.[23] Through this mechanism, the

---

[15] Report of the Commission to the General Assembly on the Work of Its Twenty-ninth Session, (1977) *Yearbook of the International Law Commission* 2:2, p. 21.

[16] *International Covenant on Economic, Social and Cultural Rights* (adopted 16 December 1966, entered into force 3 January 1967), 993 UNTS 3 (ICESCR).

[17] UN ESCR Committee, General Comment No. 3: The Nature of States Parties' Obligations (Article 2(1) of the Covenant), E/1991/23 (1990), para. 2.

[18] See, for example, CRC arts. 2(2), 11(1), 21(d), 22(1), 24(2) and (3), 27(3) and (4), 28(2), 34, 35, 38(2), 39; UN Committee on the Rights of the Child (CRC Committee), General Comment No. 5: General Measures of Implementation of the Convention on the Rights of the Child (arts. 4, 42 and 44(6)), CRC/GC/2003/5 (27 November 2003); Christian Tomuschat, *Human Rights: Between Idealism and Realism* (2nd ed., Oxford University Press, 2008), pp. 119–20.

[19] Tomuschat, ibid., pp. 110–11; Nisuke Ando, National Implementation and Interpretation, in Dinah Shelton (ed.), *The Oxford Handbook of International Human Rights Law* (Oxford University Press, 2013), p. 702.

[20] Galligan and Sandler (n. 4), pp. 27–8.

[21] Ibid., p. 32.

[22] Ibid., p. 28.

[23] David Kinley, Bendable Rules: The Development Implications of Human Rights Pluralism, in Brian Tamanaha, Caroline Sage and Michael Woolcock (eds.), *Legal Pluralism*

3.2 HUMAN RIGHTS TREATIES AND STATE DISCRETION 69

international human rights system provides scope for states to tailor human rights standards and to select the most suitable implementation method based on the context of local norms and values, social structures and institutional capacities.[24] Rather than being one-size-fits-all,[25] the system is designed so as to function in the context of each society and on the basis of each state's discretion. Given the paradox that the system relies upon and grants states discretion in implementing human rights standards designed precisely to curtail what a state may do in its own jurisdiction,[26] this discretion is not unlimited.

For example, states are required by article 26 of the *Vienna Convention on the Law of Treaties* (VCLT) to give effect to their human rights obligations in good faith and according to the principle of *pacta sunt servanda* – states must abide by their duties.[27] The HRCee has reiterated this article, emphasising that states parties are required to give effect to the ICCPR in good faith.[28] The VCLT also provides general rules of treaty interpretation in article 31(1), stating that a 'treaty shall be interpreted in good faith and in accordance with the ordinary meaning to be given to terms of the treaty in their context and in the light of its object and purpose'. While treaty interpretation has subjective (the intention of parties and state practice) as well as objective elements (plain reading and object and purpose), human rights bodies stress the objective elements when interpreting human rights treaties.[29] This is because human rights treaties are recognised as having different characteristics to other international treaties.[30] For example, the European Court of Human Rights

---

and Development: Scholars and Practitioners in Dialogue (Cambridge University Press, 2012), p. 56.

[24] Galligan and Sandler (n. 4), p. 32; Kinley, ibid., p. 56.
[25] Kinley (n. 23), p. 58.
[26] Abdullahi An-Na'im, Human Rights and Islamic Identity in France and Uzbekistan: Mediation of the Local and Global (2000) *Human Rights Quarterly* 22:4, p. 935; Galligan and Sandler (n. 4), p. 25.
[27] *Vienna Convention on the Law of Treaties* (adopted 23 May 1969, entered into force 27 January 1980), 1155 UNTS 331.
[28] UN HRCee, General Comment No. 31: The Nature of the General Legal Obligations Imposed on States Parties to the Covenant, CCPR/C/21/Rev.1/Add.13 (29 March 2004), para. 3.
[29] Koen de Feyter, Law Meets Sociology in Human Rights (2011) *Development and Society* 40:1, pp. 61–3; Koen de Feyter, Treaty Interpretation and the Social Sciences, in Fons Coomans, Fred Grünfeld and Menno Kamminga (eds.), *Methods of Human Rights Research* (Intersentia, 2009), pp. 215–16.
[30] Human rights treaties differ in nature from other international treaties, such as those regulating trade, which offer reciprocal benefits to states. See International Court of

held that the object and purpose of the *European Convention on Human Rights* 'requires that its provisions be interpreted and applied so as to make its safeguards practical and effective'.[31] This reflects the principle of *effet utile*, according to which a treaty must be interpreted in a way that enables its provisions to be 'effective and useful'.[32]

It is therefore evident that international law's focus is on the effectiveness of the treaties and a state's implementation method (and not the method itself), so long as it is performed in good faith and in line with the treaty's object and purpose. On this basis, domestic implementation is an obligation of result, rather than one of means.[33] For example, the Committee Against Torture recognises that states may choose their implementation measures so long as they are 'effective and consistent with the object and purpose of the Convention'.[34] Similarly, the ESCR Committee noted that while domestic implementation is a matter for states to determine, the chosen measures should produce results consistent with the full discharge of the states' treaty obligations.[35] Regarding the ICCPR, the International Law Commission held: 'The State is free to employ some other means [than legislation] if it so desires, provided that those means also enable

---

Justice, Reservations to the Convention on the Prevention and Punishment of the Crime of Genocide, Advisory Opinion, General List No. 12 (28 May 1951), 12; UN HRCee, General Comment No. 24: Issues relating to reservations made upon ratification or accession to the Covenant or the Optional Protocols thereto, or in relation to declarations under article 41 of the Covenant, CCPR/C/21/Rev.1/Add. 6 (1994), para. 17.

[31] *Loizidou* v. *Turkey*, App. No. 15318/89 (ECtHR, 23 March 1995), para. 72. See also the landmark case of *Soering* where the Court held: 'In interpreting the Convention regard must be had to its special character as a treaty for the collective enforcement of human rights and fundamental freedoms...Thus, the object and purpose of the Convention as an instrument for the protection of individual human beings require that its provisions be interpreted and applied so as to make its safeguards practical and effective': *Soering* v. *UK* (ECtHR, 7 July 1989) Series A No. 161, para. 87.

[32] Antonio Cassese, *International Law in a Divided World* (Oxford University Press, 1986), p. 191.

[33] Oscar Schachter, The Obligation of the Parties to Give Effect to the Covenant on Civil and Political Rights (1979) *The American Journal of International Law* 73:3, p. 462. See also UN ESCR Committee, General Comment No. 3 (n. 14), para. 9; Seibert-Fohr (n. 14), pp. 401–3; Tomuschat (n. 18), p. 111.

[34] UN Committee Against Torture, General Comment No. 2: Implementation of Article 2 by States Parties, CAT/C/GC/2/CRP. 1/Rev.4 (2007), para. 6; *Convention against Torture and Other Cruel, Inhuman or Degrading Treatment or Punishment* (adopted 10 December 1984, entered into force 26 June 1987), 1465 UNTS 85 (CAT).

[35] UN ESCR Committee, General Comment No. 9: The Domestic Application of the Covenant, E/C.12/1998/24 (3 December 1998), para. 5.

it to achieve in concrete the full realization of the individual rights provided for by the Covenant'.[36] Therefore, as long as states fulfil their international obligations, it is their prerogative to determine the manner in which to do so. Whether the measures have been effective and whether states have complied with their obligations is subject to supervision by the treaty bodies, as well as other states entitled to raise complaints.[37]

3.2.2 Preference for Domestic Legal Incorporation

Despite states' discretion, what is most commonly (and sometimes solely) conceived of for implementation of human rights treaties is incorporation or codification into the domestic legal system. This involves different measures depending on whether the national system is monist or dualist, but generally entails the transformation of international norms into domestic law. This can involve constitutional amendments, the passage of legislation, as well as ancillary regulatory and procedural measures. While most, if not all, international human rights obligations can be legally incorporated nationally, sometimes treaties specifically stipulate that the relevant obligations *must* be implemented through legal measures. This represents an obligation of conduct as well as result.[38] For example, the ICCPR requires the right to life to be protected by law, as well as legal protections against any propaganda for war or advocacy of national, racial or religious hatred that constitutes incitement to discrimination, hostility or violence.[39] The HRCee further held that some rights require legal implementation, including the privacy-related guarantees in article 17.[40] Similarly, article 2(a) CEDAW requires states 'to embody the principle of the equality of men and

---

[36] (n. 15), p. 21.
[37] See, for example, the provisions for inter-state complaints in ICCPR, arts. 41–43 and the Optional Protocol to ICESCR, art. 10. Such mechanisms are very rarely employed. However, in the context of the Universal Periodic Review by the UN Human Rights Council, states do present critiques of each other's human rights protections.
[38] Seibert-Fohr notes that 'the mere non-adoption of this course of conduct is a breach of the international obligations irrespective of the consequences of the non-adoption of legislation'. Seibert-Fohr (n. 14), pp. 401–2, fn. 10.
[39] ICCPR, arts. 6(1), 20(1) and (2). See also ICCPR, arts. 14 and 26.
[40] UN HRCee, General Comment No. 31: The Nature of the General Legal Obligations Imposed on States Parties to the Covenant, CCPR/C/21/Rev.1/Add.13 (29 March 2004), para. 8.

women in their national constitutions or other appropriate legislation'.[41] The CEDAW Committee held that states must also pass legislation prohibiting discrimination in all areas of women's lives and throughout their lifespan.[42]

While states parties are sometimes explicitly required to legally incorporate human rights provisions nationally such as in these examples, there is no general obligation to legally incorporate *all* treaty provisions.[43] Despite this, some have argued that such incorporation is preferable. It is clear from their General Comments and Concluding Observations that the UN treaty bodies prefer and encourage legal incorporation. For example, the HRCee can be seen to favour incorporation, arguing that the ICCPR's provisions may have enhanced protection in states where it is specifically part of the national legal system.[44] The HRCee invites states to consider incorporation, noting that while article 2 ICCPR does not require it, the 'Covenant cannot be viewed as a substitute for domestic criminal or civil law'.[45] Regarding that article, the International Law Commission held that 'legislative means are expressly indicated at the international level as being the *most normal and appropriate* for achieving the purpose of the Covenant in question, though recourse to such means is not specifically or exclusively required'.[46] The HRCee often requests states to codify rights domestically, and some have argued that the Committee interprets the ICCPR as creating obligations of conduct regarding legal recognition and direct applicability.[47]

Similarly, the ICESCR in article 2(1) provides that each state party undertakes to realise Covenant rights 'by all appropriate means, including particularly the adoption of legislative measures'. As with the HRCee, the ESCR Committee welcomes the incorporation of the ICESCR into domestic law, despite no such formal obligation on states. The Committee noted that there is no provision in ICESCR that obliges 'its

---

[41] *Convention on the Elimination of All Forms of Discrimination against Women* (adopted 18 December 1979, entered into force 3 September 1981), 1249 UNTS 13 (CEDAW).
[42] UN CEDAW Committee, General Recommendation No. 28 on the Core Obligations of States Parties under article 2 of the Convention on the Elimination of All Forms of Discrimination against Women, CEDAW/C/GC/28 (16 December 2010), para. 31.
[43] Schachter claims that the preparatory work to the ICCPR 'shows the mandatory incorporation into domestic law was not intended'. Schachter (n. 33), p. 462, fn. 2. UN ESCR Committee, General Comment No. 9 (n. 35), para. 8.
[44] UN HRCee, General Comment No. 31 (n. 40), paras. 13, 15.
[45] Ibid., paras. 13, 8.
[46] Emphasis added (n. 15), p. 21.
[47] Tomuschat (n. 18), pp. 117–19; Seibert-Fohr (n. 14), pp. 429–38, 450, 467.

comprehensive incorporation or requiring it to be accorded any specific type of status in national law'.[48] However, the Committee stated that 'in many instances legislation is highly desirable and in some cases may even be indispensable'.[49] The ESCR Committee argues that incorporation 'can significantly enhance the scope and effectiveness of remedial measures and should be encouraged in all cases'.[50] The Committee views domestic legal incorporation as beneficial because it can avoid subsequent problems arising regarding the translation or understanding of treaty provisions in national law, and as it enables claimants to rely directly upon Covenant rights before national courts.[51] On this basis, the ESCR Committee 'strongly encourages formal adoption or incorporation of the Covenant in national law'.[52]

Like the HRCee and the ESCR Committee, other UN treaty bodies can also be seen to favour domestic incorporation and legal implementation of the treaties. The Committee on the Rights of the Child explicitly welcomes the legal incorporation of the CRC, noting that this is 'the traditional approach' to implementation in some, but not all, states.[53] The Committee reiterates the advantages of incorporation, including the ability for Convention provisions to be invoked before national courts and applied by domestic authorities.[54] Welcoming also the incorporation of some provisions into national constitutions,[55] the Committee on the Rights of the Child notes that states parties need to ensure that the CRC's provisions 'are given legal effect within their domestic legal system'.[56] Similarly, the CEDAW Committee submits that Convention rights 'may receive enhanced protection' in states where it is enshrined in domestic law, and urges states parties to 'consider incorporation to facilitate the

---

[48] UN ESCR Committee, General Comment No. 9 (n. 35), para. 5.
[49] UN ESCR Committee, General Comment No. 3 (n. 17), para. 3.
[50] UN ESCR Committee, General Comment No. 12: The Right to Adequate Food, E/C.12/1999/5 (12 May 1999), para. 33; UN ESCR Committee, General Comment No. 14: The Right to the Highest Attainable Standard of Health, E/C.12/2000/4 (11 August 2000), para. 60; UN ESCR Committee, General Comment No. 15: The Right to Water, E/C.12/2002/11 (20 January 2003), para. 57; UN ESCR Committee, General Comment No. 18: The Right to Work, E/C.12/GC/18 (6 February 2006), para. 49.
[51] UN ESCR Committee, General Comment No. 9 (n. 35), paras. 4, 8.
[52] Ibid., para. 8.
[53] UN CRC Committee, General Comment No. 5: General Measures of Implementation of the Convention on the Rights of the Child (arts. 4, 42 and 44(6)), CRC/GC/2003/5 (27 November 2003), para. 20.
[54] Ibid.
[55] Ibid., para. 21.
[56] Ibid., para. 19.

full realization of Convention'.[57] The CEDAW and CRC Committees jointly provided that states parties are obliged to establish legal frameworks for the protection and promotion of human rights, and that an 'important first step in doing so' is domestic incorporation.[58]

The *Convention on the Elimination of All Forms of Racial Discrimination* (CERD) requires states parties to eliminate racial discrimination by 'all appropriate means, including legislation as required by circumstance' and to 'rescind or nullify any laws' perpetuating racial discrimination.[59] CERD requires states to legislate regarding some obligations, such as making the dissemination of ideas based on racial superiority or hatred, acts of violence and their incitement punishable by law.[60] The Committee supervising CERD's implementation held: 'As a minimum requirement, and without prejudice to further measures, comprehensive legislation against racial discrimination ... is indispensable to combating racist hate speech effectively'.[61] Similarly, the *Convention Against Torture* (CAT) obliges states to take measures including legislation to give effect to the treaty, and to ensure that acts of torture constitute offences under criminal law.[62] The Committee Against Torture submits that codification emphasises the gravity of the crime, strengthens the deterrent effect, and enables and empowers monitoring and accountability.[63] The Committee requires states parties to enact legislation enabling the prosecution or extradition of alleged perpetrators, and providing victims with an

---

[57] UN CEDAW Committee, General Recommendation No. 28 on the Core Obligations of States parties under article 2 of the Convention on the Elimination of All Forms of Discrimination against Women, CEDAW/C/GC/28 (16 December 2010), para. 31.

[58] UN CEDAW Committee and CRC Committee, Joint General Recommendation No. 31 of the Committee on the Elimination of Discrimination against Women/General Comment No. 18 on the Committee on the Rights of the Child on Harmful Practices, CEDAW/C/GC31-CRC/C/GC/18 (14 November 2014), para. 12.

[59] *Convention on the Elimination of All Forms of Racial Discrimination* (adopted 21 December 1965, entered into force 4 January 1969), 660 UNTS 195 (CERD), art. 2(1)(c) and (d).

[60] CERD, art. 4(a) and (b). The CERD Committee notes that the language of art. 4 is mandatory, not self-executing, and requires states to adopt legislation. UN CERD Committee, General Recommendation XV on article 4 of the Convention, Forty-second session (1993), paras. 1–7; UN CERD Committee, General Recommendation No. 35: Combating racist hate speech, CERD/C/GC/35 (26 September 2013), paras. 10, 13, 15.

[61] UN CERD Committee, General Recommendation No. 35, ibid., para. 9.

[62] *Convention against Torture and Other Cruel, Inhuman or Degrading Treatment or Punishment* (adopted 10 December 1984, entered into force 26 June 1987), 1465 UNTS 85 (CAT), arts. 2(1) and 4(1). See also art. 14; UN Committee Against Torture, General Comment No. 2: Implementation of Article 2 by States Parties, CAT/C/GC/2/CRP.1/Rev.4 (2007), paras. 8–11.

[63] UN Committee Against Torture, General Comment No. 2, ibid., para. 11.

3.2 HUMAN RIGHTS TREATIES AND STATE DISCRETION

effective remedy.[64] The Committee encourages states parties to continually review and improve their legislation.[65]

As seen from these examples, the UN treaty bodies prioritise legal implementation measures on the assumption that a treaty's effectiveness is best ensured by being incorporated into national law. This view is supported by numerous scholars,[66] some of whom claim that the 'crucial element' to making rights realisable is the extent to which they have been legally incorporated.[67] In fact, often the only measures discussed in the literature regarding human rights implementation are legal measures, with no or little consideration given to other methods. While legal measures can certainly be effective, such measures alone will not necessarily advance the human rights situation in a given state. The HRCee itself has noted that 'implementation does not depend solely on constitutional or legislative enactments, which in themselves are often not per se sufficient'.[68] There are numerous examples of states with human rights protection on the books but not in practice. A survey of the HRCee's Concluding Observations reveals numerous gaps between states' constitutional guarantees and the reality of human rights violations.[69] This invites a re-assessment of the assumption that legislative measures are indeed the most effective in implementing human rights treaties, and leads to the conclusion that they in fact need to be supplemented by other measures. After all, effectiveness – and not necessarily legal incorporation – is key.[70]

Despite the clear preference for domestic legal incorporation, it is evident in international human rights law that the treaties can – and it is submitted should – be implemented in other ways. For example, the CEDAW and CRC Committees jointly called upon states parties to

---

[64] UN Committee Against Torture, General Comment No. 3: Implementation of Article 14 by States Parties, CAT/C/GC/3 (13 December 2012), paras. 20–22.
[65] UN Committee Against Torture, General Comment No. 2 (n. 62), para. 4.
[66] Hathaway (n. 3), p. 593; Tomuschat (n. 18), p. 120; Heyns and Viljoen (n. 8), p. 527; Galligan and Sandler (n. 4), p. 49; Rhona K. M. Smith, *Textbook on International Human Rights* (Oxford University Press, 2012), p. 177.
[67] Joshua Castellino, Application of International Standards of Human Rights Law at Domestic Level, in Azizur Rahman Chowdhury and Jahid Hossain Bhuiyan (eds.), *An Introduction to International Human Rights Law* (Nijhoff, 2012), p. 253.
[68] UN HRCee, General Comment No. 3: Article 2 Implementation at the National Level (29 July 1981), para. 1. This General Comment was subsequently replaced by UN HRCee, General Comment No. 31 (n. 40).
[69] Smith (n. 66), p. 49.
[70] Seibert-Fohr (n. 14), p. 432.

prohibit harmful traditional practices by law, while noting that legislation alone will be insufficient to effectively combat such practices.[71] Therefore, they advocate a holistic strategy, including legislative, policy and social measures combined with political commitment and accountability.[72] Such a holistic approach requires organisation and coordination on the local, regional and national levels between the various actors, including traditional and religious communities and their leaders, health and education professionals, and members of civil society.[73] In similar ways, non-legislative implementation measures can also be helpful or even vital in the effective implementation of some if not all other treaty provisions. For this reason, it is necessary to look beyond this preference for and focus on domestic legal incorporation and to explore other effective measures of implementation.

3.2.3 Legalisation of Human Rights

In fact, scholars have questioned the apparent preoccupation with the law and challenged the so-called legalisation of human rights. Legalisation refers to 'the practice of formulating human rights claims as legal claims and pursuing human rights objectives through legal mechanisms'.[74] It is contended that the legalisation of human rights developed out of the UDHR and occurred at the international, regional and national levels with the creation of legally binding human rights instruments.[75] In this way, law and the legal discipline became entrenched and generally

---

[71] UN CEDAW Committee and CRC Committee, Joint General Recommendation No. 31 of the Committee on the Elimination of Discrimination against Women/General Comment No. 18 on the Committee on the Rights of the Child on Harmful Practices, CEDAW/C/GC31-CRC/C/GC/18 (14 November 2014), paras. 13, 40, 41.
[72] Ibid., para. 33.
[73] Ibid., paras. 34, 36.
[74] Jack Donnelly, The Virtues of Legalization, in Saladin Meckled-García and Başak Çali (eds.), *The Legalization of Human Rights: Multidisciplinary Perspectives on Human Rights and Human Rights Law* (Routledge, 2006), p. 67.
[75] De Feyter (n. 29), p. 50. Başak Çali and Saladin Meckled-García, Introduction: Human Rights Legalized – Defining, Interpreting, and Implementing an Ideal, in Saladin Meckled-García and Başak Çali (eds.), *The Legalization of Human Rights: Multidisciplinary Perspectives on Human Rights and Human Rights Law* (Routledge, 2006), p. 1. An-Na'im argues that the UDHR was 'hijacked' by states who transformed human rights into legal obligations in international treaties. Abdullahi Ahmed An-Na'im, The Spirit of Laws Is Not Universal: Alternatives to the Enforcement Paradigm for Human Rights (2016) *Tilburg Law Review* 21, p. 274.

3.2 HUMAN RIGHTS TREATIES AND STATE DISCRETION

seen as *the* way in which to view and address human rights issues.[76] The legal focus overshadowed other implementation methods that may be equally or even more effective in domestically protecting human rights. While legal mechanisms are important, they are not a prerequisite for better human rights behaviour.[77] Rather, what is important is how domestic stakeholders employ and realise rights.[78] Institutional, top-down processes at the national level are not necessarily better at protecting rights than other, less formal processes.[79] State law is one normative order that can be used to implement rights, but the law alone may be insufficient (or even counter-productive),[80] and the state may be unwilling or unable to enforce it.

Scholars have criticised legalism, arguing that it is not clear why all human rights should be most appropriately advanced by legal measures.[81] They suggest that evidence from real world observation rebuts such an assumption in favour of the law and confidence in its superiority in all situations.[82] For example, across many jurisdictions practices including rape and domestic violence persist despite legislation enacted to eliminate them.[83] Such laws can give the impression that complex and entrenched power differentials and inequalities have been resolved, when in fact they persist.[84] Forsythe labelled the legal-rights approach with its strong emphasis on adjudication by courts as 'judicial romanticism',[85] which highlights the unrealistic expectations placed upon the law and its

---

[76] Anthony Woodiwiss, The Law Cannot Be Enough: Human Rights and the Limits of Legalism, in Saladin Meckled-García and Başak Çali (eds.), *The Legalization of Human Rights: Multidisciplinary Perspectives on Human Rights and Human Rights Law* (Routledge, 2006), p. 32.

[77] Dai (n. 6), p. 98.

[78] Ibid., p. 99.

[79] Galligan and Sandler (n. 4), p. 48.

[80] State-led legal approaches that fail to take account of local norms and engage with communities may in turn lead to grass-roots resistance. Kieran McEvoy, Beyond Legalism: Towards a Thicker Understanding of Transitional Justice (December 2007) *Journal of Law and Society* 34:4, p. 424.

[81] Çali and Meckled-García (n. 75), p. 1.

[82] David Forsythe, Human Rights Studies: On the Dangers of Legalistic Assumptions, in Fons Coomans, Fred Grünfeld and Menno Kamminga (eds.), *Methods of Human Rights Research* (Intersentia, 2009), pp. 65–6.

[83] Ratna Kapur, Revisioning the Role of Law in Women's Human Rights Struggles, in Saladin Meckled-García and Başak Çali (eds.), *The Legalization of Human Rights: Multidisciplinary Perspectives on Human Rights and Human Rights Law* (Routledge, 2006), p. 101.

[84] Ibid., p. 111.

[85] Forsythe (n. 82), pp. 65–6.

enforcement. A central critique of the legalisation of rights is that its preoccupation with and romanticisation of the law typically leads to a disinclination to acknowledge the limits of the law. By engaging lawyers and working within a legal framework to address human rights problems, the question automatically becomes: what *legal* solution or remedy is most appropriate? This 'closed system of thinking'[86] fails to consider solutions outside the law, or to recognise that the law may not be able to present a suitable remedy in the situation.

For instance, in many areas, the state may not be the locus of authority and may lack capacity to implement its laws and policies. In such circumstances, the state-centric system of international law is misaligned and handicapped in delivering effective human rights protection. For example, the modern state model does not capture the reality of organisation, belonging or power in many contexts, such as one in which a village chief or religious leader has more influence than the official head of state. In these situations, state law claims to prevail, but fails to in practice. Many states have what Risse and Börzel call 'areas of limited statehood', in which the state is not unwilling to implement international norms, but rather lacks the practical capacity to do so.[87] As such, there may be gaps or holes in legal orders.[88] They recommend taking limited statehood into consideration when implementing rights as it can be a significant obstacle.[89] Alternatively, rather than seeing it as an obstacle, situations of limited statehood also present the opportunity to recognise the non-state norms and power structures existing in those areas and their ability to be engaged to implement rights (in conjunction with or in place of the state). In this way, it is possible to move away from a solely top-down, state-centric model of implementation to a more diffuse and bottom-up one that may be more effective in the circumstances.

---

[86] McEvoy (n. 80), p. 417.
[87] They claim that this characterises most states in the contemporary international system and in particular the developing states. Tanja A. Börzel and Thomas Risse, Human Rights in Areas of Limited Statehood: The New Agenda, in Thomas Risse, Stephen Ropp and Kathryn Sikkink (eds.), *The Persistent Power of Human Rights: From Commitment to Compliance* (Cambridge University Press, 2013), pp. 63, 66. See also Brian Tamanaha, Understanding Legal Pluralism: Past to Present, Local to Global (2008) *Sydney Law Review* 30, pp. 385, 401; Sally Engle Merry, International Law and Sociolegal Scholarship: Toward a Spatial Global Legal Pluralism, in Michael A. Helfand (ed.), *Negotiating State and Non-State Law: The Challenge of Global and Local Legal Pluralism* (Cambridge University Press, 2016), pp. 72–3.
[88] Merry (2016), ibid., p. 77.
[89] Börzel and Risse (n. 87), pp. 64–5.

3.2 HUMAN RIGHTS TREATIES AND STATE DISCRETION

The legalisation of human rights also necessarily implies a focus on the modern state as the authority responsible for the creation and enforcement of positive state law. While there are, of course, other forms of law beneath and beyond the state (like customary and religious law), the legalisation of human rights has focused on the central role of state law, positioning it as *the* law.[90] Legalisation is therefore rightly criticised for being state-centric. Rather than being universal, the state-centric legality model is relative and can be foreign in many places where other normative systems exist that should be recognised and taken into account.[91] One of the reasons why human rights reflect Western rather than other values is because 'the primary method of securing rights is through legalism where rights are claimed and adjudicated upon, not through reconciliation, repentance or education'.[92] Legalism's focus on state law and top-down measures means that other mechanisms, as well as the role of other norms and actors therein, remain under-explored and under-exploited. For example, economic mechanisms and private economic actors, which also have a profound influence on people's lives, have been marginalised.[93] Human rights need not be solely the business of states, and portraying them in this way distances and disconnects other relevant norms and actors.

Finally, legalisation secured the position of law as the dominant discipline regarding human rights, rendering others irrelevant or merely of secondary importance.[94] For example, the members of the UN treaty

---

[90] The positivist positioning of state law as *the* law is one of the embedded creeds of Western legal culture. However, agreed definitions of 'law' are elusive. See William Twining, Legal Pluralism 101, in Brian Tamanaha, Caroline Sage and Michael Woolcock (eds.), *Legal Pluralism and Development: Scholars and Practitioners in Dialogue* (Cambridge University Press, 2012), p. 114; McEvoy (n. 80), p. 416; Merry (2016) (n. 87), p. 68.

[91] An-Na'im (n. 75), p. 257. According to Twining, 'the near monopoly of coercive power by a centralised bureaucratic state is a modern exception, largely confined to the Northern Hemisphere for less than two hundred years'. Twining (n. 90), pp. 120, 126. See also Tamanaha (2008) (n. 87), p. 379.

[92] Bonny Ibhawoh, Cultural Relativism and Human Rights: Reconsidering the Africanist Discourse (2001) *Netherlands Quarterly of Human Rights* 19:1, p. 53, citing Surya Prakash Sinha, Human Rights: A Non-Western View Point (1981) *Archiv fur Rechts- und Sozialphilosophie* 67, p. 77.

[93] Jane Cowan, Anthropology and Human Rights: Do Anthropologists Have an Ethical Obligation to Promote Human Rights? An Open Exchange, in Mark Goodale (ed.), *Human Rights: An Anthropological Reader* (Blackwell, 2009), p. 205.

[94] De Feyter (2011) (n. 75), p. 51; Michael Freeman, Putting Law in Its Place: An Interdisciplinary Evaluation of National Amnesty Laws, in Saladin Meckled-García and Başak Çali (eds.), *The Legalization of Human Rights: Multidisciplinary Perspectives on Human Rights and Human Rights Law* (Routledge, 2006), p. 52.

bodies overwhelmingly have legal qualifications.[95] While not necessarily rejecting the role of law in human rights,[96] scholars have questioned its near monopoly, reiterating the value of other disciplines' contributions. While the law is not designed to explain the gaps between human rights norms and their enjoyment in practice, the social sciences are designed precisely to explain these aspects.[97] Social science research has begun to challenge law's predominance and has provided insights into the social, cultural, political, economic and other obstacles to be overcome in order to implement human rights.[98] Combining insights from different disciplines such as anthropology and sociology with those from law can create a fuller understanding of human rights in context and their interrelationship with other social forces.[99] However, in the last seventy years anthropologists have been largely uninvolved in human rights, due in part to the dominance of the legal discourse.[100]

3.2.4 Other Measures for Implementing Human Rights

Given the critiques of legalism and the need to close the implementation gap to ensure human rights enjoyment in practice, it is necessary to incorporate insights from disciplines other than law and to explore other methods of implementation. Therefore, this section considers six of the main UN human rights treaties as well as their treaty bodies' General Comments to determine the extent to which human rights obligations can be domestically implemented through measures other than legislative ones. For example, article 2(2) ICCPR obliges states parties to take steps 'to adopt legislative or other measures to give effect' to Covenant rights.

---

[95] For example, as of the membership in August 2019, only one out of eighteen HRCee members does not have a legal degree; four out of eighteen members of the ESCR Committee do not have law degrees; four out of eighteen members of the CERD Committee do not have law degrees; five out of eighteen members of the CRC Committee do not have law degrees; four out of ten members of the CAT Committee do not have law degrees; and eleven out of twenty-three members of the CEDAW Committee do not have law degrees.

[96] Some in fact defend its role and even its dominance – see Donnelly (n. 74), pp. 67–80.

[97] Freeman (n. 94), pp. 50, 62. See also de Feyter (2011), (n. 75) pp. 53–4.

[98] Todd Landman, Social Science Methods and Human Rights, in Fons Coomans, Fred Grünfeld and Menno T. Kamminga (eds.), *Methods of Human Rights Research* (Intersentia, 2009), p. 19.

[99] De Feyter 2011 (n. 75), p. 65; Galligan and Sandler (n. 4), p. 25.

[100] Ann-Belinda Preis, Human Rights as Cultural Practice: An Anthropological Critique (1996) *Human Rights Quarterly* 18, p. 287.

This article sets the overarching framework within which rights are to be guaranteed, and requires states parties to take 'legislative, judicial, administrative, educative and other appropriate measures'.[101] The HRCee has stressed the importance of other measures including awareness-raising among state officials and the general public, and the use of economic, social and cultural measures to ensure that children enjoy their rights.[102] Such treaty provisions requiring states to adopt 'other measures' of implementation are common across many international and regional human rights treaties.[103] Some of these from the international level are considered further below.

The ICESCR also permits the use of other, non-legislative implementation measures. Indicating a very broad scope, the ESCR Committee held that the term 'all appropriate means' in article 2(1) needs to 'be given its full and natural meaning'.[104] The Committee emphasised that taking legislative measures alone will not suffice, holding that 'the adoption of legislative measures, as specifically foreseen by the Covenant, is by no means exhaustive of the obligations of States parties'.[105] To avoid violating the Covenant, states parties must take *all* necessary steps to ensure the rights are realised.[106] The ESCR Committee held that steps taken by states parties must be 'deliberate, concrete and targeted as clearly as possible towards meeting' the Covenant's obligations.[107] Such measures may include 'administrative, financial, educational and social measures'.[108] For example, article 6(2) identifies steps to be taken by states regarding the right to work, including 'technical and vocational guidance and training programmes'. The ESCR Committee foresees a role for public as well as private actors in implementation, recalling, for example, the

---

[101] UN HRCee, General Comment No. 31 (n. 40), paras. 5, 7. See generally discussion of legislative and other measures by Seibert-Fohr (n. 14), pp. 453–66.
[102] UN HRCee, General Comment No. 31 (n. 40), para. 7; UN HRCee, General Comment No. 17: Article 24 (Rights of the Child) (Thirty-fifth session 1989), para. 6.
[103] See, for example: *Convention on the Rights of Persons with Disabilities* (adopted 13 December 2006, entered into force 3 May 2008), 2515 UNTS 3, art. 4(1)(a); *American Convention on Human Rights* (adopted on 22 November 1969, entered into force 18 July 1978), art. 2; *Arab Charter on Human Rights* (adopted on 15 September 1994), reprinted in 18 *Human Rights Law Journal* 151 (1997), art. 44; *African Charter on Human and Peoples' Rights* (adopted 27 June 1981, entered into force 21 October 1986) (Banjul Charter) CAB/LEG/67/3 rev. 5, 21 ILM 58 (1982), art. 1.
[104] UN ESCR Committee, General Comment No. 3 (n. 17), para. 4.
[105] Ibid.
[106] UN ESCR Committee, General Comment No. 14 (n. 50), paras. 51–3.
[107] UN ESCR Committee, General Comment No. 3 (n. 17), para. 2.
[108] Ibid., para. 7.

responsibilities of 'all members of society' in realising the right to health.[109] Notably, the ESCR Committee has acknowledged that the implementation measures adopted by states will vary, with each state enjoying discretion in determining the measures most suited to its circumstances.[110]

The CAT provides in article 2(1) that states parties 'should take effective legislative, administrative, judicial or other measures to prevent acts of torture'. While CAT is predominately focused on legal measures (such as criminalisation and prosecution), it also foresees other measures of implementation such as education, training and information dissemination in article 10. The Committee Against Torture has emphasised education and training on human rights law, particularly for law enforcement officials and military and security forces.[111] Reiterating the obligation of result rather than conduct, the Committee noted that measures taken 'must, in the end, be effective in preventing' torture.[112] If the measures adopted by a state fail to eradicate torture, 'the Convention requires that they be revised and/or that new, more effective measures be adopted'.[113] This again reinforces the view that the main criterion for selecting and assessing implementation measures is their effectiveness in practice. This conclusion is supported by an analysis of the *Convention on the Elimination of Racial Discrimination* (CERD), which also permits a wide range of other, non-legislative measures of implementation.

Article 2(1)(d) CERD requires states parties to pursue 'all appropriate means' to eliminate racial discrimination. States are obliged in article 9 to report to the Committee on the Elimination of Racial Discrimination (CERD Committee) on 'the legislative, judicial, administrative or other measures' adopted to implement the Convention. Article 7 provides that states parties shall adopt 'immediate and effective measures, particularly in the fields of teaching, education, culture and information, with a view to combating prejudices'. The Committee noted that article 7 is phrased in mandatory language and that the fields of activity listed are not 'exhaustive of the undertakings required'.[114] The Committee has stressed

---

[109] See UN ESCR Committee, General Comment No. 14 (n. 50), para. 42.
[110] Ibid., para. 53; UN ESCR Committee, General Comment No. 3 (n. 17), para. 4.
[111] UN Committee Against Torture, General Comment No. 2: Implementation of Article 2 by States Parties, CAT/C/GC/2/CRP. 1/Rev.4 (2007), paras. 24–25; UN Committee Against Torture, General Comment No. 3 Implementation of article 14 by States parties, CAT/C/GC/3 (13 December 2012), paras. 18, 34, 35.
[112] UN Committee Against Torture, General Comment No. 2, (n. 111), para. 2.
[113] Ibid., para. 4.
[114] UN CERD Committee, General Recommendation No. 35 (n. 60), para. 31.

the importance of education, including intercultural education and dialogue; informed school curricula promoting understanding and tolerance; and information campaigns engaging the public and civil society (including religious and community associations).[115] A state party may protect Convention rights in different ways, 'be it by the use of public institutions or through the activities of private institutions'.[116] The CERD Committee clearly envisages both state and non-state actors to be involved in implementation, highlighting the media's role in countering hate speech and encouraging states to engage sports associations to eradicate racism.[117]

Further examples of other, non-legislative measures of implementation can be found in the CRC. Article 4 provides that states parties shall 'undertake all appropriate legislative, administrative and other measures' to implement the Convention, while article 19(1) additionally highlights 'social and educational measures'.[118] The CRC Committee notes that it 'cannot prescribe in detail the measures which each or every State party will find appropriate to ensure effective implementation of the Convention'.[119] However, on the basis of their experience reviewing state reports, the Committee has identified a broad range of necessary measures for effective implementation.[120] These include: a comprehensive national strategy; information dissemination and awareness-raising; training and capacity-building (including for the community, religious leaders and teachers); and cooperation with civil society.[121] As with the CERD Committee, the CRC Committee also highlights the important role of education and NSAs like the media.[122] Going a step further, the Committee notes that the CRC's implementation requires input from all sectors of society, recalling the responsibilities on all organs of society for the realisation of human rights in the UDHR.[123]

---

[115] Ibid., paras. 32–4, 36–7; UN CERD Committee, General Recommendation No. XXVII on Discrimination against Roma (16 August 2000), para. 11.
[116] UN CERD Committee, General Recommendation XX on article 5 of the Convention (Forty-eighth session 1996), para. 5.
[117] UN CERD Committee, General Recommendation No. 35 (n. 60), paras. 39–41, 43.
[118] See also CRC, art. 32(2) regarding economic exploitation of children and art. 33 regarding drug use.
[119] UN CRC Committee, General Comment No. 5 (n. 53), para. 26.
[120] Ibid., para. 1.
[121] Ibid., paras. 9, 28–59, 66–70.
[122] Ibid., paras. 59, 66–70.
[123] Ibid., para. 56. See UDHR preamble.

Finally, CEDAW contains numerous provisions permitting a state's use of other, non-legislative implementation measures. In several articles, CEDAW obliges states parties to take 'all appropriate measures' to guarantee Convention rights.[124] Article 3 provides that states parties 'shall take in all fields, in particular the political, social, economic and cultural fields, all appropriate measures, including legislation'. The CEDAW Committee held that states parties must adopt a 'comprehensive range of measures', and continuously build upon them 'in the light of their effectiveness'.[125] The Committee focuses on the practical realisation of equality, holding that states should employ 'the entire range of measures that are appropriate and necessary in the particular circumstances'.[126] States will have to justify to the Committee the appropriateness of the measures they adopted, demonstrating whether they achieved the intended 'effect and result'.[127] These statements reinforce the primacy of effectiveness, and the obligation of result not conduct. Like the UDHR, CERD and CRC Committees, the CEDAW Committee recognises a role for NSAs, such as business, the media, community groups, and individuals, and requires states to enlist them in adopting measures that fulfil Convention goals.[128]

Some of the best examples of other, non-legislative implementation measures stem from the obligation on states parties under the CRC and CEDAW to combat harmful practices like female genital mutilation/cutting (FGM/C) and child marriage.[129] In addition to legislative measures,[130] the CRC and CEDAW Committees recommend that states parties' efforts to combat such harmful practices and to change the 'underlying social norms are holistic, community based and founded on a rights-based approach that includes the active participation of all relevant stakeholders'.[131] They specifically refer to measures including education (including non-formal education); training; awareness-raising

---

[124] See CEDAW, arts. 2, 3, 5–8, 10, 11(1), 12(1), 13, 14(2), 16(1), 18, 24.
[125] UN CEDAW Committee, General Recommendation No. 28 (n. 57), paras. 24, 37, 38.
[126] Ibid., para. 25.
[127] Ibid., para. 23.
[128] Ibid., para. 28. See also UN CEDAW Committee General Recommendation No. 37 (2018) on the Gender-Related Dimensions of Disaster Risk Reduction in the Context of Climate Change, CEDAW/C/GC/37 (13 March 2018), paras. 47–51.
[129] See CRC, art. 24(3); CEDAW, arts. 2(f) and 5(a).
[130] UN CEDAW Committee and CRC Committee, Joint General Recommendation (n. 58), para. 55.
[131] Ibid., para. 60.

and information programmes; microcredit programmes; the creation of safe spaces for women and girls; engaging the media; creating public dialogue and debate; and the use of theatre, television programmes, art and music.[132] The Committees advocate culturally sensitive interventions to address harmful practices on the basis that such interventions can lead to sustainable and large-scale reduction of such practices and the acceptance of new social norms.[133] The CRC and CEDAW Committees highlight that:

> awareness-raising campaigns can provide an opportunity to initiate public discussions about harmful practices with a view to collectively exploring alternatives that do not cause harm or violate the human rights of women and children and reaching agreement that the social norms underlying and sustaining harmful practices can and should be changed. The collective pride of a community in identifying and adopting new ways to fulfil its core values will ensure the commitment and sustainability of new social norms that do not result in the infliction of harm or violate human rights. The most effective efforts are inclusive and engage relevant stakeholders at all levels, especially girls and women from affected communities and boys and men. Moreover, those efforts require the active participation and support of local leaders, including through the allocation of adequate resources. Establishing or strengthening existing partnerships with relevant stakeholders, institutions, organizations and social networks (religious and traditional leaders, practitioners and civil society) can help to build bridges between constituencies.[134]

These recommendations clearly echo the scholarship on culturally sensitive approaches to human rights discussed in Chapter 2, in that they promote home-grown solutions reliant upon culture's dynamism to further human rights compliance. They align specifically with Nyamu and An-Na`im's proposals for communities to collectively explore alternatives to the dominant norm/practice that do not cause harm, but remain culturally compatible and legitimate.[135] Like culturally sensitive approaches to human rights, these CEDAW and CRC recommendations emphasise that community-based measures are beneficial due to their

---

[132] Ibid., paras. 63–81.
[133] Ibid., para. 59.
[134] Ibid., paras. 76–7.
[135] Celestine Nyamu, How Should Human Rights and Development Respond to Cultural Legitimization of Gender Hierarchy in Developing Countries? (2000) *Harvard International Law Journal* 41:2, p. 413; Abdullahi Ahmed An-Na`im, Conclusion, in Abdullahi Ahmed An-Na`im (ed.), *Human Rights in Cross-Cultural Perspectives: A Quest for Consensus* (University of Pennsylvania Press, 1992), p. 432.

effectiveness and ability to ensure commitment and sustainability of human rights compliant norms. These Committees recognise the value of inclusive engagement with and dialogue between stakeholders and developing broad community partnerships. The Committees refrain from merely recommending top-down measures like legislative bans, which may provoke a community backlash and place women and children in an even more vulnerable position. Through these recommendations, the Committees demonstrate a sophisticated view of culture, their understanding of the limitations of legislative measures, and that the state is not able to fully implement the Conventions on its own.

These CRC and CEDAW recommendations acknowledge the pre-existing social structures, institutions and normative systems in a given context and their relevance for human rights implementation. International human rights law is not implemented in a vacuum, but must interact and contend with well-entrenched local norms and institutions. Competition between such norms is inevitable, given that some local norms will be required to change – sometimes fundamentally.[136] This conflict can be exacerbated if the local community perceives human rights as foreign or illegitimate norms – or even a form of Western imperialism.[137] Therefore, domestic constituents who are able to vernacularise or translate human rights into local concepts are crucial. Research has shown that human rights treaties have the greatest impact where there is a minimum level of domestic commitment to rights, including from government officials, judges, civil society and the media.[138] The true test of effectiveness is the acceptance and adoption of human rights norms as authoritative by those to whom they apply.[139] Not only do international norms need to be internalised by rights-holders, but beneficiaries also need to commit to 'a continuing political struggle on the ground to realize human rights'.[140]

---

[136] 'At its very core, implementation involves the replacement of those competing norms or at least the evolution of existing norms to allow for the incorporation of human rights standards, and the cognitive understanding that accompany them': Galligan and Sandler (n. 4), pp. 29–30, 38, 45.

[137] Heyns and Viljoen (n. 8), p. 520.

[138] Ibid., p. 522.

[139] Makau Mutua, Book Review (2001) *American Journal of International Law* 95, p. 256; Galligan and Sandler (n. 4), p. 29.

[140] Patrick Schmidt and Simon Halliday, Introduction: Socio-legal Perspectives on Human Rights in the National Context, in Simon Halliday and Patrick Schmidt (eds.), *Human Rights Brought Home: Socio-legal Perspectives on Human Rights in the National Context* (Hart Publishing, 2004), p. 3. See Richard Falk, *Human Rights Horizons: The Pursuit of Justice in a Globalizing World* (Routledge, 2000), p. 61.

As such, rights implementation is likely to be ineffective if human rights norms do not enjoy local acceptance by a domestic constituency committed to their advocacy. Particularly in this regard, other, non-legislative measures of implementation are vital.

3.2.5 Other Measures of Implementation: Permitted but Peripheral

This section demonstrated that while states parties are legally obliged to domestically implement human rights treaty norms, they have significant discretion regarding the manner of implementation. According to the obligation of result, so long as the state effectively protects the human rights standards in the treaties, the method of doing so remains largely at its discretion. Despite this, a state's incorporation or codification of treaty obligations into national law is the primary focus and preferred manner of implementation. This is apparent from a review of the treaties, the treaty bodies' General Comments, as well as the relevant literature. Domestic incorporation and other legal measures can be useful tools for implementation; however, they are not the only tools. While domestic legal incorporation has unique benefits and is sometimes prescribed by the treaties, such legal measures alone will not necessarily advance human rights enjoyment. For this reason, the legalisation of human rights has been rightly criticised for excluding useful insights from other disciplines, and overshadowing other effective implementation methods. The focus on legislation also necessarily implies a focus on the state, which detracts from or obscures other relevant non-state actors and norms like social institutions. Despite this preoccupation with the state and its legal mechanisms, the human rights treaties all provide for domestic implementation via other measures.

As seen from the above survey, the scope for other non-legislative measures is very broad and even open-ended, so long as the measures effectively protect the rights in question. Of the UN treaty bodies, the HRCee and the Committee Against Torture are the most legalistic in their approach. This can likely be explained by the fact that civil and political rights have traditionally been seen (in the West) as justiciable rights entailing negative obligation on states, and that almost all of the HRCee members typically have law degrees. The Committee Against Torture may take such a legalistic approach given the absolute nature of the prohibition on torture, and the frequent obligations in CAT to criminalise such acts and prosecute perpetrators. As demonstrated by the example of combating harmful practices, the CEDAW and CRC Committees are the most open to other measures of implementation. This more holistic approach is perhaps due to their explicit focus on modifying culture,[141] and relatively diverse Committee memberships. Holistic approaches include legal and other measures, recognising and engaging with a multiplicity of norms and actors impacting upon the effectiveness of implementation measures. The appeal of such an approach is its ability to deliver more effective protection where legal measures cannot, or cannot do so in isolation.

3.3 UN Human Rights Treaty Bodies and Other Measures of Implementation

As seen in the last section, while permitting 'legislative or other measures', the UN human rights treaties only give very general instructions regarding domestic implementation. It therefore falls to the treaty bodies to expand upon and elucidate the types of measures required to domestically implement the treaties. This section turns to focus specifically on 'other measures' in the practice of the UN treaty bodies when supervising states parties' implementation. Ratification of the main UN human rights treaties includes an obligation to participate in the international monitoring procedures before the treaty bodies, which are the only entities in the UN system mandated to monitor states parties' treaty compliance.[142] States must periodically report to the relevant treaty body regarding the status of human rights in their jurisdiction, explaining and defending the implementation measures employed.[143] The treaty bodies have promulgated reporting guidelines to assist states with the preparation of their reports, and also send specific lists of issues to the states. Following consideration of these reports, the treaty bodies discuss them with state representatives in an open dialogue – rather than an adversarial process.[144] For example, the HRCee intends its consideration of a report

---

[141] See, for example, CEDAW, art. 5(a); CRC, art. 24(3).
[142] Ilias Bantekas and Lutz Oette, *International Human Rights Law and Practice* (Cambridge University Press, 2013), pp. 181–2.
[143] See ICCPR, art. 40; ICESCR, arts. 16–17; CERD, art. 9; CEDAW, art. 18; CAT, art. 19; CRC, art. 44.
[144] 'At the international level, the reporting process creates a basis for constructive dialogue between States and the treaty bodies. The treaty bodies, in providing these guidelines, wish to emphasize their supportive role in fostering effective national implementation of the international human rights instruments': UN, Report of the Inter-Committee

3.3 HUMAN RIGHTS TREATIES & OTHER MEASURES

to be a 'constructive discussion' with the state party in the aim of improving their human rights situation.[145]

Following this hearing, the treaty body evaluates the state's human rights situation and determines whether the domestic protection offered meets the requisite standards. The treaty body's views are published as Concluding Observations, which identify positive elements as well as any problems in implementation along with proposed remedial actions. In a quasi-judicial manner, the treaty bodies determine whether a state party has met its international obligations or not. However, the treaty body decisions are not legally binding, and, as such, states retain discretion in implementing them.[146] Despite not being binding, the treaty body decisions are highly persuasive as the authoritative interpretations of the treaties.[147] While not a flawless system,[148] the treaty bodies' production of General Comments, their ongoing examination of state reports, and the Concluding Observations thereon clarify the scope of the treaties as living instruments.[149] Focusing on the HRCee, ESCR Committee and the CEDAW Committee,

---

Technical Working Group, Harmonized Guidelines on Reporting to the International Human Rights Treaty Monitoring Bodies, HRI/MC/2006/3 (10 May 2006), para. 11.

[145] UN, Report of the Secretary-General, Compilation of Guidelines on the Form and Content of Reports to Be Submitted by States Parties to the International Human Rights Treaties, HRI/GEN/2/Rev.6 (3 June 2009), Chapter III Human Rights Committee, para. G.1. See also Boerefijn (n. 9), pp. 201–3.

[146] Ando (n. 19), p. 712. However, a 2018 decision by the Spainish Supreme Court held that the views of the CEDAW Committee were indeed legally binding on Spain. See analysis by Machiko Kanetake, *María de los Ángeles González Carreño v. Ministry of Justice*, Judgment No. 1263/2018 of 17 July 2018 (ROJ: STS 2747/2018) *American Journal of International Law* (2019) 113:3, pp. 586–92.

[147] See Martin Scheinin, International Mechanisms and Procedures for Monitoring, in Catarina Krause and Martin Scheinin (eds.), *International Protection of Human Rights: A Textbook* (Turku/Åbo: Åbo Akademi University, Institute for Human Rights, 2009), pp. 617, 619; UN HRCee, General Comment No. 33: The Obligations of States Parties under the Optional Protocol to the International Covenant on Civil and Political Rights, CCPR/C/GC/33 (5 November 2008), para. 13.

[148] There has been much critique of the UN treaty body system, for example their slow process, complexity of and duplication in the reporting procedure, the non-binding status of their decisions, and that states often fail to report or to comply with decisions. In response, the UN General Assembly in 2012 commenced (and subsequently extended) an intergovernmental process on strengthening and enhancing the effective functioning of the human rights treaty body system: see UN General Assembly, Resolution A/RES/66/254 (23 February 2012); UN General Assembly, Resolution A/RES/68/268 (9 April 2014).

[149] Smith (n. 66), p. 154. Where ratified by states, the treaty bodies can also have jurisdiction to determine individual complaints against states, which also contributes to the treaties' interpretation.

this section analyses the types of implementation measures recommended by the treaty bodies, with a focus on other measures and the role of non-state actors therein.

3.3.1 UN Treaty Bodies' Reporting Guidelines

Over the years, each treaty body has provided guidance to states parties regarding reporting on their specific instrument. In addition to these guidelines, in 2006 the UN Inter-Committee Technical Working Group created standardised guidelines regarding reporting under the various treaties. These so-called Harmonised Guidelines apply to the seven main human rights treaties generally, as well as having specific guidance to states for reporting under each treaty.[150] For example, the guidelines advise states on what they are to report on in order to give the treaty bodies a complete picture of the implementation of the relevant treaties, as well as practical information like length and format. The Harmonised Guidelines are intended to strengthen states' capacity to effectively and efficiently fulfil their reporting obligations, for example by reducing unnecessary duplication, which helps to improve the efficacy of the treaty monitoring system in general.[151]

While the Harmonised Guidelines foresee a variety of implementation measures, they focus on legal measures. For example, states are to report on which rights 'are protected either in the constitution, a bill of rights, a basic law, or other national legislation'.[152] They are additionally required to report on whether the treaties have been incorporated domestically; which judicial, administrative or other authorities have competence over human rights matters; whether provisions can be directly invoked before courts, tribunals, etc.; and whether the state has signed up to regional courts or other such mechanisms.[153] However, the Harmonised Guidelines also provide that states parties are to elaborate on not just the legal but also the de facto situation regarding treaty implementation. As such,

---

[150] The Harmonised Guidelines apply to the ICCPR; ICESCR; CERD; CAT; CEDAW; CRC; *International Convention on the Protection of the Rights of All Migrant Workers and Members of Their Families* (adopted 18 December 1990, entered into force 1 July 2003), 2220 UNTS 3.

[151] UN, Report of the Secretary-General, Compilation of Guidelines on the Form and Content of Reports to be Submitted by States Parties to the International Human Rights Treaties, HRI/GEN/2/Rev.6 (3 June 2009) (Harmonised Guidelines), para. 4.

[152] Ibid., para. 42(a).

[153] Ibid., para. 42.

state reports should indicate how the legal instruments adopted 'are reflected in the actual political, economic, social and cultural realities and general conditions existing in the country'.[154] States should also report on implementation measures such as dissemination of information, awareness-raising, engaging the media, education, development cooperation and assistance, and allocation of budgetary resources.[155]

While the implementation measures are typically actions to be taken by the state, the Harmonised Guidelines also foresee a role for NSAs in implementation, such as civil society and non-governmental organisations (NGOs). States parties are encouraged to report on:

> [t]he extent of the participation of civil society, in particular non-governmental organizations, in the promotion and protection of human rights within the country, and the steps taken by the Government to encourage and promote the development of a civil society with a view to ensuring the promotion and protection of human rights.[156]

As this demonstrates, in addition to their legal focus, the Harmonised Guidelines foresee a variety of other implementation measures and also a role for NSAs.

In addition to these Guidelines, the ESCR Committee provided specific guidance to states regarding reporting on ICESCR's implementation. The ESCR Committee's Guidelines envisage states parties reporting on various implementation measures including: legislation; legal safeguards; constitutional guarantees; policies; programmes; administrative provisions; training; public awareness raising; and national action plans.[157] States parties are instructed to report on legal measures,[158] however with the caveat that simply listing legal instruments is insufficient without providing further information on implementation in both law and fact.[159] The

---

[154] Ibid., para. 25.
[155] Ibid., para. 43.
[156] Ibid., para. 43(g).
[157] UN Economic and Social Council, Guidelines on Treaty-Specific documents to be submitted by States Parties under Articles 16 and 17 of the ICESCR, E/C.12/2008/2 (24 March 2009), Annex.
[158] For example, states parties should report on the 'incorporation and direct applicability of each Covenant right in the domestic legal order, with reference to specific examples of relevant case law'. Ibid., Annex, para. 3(d).
[159] Ibid., Annex, para. 2. The HRCee also includes this stipulation: see UN HRC, Guidelines for the treaty-specific document to be submitted by States parties under article 40 of the International Covenant on Civil and Political Rights, CCPR/C/2009/1 (22 November 2010), para. 26.

Committee emphasises practical information including disaggregated and comparative statistical data. Such information is especially useful for the creation of benchmarks and indicators to monitor progress or identify gaps in implementation.[160] Importantly, the ESCR Committee Guidelines are not prescriptive and frequently request states to report on the general or unspecified implementation measures they have taken such as: steps; effective measures; other measures/mechanisms/strategies; and ways and means.

Like the ESCR Committee's, the HRCee's Guidelines are not prescriptive and foresee the possibility for states to use unspecified implementation measures like steps, measures, or ways and means. It also requests statistical data and practical information on the actual enjoyment of Covenant rights. However, it appears that the main focus of the HRCee's Guidelines is on legal measures of implementation. For example, regarding article 2 ICCPR – which refers to both legal and other measures – states are instructed to report on the principal legal measures taken; whether and to what extent the rights are guaranteed in the constitution or other laws; whether and to what extent the Covenant is incorporated into domestic law making it directly applicable and enforceable; and which 'judicial, administrative and other competent authorities have jurisdiction to secure Covenant rights' and to provide examples of cases.[161] The only non-legal measures of implementation mentioned in relation to this article are national or official institutions or machinery responsible for implementation, and awareness-raising and dissemination of information on the Covenant.[162] As such, it is apparent that the HRCee largely conceives of the ICCPR's implementation through the prism of state law and other legal measures.

Under article 18 CEDAW, states have to report on the legislative, judicial, administrative and other measures they have adopted to give effect to the Convention. This requirement is echoed in the CEDAW Committee's Reporting Guidelines to states for the preparation of their

---

[160] See Neumayer (n. 3), p. 934; Paul Hunt, Judith Bueno de Mesquita, Joo-Young Lee and Sally-Anne Way, Implementation of Economic, Social and Cultural Rights, in Scott Sheeran and Sir Nigel Rodley (eds.), *Routledge Handbook of International Human Rights Law* (Routledge, 2013), p. 558.
[161] UN HRC, Guidelines for the treaty-specific document to be submitted by States parties under article 40 of the International Covenant on Civil and Political Rights, CCPR/C/2009/1 (22 November 2010), para. 29.
[162] Ibid., paras. 30–2.

reports.[163] Like the others above, the CEDAW Committee's Guidelines commence with a focus on legal measures, requiring that states explain whether CEDAW is directly applicable in domestic law; incorporated nationally; guaranteed in the constitution or other law; and able to be invoked before courts, tribunals and administrative authorities.[164] While this information is required, the Committee's Guidelines also go on to note that an explanation of legal norms alone is insufficient, and that the 'factual situation and the practical availability, effect and implementation of remedies for violations of provisions of the Convention should be explained or exemplified'.[165] In this way, states have to provide detailed information on the *de facto* situation of rights enjoyment in their jurisdiction. Like the Harmonised Guidelines, the CEDAW Committee's Guidelines refer to the role of civil society, inviting states to report on 'the situation of non-governmental organizations and women's associations and their participation in the implementation of the Convention'.[166]

Overall, the various reporting guidelines are quite similar. States are primarily required to report on their legal measures of implementation, but also on other measures like awareness-raising. Despite sometimes specifying in detail what states are to report on, the guidelines also frequently and generically refer to implementation 'measures' or 'steps'. This reinforces the earlier contention that while some (legal) measures are prescribed, generally states parties retain significant discretion in the method of domestic implementation. The guidelines are also all focused on practical matters and on the actual situation of rights enjoyment in the state, rather than simply on the situation *de jure*. This reiterates the view that effectiveness is the key criterion for implementation measures. Importantly, the Harmonised Guidelines, which apply to seven human rights treaty bodies, also foresee NSAs such as civil society as playing a role in implementation. However, of the three Committees, only the CEDAW Committee elaborates upon this further in its own reporting guidelines. These conclusions are reinforced by an analysis of a sample of the HRCee and the ESCR and CEDAW Committee's Concluding Observations to state reports.

---

[163] UN, Compilation of Guidelines on the Form and Content of Reports to Be Submitted by States Parties to the International Human Rights Treaties Addendum: CEDAW, HRI/GEN/2/REV.1/Add.2 (5 May 2003), para. B.1.
[164] Ibid., para. D.2.2.
[165] Ibid., para. D.2.1. See also UN HRC, Guidelines for the treaty-specific document (n. 161), para. 26.
[166] UN, Compilation of Guidelines (n. 163), para. D.2.6.

3.3.2 UN Treaty Bodies' Concluding Observations

Following the constructive dialogue with states regarding their periodic report, the treaty bodies draft, adopt and publicly promulgate Concluding Observations. These Observations are made based on the state reports, as well as other material sourced, *inter alia*, from national human rights institutions (NHRIs), other UN bodies, national and international civil society, and the media.[167] Unlike the Reporting Guidelines that apply generically to all states parties, these Concluding Observations relate specifically to the state party reporting and to their implementation status. As such, these Observations are tailored to the state party, its particular national context, as well as level of treaty implementation. Through these Observations, the treaty bodies respond to contemporary affairs in the state and to particular issues regarding the protection of rights. The treaty bodies both welcome positive steps taken by the state to implement the treaty, and identify areas of concern along with the proposed remedial measures. In this way, the Concluding Observations provide useful insights regarding how the treaty bodies conceive of and understand the process of domestic implementation, and what measures they consider to be available under the treaties and effective in practice. This part analyses in turn a sample of Concluding Observations by the HRCee, ESCR Committee and the CEDAW Committee.

Human Rights Committee's Concluding Observations

The legal, state-centric focus apparent in the HRCee's General Comments is also found in its Concluding Observations to state reports. As noted above, the Committee frequently requests states to legally incorporate the Covenant, and also requests specific legislation be enacted, such as criminalising marital rape; proscribing torture; setting a minimum age for marriage; and anti-discrimination legislation.[168] The HRCee also

---

[167] See further Boerefijn (n. 9), pp. 209–22.
[168] These are all topics that the ESCR and CEDAW Committees also frequently raise with states parties and request legislation. Regarding the HRCee, see: Concluding observations on the fourth periodic report of the Republic of Korea, CCPR/C/KOR/CO/4 (3 December 2015), paras. 13, 19, 27; Concluding observations on the second periodic report of the Niger, CCPR/C/NER/CO/2 (16 May 2019), paras. 19, 23(c), 31; Concluding observations on the third periodic report of Suriname, CCPR/C/SUR/CO/3 (3 December 2015), para. 16; Concluding observations on Saint Vincent and the Grenadines in the absence of its second periodic report, CCPR/C/VCT/CO/2Add.1 (9 May 2019), para. 37; Concluding observations on the second periodic report of Angola, CCPR/C/AGO/CO/2 (8 May 2019), para. 20(c).

refers in their Concluding Observations to other measures of implementation, such as state institutional measures like creating NHRIs and national strategies or action plans. For example, the HRCee welcomed Benin's adoption of the National Child Protection Policy; Suriname's Integral Gender Action Plan; and Austria's adoption of a Roma strategy.[169] The HRCee consistently refers to the Paris Principles and encourages states to 'take measures to ensure the effective functioning of the National Human Rights Institute with a broad human rights mandate, and provide it with adequate financial and human resources'.[170] Such recommendations regarding NHRIs are also made by the ESCR and CEDAW Committees, which indicates that all three Committees view such national institutions as important for the domestic implementation of human rights.

Other non-legal measures of implementation frequently recommended by the HRCee are awareness-raising measures, education and training. According to Seibert-Fohr, education and information dissemination have long been emphasised by the HRCee.[171] In fact, these measures are often recommended by the Committee in conjunction with legal measures. For example, the HRCee stated that Austria 'should ensure that all rights protected under the Covenant are given full effect in domestic law and that judges and law enforcement officers receive adequate training'.[172] Suriname was advised to take practical steps, including legislative measures, to end corporal punishment of children, and to undertake 'public information campaigns to raise awareness about the harmful effects of

---

[169] UN HRCee, Concluding observations on the second periodic report of Benin, CCPR/C/BEN/CO/2 (23 November 2015), para. 3(d); UN HRCee, Concluding observations on Suriname (n. 168), para. 3(b); UN HRCee, Concluding observations on the fifth periodic report of Austria, CCPR/C/AUT/CO/5 (3 December 2015), para. 3(a). Typically the Human Rights, ESCR and CEDAW Committees commence their Observations by welcoming measures taken by states parties, including institutional measures and action plans.

[170] UN HRCee, Concluding observations on Suriname (n. 168), para. 10; UN HRCee, Concluding observations on Austria (n. 169), para. 10; UN HRCee, Concluding observations on the third periodic report of San Marino CCPR/C/SMR/CO/3 (3 December 2015), para. 7; UN HRCee, Concluding observations on the fifth periodic report of Iraq, CCPR/C/IRQ/CO/5 (3 December 2015), para. 8; UN HRCee, Concluding observations on Benin (n. 169), para. 9; UN HRCee, Concluding observations on Niger (n. 168), para. 9; UN HRCee Concluding observations on Angola (n. 168), para. 10.

[171] Seibert-Fohr (n. 14), pp. 464–6.

[172] UN HRCee, Concluding observations on Austria (n. 169), para. 6. See also UN HRCee, Concluding observations on Saint Vincent and the Grenadines (n. 168), para. 9.

corporal punishment'.[173] San Marino was recommended to strengthen their 'legal framework against discrimination, in particular by enacting comprehensive anti-discrimination legislation ... [and] make vigorous efforts to raise awareness among the general public and train judges and lawyers on the existing criminal provisions against discrimination'.[174]

The HRCee uses the same approach of teaming legislative measures with awareness-raising and education in relation to socio-cultural matters like combating stereotypes and harmful practices. For example, the Committee first advised Macedonia to amend its law to prohibit discrimination based on sexual orientation and gender identity, and to ensure 'that perpetrators of violence on the grounds of sexual orientation are prosecuted and sanctioned'.[175] Macedonia was then also recommended to intensify efforts to eliminate stereotypes and prejudice against LGBTQI persons by providing training to public officials and organising awareness-raising campaigns targeting the general public.[176] Iraq was advised to take 'vigorous measures to generate public awareness about' the negative effects of harmful practices discriminating against women and girls, and to ensure that the relevant criminal legislation is efficiently enforced.[177] Similarly, the HRCee advised Greece to ensure its legislation prohibits racial and religious hatred and that such cases are prosecuted, and to conduct 'public awareness campaigns to promote tolerance and respect for diversity'.[178]

Particularly in relation to violence against women, the HRCee has been more holistic in its recommendations. For example, Iraq was advised to protect women by enacting legislation; increasing awareness-raising activities; providing access to shelters; initiating behaviour-change programmes for perpetrators; and reinforcing training in order for state

---

[173] UN HRCee, Concluding observations on Suriname (n. 168), para. 46. See also UN HRCee, Concluding observations on Saint Vincent and the Grenadines (n. 168), para. 31.

[174] UN HRCee, Concluding observations on San Marino (n. 170), para. 9. See also UN HRCee, Concluding observations on Angola (n. 168), para. 14.

[175] UN HRCee, Concluding observations on the third periodic report of the former Yugoslav Republic of Macedonia, CCPR/C/MKD/CO/3 (17 August 2015), para. 7.

[176] Ibid. See also UN HRCee, Concluding observations on the second periodic report of Greece, CCPR/C/GRC/CO/2 (3 December 2015), para. 12; UN HRCee, Concluding observations on the Republic of Korea (n. 168), para. 15.

[177] HRCee, Concluding observations on Iraq (n. 170), para. 16.

[178] UN HRCee, Concluding observations on Greece (n. 176), para. 14. See also para. 12 regarding LGBTQI persons.

3.3 HUMAN RIGHTS TREATIES & OTHER MEASURES

officials to respond effectively.[179] Similarly, Macedonia was advised to enact legislation; prosecute perpetrators; provide remedies to victims; ensure access to specialised assistance including access to shelters; carry out awareness-raising campaigns; and organise training for local authorities, law enforcement officials, social workers and medical personnel.[180] These more comprehensive or holistic recommendations likely reflect the HRCee's understanding that issues like violence against women are often complex and embedded problems relating to culture, tradition and power, and cannot be easily resolved by legislation alone. While these recommendations represent some of the more holistic ones by the HRCee, they fall short of the recommendations made by the CEDAW Committee.

Whereas the CEDAW Committee combines a variety of measures to implement rights related to harmful practices (as seen below), the HRCee tends to maintain the approach of legal measures combined with awareness-raising and education, as well as support for victims. In fact, sometimes the HRCee is very vague in its recommendations to states parties, simply instructing them to 'take concrete measures to eliminate gender biases and stereotypes regarding the roles and responsibilities of men and women in the family and society'.[181] Unlike the CEDAW Committee, the HRCee does not focus on community consultation, dialogue or empowerment. For example, even when the HRCee acknowledged the need to engage local leaders in Benin to combat stereotypes and practices harmful to women, it recommended 'public awareness campaigns, especially among religious and traditional leaders',[182] rather than engaging with them in dialogue and consultation, or working with communities to identify alternative practices. The HRCee's top-down approach was for the Benin Government to teach local leaders about human rights, rather than engaging in a two-way dialogue with them about the issues. While the HRCee's recommendations do not preclude states from taking a holistic approach in their discretion, they do not actively encourage states parties to do so as the CEDAW Committee does.

---

[179] UN HRCee, Concluding observations on Iraq (n. 170), para. 26.
[180] UN HRCee, Concluding observations on the former Yugoslav Republic of Macedonia (n. 175), para. 10. See also UN HRCee, Concluding observations on Greece (n. 176), para. 20; UN HRCee, Concluding observations on Niger (n. 168), para. 23; UN HRCee Concluding observations on Angola (n. 168), para. 18.
[181] UN HRCee, Concluding observations on Suriname (n. 168), para. 14.
[182] UN HRCee, Concluding observations on Benin (n. 169), para. 13. See the similar approaches taken by the HRCee regarding Angola and Niger: Concluding observations on Niger (n. 168), para. 45(b); Concluding observations on Angola (n. 168), para. 20(b).

While the HRCee's usual approach is to be generic in its recommendations to states parties, it is at times rather specific. For example, France was advised 'to reduce prison overcrowding ... by increasing the use of adjusted sentences',[183] and Greece was advised to 'ensure that, in all cases involving refoulement, appeals to the courts have a suspensive effect'.[184] However, such specific recommendations are exceptional, with the Committee typically making generic recommendations. As an illustration, the HRCee advised states to 'take measures' to ensure that rights are fully respected;[185] to ensure that all persons are 'effectively protected' from discrimination;[186] and to 'step up its efforts' to enable disadvantaged persons to participate in publicly elected bodies.[187] The HRCee has also advised adopting, if necessary, 'temporary special measures' to address women's under-representation in decision-making positions.[188] As seen here, the HRCee refrains from prescribing the type of implementation measures that states should take to achieve these goals, rather reiterating the standards in the treaty to be met. This reflects the obligation of result – and not of conduct – regarding domestic treaty implementation.

An apt example of the HRCee's generic recommendations relates to providing remedies for victims of rights violations. Remedies are typically only of a general nature as, according to the principle of subsidiarity, the international system has limited authority to delineate remedies for victims.[189] As such, the HRCee's Concluding Observations often require

---

[183] UN HRCee, Concluding observations on the fifth periodic report of France, CCPR/C/FRA/CO/5 (17 August 2015), para. 17. See also UN HRCee, Concluding observations on Angola (n. 168), para. 32(a).

[184] UN HRCee, Concluding observations on Greece (n. 176), para. 30.

[185] UN HRCee, Concluding observations on the former Yugoslav Republic of Macedonia (n. 175), para. 16.

[186] UN HRCee, Concluding observations on Greece (n. 176), para. 44.

[187] UN HRCee, Concluding observations on Austria (n. 169), para. 18; UN HRCee, Concluding observations on Greece (n. 176), para. 8.

[188] See, for example, UN HRCee, Concluding observations on Suriname (n. 168), para. 14; UN HRCee, Concluding observations on the former Yugoslav Republic of Macedonia (n. 175), para. 9; UN HRCee, Concluding obserations on Saint Vincent and the Grenadines (n. 168), para. 15; UN HRCee Concluding observations on Angola (n. 168), para. 16(a).

[189] Galligan and Sandler (n. 4), p. 42. See also Valeska David, Reparations at the Human Rights Committee: Legal Basis, Practice and Challenges (2014) *Netherlands Quarterly of Human Rights* 32:1, pp. 8–43; Gerald Neuman, Subsidiarity, in Dinah Shelton (ed.), *The Oxford Handbook of International Human Rights Law* (Oxford University Press, 2013), pp. 372–4.

states parties to ensure that victims have access to 'adequate'[190] or 'effective remedies'.[191] While sometimes adding that remedies should include 'rehabilitation and compensation',[192] the Committee falls short of prescribing specific types of remedies, their composition or value. This is typical also for the ESCR[193] and CEDAW Committees; however, the latter tends to be more detailed. For example, the CEDAW Committee recommended to Slovakia 'that victims of such practices [forced sterilisation] have access to remedies and redress that are adequate, effective, promptly granted, holistic and proportionate to the gravity of the harm suffered'.[194] While providing additional details as to the required standard of the remedies, the CEDAW Committee still refrained from prescribing any particular type or modality of remedy. This leaves important scope for state discretion to determine the most appropriate remedies depending upon the national context.

ESCR Committee's Concluding Observations

Like the HRCee, the ESCR Committee typically commences their Concluding Observations to states parties reports with a focus on legal measures of implementation. The ESCR Committee often recommends states incorporate the Covenant, or take the necessary steps to give effect to it in the domestic legal system.[195] In addition, the Committee advises states parties to enact specific legislation, such as to enable indigenous

---

[190] UN HRCee, Concluding observations the former Yugoslav Republic of Macedonia (n. 175), para. 23.
[191] UN HRCee, Concluding observations on Iraq (n. 170), para. 16.
[192] UN HRCee, Concluding observations on the Republic of Korea (n. 168), para. 27; UN HRCee, Concluding observations on Suriname (n. 168), para. 30.
[193] See, for example, UN ESCR Committee, Concluding observations on the initial report of Burundi, E/C.12/BDI/CO/1 (16 October 2015), paras. 16(b), 46(c); UN ESCR Committee, Concluding observations on the fourth periodic report of Morocco, E/C.12/MAR/CO/4 (22 October 2015), paras. 32, 38; UN ESCR Committee, Concluding observations on the second periodic report of Sudan, E/C.12/SDN/CO/2 (27 October 2015), paras. 8, 20, 48.
[194] UN CEDAW Committee, Concluding observations on the combined fifth and sixth periodic reports of Slovakia, CEDAW/C/SVK/CO/5-6 (20 November 2015), para. 33(d).
[195] See, for example, UN ESCR Committee, Concluding observations on Morocco (n. 193), para. 10; UN ESCR Committee, Concluding observations on Sudan (n. 193), para. 6; UN ESCR Committee, Concluding observations on the fourth periodic report of Iraq, E/C.12/IRQ/CO/4 (27 October 2015), para. 8; UN ESCR Committee, Concluding observations on the fifth periodic report of Italy, E/C.12/ITA/CO/5 (28 October 2015), para. 7; UN ESCR Committee, Concluding observations on the third periodic report of Estonia, E/C.12/EST/CO/3 (27 March 2019), para. 5(a).

peoples to access/claim land;[196] criminalise domestic violence;[197] and regulate housing, evictions and rent control.[198] The Committee also regularly recommends states adopt anti-discrimination legislation covering the grounds in article 2(2) ICESCR,[199] including other additional measures. For example, the Committee has advised states parties to employ administrative mechanisms, undertake education and training, temporary special measures, and awareness-raising campaigns. The Committee recommended Burundi tackle inequality by taking steps to dispel gender stereotypes through information campaigns to promote the sharing of family responsibilities and by conducting awareness campaigns to reshape traditional attitudes.[200] Italy was advised to 'step up' efforts to combat gender inequality and stereotypes by embarking on national awareness-raising campaigns (including through the media), and by employing temporary special measures such as quotas.[201]

In fact, the ESCR Committee often recommends that states parties adopt national strategies or action plans to set out and coordinate the various implementation measures. In relation to the right to housing, the Committee recommended that states adopt a 'national strategy to enquire into the causes and the extent of homelessness ... and adopt

---

[196] UN ESCR Committee, Concluding observations on the fourth periodic report of Paraguay, E/C.12/PRY/CO/4 (20 March 2015), para. 6(d); UN ESCR Committee, Concluding observations on the combined second to fourth periodic report of Guyana, E/C.12/GUY/CO/2–4 (28 October 2015), para. 15.

[197] UN ESCR Committee, Concluding observations on the fourth report of Tajikistan, E/C.12/TJK/CO/2–3 (25 March 2015), para. 25; UN ESCR Committee, Concluding observations on the second periodic report of Kazakhstan, E/C.12/KAZ/CO/2 (29 March 2019), para. 37; UN ESCR Committee, Concluding observations on the fourth periodic report of Cameroon, E/C.12/CMR/CO/4 (25 March 2019), para. 47.

[198] UN ESCR Committee, Concluding observations on Italy (n. 195), paras. 41(a), 43(a); UN ESCR Committee, Concluding observations on Tajikistan (n. 197), para. 27; UN ESCR Committee, Concluding observations on Guyana (n. 196), para. 45; UN ESCR Committee, Concluding observations on Cameroon (n. 197), para. 54.

[199] See, for example, UN ESCR Committee, Concluding observations on Paraguay (n. 196), para. 13; UN ESCR Committee, Concluding observations on Tajikistan (n. 197), para. 13; UN ESCR Committee, Concluding observations on Estonia (n. 195), para. 11; UN ESCR Committee, Concluding observations on Cameroon (n. 197), para. 22.

[200] UN ESCR Committee, Concluding observations on the initial report of Burundi, E/C.12/BDI/CO/1 (16 October 2015), paras. 20(a), 22. See also UN ESCR Committee, Concluding observations on Estonia (n. 195), para. 19.

[201] UN ESCR Committee, Concluding observations on Italy (n. 195), para. 23. See also UN ESCR Committee, Concluding observations on the fifth periodic report of Mauritius, E/C.12/MUS/CO/5 (5 April 2019), para. 24; UN ESCR Committee, Concluding observations on Cameroon (n. 197), para. 26.

more effective measures to address homelessness';[202] 'take all appropriate steps to improve the supply of affordable housing ... by adopting and implementing a national housing strategy';[203] and 'adopt a human rights-based national housing strategy outlining the measures to be taken and the resources involved to progressively address the housing shortage'.[204] Given that the functioning of such national strategies is dependent in part upon their resources, the ESCR Committee often urges the creation of such strategies coupled with the provision of adequate resources. For example, regarding poverty reduction, the Committee recommended that states adopt a human rights-based strategy and allocate sufficient financial and other resources for its implementation.[205] These recommendations for national strategies and action plans demonstrate the Committee's view that implementing economic, social and cultural rights can be complex and requires multifaceted, coordinated responses beyond just legislation.

Sometimes, the ESCR Committee is rather specific in its recommendations to states parties regarding ICESCR's implementation. For example, the Committee recommended Iraq to 'take preventive measures to control and stop the spread of diarrhoea and cholera, including by providing vaccinations and information on basic sanitation procedures'.[206] Tajikistan was recommended to 'take all the necessary measures to improve the quality of education, through allocating sufficient resources, increasing the number of qualified teachers and their remuneration, and improving infrastructure and teaching materials'.[207] Italy was recommended to 'redouble its efforts to combat obesity' by increasing taxes on junk food and sweet beverages, and to 'consider adopting strict regulations on the marketing of such products, while ensuring improved access to healthy diets'.[208] While these recommendations are quite specific, they nonetheless leave a measure of discretion to

---

[202] UN ESCR Committee, Concluding observations on Italy (n. 195), para. 41(b).
[203] UN ESCR Committee, Concluding observations on Burundi (n. 200), para. 48.
[204] UN ESCR Committee, Concluding observations on Sudan (n. 193), para. 46.
[205] UN ESCR Committee, Concluding observations on Morocco (n. 193), para. 42; UN ESCR Committee, Concluding observations on Iraq (n. 195), para. 46.
[206] UN ESCR Committee, Concluding observations on Iraq (n. 195), para. 52.
[207] UN ESCR Committee, Concluding observations on Tajikistan (n. 197), para. 35. Paraguay was advised to improve education infrastructure, 'including, in particular, separate toilet facilities for each sex'. UN ESCR Committee, Concluding observations on Paraguay (n. 196), para. 30.
[208] UN ESCR Committee, Concluding observations on Italy (n. 195), para. 51.

the state, and continue to be presented as 'recommendations'. Despite these examples of the ESCR Committee being direct in their recommendations for improving treaty implementation, such examples are in the minority.

What is most common is for the ESCR Committee – like the HRCee – to be generic in its recommendations, requiring a state party, for example, to 'spare no efforts to eliminate the causes of inter-ethnic discrimination';[209] 'take all the necessary measures' to improve access to drinking water, sanitation and electricity;[210] or to 'adopt all necessary measures to improve the availability and supply of low-cost housing'.[211] Here, the Committee refrains from being prescriptive and provides only vague guidance regarding the treaty standard to be achieved. Often, the ESCR Committee advises states generally to improve services or infrastructure, or to allocate adequate resources. For example, Burundi was recommended to 'intensify its efforts to combat poverty ... by ensuring that targeted social programmes are implemented ... and are endowed with the necessary resources'.[212] Greece was recommended to 'increase health-care expenditure as a proportion of gross domestic product ... [t]ake effective measures to ensure that there are sufficient health-care professionals ... [and] take measures to further improve the infrastructure of the primary health-care system'.[213] In such examples, the Committee indicates the areas for improvement, but refrains from specifying the measures states parties should take or the amount of resources to be allocated.

Finally, the ESCR Committee also foresees in its Concluding Observations a role for NSAs like civil society in implementation. Regarding victims of gender-based violence, Iraq was advised to empower 'civil society to continue providing shelters and other related services, including awareness-raising and information campaigns'.[214] Sudan was encouraged to cooperate with NGOs to provide asylum seekers and refugees with access to healthcare and education, and to cooperate with the private sector to address the housing shortage.[215] Tajikistan was recommended to

---

[209] UN ESCR Committee, Concluding observations on Guyana (n. 196), para. 21.
[210] UN ESCR Committee, Concluding observations on Tajikistan (n. 197), para. 28.
[211] UN ESCR Committee, Concluding observations on Paraguay (n. 196), para. 27.
[212] UN ESCR Committee, Concluding observations on Burundi (n. 200), para. 44.
[213] UN ESCR Committee, Concluding observations on the second periodic report of Greece, E/C.12/GRC/CO/2 (27 October 2015), para. 36.
[214] UN ESCR Committee, Concluding observations on Iraq (n. 195), para. 40(b).
[215] UN ESCR Committee, Concluding observations on Sudan (n. 193), paras. 26 and 46.

'make every effort to ensure that amendments to the Law [on Public Associations] strengthen freedom of association and contribute to a more active role for civil society, and thus to the enjoyment of economic, social and cultural rights'.[216] New Zealand was advised to work in partnership with Indigenous people and representatives as well as civil society organisations.[217] The ESCR Committee clearly recognises that states are not the only actors in human rights implementation, and that they should facilitate and collaborate with private actors. While these references to other NSAs are similar to those made by the CEDAW Committee (discussed below), they exceed those made by the HRCee in their Concluding Observations, which tend to be overwhelmingly state-centric.

CEDAW Committee's Concluding Observations

Demonstrating a coherent approach between the treaty bodies, the CEDAW Committee's Concluding Observations are similar in many ways to those of the HRCee and ESCR Committee. For example, the CEDAW Committee commences its observations on state reports with a focus on legal measures of implementation, such as commenting upon Conventions ratified and national legislation enacted. Going a step further, the CEDAW Committee repeatedly emphasises 'the crucial role of the legislative power in ensuring the full implementation of the Convention'.[218] The Committee frequently invites states to incorporate CEDAW into the national legal system and to make its provisions directly applicable before national courts. Like the HRCee and ESCR Committee, the CEDAW Committee also recommends states enact legislation regarding specific issues, and welcomes efforts to improve national institutional and

---

[216] UN ESCR Committee, Concluding observations on Tajikistan (n. 197), para. 10. Regarding a role for civil society generally, see UN ESCR Committee, Concluding observations on Kazakhstan (n. 197), para. 9; UN ESCR Committee, Concluding Observations on the sixth periodic report of Bulgaria, E/C.12/BGR/CO/6 (29 March 2019), para. 13(a); UN ESCR Committee, Concluding observations on the inital report of Bangladesh, E/C.12/BGD/CO/1 (18 April 2018), para. 14; UN ESCR Committee, Concluding observations on Paraguay (n. 196), para. 8.

[217] UN ESCR Committee, Concluding observations on the fourth periodic report of New Zealand, E/C.12/NZL/CO/4 (1 May 2018), paras. 9(a), 13(b) and 45.

[218] See, for example, the UN CEDAW Committee, Concluding observations on the combined seventh and eighth periodic reports of Liberia, CEDAW/C/LBR/CO/7-8 (20 November 2015), para. 8; Concluding observations on the combined second and third periodic reports of Timor-Leste, CEDAW/C/TLS/CO/2-3 (24 November 2015), para. 7; Concluding observations on the eighth periodic report of Australia, CEDAW/C/AUS/CO/8 (20 July 2018), para. 8; Concluding observations on the fifth periodic report of Turkmenistan, CEDAW/C.TKM/CO/5 (20 July 2018), para. 7.

policy frameworks for implementing rights. The types of measures referred to here include the establishment of NHRIs, national strategies, and action plans. While all three Committees envisage other, non-legal measures of implementation like education, training and awareness-raising, the CEDAW Committee can be seen as the most progressive in this regard.

In particular, the CEDAW Committee's Concluding Observations can be distinguished by its recommendations for consultation, dialogue and collaboration with NSAs, such as the media, civil society, community groups, and traditional and religious leaders. For example, the United Arab Emirates were advised to develop 'a comprehensive strategy, in collaboration with civil society and the media, to eliminate discriminatory stereotypes on the roles and responsibilities of women and men in society and the family'.[219] Portugal was recommended to provide adequate support (including funding) to NGOs working on women's rights and gender equality, and to consult with them systematically.[220] Timor-Leste and Liberia were called upon to regulate the relationship between state and traditional legal systems 'after an open dialogue with civil society, including women's organizations, on the impact of such legislation on the enjoyment of women's rights'.[221] Both the United Arab Emirates and Lebanon were advised to initiate dialogue with religious leaders and scholars to work towards withdrawing their reservations to CEDAW.[222]

In addition to this consultative role, the CEDAW Committee – like the ESCR Committee – foresees NSAs playing a role in implementation. The CEDAW Committee frequently advises states parties to facilitate, collaborate or partner with civil society. For example, Slovenia was recommended to 'develop and implement a comprehensive policy ... to overcome stereotypical attitudes towards the roles and responsibilities

---

[219] UN CEDAW Committee, Concluding observations on the combined second and third periodic reports of the United Arab Emirates, CEDAW/C/ARE/CO/2–3 (24 November 2015), para. 24.
[220] UN CEDAW Committee, Concluding observations on the combined eighth and ninth periodic reports of Portugal, CEDAW/C/PRT/CO/8–9 (24 November 2015), para. 17.
[221] UN CEDAW Committee, Concluding observations on Timor-Leste (n. 218), para. 9(c), and see also para. 35(c); UN CEDAW Committee, Concluding observations on Liberia (n. 218), para. 14(a).
[222] UN CEDAW Committee, Concluding observations on the combined fourth and fifth periodic reports of Lebanon, CEDAW/C/LBN/CO/4–5 (24 November 2015), para. 16(c); UN CEDAW Committee, Concluding observations on the United Arab Emirates (n. 219), para. 10.

of women and men ... and engage civil society organizations and the mass media in its implementation'.[223] Slovakia was recommended to ensure the 'active and meaningful' participation of women's organisations in the development and implementation of a comprehensive programme on sexual and reproductive health.[224] Colombia was advised to '[c]onduct inclusive awareness-raising campaigns on the principles of non-discrimination and gender equality, through cooperation with civil society and women's organizations, political parties, education professionals and the media'.[225] Turkmenistan was advised to '[s]eek and strengthen cooperation with civil society organizations in the implementation of all areas covered by the Convention'.[226] In recognition of their role, states are advised to 'adopt concrete measures, including legal amendments, to create and ensure an enabling environment in which civil society and women's rights groups may be established and may freely conduct their programmes and activities'.[227]

Other measures of implementation foreseen by the CEDAW Committee include measures to promote women's financial and political empowerment. Numerous recommendations aim to promote women's economic entrepreneurship and access to finance, through measures like vocational and technical training, counselling and placement services (not limited to traditional employment areas), and expanding women's access to micro-finance.[228] The Committee has advised ancillary social measures to facilitate women's economic activities, such as sensitising employers to discrimination, providing incentives for employers to

---

[223] UN CEDAW Committee, Concluding observations on the combined fifth and sixth periodic reports of Slovenia, CEDAW/C/SVN/CO/5-6 (24 November 2015), para. 18(a).
[224] UN CEDAW Committee, Concluding observations on Slovakia (n. 194), para. 31(a).
[225] UN CEDAW Committee, Concluding observations on the ninth periodic report of Colombia, CEDAW/C/COL/CO/9 (14 March 2019), para. 42(c).
[226] UN CEDAW Committee, Concluding observations on Turkmenistan (n. 218), para. 29 (c). See also UN CEDAW Committee, Concluding observations on the eighth periodic report of Ethiopia, CEDAW/C/ETH/CO/8 (14 March 2019), para. 14(b).
[227] UN CEDAW Committee, Concluding observations on the eighth periodic reports of the Russian Federation, CEDAW/C/RUS/CO/8 (20 November 2015), para. 16; UN CEDAW Committee, Concluding observations on the United Arab Emirates (n. 219), para. 20; UN CEDAW Committee, Concluding observations on the eighth periodic report of Ethiopia, CEDAW/C/ETH/CO/8 (14 March 2019), para. 30.
[228] See, for example, the UN CEDAW Committee, Concluding observations on Lebanon (n. 222), para. 36(d); Concluding observations on the Russian Federation (n. 227), para. 34(a); Concluding observations on Liberia (n. 218), para. 42(b); UN CEDAW Committee, Concluding observations on the seventh periodic report of Malawi, CEDAW/C/MWI/CO/7 (24 November 2015), para. 39.

recruit women, 'promoting equal sharing of family responsibilities between women and men', and 'increasing the availability of child care and pre-school education'.[229] The CEDAW Committee promotes women's political empowerment through measures including temporary special measures (such as quotas), awareness-raising campaigns, capacity building and training programmes, mentoring programmes, and financial support.[230]

As seen from this survey of recommendations, the CEDAW Committee tends to be the most holistic and inclusive of the three Committees in its approach to implementation. This suggests that the CEDAW Committee views law alone to be insufficient for fully implementing women's rights, and that a combination of legal and other measures is necessary. This approach is most apparent in relation to the Committee's recommendations regarding combating stereotypes and harmful practices. In addition to recommending effective legal measures to end harmful practices, the Committee encouraged Liberia to step up 'media and other awareness-raising efforts to sensitize the public about existing discriminatory gender stereotypes', and to '[e]xpand public education programmes on the negative impact of such stereotypes', including targeting traditional leaders who are 'the custodians of customary values'.[231] Liberia was further recommended to develop entrepreneurial programmes for the traditional practitioners of FGM/C to facilitate them abandoning the practice and finding alternative livelihoods.[232] These holistic recommendations comprising a range of implementation measures illustrate the CEDAW Committee's appreciation of the complex nature of implementing women's rights and the need for comprehensive and multifaceted approaches involving a range of actors.

Arguably given this complexity, the CEDAW Committee highlights the importance of studies and data that may assist in understanding

---

[229] UN CEDAW Committee, Concluding observations on the Russian Federation (n. 227), para. 34(a); UN CEDAW Committee, Concluding observations on the fifth periodic reports of Uzbekistan, CEDAW/C/UZB/CO/5 (20 November 2015), para. 26(a); UN CEDAW Committee, Concluding observations on Lebanon (n. 222), para. 36.
[230] See, for example, the UN CEDAW Committee, Concluding observations on the Russian Federation (n. 227), para. 28(a), (b); Concluding observations on the United Arab Emirates (n. 219), para. 34; Concluding observations on Timor-Leste (n. 218), para. 23 (b); Concluding observations on the Russian Federation (n. 227), para. 28(c); Concluding observations on Uzbekistan (n. 229), para. 22(b).
[231] UN CEDAW Committee, Concluding observations on Liberia (n. 218), para. 22(a)–(c).
[232] Ibid., para. 24(d).

discrimination against women and its root causes. As noted above, such data also helps to establish a benchmark from which to measure progress and the effectiveness of states' implementation measures. The Committee therefore urged several states to undertake studies on trafficking and prostitution, including by collecting data to identify, and then address, their root causes.[233] The Committee recommended Slovenia study child, early and forced marriage in order to assess its magnitude and determine the root causes.[234] Russia was urged to undertake 'research on the extent of harmful practices in the Northern Caucasus and develop a comprehensive strategy to eliminate them including through education and awareness-raising campaigns for community and religious leaders and the general public'.[235] Detailed and accurate information about the situation on the ground is important to the CEDAW Committee given its utility in devising effective strategies to secure women's enjoyment of their rights in practice. While the other two Committees also request statistics and data from states parties,[236] CEDAW does so more consistently and in more detail.

As demonstrated in this section, the CEDAW Committee is also more prescriptive than either the HRCee or the ESCR Committee in its recommendations to states regarding implementation measures. While sometimes its recommendations are general and non-descript, often they are more specific, detailing a variety of measures to be taken and outcomes to be achieved.[237] However, even the more prescriptive recommendations remain somewhat generic with scope therein for

---

[233] UN CEDAW Committee, Concluding observations on Uzbekistan (n. 229), para. 20(a); UN CEDAW Committee, Concluding observations on Malawi (n. 228), para. 25(d); UN CEDAW Committee, Concluding observations on Timor-Leste (n. 218), para. 21(b).

[234] UN CEDAW Committee, Concluding observations on the combined fifth and sixth periodic reports of Slovenia, CEDAW/C/SVN/CO/5-6 (24 November 2015), para. 40(e). See also para. 28(b).

[235] UN CEDAW Committee, Concluding observations on the Russian Federation (n. 227), para. 24(a).

[236] See, for example, UN ESCR Committee, Concluding observations on the initial report of Gambia, E/C.12/GMB/CO/1 (20 March 2015), paras. 8, 22; UN ESCR Committee, Concluding observations on the second periodic report of Greece, E/C.12/GRC/CO/2 (27 October 2015), para. 10; UN ESCR Committee, Concluding observations on the combined second to fourth periodic report of Guyana, E/C.12/GUY/CO/2-4 (28 October 2015), paras. 6-7; UN HRCee, Concluding observations on the Republic of Korea (n. 168), para. 25; UN HRCee, Concluding observations on Austria (n. 169), para. 26.

[237] See, for examples, the UN CEDAW Committee, Concluding observations on the United Arab Emirates (n. 219), para. 38; Concluding observations on Timor-Leste (n. 218), paras. 27(a), 39(c).

variety and divergence. Furthermore, all of the CEDAW Committee's recommendations are phrased as recommendations only and are not binding, respecting the states parties' discretion to implement them. As with the HRCee and ESCR Committee's Concluding Observations, this reinforces the above contention that states enjoy rather broad discretion under the treaties to determine the most appropriate way in which to implement their obligations and may use a wide range of measures to do so.

3.3.3   UN Treaty Bodies and Other Measures: Always an Afterthought?

Despite commencing with a legal focus, welcoming legislation and recommending domestic incorporation of treaty provisions, it is clear that all three treaty bodies also recommend other, non-legislative measures of implementation in their Concluding Observations. However, this prioritisation of legal measures is not required in the treaties, but rather is symptomatic of the legalisation of human rights. The Concluding Observations sampled above illustrate the extent to which the Committees prize legal measures of implementation and treat other measures as secondary add-ons. Other measures remain an afterthought, stuck in the shadow of legal measures of implementation. This is most apparent from the HRCee's Concluding Observations, but also applies to those of the ESCR and CEDAW Committees. In this way, the Committees' implementation recommendations all tend to be legalistic, state-centric and top-down. Of the three Committees, the CEDAW Committee advocates the most holistic approaches to implementation combining legal and a variety of other measures.

What distinguishes the CEDAW Committee's approach, as seen also in section one above, is its focus on consultation, dialogue and collaboration with NSA like civil society, the media and community groups. Rather than implementation being solely the top-down imposition of a human rights regime, the CEDAW Committee most overtly values the involvement of local private actors and grassroots supporters of human rights. In this way, it is the least state-centric of the three Committees. The CEDAW Committee (and to a lesser extent the ESCR Committee) envisages a role for civil society in implementing rights, which is also borne out in the Harmonised Reporting Guidelines. These Guidelines apply to seven of the UN treaty bodies, including the HRCee. However, the only reference to NGOs or civil society typically made in the HRCee's

3.3 HUMAN RIGHTS TREATIES & OTHER MEASURES

Observations comes at the end, where states are requested to consult with them when preparing their next reports.[238]

It is perhaps understandable that the CEDAW Committee is more inclusive of NSAs as it addresses discrimination by private as well as public actors, and states are mandated in Article 5(a) to modify social and cultural patterns deemed incompatible with the Convention. This includes discrimination in the home, violence by domestic partners, and harmful practices like FGM/C. However, the HRCee similarly deals with discrimination, violence and other violations by private actors, and is also tasked with remedying (cultural) practices incompatible with the ICCPR (including FGM/C). While the ICCPR does not explicitly identify an obligation of cultural modification, it is nonetheless implicitly required to implement many of the rights therein. As elaborated in Chapter 2, human rights are themselves part of culture, and nearly all rights have a cultural dimension. It is a misconception and misrepresentation to intimate that civil and political rights are somehow more 'objective' or 'neutral' than women's rights or economic, social and cultural rights. The differences in the Committee's approaches are therefore not a product of their different mandates, but rather a result of the composition and established practices of the Committees.

While sometimes more specific regarding what measures to take (particularly the CEDAW Committee), in the main the three Committees make open, generic recommendations to states parties. In fact, the treaty bodies have been criticised for being insufficiently clear or specific in their Concluding Observations.[239] However, this lack of specificity reflects the discretion states retain in selecting their method of implementation. Given this discretion, it may be impractical and even inappropriate for the Committees to prescribe implementation measures in great detail.[240] This conclusion is also supported by the language of the Observations, as the Committees 'recommend', 'call upon', or 'urge' states to take certain actions. An important distinction in this regard is that while the ESCR and CEDAW Committees almost exclusively use this language, the HRCee provides that the state party 'should' undertake

---

[238] UN HRCee, Concluding observations on Benin (n. 169), para. 39; UN HRCee, Concluding observations on Austria (n. 169), para. 37; UN HRCee, Concluding observations on Iraq (n. 170), para. 45.

[239] Scheinin notes that the Observations 'may appear as overly cautious, ambiguous or vague': Scheinin (n. 147), p. 605.

[240] Boerefijn (n. 9), p. 598.

certain measures. While this language is more direct than that used by the other Committees, it is still advisory rather than instructive (i.e. must or shall). This language emphasises that the Concluding Observations are not binding, but recommendations subject to a state's discretion. While the treaty bodies are well placed to monitor and advise states parties, states themselves are best placed to determine the methods most suited to their context and likely to be effective in practice.

Given that implementation is an obligation of result (and not conduct), the controlling feature upon which to select or assess implementation measures is effectiveness. Scholars agree, noting that as the treaties' overriding purpose is the effective protection of rights, the 'only acceptable yardstick' for judging implementation measures is their effectiveness.[241] According to Tomuschat, the HRCee has employed the substantive criterion of effectiveness as *the* guiding principle in its assessment of states' implementation measures.[242] Despite the HRCee's penchant for legal measures, states parties are not required to domestically incorporate the ICCPR, 'provided that its effectiveness does not suffer therefrom'.[243] Other than where it would be effective, there is no reason under the Covenant to require domestic legal codification.[244] This analysis can be extrapolated and applied to both the ICESCR and CEDAW and their treaty bodies. All three Committees can be seen from the present study to require actual impact of the measures on the ground, emphasising the de facto implementation of the treaties and enjoyment of rights.

In this way, while it is largely the states' prerogative to determine domestic implementation measures, they do not have free rein and must report to the treaty bodies. Like the treaties themselves, the treaty bodies do not dictate the measures to be taken by states to implement their human rights obligations, but rather play a safeguarding role seeking to ensure that states employ effective measures of implementation. Despite the focus here on the outcome rather than on the methodology *per se*, the treaty bodies all possess an observable bias towards legislative measures. This bias detracts from other measures of implementation that may also

---

[241] Tomuschat (n. 18), p. 119; Seibert-Fohr (n. 14), p. 425, fn. 126.
[242] Tomuschat (n. 18), p. 117.
[243] Tomuschat (n. 18), p. 117; Seibert-Fohr (n. 14), p. 469. See also *Roberts v. Barbados*, Communication No. 504/1992, Doc. CCPR/C/51/D/504/1992 (1992), para. 6.3.
[244] 'It is doubtful why codification should be an important element of protection when reliance on unwritten rules would be also effective.' Seibert-Fohr (n. 14), p. 432.

be effective, or even more effective in practice. As seen in this study, legalisation has curtailed the imagination and promotion of other methods of implementing human rights, and shunned the germane and necessary insights of other disciplines. This has not occurred necessarily by mal-intent or design, but perhaps rather incidentally and even with misplaced good intentions.

3.4 Conclusions: Legislative and Other Effective Implementation Measures

Human rights treaties are difficult to implement. More often than not, they require far-reaching reforms and dramatic changes to socio-economic systems, political structures, and cultural norms and practices. As a result, human rights implementation remains a challenge for states all around the world. As seen in Chapter 2, the national context is highly relevant for the design and success of implementation measures. Without being purpose-built to fit the specific context, the implementation measure may be a blunt instrument of limited effect – or even counter-productive. While states parties are obliged to implement their international treaty norms, they have near exclusive right to determine the manner of such implementation. In this way, the international system grants states discretion to tailor implementation measures to their context of local norms, socio-economic structures and institutional capabilities. This upholds states' sovereignty and ensures flexibility in the system to accommodate and respond to diversity both between and within states.

An outcome of this discretion is that states parties are likely to adopt a diversity of methods to implement human rights. States may amend their constitutions, enact laws or empower their judiciaries. They may also create NHRIs, implement national action plans, provide education and training, engage the media, partner with religious groups, or fund community initiatives. This is not problematic, as, despite human rights being universally applicable, international law does not expect let alone require uniformity in implementation. Of course, however, this discretion is not unlimited and is subject to the treaties and supervision by the treaty bodies. It is evident from this chapter that the focus in international law is on the effectiveness of the implementation method (and not the method itself), so long as it is performed in good faith and in line with the object and purpose of the treaty. The controlling criterion for implementation measures is their effectiveness in practice.

Despite this broad scope, it is clear from a review of the treaties, treaty body documents and literature that legal incorporation of treaty obligations into national law is the primary focus and preferred manner of implementation. This reflects the legalisation of human rights and the tendency to conceive of it primarily through the lens of the legal discipline. This myopic approach fails to acknowledge the law's limitations, as well as the utility and necessity of multidisciplinary perspectives on rights and other methods of implementation. While legal incorporation undoubtedly has certain benefits (and is sometimes prescribed by the treaties), legal measures alone will not advance rights in all circumstances. Woodiwiss claims that 'just as there is far more in rights than law alone, so for rights to work far more than law itself is required'.[245] By focusing so predominantly on legal measures, the treaty bodies are doing states parties a disservice by neglecting the many other tools for implementing rights.

As such, the focus should shift to become more inclusive in order to better understand human rights in context and how to implement them more effectively in practice. It is necessary to look to other disciplines for their insights into human rights protection in the diverse societies around the world, and to explore other measures than state law for implementation. For example, other measures may include employing culturally sensitive approaches such as engaging with social institutions like religious norms and actors. The attractiveness of such culturally sensitive measures is their ability to potentially implement human rights more effectively than legal measures – or legal measures alone. As the CEDAW Committee acknowledges by recommending numerous other measures, changing a cultural community's norms is not a straightforward process, but rather requires engagement, consultation and dialogue with members and leaders. Such an approach can be effective in building domestic constituents for human rights and creating sustainable protections.

While utilising a variety of implementation measures tailored to specific contexts is done with the aim of improving effectiveness, it is also important from a normative position: valuing diversity. If the international human rights system were to promote a particular method of implementation from only one tradition in the world, this would be unacceptable as hegemonic or imperialistic. In rejecting imperialism and embracing diversity, human rights seek to allow all humans 'to

---

[245] Woodiwiss (n. 76), p. 37.

pursue their own visions of the good life'.[246] According to Donnelly, so long as the choices remain 'consistent with comparable rights for others and reflect a plausible vision of human flourishing', then they deserve respect.[247] Allowing and encouraging states parties to employ other measures of human rights implementation that stem from or align with their own worldviews and social ordering is part of this endeavour.

On this basis, the UN treaty bodies should recommend states parties explore and employ the full variety of implementation measures available in their societies. As this chapter has shown, this is particularly relevant for the HRCee and, to a lesser extent, the ESCR Committee. A lot could be learned from the CEDAW Committee and its progressive focus on other measures, holistic approaches and engaging with social institutions. However, all three Committees continue to preference legal measures. While legal measures cast the state as the central actor, other measures better recognise and facilitate the role of private actors and social institutions in human rights implementation. While state measures are necessarily top-down, the bottom-up resources and initiatives of non-state actors and norms can be effective in developing a wider culture of rights. While it is apparent from this chapter that NSAs play a role in implementation, what remains to be seen is how the international law framework applies in such situations.

---

[246] Jack Donnelly, The Relative Universality of Human Rights (May 2007) *Human Rights Quarterly* 29:2, p. 303.
[247] Ibid.

4

Domestic Implementation of International Human Rights Treaties: The Role of Public and Private Actors

4.1 Introduction

International human rights law, as a branch of public international law, is inherently state-centric. This fact has become increasingly problematic in the last half century; however, it is questionable whether international law's state-centricity was ever an accurate reflection of or an appropriate structure for human rights. As far-reaching and pervasive norms, human rights impact upon and are influenced by a multiplicity of actors beyond just the state. Despite this, only states parties to international human rights treaties are legally obliged to respect, protect and fulfil the rights therein and can be held accountable by the UN treaty bodies for failing to do so.[1] States may, however, lack the will to implement international human rights standards, or the capacity to do so. For example, states may be too weak to enforce human rights standards against large transnational corporations or powerful armed opposition groups.[2] Despite these apparent design and practical shortcomings, international human rights law remains firmly centred around the state, its tools and actors. Scholars have therefore problematised the nature of international law and a human rights system obsessed with the obligations on states to the exclusion of all other actors.[3]

---

[1] Both international humanitarian law and international criminal law can apply to non-state actors, and in certain circumstances NSAs can also be bound by international human rights law. See, for example, UN Committee on the Elimination of Discrimination Against Women (CEDAW Committee), General Recommendation No. 30 on Women in Conflict Prevention, Conflict and Post-conflict Situations, CEDAW/C/GC/30 (1 November 2013), para. 16. In relation to armed groups, see Katharine Fortin, *The Accountability of Armed Groups under Human Rights Law* (Oxford University Press, 2017), Part III.

[2] Other obstacles may include socio-economic factors like poverty and illiteracy; political instability; conflicting customary or religious norms and practices; and the lack of an independent and capable judiciary and media. Christof Heyns and Frans Viljoen, The Impact of the United Nations Human Rights Treaties on the Domestic Level (2001) *Human Rights Quarterly* 23:3, pp. 518–19.

[3] Adam McBeth, Every Organ of Society: The Responsibility of Non-State Actors for the Realization of Human Rights (2008–9) *Journal of Public Law & Policy* 30:1, p. 66.

While the state plays a central role in international human rights law, in practice, the stage is shared with a cast of actors. This involvement of NSAs in human rights is not a new phenomenon. For example, social institutions like kinship groups and religious organisations have been providing education and healthcare services in many places long before the state ever became involved. Despite this long involvement, NSAs have become particularly important in the last three decades due to several factors. These factors include privatisation and globalisation, along with the expansion of multilateral institutions (like the United Nations), the growth of civil society, the changing nature of conflicts, and the progress around women's rights and dismantling the private/public divide.[4] International law's traditional focus on states as both protectors and violators of rights and individuals as the beneficiaries/victims insufficiently addresses the reality of NSAs in human rights.[5] The importance of and focus on NSAs in human rights is unlikely to change in coming years. Scholars have, therefore, identified the need to make space in international law to better account for the role of NSAs, creating counter-narratives and debunking myths of the state.[6]

This chapter contributes to this endeavour by analysing the role of NSAs in human rights implementation as recognised by the treaties and treaty bodies and set out in Chapter 3. While the relationship between human rights and non-governmental organisations (NGOs), corporations and armed groups has received significant scholarly attention, other NSAs have received markedly less. Further, with the exception of NGOs, much of the scholarship considers only NSAs as abusers or violators of rights, and not their role in promoting or protecting rights. Social institutions in general are relatively poorly considered in the literature and warrant further examination of their potential and actual

---

[4] Philip Alston, The 'Not-a-Cat' Syndrome: Can the International Human Rights Regime Accommodate Non-State Actors? in Philip Alston (ed.), *Non-State Actors and Human Rights* (Oxford University Press, 2005), pp. 17–18; Andrew Clapham, *Human Rights Obligations of Non-State Actors* (Oxford University Press, 2006), p. 3.

[5] David Weissbrodt, Roles and Responsibilities of Non-State Actors, in Dinah Shelton (ed.), *The Oxford Handbook of International Human Rights Law* (Oxford University Press, 2013), p. 719.

[6] Manisuli Ssenyonjo, Non-State Actors and Economic, Social, and Cultural Rights, in Mashood Baderin and Robert McCorquodale (eds.), *Economic, Social, and Cultural Rights in Action* (Oxford University Press, 2007), pp. 109, 134; Cedric Ryngaert, Non-State Actors: Carving out a Space in a State-Centred International Legal System (2016) *Netherlands International Law Review* 63, p. 185, citing Mariana Valverde, *Chronotopes of the Law: Jurisdiction, Scale and Governance* (Routledge, 2015).

positive impact upon human rights enjoyment. Rather than proposing amendments to international law to directly oblige a wider range of actors, which is widely debated, this chapter demonstrates the preexisting scope in international law for NSAs to domestically implement human rights treaty obligations.

This chapter proceeds in three main sections. The first necessarily dissects the term 'non-state actor' and briefly explores the range of actors encompassed, including social institutions. The next section considers the responsibilities and obligations on NSAs under international human rights law. This involves an examination of international law sources (notably the Universal Declaration of Human Rights[7] and six of the main UN human rights treaties) to discern any responsibilities or obligations on NSAs and their role in implementing treaty obligations. The final section addresses the situation under international law of states delegating or outsourcing the implementation of their human rights treaty obligations to NSAs. This section analyses the legal obligations on both states and NSAs providing human rights related services using the example of healthcare. The chapter concludes by reflecting on the fact that while NSAs have no direct obligations under international law, they have numerous responsibilities and indirect obligations regarding the enjoyment of human rights.

4.2 The State versus Everyone Else: Unhelpful Dichotomies in Human Rights

First, the term 'non-state actor' requires explication. It is a broad and amorphous term covering a contested and unfixed category of actors, which develops over time as new actors emerge. For example, it includes individuals, families, indigenous peoples, civil society, NGOs, sporting associations, religious organisations, media, political parties, trade unions, businesses, international organisations and armed groups. Clearly, 'NSA' is an umbrella term, covering a huge – virtually unlimited – variety of private actors. Alston famously diagnosed the term with the 'not-a-cat syndrome', likening the categorisation to a distinction in the animal kingdom between cats and everything else.[8] Such a distinction is so broad and virtually open-ended that it is of questionable utility.

---

[7] Universal Declaration of Human Rights (adopted 10 December 1948), UNGA Res. 217 A(III) (UDHR).

[8] Alston (n. 4), p. 3.

As Rodley notes, '[t]here is and can be nothing relevant in common between every individual and every entity that is not a state'.[9] The characterisation is therefore normative, reiterating the dominant position of the state as the primary actor in international law, and necessarily reducing every other actor to an afterthought.[10] Today, and as seen in Chapter 3, there is still great fidelity to this traditional state-centric approach, 'despite its ever-diminishing capacity to describe the evolving reality'.[11]

As explained in the book's introduction, social institutions are loosely categorised along with NSAs for the purposes of the present analysis of international law. This categorisation is not entirely satisfying and reflects the difficulty of multidisciplinary work where concepts do not neatly align across disciplines. For example, social institutions like women's associations, savings clubs, families, religious organisations and sporting clubs certainly are NSAs. While such actors have little to do with intergovernmental organisations like the European Union or armed groups like Boko Haram, as they are all private actors compared to the state, they fall into the category of NSAs under international law. Other social institutions, like languages, customs or religious law, are certainly not actors. However, while some social institutions are not themselves actors (such as norms and conventions), they motivate, guide or enable actors. In this way, while the categories of NSAs and social institutions overlap to an extent, not all social institutions are actors and not all NSAs are social institutions.

While social institutions may not necessarily identify their purpose or function in terms of human rights, they nonetheless often address human rights issues. For example, women's associations exist in numerous forms and have strong traditional foundations across many parts of the world including Africa.[12] They are usually formed and led by women, and function in support of women and girls as 'mutual help associations'.[13]

---

[9] Sir Nigel Rodley, Non-State Actors and Human Rights, in Scott Sheeran and Sir Nigel Rodley (eds.), *Routledge Handbook of International Human Rights Law* (Routledge, 2013), p. 524.

[10] Cedric Ryngaert, Math Noortmann and August Reinisch, Concluding Observations, in Math Noortmann, August Reinisch and Cedric Ryngaert, *Non-State Actors in International Law* (Hart, 2015), p. 369; Alston (n. 4), p. 19.

[11] Alston (n. 4), p. 20.

[12] Prudence Woodford-Berger, Associating Women: Female Linage, Collective Identities and Political Ideology, in Eva Evers Rosander (ed.), *Transforming Female Identities: Women's Organizational Forms in West Africa* (Nordiska Afrikainstitutet, 1997), p. 41.

[13] Ebbe Prag, *Women Making Politics in Rural Senegal: Women's Associations, Female Politicians and Development Brokers* (LAP LAMBERT Academic Publishing, 2010), p. 264.

Often associations provide entertainment and social support for women and function as a kind of social security system. They usually address the common needs of their members, which may be economic, political, cultural or social. Like other NSAs, while able to promote and protect human rights, social institutions can also oppose or abuse human rights. For example, religious groups may provide free or affordable education, healthcare and childcare services in their communities. While these may be vital services welcomed by the community, the religious groups may also abuse rights by discriminating against those who may access or perform the services. The language used here again illustrates the distinction between states and everyone else: whereas states 'violate' rights, NSAs are considered to 'abuse' them.

One type of NSA that is particularly important for human rights is NGOs. While some forty years ago many states lacked significant NGO activity, nowadays 'the associative spirit is nearly universal'.[14] However, NGOs are also a nebulous category representing a variety of interests in a variety of structures. As with the term NSA, NGOs are primarily defined by what they are not: governmental. Therefore, it is not an easy task to define an NGO, and an agreed definition has proved elusive.[15] Typically, an NGO is a private, independent, non-profit, goal-oriented group not founded or controlled by a government, which may include research institutes, religious organisations, neighbourhood associations, political groups or trade unions.[16] As these examples show, NGOs are groups of individuals who have voluntarily associated in order to pursue particular objectives outside the scope of governmental action.[17] As these examples show, NGOs can also be social institutions.

Despite definitional issues, NGOs have proven indispensable to human rights over the last century. Their contribution has oft been

---

[14] Steve Charnovitz, Nongovernmental Organizations and International Law (2006) *American Journal of International Law* 100, p. 350.

[15] Kerstin Martens, Mission Impossible? Defining Nongovernmental Organizations (2002) *Voluntas: International Journal of Voluntary and Nonprofit Organizations* 13:3, pp. 272, 277.

[16] George Edwards, Attributes of Successful Human Rights Non-governmental Organisations (NGOs) – 60 Years after the 1948 Universal Declaration of Human Rights, in Azizur Rahman Chowdhury and Jahid Hossain Bhuiyan (eds.), *An Introduction to International Human Rights Law* (Martinus Nijhoff Publishers, 2012), p. 148; Martens (n. 15), p. 282.

[17] Nigel Rodley, Human Rights NGOs: Rights and Obligations (Present Status and Perspectives) (1997) *SIM Special* 19, p. 45.

noted, with some claiming that, but for NGOs, there might not have been the explosion of international human rights law that occurred since the 1940s.[18] NGOs have been part of the engine driving 'the development of human rights as an international concern', shepherding the evolution of human rights norms and laws.[19] NGOs were heavily involved and influential in the drafting of UN human rights instruments in the last half century. For example, they were involved in drafting the UN Charter, successfully lobbying for and securing official status for NGOs in article 71.[20] Since then, NGOs have been active within the human rights system in various ways, being involved in almost every aspect of human rights practice at the international level.[21] NGOs play a variety of roles regarding human rights, including advocacy and lobbying, standard and norm setting, implementation, monitoring and enforcement, as well as advisory services and technical assistance. NGOs, of course, can also be implicated in human rights abuses.

However, when discussing human rights abuses in current debates the archetype NSA is corporations. Given their increasing power and influence over human rights issues around the world, corporations have gained attention in recent decades. While also positively contributing to human rights enjoyment at times, examples of abuse including slave labour, environmental pollution and workplace fatalities are not hard to find. Therefore, initiatives to constrain corporations and find pathways for their accountability under national and international law have been made. In 2003, the UN produced the *Norms on the Responsibilities of Transnational Corporations and Other Business Enterprises with Regard to Human Rights*, which confirmed that corporations are 'organs of

---

[18] Ibid., p. 41; Menno Kamminga, The Evolving Status of NGOs under International Law: A Threat to the Inter-State System?, in Philip Alston (ed.), *Non-State Actors and Human Rights* (Oxford University Press, 2005), p. 101.

[19] Rodley (n. 17), p. 45.

[20] *Charter of the United Nations* (24 October 1945), 1 UNTS XVI ch. X art. 71. See also Charnovitz (n. 14), p. 358; Claire Breen, Rationalising the Work of UN Human Rights Bodies or Reducing the Input of NGOs? The Changing Role of Human Rights NGOs at the United Nations (2005) *Non-State Actors and International Law* 5, p. 103.

[21] See Andrew Clapham, The Use of International Human Rights Law by Civil Society Organisations, in Scott Sheeran and Sir Nigel Rodley (eds.), *Routledge Handbook of International Human Rights Law* (Routledge, 2013); Weissbrodt (n. 5), p. 721; Brianne McGonigle Leyh, Changing Landscapes in Documentation Efforts: Civil Society Documentation of Serious Human Rights Violations (2017) *Utrecht Journal of International and European Law* 33:84, pp. 44–58.

society' bearing human rights responsibilities.[22] In 2011, the UN endorsed the *Guiding Principles on Business and Human Rights* (Ruggie Principles), which recognised that businesses should respect human rights.[23] Despite this progress, the regulation of corporations remains problematic, with measures to date criticised as too business-friendly or for having weak – or even non-existent – enforcement mechanisms.[24]

Clearly, NSAs play a virtually unlimited number of roles regarding human rights. Despite this, they have not been formally recognised in international law and their position and status is unclear. The roles of NSAs in human rights are contested, with critical questions raised regarding the influence, legitimacy and accountability of such actors. For example, while NGOs have undoubtedly had a profound influence on international law, their role and contribution remains puzzling as, 'doctrinally, international law is understood to be a product of State positivism'.[25] This is due to traditional Westphalian conceptions of states and their positioning as the primary subjects of international law. The result is that NSAs fall into obscurity in international law – the porous definition being only one symptom. However, scholars have noted that with the increasing role and influence of NSAs in recent decades, states have perhaps begun to retreat as the prime guarantors of rights and may no longer be the sole addressees of international obligations.[26] Given the range of NSAs involved in human rights protection, as well as implicated in their abuse, it is necessary to examine their responsibilities and obligations under international law.

4.3 NSAs: Human Rights Responsibilities and (Indirect) Obligations

Despite NSAs being integral to human rights, they are marginalised in international law. This can be seen from article 38 of the *Statute of the*

---

[22] UN Sub-Commission on the Promotion and Protection of Human Rights, Norms on the Responsibilities of Transnational Corporations and Other Business Enterprises with Regard to Human Rights, E/CN.4/Sub.2/2003/12/Rev.2 (13 August 2003), preamble.
[23] UN Human Rights Council, Resolution 17/4, Guiding Principles on Business and Human Rights A/HRC/17/31 (16 June 2011), Principles 11–15.
[24] August Reinisch, The Changing International Legal Framework for Dealing with Non-State Actors, in Philip Alston (ed.), *Non-State Actors and Human Rights* (Oxford University Press, 2005), p. 52.
[25] Charnovitz (n. 14), p. 348.
[26] Reinisch (n. 24), p. 75.

International Court of Justice, which places states at the centre of sources of international law.[27] Despite this state-centric system, international law has granted NSAs piecemeal recognition and assigned them various roles, responsibilities and obligations. Again, the distinction between states and everyone else is apparent here based on the language. While states clearly have human rights obligations under international law, NSAs are considered to have 'responsibilities', an implicitly lesser yet undefined subcategory of obligation. The human rights responsibilities on NSAs vary not only in their degree of recognition and elaboration, but also in their success in implementation and enforcement. To date, there remains 'no general theory on NSAs' international obligations; their scope and extent depend on the specific regime and the actor in question'.[28] This section examines any responsibilities and obligations on NSAs under international human rights law by considering UN declarations, instruments and treaties. It focuses on the six main UN human rights treaties and the views of their corresponding treaty bodies to determine whether and how NSAs are addressed, as well as their role in relation to treaty implementation.

4.3.1 NSAs' Obligations and Responsibilities under UN Declarations and Principles

The United Nations and its member states have recognised the human rights responsibilities of NSAs in various declarations and instruments over the years. Pre-eminent among them is the UDHR. As the foundation of the international human rights system and declaration of the universal standard, the UDHR is a key document to understanding human rights. The UDHR provides concrete insights regarding the system of human rights envisaged and the relevant actors therein. One of the central paragraphs in this regard is in the UDHR's preamble, which is highly inclusive of diverse actors, stating that:

> every individual and every organ of society, keeping this Declaration constantly in mind, shall strive by teaching and education to promote respect for these rights and freedoms and by progressive measures, national and international, to secure their universal and effective recognition and observance, both among the peoples of Member States themselves and among the peoples of territories under their jurisdiction.

---

[27] UN, *Statute of the International Court of Justice* (adopted 26 June 1945, entered into force 24 October 1945), 33 UNTS 993.
[28] Ryngaert (n. 6), p. 191.

Prima facie, according to the UDHR, both state and NSAs are responsible for the realisation of international human rights. Furthermore, article 29 UDHR provides that '[e]veryone has duties to the community', which McBeth refers to as the Declaration's *erga omnes* character, meaning that rights are not simply claimable against states but against everyone.[29] In fact, the UDHR fails to strongly differentiate between state and NSAs, simply proclaiming human rights without necessarily identifying a duty-bearer.[30] Only in two articles does the UDHR refer to the state,[31] with 'State' only mentioned six times in total. Therefore, the UDHR's approach 'is to enumerate entitlements for every human being ... and to assume a correlative imperative on society as a whole to secure and deliver those entitlements'.[32] This aligns with the view of the UDHR as a document of the people (rather than states), deliberately re-named 'universal' from 'international' to highlight this approach.[33] Cassin, one of the UDHR's drafters, reportedly proposed this change to 'universal' to indicate that the Declaration was addressed to all of humanity and morally binding upon everyone, not just governments.[34]

Since its drafting, scholars have debated the UDHR and its implications for NSAs, with some suggesting that it has been underutilised as a source of NSAs' human rights responsibilities.[35] According to Clapham, the UDHR supports the view that human rights are to be respected by all persons, and that if they were only the duties of states, the UDHR would have stipulated this explicitly.[36] Others have concluded that both states and NSAs have duties under the UDHR, however, the precise nature of those duties remains unclear. Some scholars submit that the UDHR does not imply a positive duty on NSAs to protect, promote or fulfil rights,[37]

---

[29] McBeth (n. 3), p. 42.
[30] Clapham (n. 4), p. 34; Manfred Nowak and Karolina Miriam Januszewski, Non-State Actors and Human Rights, in Math Noortmaan, August Reinisch and Cedric Ryngaert, *Non-State Actors in International Law* (Hart, 2015), p. 139; McBeth (n. 3), p. 40.
[31] UDHR, art. 16(3) regarding the family's entitlement to protection from society and the state; and UDHR, art. 22 regarding an individual's entitlement from the state for social security.
[32] McBeth (n. 3), p. 41.
[33] Mary Ann Glendon, *A World Made New* (Random House, 2002), pp. 93, 113, 161; Johannes Morsink, *The Universal Declaration of Human Rights: Origins, Drafting, and Intent* (Pennsylvania Studies in Human Rights, 1999), pp. 33–5, 324.
[34] Glendon (n. 33), p. 161; Morsink (n. 33), p. 33.
[35] McBeth (n. 3), p. 87.
[36] Clapham (n. 4), pp. 29–30, 34.
[37] McBeth (n. 3), pp. 84–5.

while others contend that NSAs have more than just negative duties as they are obliged to 'secure' the observance of rights.[38] Others reject such positions, claiming that any duties in the UDHR on NSAs are not made in the language of binding legal obligations.[39] This ongoing debate regarding whether or not the UDHR creates obligations for NSAs is made more important by the suggestion that the Declaration has gained the status of customary international law (CIL). While some argue that the UDHR has become binding through custom, others contest this, and the precise legal significance of the Declaration remains unclear.[40]

The UN and its member states have subsequently recognised the role of NSAs in human rights in other instruments. For example, the 1993 World Conference on Human Rights in Vienna recognised in its concluding Declaration the important role of NGOs in the promotion of human rights.[41] Significantly, the World Conference recognised the important role of NGOs in the effective implementation of *all* human rights instruments.[42] NGOs' contribution to education, training and research was highlighted, with dialogue and cooperation between NGOs and states encouraged.[43] In the section on implementation, the Conference urged states *inter alia* 'to strengthen national structures, institutions and organs of society which play a role in promoting and safeguarding human rights'.[44] The World Conference emphasised measures to assist in building and strengthening institutions relating to human rights and to a pluralistic civil society.[45] This recognition of NSAs came despite the Vienna Declaration's reiteration that the protection and promotion of human rights is first the responsibility of states.[46] The Declaration therefore supports the view that NSAs have a role to play in human rights, but that primary obligations rest with states.

---

[38] Ssenyonjo (n. 6), p. 123.
[39] Nigel Rodley, Can Armed Opposition Groups Violate Human Rights?, in Kathleen Mahoney and Paul Mahoney (eds.), *Human Rights in the Twenty-First Century: A Global Challenge* (Martinus Nijhoff Publishers, 1993), pp. 305–6.
[40] See McBeth (n. 3), pp. 53, 84; William Schabas, *The Universal Declaration of Human Rights* (Cambridge University Press, 2013), pp. cxix–cxx, cxiii.
[41] World Conference on Human Rights, *Vienna Declaration and Programme of Action* A/CONF.157/23 (12 July 1993).
[42] Ibid., pt II, art. 52.
[43] Ibid., pt I, art. 38.
[44] Ibid., pt II, art. 83.
[45] Ibid., pt II, art. 67.
[46] Ibid., pt I, art. 1.

Similarly, the UN General Assembly adopted by consensus a further declaration in 1999 on the *Right and Responsibility of Individuals, Groups and Organs of Society to Promote and Protect Universally Recognized Human Rights and Fundamental Freedoms*.[47] This Declaration recognises in article 18 that NSAs have duties to the community and a responsibility in promoting human rights. While the Declaration can be seen as an important recognition of NSAs' responsibilities, others downplay its significance suggesting that, like the Vienna Declaration, it simply affirms the primary role of states. For example, as a declaration it is not legally binding, and, given that it contains only general provisions for NSAs, it is unlikely that liability under international law could be based on those provisions, even if it was assumed that they contained binding obligations.[48] Rodley argued that this Declaration provided the opportunity for states to bestow NSAs with responsibilities under international law, but that they specifically chose not to do so. He claims '[t]he absence of any language suggesting a legal obligation on groups and individuals is evident, as is the absence of any kind of obligation to *protect or comply with* human rights, as opposed to *promoting (respect for)* human rights'.[49] As such, the Declaration can be seen to uphold the traditional view that states are the primary actors and subjects of international law, with NSAs having a secondary, important yet ill-defined role.

Finally, the UN Human Rights Council endorsed in 2011 the *Guiding Principles on Business and Human Rights* (Ruggie Principles). While these Principles are landmark in their recognition that businesses should respect human rights, they do not create new legal obligations on NSAs.[50] As such, there remains at present 'no international legally binding instrument on the business sector's responsibilities vis-à-vis human rights'.[51] Indeed, the Ruggie Principles refer to, derive from,

---

[47] UN General Assembly Resolution 53/144, Declaration on the Right and Responsibility of Individuals, Groups and Organs of Society to Promote and Protect Universally Recognized Human Rights and Fundamental Freedoms, A/RES/53/144 (8 March 1999).

[48] Kamminga (n. 18), p. 108.

[49] Rodley (n. 9), p. 534. See, for example, arts. 2 and 3 of the Declaration, which clearly establish the state's prime responsibility and how the Declaration is to be realised based on domestic law.

[50] UN Human Rights Council, Resolution 17/4, Guiding Principles on Business and Human Rights ('Ruggie Principles') A/HRC/17/31 (16 June 2011): see General Principles and Principle 11.

[51] UN Committee on the Rights of the Child (CRC Committee), General Comment No. 16 (2013) on State Obligations Regarding the Impact of the Business Sector on Children's Rights, CRC/C/GC/16 (17 April 2013), para. 8.

and elaborate upon states' existing human rights obligations under international law. As such, while a welcome addition as a mechanism intended to assist in addressing the role and (adverse) impact of business on human rights, the Principles reinforce states' primary role as duty-bearers under international law. Despite this, such instruments are important as they often provide guidance to actors and point the way for future treaties and monitoring procedures.[52] For example, the Principles may herald the development by states of binding human rights obligations for businesses in the form of a treaty.[53] While such a paradigm shift has not yet occurred, it may do so if states wish it to.[54] Until that time, UN human rights treaties will continue to focus their obligations on states parties, as seen in the analysis below.

4.3.2 NSAs' Obligations and Responsibilities under UN Human Rights Treaties

While the UN instruments discussed above clearly articulate a role and responsibility for both states and NSAs in human rights, the treaties are more squarely concentrated on the obligations of states parties. However, like the UDHR, the treaties also create rights without necessarily identifying the state or any other duty-bearer, as seen in statements like 'everyone has a right to life', and 'no one will be subject to discrimination'.[55] This implies that such rights are to be protected against the world at large, implicating all organs of society as set out in the UDHR. Therefore, some have 'asserted that a contemporary reading of human rights instruments shows that non-state actors are also addressees of human rights norms'.[56] This can also be seen in the treaty body comments regarding the responsibilities on NSAs to both promote human rights and protect against their violation. However, as discussed below, the treaties only create accountability and enforcement mechanisms for states – and not NSAs. This reflects the classic 'vertical' conceptualisation

---

[52] Clapham (n. 4), pp. 99–100.
[53] See UN Human Rights Council, Resolution 26/9, Elaboration of an international legally binding instrument on transnational corporations and other business enterprises with respect to human rights, A/HRC/RES/26/9 (26 June 2014).
[54] Rodley (n. 9), p. 536; Nowak and Januszewski (n. 30), p. 118; Reinisch (n. 24), p. 87.
[55] Clapham (n. 4), p. 34; Nicolas Carrillo Santarelli, Non-State Actors' Human Rights Obligations and Responsibility under International Law (2008) *Revista Electronica de Estudios Internacionales* 15, p. 8.
[56] Reinisch (n. 24), pp. 72–3.

of rights as obliging a governing actor (the state or its agents) towards individuals (or groups of individuals) within a state's jurisdiction.[57] As such, horizontal obligations directly on NSAs are virtually absent in the treaties.

Accountability for the obligations set out in international human rights law applies directly to the states parties to those treaties. Such state accountability can be engaged in various ways. First, states are accountable for their own direct violations of their treaty obligations, by act or omission. Secondly, states are accountable for the violations of private actors who were acting on behalf of the state or where the state controls or directs their actions. This kind of liability arises under the *2001 Draft Articles on Responsibility of States for Internationally Wrongful Acts*, which deals with the exercise of state 'authority and the attribution of the conduct of otherwise private actors to the state'.[58] Under these principles, the conduct of state agents and organs is attributable to the state, but also attributable is the conduct of NSAs exercising government authority.[59] For example, the conduct of private security actors, such as running private prisons, may be attributed to the state under these principles. For both of these first two types of accountability, the state is directly liable under international law for its own conduct and for conduct attributed to it.

States can also be accountable under international law for human rights abuse by NSAs that the state failed to prevent or punish. It is well established, both internationally and regionally,[60] that states can be

---

[57] Ssenyonjo (n. 6), p. 109.
[58] See International Law Commission, Draft Articles on Responsibility of States for Internationally Wrongful Acts, Supplement No. 10, A/56/10 (November 2001), arts. 5–11. These Articles essentially codify customary international law on state responsibility based on International Court of Justice (ICJ) jurisprudence such as: *Case Concerning Military and Paramilitary Activities in and against Nicaragua (Nicaragua v. United States of America); Merits* (27 June 1986); *Case Concerning United States Diplomatic and Consular Staff in Tehran (United States of America v. Iran); Order*, 12 V 81 (12 May 1981) (*Tehran Hostages* case).
[59] See, for example, UN Committee against Torture, General Comment No. 2: Implementation of Article 2 by States Parties, CAT/C/GC/2 (24 January 2008), paras. 7, 15; UN ESCR Committee, General Comment No. 24 on State Obligations under the International Covenant on Economic, Social and Cultural Rights in the Context of Business Activity, E/C.12/GC/24 (10 August 2017), para. 11, fn. 31.
[60] See, for example: from the Inter-American Court of Human Rights (IACtHR), *Velasquez Rodriguez v. Honduras*, Series C no. 4 (29 July 1988); *Ximenes-Lopes v. Brazil*, Series C no. 149 (4 July 2006); from the European Court of Human Rights, *Osman v. United Kingdom*, Case no. 87/1997/871/1083, Reports 1998-VIII (28 October 1998);

liable under primary international obligations for failing to protect those within their jurisdiction from abuse by NSAs. This includes abuse such as domestic violence, enforced disappearances, and violations of economic, social and cultural rights. Such state liability under international law is typically engaged by state omissions, where it fails to regulate, monitor, prevent, investigate, prosecute, punish and repair abuse by NSAs. As such, the state is not liable for the actions of the NSAs, but for its own (in)action in failing to protect against human rights abuse. Such duties on states are referred to as positive obligations, as well as duties to protect or due diligence. Due diligence is in fact an obligation on states under customary international law.[61] This application to third parties is known as the indirect horizontal effect of international law – or *Drittwirkung*.

According to these obligations, states must regulate NSAs in their jurisdiction via measures such as legislation, regulations and contractual obligations. On this basis, NSAs may have enforceable domestic human rights obligations, even if they lack a human rights label.[62] The state is required under international law to hold any NSAs abusing rights to account at the domestic level, while the state remains accountable internationally for a failure to do so. Rather than being held directly accountable under the treaty, NSAs are 'only bound to the extent that obligations accepted by states can be applied to them by states'.[63] As such, the human rights obligations on NSAs arise under national instead of international law, a form of indirect accountability. While this national regulation lacks the status of international law, it 'may nevertheless command legitimacy and compliance at a level only aspired to by international law'.[64] In this way, NSAs are beyond the direct reach of international law, and, as such, finding specific international obligations on NSAs is like searching 'for a needle in a haystack'.[65] This next part dives into the haystack to analyse the text of the six main human rights treaties as well as the General Comments by their respective treaty bodies

---

Costello-Roberts v. *United Kingdom*, App. no. 13134/87 (25 March 1993); *Matthews* v. *United Kingdom*, App no. 24833/94 (18 February 1999); African Commission on Human and Peoples' Rights, *Social and Economic Rights Action Centre and Another* v. *Nigeria* (2001) AHRLR 60.
[61] ICJ, *Tehran Hostages* case (n. 58).
[62] McBeth (n. 3), p. 61.
[63] Ssenyonjo (n. 6), p. 110.
[64] Ryngaert, Noortmann, and Reinisch (n. 10), p. 376.
[65] Nowak and Januszewski (n. 30), p. 117; Ssenyonjo (n. 6), p. 109.

to determine the roles, responsibilities, and – where possible – the obligations on NSAs.

International Covenant on Civil and Political Rights

The *International Covenant on Civil and Political Rights* (ICCPR) focuses overwhelmingly on the obligations of states parties, with a few exceptions regarding individuals, groups and society. For example, like that of the UDHR, the ICCPR's preamble provides duties and responsibilities for individuals, reading: 'Realizing that the individual, having duties to other individuals and to the community to which he [sic] belongs, is under a responsibility to strive for the promotion and observance of the rights recognized in the present Covenant'. Secondly, article 5(1) ICCPR (as well as article 30 UDHR and article 5(1) ICESCR) provides that no 'state, group or person' may destroy the rights therein. These provisions clearly apply to state as well as NSAs, prohibiting any activity aimed at the destruction or abuse of rights.[66] Furthermore, article 23(1) ICCPR provides that '[t]he family is the natural and fundamental group unit of society and is entitled to protection by society and the State'. Finally, article 24(1) ICCPR provides that '[e]very child shall have ... the right to such measures of protection as are required by his [sic] status as a minor, on the part of his [sic] family, society and the State'. Extending responsibilities to families and society in terms of protecting children is befitting, and is also reflected in the CRC (discussed below).

The UN Human Rights Committee (HRCee), in its task of supervising states parties' implementation of the ICCPR, has elaborated on the role of NSAs. For example, the HRCee noted that state reports should 'indicate how society, social institutions and the State are discharging their responsibility to assist the family in ensuring the protection of the child'.[67] The Committee therefore envisages NSAs playing a protective role regarding human rights, but also as capable of abusing the rights of others in various circumstances. States parties were urged by the Committee to prohibit discrimination against women 'by private actors in areas such as employment, education, political activities and the provision of accommodation, goods and services'.[68] The HRCee further commented on the

---

[66] Ssenyonjo (n. 6), p. 125.
[67] UN HRCee, General Comment No. 17: Article 24 Rights of the Child (1989), para. 6.
[68] UN HRCee, General Comment No. 28: Article 3 The Equality of Rights between Men and Women, HRI/GEN/1/Rev.9 (vol. I) (29 March 2000), para. 31; UN HRCee, General Comment No. 18: Non-discrimination (10 November 1989), para. 9.

ability of women's right to privacy to be violated by private actors, including their relatives or employers.[69] Additionally, the Committee's references in the General Comment on torture to 'private capacity' make clear that article 7 ICCPR also addresses acts committed by NSAs.[70]

Despite these references to NSAs in their General Comments, the HRCee has in fact taken a rather restrictive approach to the responsibilities of NSAs under the ICCPR.[71] Clapham argues that more so than the other treaty bodies, the HRCee has stressed that the Covenant does not create direct obligations on NSAs, holding rather that the obligations are binding on states parties and do *not* have direct horizontal effect.[72] While NSAs may have obligations under international law, such obligations do not stem from the ICCPR, which merely generates direct obligations for states – albeit ones that apply both in public and private spheres.[73] As such, the human rights obligations on NSAs under the ICCPR operate indirectly as enforced by states parties. As with the treaties discussed below, the ICCPR creates due diligence obligations for states parties to protect, prevent, investigate and repair violations caused by NSAs.[74] For example, article 20 ICCPR requires states to prohibit in law any propaganda for war as well as '[a]ny advocacy of national, racial or religious hatred that constitutes incitement to discrimination, hostility or violence'. This clearly includes an obligation on states regarding propaganda or advocacy by both state and NSAs.

International Covenant on Economic, Social and Cultural Rights

The ICESCR's preamble is identical to that of the ICCPR regarding the duties owed by individuals to promote and observe Covenant rights. And, like the ICCPR, while the ICESCR creates rights that can be violated by both state and NSAs, the treaty obligations are placed on the state with

---

[69] UN HRCee, General Comment No. 16: Article 17 Right to Privacy (8 April 1988), paras. 1, 10; UN HRCee, General Comment No. 28: Article 3 The Equality of Rights between Men and Women, HRI/GEN/1/Rev.9 (vol. I) (29 March 2000), para. 20.
[70] UN HRCee, General Comment No. 20: Article 7 Prohibition of Torture, or Other Cruel, Inhuman or Degrading Treatment or Punishment (10 March 1992), para. 2; Clapham (n. 4), p. 330.
[71] Clapham (n. 4), p. 328.
[72] Ibid.; UN HRCee, General Comment No. 31: The Nature of the General Legal Obligations Imposed on States Parties to the Covenant, CCPR/C/21/Rev.1/Add.13 (29 March 2004), para. 8.
[73] Clapham (n. 4), p. 329.
[74] UN HRCee, General Comment No. 31 (n. 72), para. 8.

regards to both actors. Despite the paucity of direct references in the Covenant to the responsibilities of NSAs, the treaty body supervising the Covenant's implementation, the Economic, Social and Cultural Rights (ESCR) Committee, has further articulated these in greater detail. In fact, the ESCR Committee has been one of the most progressive in recognising the role and human rights responsibilities of NSAs. For example, in relation to the rights to cultural life, food, work and health, the ESCR Committee has explicitly recognised the responsibilities of various organs of society, echoing the language of the UDHR preamble.[75] Regarding the right to health, the ESCR Committee held that:

> While only States are parties to the Covenant and thus ultimately accountable for compliance with it, all members of society – individuals, including health professionals, families, local communities, intergovernmental and non-governmental organizations, civil society organizations, as well as the private business sector – have responsibilities regarding the realization of the right to health. State parties should therefore provide an environment which facilitates the discharge of these responsibilities.[76]

In this way, the ESCR Committee has directly identified the following NSAs as holding human rights responsibilities: individuals, families, local communities, indigenous peoples, civil society, religious bodies, NGOs, trade unions, health professionals, the private business sector and intergovernmental organisations. In fact, many of the ESCR General Comments conclude with a dedicated section on the human rights obligations of actors other than states. The Committee has specifically noted the role *inter alia* of the World Health Organization, UN Development Programme, UNICEF, International Labour Organization, World Trade Organization, World Bank, International Monetary Fund (IMF), the Red Cross and NGOs in implementing the right to water at the national level, as well as the rights to education, health and work.[77] Not only do

---

[75] UN ESCR Committee, General Comment No. 12: The Right to Adequate Food, E/C.12/1999/5 (12 May 1999), para. 20; UN ESCR Committee, General Comment No. 14: The Right to the Highest Attainable Standard of Health, E/C.12/2000/4 (11 August 2000), para. 42; UN ESCR Committee, General Comment No. 18: The Right to Work, E/C.12/GC/18 (6 February 2006), para. 52; UN ESCR Committee, General Comment No. 21: Rights of Everyone to Take Part in Cultural Life, E/C.12/GC/21 (21 December 2009), para. 73; UN ESCR Committee, General Comment No. 23 on the Right to Just and Favourable Conditions of Work (Article 7), E/C.12/GC/23 (27 April 2016), para. 74.

[76] UN ESCR Committee, General Comment No. 14 (n. 75), para. 42.

[77] UN ESCR Committee, General Comment No. 13: The Right to Education, E/C.12/1999/10 (8 December 1999), para. 60; UN ESCR Committee, General Comment No. 14 (n. 75), paras. 64–5; UN ESCR Committee, General Comment No. 15: The Right to Water,

4.3 RESPONSIBILITIES & (INDIRECT) OBLIGATIONS 131

these NSAs have these responsibilities, but states are obliged to facilitate them in discharging their responsibilities. For example, the ESCR Committee requires states to respect, protect and facilitate 'the work of human rights advocates and other members of civil society who assist vulnerable groups in the realization of their right to adequate food', as well as to water, social security and work.[78]

The ESCR Committee has commented particularly on the role of NSAs in the context of the right to work, such as trade unions, businesses and corporations. The Committee held that while not bound by the Covenant, national and multinational private enterprises 'have a particular role to play in job creation, hiring policies and non-discriminatory access to work'.[79] They held that the promotion of employment requires the effective involvement of the community and associations dedicated to workers' rights and trade unions 'in the definition of priorities, decision-making, planning, implementation and evaluation of the strategy to promote employment'.[80] Despite their responsibilities and role in implementing the right to work, the Committee noted that states are obliged to 'effectively regulate and enforce that right, and sanction non-compliance by public and private employers'.[81] For example, states should prohibit forced or compulsory labour by NSAs.[82] As part of their due diligence obligations, states should create and enforce regulations, ensuring remedies in case of violations by NSAs through legitimate processes.[83]

Having recognised NSAs' responsibilities, the ESCR Committee obliges states to regulate their activities and to protect against their violation of rights. The Committee advises states to monitor and regulate NSAs 'to ensure that they do not violate the equal right of men and

---

E/C.12/2002/11 (20 January 2003), para. 60; UN ESCR Committee, 'General Comment No. 18 The Right to Work' E/C.12/GC/18 (6 February 2006), para. 53; UN ESCR Committee, General Comment No. 22 on the Right to Sexual and Reproductive Health (article 12) E/C.12/GC/22 (2 May 2016), para. 53.

[78] UN ESCR Committee, General Comment No. 12 (n. 75), para. 35; UN ESCR Committee, General Comment No. 15 (n. 77), para. 59; UN ESCR Committee, General Comment No. 18 (n. 77), para. 51; UN ESCR Committee, General Comment No. 19: The Right to Social Security, E/C.12/GC/19 (4 February 2008), para. 81; UN ESCR Committee, General Comment No. 23 (n. 75), para. 49.
[79] UN ESCR Committee, General Comment No. 18 (n. 77), para. 52.
[80] Ibid., para. 42.
[81] UN ESCR Committee, General Comment No. 23 (n. 75), para. 51.
[82] UN ESCR Committee, General Comment No. 18 (n. 77), paras. 25 and 35.
[83] UN ESCR Committee, General Comment No. 23 (n. 75), para. 75. See also UN ESCR Committee, General Comment No. 18 (n. 77), para. 52.

women to enjoy economic, social and cultural rights'.[84] As with the ICCPR, the ICESCR obliges states to protect generally against discrimination by third parties.[85] The Committee held that states should protect against and prevent violations of rights by NSAs, such as the right to food and water, and to implement an effective regulatory system.[86] In this way, the ESCR Committee recognises the responsibilities and role of NSAs, but places the obligations on states regarding their domestic regulation. This obligation to regulate NSAs applies particularly 'in cases where public services have been partially or fully privatised'.[87] Article 13 ICESCR expressly envisages education being provided by private actors.[88] While the ESCR Committee recognised the role of religious institutions and other NSAs providing education, it emphasised the obligation on states to monitor them.[89]

In 2017, the ESCR Committee specifically acknowledged the human rights obligations and responsibilities on the business sector in their General Comment No. 24.[90] Having noted the important role of businesses in realising economic, social and cultural rights, the Comment then focuses almost overwhelmingly on their negative role in violating rights. Furthermore, while clearly outlining the corresponding obligations on states parties to respect, protect and fulfil human rights, the Comment 'only deals with the conduct of private actors – including business entities – indirectly'.[91] Definitively, as with the ICCPR, the ICESCR creates indirect obligations on NSAs and enforces them via the state, holding it liable for any failure to uphold rights guaranteed by the Covenant in its jurisdiction. This demonstrates that while the ESCR Committee has recognised the broad responsibilities of a wide

[84] UN ESCR Committee, General Comment No. 16: The Equal Right of Men and Women to the Enjoyment of all Economic, Social and Cultural Rights, E/C.12/2005/4 (11 August 2005), para. 20.
[85] Ibid., para. 19. See also UN ESCR Committee, General Comment No. 18 (n. 77), para. 22; UN ESCR Committee, General Comment No. 24 (n. 59), para. 7.
[86] UN ESCR Committee, General Comment No. 12 (n. 75), paras. 15, 19; UN ESCR Committee, General Comment No. 15 (n. 77), paras. 23–4. See also UN ESCR Committee, General Comment No. 14 (n. 75), para. 51.
[87] UN ESCR Committee, General Comment No. 16: The Equal Right of Men and Women to the Enjoyment of All Economic, Social and Cultural Rights, E/C.12/2005/4 (11 August 2005), para. 20.
[88] See also UN ESCR Committee, General Comment No. 13 (n. 77), paras. 29–30.
[89] Ibid., paras. 41, 47, 49, 54, 59.
[90] UN ESCR Committee, General Comment No. 24 (n. 59), para. 5.
[91] Ibid., para. 11.

range of NSAs and their instrumental role in implementing human rights, the treaty obligations remain upon states parties.

Convention on the Elimination of All Forms of Racial Discrimination

The *Convention on the Elimination of All Forms of Racial Discrimination* (CERD) maintains the centrality of the state and its responsibility for the actions of NSAs, but also recognises the crucial role of NSAs in combating racial discrimination. For example, the Convention obliges states parties to 'prohibit and bring to an end, by all appropriate means, including legislation as required by circumstances, racial discrimination by any persons, group or organization'.[92] Furthermore, the Convention obliges states to 'declare illegal and prohibit organizations, and also organized and all other propaganda activities, which promote and incite racial discrimination, and shall recognize participation in such organizations or activities as an offence punishable by law'.[93] According to article 5(b), states undertake to prohibit and eliminate all forms of racial discrimination, including 'protection by the State against violence or bodily harm, whether inflicted by government officials or by any individual group or institution'. As such, CERD protects individuals against racial discrimination of any kind, not just that perpetrated by the state or its agents. This has been reiterated by the CERD Committee, which found Denmark in violation for failing to protect a person from racial discrimination by a bank in refusing a loan.[94] The Committee has called for states to ensure that perpetrators of racial discrimination, 'be they public officials or other persons, do not enjoy any degree of impunity'.[95]

Conversely, both the CERD and the Committee recognise the role of NSAs in protecting against discrimination. The Convention obliges states parties to 'encourage, where appropriate, integrationist multiracial organizations and movements and other means of eliminating barriers between races, and to discourage anything which tends to strengthen racial division'.[96] The CERD Committee held that 'protection may be achieved in different ways, be it by the use of public institutions or

---

[92] CERD, art. 2(1)(d).
[93] CERD, art. 4(b).
[94] UN CERD Committee, Communication No. 10/1997, CERD/C/54/D/10/1997 (6 April 1999).
[95] UN CERD Committee, General Recommendation XXVII on discrimination against Roma (16 August 2000), para. 12.
[96] CERD, art. 2(1)(e).

through the activities of private institutions'.[97] The Committee stressed the role of NSAs in implementation, including the vital role of NGOs in the struggle against discrimination,[98] as well as that of an '[i]nformed, ethical and objective media, including social media and the Internet'.[99] Noting that free expression 'carries with it special duties and responsibilities',[100] the Committee encouraged politicians and other public opinion-formers 'to adopt positive approaches directed to the promotion of intercultural understanding and harmony'.[101] The Committee advised states to enact legislation for the media in line with international standards and to encourage the media to adopt codes of professional ethics incorporating respect for human rights.[102] Despite specifically envisaging a role for NSAs in both protecting against – as well as perpetrating – racial discrimination, the CERD Committee reiterated that 'it is the obligation of the state party concerned to ensure the effective implementation of the Convention'.[103]

Convention against Torture

In contrast to the ICESCR and CERD, the *Convention against Torture* (CAT) and its Committee take an approach more in line with that of the ICCPR and the HRCee. In fact, CAT does not refer to NSAs, with the exception of noting that individuals can bring complaints of violations to the Committee against Torture.[104] This blinkered focus on the state reflects the analysis above in Chapter 3. While CAT is state-centric, the Committee against Torture also maintains this approach, being 'careful not to stretch the Convention beyond acts with a state nexus or where the direct perpetrators have a quasi-governmental function'.[105] However, the Committee has taken a progressive approach in determining the state

---

[97] UN CERD Committee, General Recommendation XX on article 5 CERD (1996), para. 5.
[98] UN CERD Committee, General Recommendation XXVIII on the follow-up to the World Conference against Racism, Racial Discrimination, Xenophobia and Related Intolerance (19 March 2002), preamble.
[99] UN CERD Committee, General Recommendation No. 35: Combating Racist Hate Speech, CERD/G/GC/35 (26 September 2013), para. 39. See also UN CERD Committee, General Recommendation XXVII on discrimination against Roma (16 August 2000), para. 37.
[100] UN CERD Committee, General Recommendation No. 35, ibid., para. 26.
[101] Ibid., para. 15.
[102] Ibid., para. 39.
[103] UN CERD Committee, General Recommendation XX (n. 97), para. 5.
[104] CAT, art. 22.
[105] Clapham (n. 4), p. 346.

nexus, holding states parties responsible for due diligence failures that result in torture or inhumane treatment by NSAs. The Committee against Torture held that:

> where State authorities or others acting in official capacity or under colour of law, know or have reasonable grounds to believe that acts of torture or ill-treatment are being committed by non-State officials or private actors and they fail to exercise due diligence ... the State bears responsibility and its officials should be considered as authors, complicit or otherwise responsible under the Convention for consenting to or acquiescing in such impermissible acts. Since the failure of the State to exercise due diligence to intervene to stop, sanction and provide remedies to victims of torture facilitates and enables non-State actors to commit acts impermissible under the Convention with impunity, the State's indifference or inaction provides a form of encouragement and/or de facto permission.[106]

The Committee has applied this approach and found states liable under the Convention for failing 'to prevent and protect victims from gender-based violence, such as rape, domestic violence, female genital mutilation, and trafficking'.[107] In addition, the Committee has held that it considers the personnel in detention centres that are privately owned or run to be 'acting in an official capacity on account of their responsibility for carrying out the State function without derogation of the obligation of State officials to monitor and take all effective measures to prevent torture and ill-treatment'.[108] While these examples relate to NSAs as potentially violating the rights contained in CAT, the Committee has also recognised a (limited) role for NSAs in protecting rights. For example, the Committee recognised the role of NGOs in providing rehabilitative services to victims.[109] As this indicates, CAT only creates obligations and accountability for states, and the Committee has also refrained from identifying corresponding responsibilities on NSAs.

Convention on the Elimination of All Forms of Discrimination against Women

While CEDAW remains focused on state obligations, it also recognises the role of NSAs in women's enjoyment of their rights. For example,

---

[106] UN Committee against Torture, General Comment No. 2: Implementation of Article 2 by States Parties, CAT/C/GC/2 (24 January 2008), para. 18.
[107] Ibid.
[108] Ibid., para. 17.
[109] UN Committee against Torture, General Comment No. 3: Implementation of Article 14 by States Parties, CAT/C/GC/3 (13 December 2012), para. 15.

CEDAW's preamble highlights women's contributions to the 'welfare of the family and to the development of society', and that raising children requires a 'sharing of responsibility between men and women and society as a whole'. Similarly to CERD, CEDAW recognises the role of NSAs in combating discrimination as well as their ability to discriminate. Article 2(e) CEDAW obliges states to remove discrimination against women 'by any person, organisation or enterprise', such as ensuring equal job opportunities in the private sector.[110] According to the CEDAW Committee, this article imposes due diligence obligations on states to prevent discrimination by NSAs.[111] As with the treaties discussed above, CEDAW refers to NSAs but affixes corresponding obligations on states parties. In fact, the Committee 'has been at the forefront of efforts to develop international human rights law to make it clear that states have positive duties to protect individuals from the violent acts of other individuals and groups'.[112] The CEDAW Committee has addressed the role and relevance of NSAs in greater detail in its General Comments.

The CEDAW Committee has acknowledged that the 'social positioning of women and men is affected by political, economic, cultural, social, religious, ideological and environmental factors and can be changed by culture, society and community'.[113] On this basis, numerous NSAs well beyond the state are implicated in women's enjoyment of their rights. For example, the CEDAW Committee held that strategies adopted by states to end harmful practices need to involve a broad range of stakeholders, including civil society, national human rights institutions, professionals in health, education and law enforcement, and those who engage in harmful practices.[114] The Committee recognises not only

---

[110] See CEDAW, arts. 13 and 14.
[111] UN CEDAW Committee, General Recommendation No. 28 on the core obligations of States parties under article 2, CEDAW/C/GC/28 (16 December 2010), paras. 9, 10, 13. See also the UN CEDAW Committee, General Recommendation No. 19: Violence against Women (1992), para. 9, and General Recommendation No. 35 on Gender-based Violence against Women, Updating General Recommendation No. 19, CEDAW/C/GC/35 (14 July 2017).
[112] Clapham (n. 4), p. 333.
[113] UN CEDAW Committee, General Recommendation No. 28 (n. 111), paras. 5, 17.
[114] UN CEDAW Committee and CRC Committee, Joint General Recommendation No. 31 of the Committee on the Elimination of Discrimination against Women/General Comment No. 18 on the Committee on the Rights of the Child on Harmful Practices, CEDAW/C/GC31-CRC/C/GC/18 (14 November 2014), para. 36. See further Chapter 3 where this Joint Recommendation is discussed.

4.3 RESPONSIBILITIES & (INDIRECT) OBLIGATIONS 137

the role of NSAs, but also that of non-state normative systems such as religious and customary law.[115] As part of their national policy for eliminating discrimination against women, the CEDAW Committee calls for states to provide resources to ensure that NGOs 'are well-informed, adequately consulted and generally able to play an active role in the initial and subsequent development of the policy'.[116] The Committee specifically urged states to ensure that women's NGOs and civil society organisations are included in all peace negotiations, post-conflict rebuilding, and reconstruction efforts.[117] This confirms the CEDAW Committee's view that NSAs have a strong role to play in advancing women's rights.

Despite this recognition of NSAs, the Committee has reiterated that states parties to the Convention remain responsible for ensuring its full implementation in all circumstances.[118] This puts it in line with the four treaties discussed already, which, despite acknowledging NSAs to varying degrees, all place legal obligations on states parties. According to the duty to protect, CEDAW requires states to domestically regulate NSAs by exercising due diligence to 'prevent, investigate, punish and ensure redress for the acts of private individuals or entities that impair the rights enshrined in the Convention'.[119] As such, states must establish permanent coordination and monitoring mechanisms and put safeguards in place to protect against discrimination by third parties. Furthermore, the Convention requires states to regulate the activities of domestic NSAs within their effective control – including national corporations – who operate extraterritorially.[120]

---

[115] UN CEDAW Committee, General Recommendation No. 28 (n. 111), para. 33; UN CEDAW Committee, General Recommendation on Article 16 Economic Consequences of Marriage, Family Relations and Their Dissolution, CEDAW/C/GC/29 (30 October 2013), paras. 2, 10–15; UN CEDAW Committee and CRC Committee, Joint General Recommendation (n. 114), para. 43.
[116] UN CEDAW Committee, General Recommendation No. 28 (n. 111), para. 27.
[117] UN CEDAW Committee, General Recommendation No. 30 on Women in Conflict Prevention, Conflict and Post-conflict Situations, CEDAW/C/GC/30 (1 November 2013), para. 46(c).
[118] UN CEDAW Committee, General Recommendation No. 28 (n. 111), para. 39.
[119] UN CEDAW Committee, General Recommendation No. 30 (n. 117), para. 15.
[120] UN CEDAW Committee, General Recommendation No. 30 (n. 117), para. 10 and see also para. 12(b). See also UN CEDAW Committee, General Recommendation No. 37 on the Gender-related dimensions of Disaster Risk Reduction in a Changing Climate, CEDAW/C/GC/37 (7 February 2018), Parts C and D. This obligation has also been recognised by other Committees: see, for example, UN ESCR Committee, General Comment No. 24 (n. 59), Part C.

Convention on the Rights of the Child

As noted above, NGOs contributed greatly to the creation of the *Convention on the Rights of the Child* (CRC). Perhaps for this reason it is also the most progressive in terms of its acknowledgement of NSAs and even creates obligations for them – predominantly parents – in addition to the state. This is also important given that the CRC is the most ratified of all the international human rights treaties.[121] Already in its preamble, the CRC acknowledges the responsibilities or duties owed by families, holding that the family 'should be afforded the necessary protection and assistance so that it can fully assume its responsibilities within the community'. Not only does the treaty itself address NSAs, but the Committee responsible for supervising the treaty's implementation has addressed the issue in detail, including being the first UN human rights treaty body to address the role of the private sector as service providers implementing children's rights in 2002.[122]

Article 5 CRC recognises the duties of parents and members of the extended family or community responsible for the child to provide 'appropriate direction and guidance in the exercise by the child of the rights recognized in the present Convention'. The CRC provides that parents/guardians 'have the primary responsibility for the upbringing and development of the child' and the 'primary responsibility to secure, within their abilities and financial capacities, the conditions of living necessary for the child's development'.[123] In addition, states 'shall render appropriate assistance to parents and legal guardians in the performance of their child-rearing responsibilities' and 'shall in case of need provide material assistance and support programmes'.[124] Articles 20(1) and (2) provide that if a child is temporarily or permanently deprived of their family environment, states shall ensure alternative care for the child. Alternatives include care provided by

---

[121] As of 2019, the USA is the only UN member state not to have ratified the CRC.

[122] UN CRC Committee, Day of Discussion on The Private Sector as Service Provider and its Role in Implementing Child Rights (20 September 2002), Geneva, Switzerland; UN CRC Committee, Report on the Thirty-First Session, CRC/C/121 (11 December 2002), para. 640. See also the ESCR Committee's General Comment No. 24 (n. 59) of 2017 on the topic.

[123] CRC, arts. 18 and 27(2).

[124] CRC, arts. 18(2) and 27(3). Regarding health, see also UN CRC Committee, General Comment No. 15 on the Right of the Child to the Enjoyment of the Highest Attainable Standard of Health (art. 24), CRC/C/GC/15 (17 April 2013), para. 78.

4.3 RESPONSIBILITIES & (INDIRECT) OBLIGATIONS 139

private actors such as 'foster placement, kafalah of Islamic law, [or] adoption'.[125]

The CRC also recognises NSAs other than families, parents and guardians. For example, according to the CRC Committee, the media can be a valuable partner in the implementation process.[126] Article 17 CRC recognises the 'important function performed by the mass media', but still places the relevant regulatory obligations on the state. States parties are to ensure that the 'child has access to information and material from a diversity of national and international sources' and shall *inter alia* '[e]ncourage the mass media to disseminate information and material of social and cultural benefit to the child'.[127] The CRC also recognises the role of NSAs in monitoring states parties' implementation of and compliance with the Convention. It provides that the CRC Committee 'may invite the specialized agencies, the United Nations Children's Fund and *other competent bodies* as it may consider appropriate to provide expert advice on the implementation of the Convention'.[128] This made the CRC the first UN human rights treaty to expressly grant NGOs a role in monitoring its implementation.[129] Developing this role, the Committee prepared Guidelines for the *Participation of Partners (NGOs and Individual Experts) in the Pre-sessional Working Group of the Committee on the Rights of the Child*.[130]

Also in its General Comments, the CRC Committee has elaborated upon the role of NSAs in the Convention's implementation. Echoing the UDHR and the ESCR Committee, the CRC Committee held that '[w]hile it is the State that takes on obligations under the Convention, the task of

---

[125] CRC, art. 20(3). This reference to 'kafalah' was the first time an exclusively Islamic concept was recognised in a binding international instrument; see Usang Assim and Julia Sloth-Nielsen, 'Islamic Kafalah as an Alternative Care Option for Children Deprived of a Family Environment' (2014) *African Human Rights Law Journal* 14, pp. 324–5.
[126] UN CRC Committee, General Comment No. 5: General Measures of Implementation, CRC/GC/2003/5 (27 November 2003), para. 59. See also UN CRC Committee, General Comment No. 16 on State Obligations Regarding the Impact of the Business Sector on Children's Rights, CRC/C/GC/16 (17 April 2013), paras. 58–60; UN CRC Committee, General Comment No. 15 on the Right of the Child to the Enjoyment of the Highest Attainable Standard of Health (art. 24), CRC/C/GC/15 (17 April 2013), para. 84.
[127] See CRC, art. 17(a)–(e).
[128] CRC, art. 45(a). Emphasis added.
[129] Breen (n. 20), p. 109.
[130] UN CRC Committee, Report on the Twenty-second session, CRC/C/90 (7 December 1999), Annex VIII.

implementation needs to engage all sectors of society, including business, civil society and children themselves'.[131] The Committee specifically recognised the 'vital' role of NGOs in the implementation process, including child and youth-led organisations, parent and family groups, faith groups, academia, chambers of commerce and industry, trade unions, consumer associations and professional institutions.[132] The Committee urges states to collaborate and work closely with such organisations and 'to give them non-directive support and to develop positive formal as well as informal relationships with them'.[133] The CRC Committee also stressed the obligation on states to create an enabling environment for businesses to respect children's rights.[134] It is clear from these comments that the CRC Committee considers NGOs, civil society and other NSAs to be essential to the enjoyment of Convention rights.

The CRC Committee has also considered the role of NSAs as private providers of human rights related services such as education, health and childcare. The Committee emphasised that states 'have a legal obligation to respect and ensure the rights of children as stipulated in the Convention, which includes the obligation to ensure that non-State service providers operate in accordance with its provisions'.[135] While such NSAs can be seen to have indirect obligations regarding Convention rights, states have due diligence obligations to regulate, supervise and monitor their functions. The Committee has proposed states establish 'a permanent monitoring mechanism or process aimed at ensuring that all State and non-State service providers respect the Convention'.[136] Notably, the Committee also acknowledged the role that civil society can play in such monitoring and compliance.[137] Ultimately, the

---

[131] UN CRC Committee, General Comment No. 16 (2013) on State obligations regarding the impact of the business sector on children's rights, CRC/C/GC/16 (17 April 2013), para. 82; UN CRC Committee, Report on the Thirty-First Session, CRC/C/121 (11 December 2002), para. 653(6); UN CRC Committee, General Comment No. 5: General Measures of Implementation CRC/GC/2003/5 (27 November 2003), paras. 1, 56.

[132] UN CRC Committee, General Comment No. 16 (n. 131), para. 84; UN CRC Committee, General Comment No. 5 (n. 131), para. 58.

[133] UN CRC Committee, General Comment No. 16 (n. 131), para. 84; UN CRC Committee, General Comment No. 5 (n. 131), paras. 58, 59.

[134] UN CRC Committee, General Comment No. 16 (n. 131), paras. 14, 20.

[135] UN CRC Committee, General Comment No. 5 (n. 131), para. 43.

[136] Ibid., para. 44; UN CRC Committee, General Comment No. 16 (n. 131), para. 34.

[137] UN CRC Committee, General Comment No. 16 (n. 131), para. 84. See also UN GA, Report of the Special Rapporteur on the right of everyone to the enjoyment of the highest attainable standard of physical and mental health, Anand Grover, A/69/299 (11 August 2014), para. 33.

Committee recalled that while NSAs may have indirect obligations regarding the provision of services, this 'does not in any way lessen the State's obligation to ensure for all children within its jurisdiction the full recognition and realization of all rights in the Convention'.[138] As such, despite acknowledging that NSAs have duties and responsibilities regarding children's rights, the Convention and Committee principally address state obligations.

4.3.3 Hide and Seek: NSAs' Human Rights Responsibilities and Obligations

Human rights as set out in the UDHR were guaranteed to all humans owing to their dignity. They were not premised on states or other specified actors, but were identified as innate and inalienable rights. All organs of society were seen as necessary and responsible for their promotion and protection. This reflects the complex reality of rights around the world, and the various conditions, factors and stakeholders impacting upon their enjoyment. Scholars have argued that the UDHR, now potentially CIL, is a source of human rights obligations on NSAs. In several subsequent documents, the UN reiterated human rights' dependence upon a matrix of both state and NSAs and their corresponding responsibilities. Despite being initially broad, the position of NSAs in human rights was narrowed by the UN treaties. These treaties overwhelmingly create state obligations, reflecting the traditional view of the state as the addressee of public international law and duty-bearer regarding human rights. In addition to these direct obligations on states, the treaties recognise the role of NSAs in both protecting and abusing rights. While the treaties themselves do not create (m)any direct obligations on NSAs, their obligations are indirect, as applied and enforced by states.

Despite the dearth of direct obligations on NSAs in the human rights treaties, the treaty bodies have nonetheless elaborated in greater detail the role and responsibilities of NSAs. Pre-eminent among them, the ESCR Committee has articulated in General Comments the responsibility of all organs of society to realise the right therein, as has the CRC Committee regarding the rights of the child. The Committees not only recognise NSAs' responsibilities, but further oblige states to facilitate and create

---

[138] UN CRC Committee, General Comment No. 5 (n. 131), para. 44.

environments conducive to NSAs' discharge of their responsibilities. Both the CERD and CEDAW Committees have recognised the pivotal role of NSAs in ending discrimination, calling upon states to engage and collaborate with private actors, such as the media and religious groups, to promote and protect rights. While the HRCee and the Committee against Torture also recognise the role of NSAs, it is to a lesser extent than these other Committees, arguably due to the fact that the ICCPR and CAT are more focused upon 'traditional state functions' such as ensuring state security, running prisons and delivering justice. However, even in relation to these functions, NSAs play a role and an increasing one. Due to human rights privatisation, NSAs are performing functions and providing services (albeit not uncontestedly) even in these areas considered to be quintessential state functions.

In this way, the treaty bodies have repeatedly recognised and extrapolated upon NSAs' human rights responsibilities. This is despite the fact that the treaties by and large neglect the issue. Arguably, through their practical work with states and stakeholders regarding the implementation of rights, the treaty bodies were confronted by this lacuna and sought to fill it by recalling the position of NSAs as first espoused in the UDHR. Given the varied and influential role of NSAs in human rights, it would be incongruous for the treaty bodies not to recognise and account for NSAs in their supervision of states' implementation. While doing so in their General Comments does not create new legal obligations on NSAs (as they are not binding), the Comments are the most authoritative interpretations of the treaties, and therefore highly persuasive. Furthermore, despite recognising the responsibilities of NSAs, the treaty bodies cannot enforce them given their limited mandate on states parties. As such, the treaty bodies simultaneously highlight the responsibilities of NSAs yet emphasise the corresponding state obligations.

To date, controversy surrounds the legal personality of NSAs and whether they can in fact be bound by international law. While some scholars conclude that the core human right obligations bind all parts of society (including NSAs), others maintain that none of the international human rights treaties purport 'to impose obligations on entities other than states'.[139] While there does appear to be consensus that NSAs do indeed have international human rights responsibilities, their exact

---

[139] Respectively Reinisch (n. 24), p. 71; Rodley (n. 9), p. 533.

source, scope and the method of enforcement remain unclear. In this way, they are like apparitions in the shadows, more form than substance. What is clear, however, is that the UN treaties create indirect obligations on NSAs to be enforced domestically by the state party. These relate to the due diligence obligations on states to protect against violations by NSAs. These indirect obligations on NSAs and the corresponding obligations on states are explored by way of example below.

4.4 Privatising Human Rights Implementation and Shifting Obligations

Since the main international human rights treaties were drafted in the last century, the role and position of the state has changed, as has that of NSAs. As noted at the outset of this chapter, NSAs now play an increasing role in human rights due to factors including privatisation. In the context of neoliberalism, privatisation has been pursued globally, with state assets sold off or functions outsourced to private actors despite their importance in realising human rights.[140] Privatisation has occurred particularly in human rights related areas such as water, electricity, prisons, transport, education and healthcare. This was a matter of state policy and also the policies of international financial bodies like the World Bank and IMF, which advocated states decrease expenditure by selling off public assets and services 'to be run more efficiently under competitive market conditions'.[141] While privatisation is considered to be the shift in whole or part of traditional functions like education and healthcare provision from the state to private actors, in some circumstances, the state in question may never have provided these services. As such, there has been no shift away from the state, but rather a continuation of private actors performing so-called 'state functions'.

In fact, rather than being an anomaly or recent occurrence, private sector providers in a majority of countries pre-date state involvement in

---

[140] Adam McBeth, Privatising Human Rights: What Happens to the State's Human Rights Duties When Services Are Privatised? (2004) *Melbourne Journal of International Law* 5, p. 134; Manfred Nowak, *Human Rights or Global Capitalism: The Limits of Privatization* (University of Pennsylvania Press, 2017), pp. 1, 43–7.
[141] Alexis Kontos, 'Private' Security Guards: Privatized Force and State Responsibility under International Human Rights Law (2004) *Non-State Actors and International Law* 4, pp. 200, 205.

functions such as social security, health and education services.[142] Traditionally, it was primarily social institutions such as families, charities and religious organisations that provided healthcare, with the state only beginning to take a stronger role in Europe in the nineteenth century.[143] The prevalence of private provision of human rights related services may be due to the state being weak or lacking resources. The private provision of human rights related services may also be preferred by the relevant community. For example, religious groups may prefer sending their children to their own schools based on religious teachings, rather than to secular state institutions. Furthermore, private actors may have more connection and legitimacy in some communities compared to the state, and therefore be more accepted, trusted and better able to meet community members' needs. Finally, while it has seemingly been taken for granted that the state should provide essential services, it has been argued that they can be provided 'better, more cheaply, and more effectively' by private actors.[144]

Despite the long-standing practice of NSAs fulfilling certain state functions and the more contemporary trend of privatisation, international human rights law has only recently begun to pay attention.[145] This section therefore uses the example of privately provided healthcare to explore the legal issues from a human rights perspective. Rather than focusing on neoliberal privatisation and for-profit providers as has been done elsewhere, this section focuses more on the provision of healthcare by social institutions such as religious organisations, kinship groups and traditional healers. Therefore, the present discussion is not necessarily centred upon the shift from the state to the private sector, but on the role (new or pre-existing) of private actors like social institutions fulfilling functions obligated to states under international human rights treaties. This section considers whether states can collaborate with or delegate to such private actors for the domestic implementation of the right to health, and what international responsibilities and obligations apply to both states and NSAs in the situation.

---

[142] UNICEF comments for the UN CRC Committee, Day of Discussion on The Private Sector as Service Provider and its Role in Implementing Child Rights, Geneva (20 September 2002), para. 1.
[143] Nowak (n. 140), p. 69.
[144] Antenor Hallo de Wolf, Human Rights and the Regulation of Privatized Essential Services (2013) *Netherlands International Law Review* 60:2, pp. 169–71.
[145] Ibid., p. 168; Nowak (n. 140), pp. 1, 47.

4.4.1 Privatisation of Healthcare and International Human Rights Law

Historically as well as today, private providers play a major role in healthcare in both developed and developing states.[146] Arguably for this reason, the ESCR Committee recognised the responsibilities on NSAs for realising the right to health as discussed above. The involvement of NSAs in healthcare is not necessarily or inherently problematic. The main human rights concern regarding the role of private actors in service delivery is that quality, accessibility, availability and acceptability may be compromised, resulting in rights violations. Some contributions of private actors are beneficial, such as programmes run by not-for-profit organisations that improve access for marginalised communities; while other contributions can be minimal or even abuse rights. Given the diversity of private actors involved and the variety of health services provided, academic literature on the topic is inconclusive as to whether private participation has an overall positive or negative impact.[147] However, the private sector (both profit and not-for-profit) has been recognised for its constructive role in providing services.[148]

In fact, privatisation is generally advocated based on efficiency – for both the state and rights-holders. NSAs may have more expertise, may be located closer to the rights-holders, and may be able to more efficiently provide the services than the state in terms of logistics and administration. Equally, the state, for various reasons, may not be well placed to provide certain services, may lack capacity and resources, and therefore require the involvement of private actors. As seen in Chapter 2, social institutions can be important in this regard as they enjoy normative legitimacy and trust in their communities, which can help promote the acceptability of healthcare including its cultural appropriateness. The primary concern of the treaty bodies and Special Rapporteurs for health

---

[146] Audrey Chapman, The Impact of Reliance on Private Sector Health Services on the Right to Health (2014) *Health and Human Rights Journal* 16:1, p. 123; Antenor Hallo de Wolf and Brigit Toebes, Assessing Private Sector Involvement in Health Care and Universal Health Coverage in Light of the Right to Health (2016) *Health and Human Rights* 18:2, p. 80.
[147] Hallo de Wolf and Toebes, ibid., p. 82.
[148] Office of the High Commission for Human Rights (OHCHR), Submission to the UN Committee on the Rights of the Child Day of Discussion on The Private Sector as Service Provider and Its Role in Implementing Child Rights, Geneva (20 September 2002), p. 3.

has not been who provides the healthcare services, but whether such services – irrespective of the provider – are delivered in a way that fulfils the end users' rights.[149]

As set out in Chapter 3, the treaties impose obligations of result upon states parties, who enjoy wide discretion as to how to domestically implement human rights standards. International law does not dictate how a state's healthcare should be delivered or paid for, so long as the care meets human rights standards. International human rights law obliges states to manage the private provision of healthcare in their jurisdiction to ensure that, whatever mix of public and private service providers exists, the right to health is upheld. In fact, the ESCR Committee has held that the Covenant is 'neutral' and 'neither requires nor precludes any particular form of government or economic system'.[150] The Committee stated specifically that the ICESCR does not prohibit privatisation, including in the provision of healthcare.[151] This reflects the conclusions in Chapter 3 that the Committee's focus is on the effectiveness of implementation measures, rather than the type of measures per se.

The majority of scholars agree that international human rights law is agnostic as to how a state party meets its treaty obligations, and is therefore 'neither for nor against' the privatisation of service delivery.[152] For example, Bloche concluded that 'there is no human rights case against overt commodification of health services'.[153] Essentially, states are at liberty to select any mix or combination they deem suitable of

---

[149] Office of the High Commission for Human Rights (OHCHR), Submission to the UN Committee on the Rights of the Child Day of Discussion on The Private Sector as Service Provider and Its Role in Implementing Child Rights, Geneva (20 September 2002), p. 4; UN ESCR Committee, General Comment No. 14 (n. 75), para. 12(b); Andrew Clapham and Mariano Garcia Rubio, The Obligations of States with Regard to Non-State Actors in the Context of the Right to Health (2002) *Health and Human Rights Working Paper Series*, No. 3, p. 3.

[150] UN ESCR Committee, General Comment No. 3: The Nature of States Parties' Obligations, E/1991/23 (14 December 1990), para. 8.

[151] UN ESCR Committee, General Comment No. 24 (n. 28), para. 21.

[152] Chapman (n. 146), p. 125. Brigit Toebes, The Right to Health and the Privatization of National Health Systems: A Case Study of the Netherlands (2006) *Health and Human Rights* 9:1, p. 107; UN CRC Committee, Report on the Thirty-First Session (n. 131), para. 641.

[153] M. Gregg Bloche, Is Privatisation of Health Care a Human Rights Problem?, in Koen de Feyter and Felipe Gómez Isa (eds.), *Privatisation and Human Rights in the Age of Globalisation* (Intersentia, 2005), p. 221.

4.4 PRIVATISING HUMAN RIGHTS IMPLEMENTATION 147

public and private provision of healthcare to meet their international obligations.[154] However, Nowak challenges the dominant position that human rights are neutral in this way, submitting that far-reaching privatisation makes it difficult – or impossible – for states to comply with their human rights obligations.[155] He argues that if rights enjoyment suffers, privatisation may qualify as a 'deliberate retrogressive measure' prohibited under ICESCR.[156] Citing the negative effects of neoliberal privatisation and for-profit healthcare, such as growing inequality and exclusion, he refutes the claim that international human rights law is neutral regarding privatisation.[157] These arguments warrant consideration.

First, the assumption that privatisation promotes effectiveness and efficiency does not always hold. For example, NGOs may compete with one another or with the state, creating duplication and competition rather than the pooling of ideas and resources.[158] Involving for-profit healthcare service providers can weaken the public system, as the best medical staff may choose to work privately for more remuneration. In general, the greater role of the private sector can undermine both the quality and the capacity of the public system.[159] The private sector can also abuse the right to health by providing low-quality healthcare, increasing costs and making services unaffordable, or discriminating against patients. Privatisation over the last few decades provides numerous examples of increases in inequality and a deterioration in the enjoyment of rights.[160] While privatisation is often done with the assumption that it will reduce the size and cost of the government, the corresponding regulatory obligations on states can also be demanding.[161] These are explored in the next section.

---

[154] Hallo de Wolf and Toebes (n. 146), p. 84. This applies also to other rights. See, for example, regarding housing: UN ESCR Committee, General Comment No. 4: The Right to Adequate Housing (Art. 11(1) of the Covenant), E/1992/23 (1991), para. 14.
[155] Nowak (n. 140), pp. 2–3, 50–1.
[156] See ICESCR, art. 2(1); Nowak (n. 140), pp. 2–3, 50–1.
[157] Nowak (n. 140), p. 79.
[158] Save the Children UK, Submission to the Committee on the Rights of the Child Theme Day: The Private Sector as Service Provider and Its Role in Implementing Child Rights (20 September 2002), p. 7.
[159] Ibid.
[160] Nowak (n. 140), pp. 52, 77–9.
[161] Hallo de Wolf (n. 144), p. 171.

4.4.2 Privatising Health: Shifting State Obligations from Fulfilling to Protecting

As established in Chapter 3, states are the primary duty-bearers of human rights under the treaties and are obliged to effectively implement the standards therein. While states have discretion in how this is done, they are accountable to the treaty bodies and may be held liable for their own violations, those attributable to them, and violations by private actors that they failed to prevent or punish. As such, where the state determines in its discretion to collaborate with or engage NSAs to implement treaty standards, the state does not delegate or diminish in any way its treaty obligations. The treaty bodies have underlined this, stressing that states remain responsible in all circumstances for full compliance with the treaties, including where services have been outsourced.[162] The CEDAW Committee reiterated states parties' responsibility for the Convention's implementation in 'all circumstances',[163] and has held states liable for the failures of private health providers. The purpose of holding states vicariously liable for the violations of NSAs is to ensure that states 'have a direct interest in regulating the behaviour of non-state actors to whom they have transferred state tasks'.[164] Concretely, states cannot absolve themselves of their human rights obligations by delegating implementation in whole or in part to private actors.[165]

States therefore remain liable under international law for implementing the treaty standards in their jurisdiction and cannot defer to NSAs or attribute blame to them internationally for rights violations. As such, before shifting the provision of healthcare services from public to private actors, states are advised to undertake a comprehensive and transparent

---

[162] See, for example, UN CRC Committee, General Comment No. 16 (n. 131), paras. 25, 33; UN CRC Committee, General Comment No. 15 on the Right of the Child to the Enjoyment of the Highest Attainable Standard of Health (art. 24), CRC/C/GC/15 (17 April 2013), para. 75. See also UN HRCee, *Cabal and Pasini Bertran v. Australia*, Communication 1020/2001 (19 September 2003), para. 7.2, providing that outsourcing detention facilities does not absolve state responsibility.

[163] UN CEDAW Committee, General Recommendation No. 28 (n. 111), para. 39.

[164] Reinisch (n. 24), p. 81.

[165] UN CEDAW Committee, General Recommendation No. 24: Article 12 of the Convention (Women and Health) (article 12), A/54/38/Rev.1, chap. I (1999), para. 17; UN ESCR Committee, General Comment No. 5: Persons with Disabilities (1994), para. 12; UN CRC Committee, General Comment No. 15 (n. 162), para. 48. See also *Costello-Roberts v. United Kingdom*, App no. 13134/87 (25 March 1993), para. 27 (ECtHR).

4.4 PRIVATISING HUMAN RIGHTS IMPLEMENTATION 149

assessment of the human rights implications.[166] Scholars advise states to assess the impact of private provision of healthcare, recommending that privatisation occur only if it proves highly likely to lead to the progressive realisation of rights.[167] In situations where NSAs are already providing healthcare services, it is suggested that such an assessment should still be undertaken to determine the pros and cons of their involvement and any gaps. The CRC Committee recommended that states 'facilitate the participation of the local communities using the services in the assessment process, with a particular focus on children, families and vulnerable groups'.[168] In fact, the ESCR Committee has held that members of the public have a right to participate in all health-related decisions, which would include the decision to involve private actors in providing – or to continue providing – healthcare.[169]

Where NSAs are providing services and contributing to implementing the right to health, the state's obligations are not diminished, but rather shift from fulfilling to protecting rights.[170] This entails recalibrating the role of the state, in whole or in part, 'from producing and delivering services to enabling and regulating them'.[171] This role has two aspects to it as set out in the section above. First, states must create an environment that facilitates NSAs' awareness of and ability to discharge their international responsibilities regarding the right to health.[172] Secondly, based on their due diligence obligations, states must take reasonable measures to prevent, investigate, punish and remedy violations of international human rights law by private actors. For example, the CEDAW Committee held under article 2(e) that 'the State party has a due diligence obligation to take measures to ensure that the activities of private actors

---

[166] UN CRC Committee, Report on the Thirty-First Session (n. 131), para. 653(11). See also UN CRC Committee, General Comment No. 16 on State Obligations Regarding the Impact of the Business Sector on Children's Rights, CRC/C/GC/16 (17 April 2013), paras. 78–81.
[167] Hallo de Wolf and Toebes (n. 146), pp. 89–90; Toebes (n. 152), pp. 111–12. Nowak (n. 140), pp. 52–4, 79–80.
[168] UN CRC Committee, Report on the Thirty-First Session (n. 131), para. 653(12). See also CRC, art. 12.
[169] UN ESCR Committee, General Comment No. 14 (n. 75), paras. 11, 17, 23, 54. See also Declaration on the Rights of Indigenous Peoples, A/RES/61/295 (2 October 2007), art. 18.
[170] Hallo de Wolf and Toebes (n. 146), p. 84; Chapman (n. 152), p. 128.
[171] Chapman, ibid.; Hallo de Wolf (n. 144), p. 180.
[172] See, for example, UN CRC Committee, General Comment No. 15 (n. 162), paras. 76, 91, 101; UN CRC Committee, General Comment No. 16 (n. 131), paras. 29, 73.

in regard to health policies and practices are appropriate'.[173] According to scholars, the obligation on states to protect regarding the right to health involves interlinked duties with four key components:

> the obligation to *regulate* all actors in the health sector through the adoption of legislation, regulations, and policies; the obligation to *monitor*, through independent mechanisms, the behaviour of these actors; the obligation to ensure that there is *accountability* for violations committed by public and private actors; and the obligation to ensure the population's *participation* in health care decision-making.[174]

Regarding regulation, states must create a national framework requiring NSAs to comply with human rights norms, which in the case of healthcare relate to quality, accessibility, acceptability and affordability. It is through this framework that states transpose their international obligations into national obligations on NSAs. However, international documents provide little guidance as to how states are to regulate private actors.[175] This is slowly changing, with the ESCR and CRC Committees providing greater insight specifically regarding businesses.[176] For example, the CRC Committee requires states parties to 'take all necessary, appropriate and reasonable measures' to prevent businesses from abusing children's rights, including adopting a policy framework and enacting and enforcing legislation and regulations.[177] Scholars recommend that states' regulations cover: the geographic spread of clinics; non-discrimination; physical and financial accessibility for patients; medical ethics; cultural appropriateness; and quality of facilities, goods and services.[178] A rigorous registration/licensing process with an effective health information system is necessary for states to know who is providing what services to which patients where and for what price.[179] Given that states are obliged to progressively realise the right to health, regulations should ensure that NSAs continuously improve their healthcare services with no retrogressive measures.[180]

---

[173] UN CEDAW Committee, *Alyne da Silva Pimentel* v. *Brazil*, CEDAW/C/49/D/17/2008 (10 August 2011), para. 7.5.
[174] Hallo de Wolf and Toebes (n. 146), p. 84.
[175] Chapman (n. 152), pp. 131–2; Toebes (n. 167), p. 107. See also Hallo de Wolf (n. 144), p. 166.
[176] See UN CRC Committee, General Comment No. 16 (n. 131); UN ESCR Committee, General Comment No. 24 (n. 59).
[177] UN CRC Committee, General Comment No. 16 (n. 131), paras. 28–9, 53.
[178] Hallo de Wolf and Toebes (n. 146), p. 86.
[179] Chapman (n. 152), p. 128.
[180] See ICESCR, art. 2(1); Nowak (n. 140), p. 168.

4.4 PRIVATISING HUMAN RIGHTS IMPLEMENTATION 151

In addition to creating regulations for NSAs providing healthcare services, states must monitor their compliance with them. This can be achieved in various ways and by input from various actors, including NHRIs, patients and civil society. For example, states can require private actors to report publicly on their compliance, create a reporting and investigatory framework for patient complaints, and collect data in order to measure compliance and identify problems.[181] This is crucial, as states will be liable for violations arising from a failure to properly monitor NSAs providing healthcare, as in the case of *Alyne da Silva Pimentel v. Brazil*.[182] Despite the state alleging that the poor medical care leading to a pregnant woman's death was 'not imputable to it, but to the private health-care institution', the CEDAW Committee held Brazil 'directly responsible for the action of private institutions when it outsources its medical services, and that furthermore, the State always maintains the duty to regulate and monitor private health-care institutions'.[183] The Committee found Brazil to have failed in its reproductive health obligations under article 12(2) CEDAW, and to have violated its obligation to ensure effective judicial remedies and protection for victims.[184]

As this demonstrates, in addition to regulating and monitoring NSAs providing healthcare, states must also ensure that accountability mechanisms exist for NSAs and remedies for victims.[185] As part of the right to an effective remedy, states must provide remedies and reparations for victims of rights violations including those caused by NSAs.[186] Scholars

---

[181] UN CRC Committee, General Comment No. 16 (n. 131), paras. 64, 76–7. Regarding health specifically, the CRC Committee held: 'States should require businesses to undertake children's rights due diligence.' UN CRC Committee, General Comment No. 15 on the Right of the Child to the Enjoyment of the Highest Attainable Standard of Health (art. 24), CRC/C/GC/15 (17 April 2013), para. 80.

[182] UN CEDAW Committee, *Alyne da Silva Pimentel* v. *Brazil* (n. 173). Regional human rights courts have made similar findings regarding private healthcare providers. See, for example: *Storck* v. *Germany*, App. no. 61603/00 (16 June 2005) (ECtHR); *Ximenes-Lopes* v. *Brazil*, Series C No. 149 (4 July 2006) (IACtHR). See also discussion of national cases where courts have held the government accountable in Nowak (n. 140), pp. 72–4.

[183] UN CEDAW Committee, *Alyne da Silva Pimentel* v. *Brazil* (n. 173), para. 7.5.

[184] Ibid., para. 7.8. See also Rebecca Cook, Human Rights and Maternal Health: Exploring the Effectiveness of the Alyne Decision (2013) *Journal of Law, Medicine, and Ethics* 41.

[185] UN ESCR Committee, General Comment No. 22 on the Right to Sexual and Reproductive Health Article 12, E/C.12/GC/22 (2 May 2016), para. 64; UN ESCR Committee, General Comment No. 24 (n. 59), paras. 14–16, 38–57; Hallo de Wolf and Toebes (n. 146), p. 83.

[186] UN CRC Committee, General Comment No. 16 (n. 131), paras. 30–1, 66–72. For the right to a remedy, see for example art. 2(3) ICCPR or art. 14 CAT.

recommend that states create regulatory bodies to monitor NSAs' compliance with healthcare regulations, which can also serve as a venue for those seeking redress.[187] Such bodies should be independent, operate in a transparent and predictable manner, be accessible and equitable, as well as compatible with international human rights standards.[188] Other accountability mechanisms for NSAs could include judicial, quasi-judicial (i.e. NHRIs or ombudspersons), as well as administrative, political or social mechanisms (i.e. the media, NGOs, etc.).[189] To ensure accountability, these systems must be effective and able to impose penalties and sanctions on private providers that breach human rights standards.[190] If a state fails to take all 'necessary, appropriate and reasonable measures to prevent and remedy such infringements or otherwise collaborated with or tolerated the infringements', it may be found liable internationally.[191]

The above steps are necessary for a state to ensure that healthcare provided by NSAs meets international standards. These national measures are vital in ensuring that there is no accountability gap, as NSAs lack direct international human rights obligations and may have conflicting priorities and capabilities. Chapman notes that 'the goals and priorities of private health care institutions tend to differ, often significantly, from the values and norms in the human rights paradigm'.[192] For example, if they are for-profit providers, they may require extra incentives or subsidies from the state to provide certain healthcare services for certain groups or in certain locations. According to the Special Rapporteur on Health, the global trend of privatisation in healthcare 'poses significant risks to the equitable availability and accessibility of health facilities, goods and services, especially for the poor and other vulnerable or marginalized groups'.[193] While states can set minimum standards to be met and

---

[187] Hallo de Wolf and Toebes (n. 146), pp. 86, 88; Hallo de Wolf (n. 144), pp. 179–82.
[188] Similar to the requirements for NHRIs under the Paris Principles: Hallo de Wolf (n. 144), pp. 181, 190–1.
[189] Hallo de Wolf and Toebes (n. 146), p. 88; UN CRC Committee, General Comment No. 16 (n. 131), para. 61(d).
[190] Chapman notes that this is difficult, particularly in developing countries. Chapman (n. 152), pp. 128–9.
[191] UN CRC Committee, General Comment No. 16 (n. 131), para. 28.
[192] Chapman (n. 152), p. 123.
[193] UN GA, Interim report of the Special Rapporteur on the right of everyone to the enjoyment of the highest attainable standard of physical and mental health, Anand Grover, A/67/302 (13 August 2012), para. 3. For discussion of UN treaty bodies concerns regarding privatisation and health, see Nowak (n. 140), pp. 75–6.

4.4 PRIVATISING HUMAN RIGHTS IMPLEMENTATION

privatise healthcare, they also have to provide a safety net if the private providers fail to deliver all services to all people at the requisite standards.[194]

As is clear from the proceeding paragraphs, due diligence obligations on states are rarely straightforward or cheap, but involve ongoing vigilance and investment. Typically, it is not the creation of the regulatory framework but rather its monitoring and enforcement against NSAs that pose the greatest challenges.[195] For example, working with private providers 'requires management skills and complex health information systems that many governments ... often lack'.[196] Where the state is willing and able to do this and ensure private providers conform to human rights standards, the system can work well. However, low- and middle-income states in particular often have limited institutional capacity, outdated regulations and weak enforcement, which constrains their interaction with and control over private health providers.[197] As set out above, the failure to regulate private healthcare providers can give rise to human rights violations, a domestic accountability gap, and a state's international liability.

4.4.3 Privatising Health: Shifting NSAs' Obligations from National to International?

Where human rights related services are provided by the private sector, both the state and NSAs bear different but complementary obligations.[198] As set out above, NSAs have international human rights responsibilities including general responsibilities under the UDHR, as well as specific (yet undefined) responsibilities regarding realising the right to health as articulated by the ESCR Committee.[199] In addition, NSAs also have a general obligation under international law to respect the human rights of others in the course of their activities.[200] While there is consensus

---

[194] UN CRC Committee, Report on the Thirty-First Session (n. 131), para. 644; Ryngaert (n. 6), p. 193.
[195] UN CRC Committee, General Comment No. 16 (n. 131), para. 61.
[196] Chapman (n. 152), p. 123.
[197] Ibid., p. 130.
[198] McBeth (n. 140), p. 135.
[199] UN ESCR Committee, General Comment No. 14 (n. 75), para. 42.
[200] Nowak and Januszewski refer to this as 'undisputable' and McBeth as 'self-evident'. Nowak and Januszewski (n. 30), p. 159; McBeth (n. 140), p. 146. See also UN ESCR Committee, General Comment No. 24 (n. 59), para. 5; UN CRC Committee, General Comment No. 16 (n. 131), para. 8; UN Human Rights Council, Resolution 17/4, Guiding

regarding the existence of these obligations and responsibilities, their precise content remains unclear and there are presently no international mechanisms to enforce them against NSAs. This makes the national obligations on NSAs, which stem from the regulatory framework created by states, all the more important. These national and international obligations on NSAs in no way detract from or alter the concurrent primary international obligations on states.[201]

A state's regulatory framework applicable to NSAs providing healthcare may comprise legislation including criminal, tort and employment law, which can be enforced by local and/or national criminal and civil courts and other judicial bodies.[202] Such laws may prohibit a private provider from *inter alia* discriminating, committing fraud, negligent or deliberate harm, or exploitation. The states' framework may also comprise regulations regarding permissible medications and treatments, medical standards, marketing or advertising codes, medical costs, and staff training, qualifications, registration and ethics, etc. A NSA may have to report regularly regarding, for example, its patients, medications, staffing, procedures, financial management, and human rights compliance. These regulations may be enforced by specialised regulatory bodies, with conflicts adjudicated by the courts or other quasi-judicial bodies. The regulatory framework may also include contractual obligations upon NSAs who have contracted with the state to provide healthcare. These contracts may prescribe locations for health clinics, the prices and subsidies for care, hours of operation, conditions regarding sub-contractors, and be enforceable by civil courts.

The NSAs may also be required – or may do so independently – to create self-regulation mechanisms with a system of checks and balances,[203] which may include a code of ethics, developing indicators or benchmarks to measure progress and establish accountability, as well as developing a complaints mechanism.[204] Private healthcare providers should also 'engage in a continuing process of dialogue and consultation with the communities they serve ... and involve community groups in decision-making processes and, where appropriate, in service

---

Principles on Business and Human Rights, A/HRC/17/31 (16 June 2011) (Ruggie Principles), Principles 11–15.

[201] McBeth (n. 140), p. 149.
[202] UN ESCR Committee, General Comment No. 24 (n. 59), paras. 14–15.
[203] UN CRC Committee, Report on the Thirty-First Session (n. 131), para. 653(17).
[204] Ibid., para. 653(17)(i)–(v).

4.4 PRIVATISING HUMAN RIGHTS IMPLEMENTATION 155

provision itself',[205] which would help ensure that services are culturally appropriate. NSAs may create internal mechanisms to ensure human rights compliance, and impose similar requirements on their partners, employees, or sub-contractors via contractual agreements. The CRC Committee has called upon all NSAs providing healthcare to comply with the Convention and to ensure their partners comply.[206] Private providers may also subscribe to voluntary codes of conduct in line with international human rights. While these are some possible features of a national regulatory framework for NSAs providing healthcare, the systems will vary depending upon the state in question, the type, size and capacity of the NSA, and local circumstances.

Given the potential for these national obligations imposed by the state to be comprehensive, binding and enforceable, they may suffice to hold NSAs providing healthcare to account. This is how the system of due diligence is to work in theory. On this basis, some argue that there is no utility or added value of also directly obliging or holding NSAs to account under international human rights law. Rodley argues that human rights are the 'concept of rules applicable to the relations between governments and governed', and that extending human rights obligations to NSAs would confuse rights violations with crimes and diminish the special meaning of rights.[207] While such a hierarchy of liability in national and international law appears to provide protection and accountability for both state and NSAs, it is not without practical flaws. For instance, not all states will have adequate regulatory frameworks in place, and, where they do, enforcement may be problematic. States may be unable or unwilling to hold NSAs accountable for violations of their national human rights obligations. It is this potential for an accountability gap at the national level that has prompted critiques of privatisation and calls for extending international human rights obligations to NSAs.

Clearly, there are various weak spots in the current accountability model for human rights violations. First, reliance upon the state as the guardian of human rights falls down when the state lacks the will or capacity to hold NSAs to account. As noted above, the national regulation of NSAs providing healthcare can be onerous and require significant dedication of human and financial resources. Even if a state has adequate

---

[205] Ibid., para. 653(18).
[206] UN CRC Committee, General Comment No. 15 (n. 181), para. 77.
[207] Rodley (n. 39), p. 299–302. Rodley (n. 9), pp. 528–9. See discussion by Fortin (n. 1), pp. 9–10.

measures in place, it may not be able to apply them practically to a large transnational corporation (TNC) potentially registered in a different state. In this situation, a state may not be able to protect against human rights violations by NSAs or hold them to account. Particularly in the modern era of globalisation and neoliberal privatisation to for-profit private actors, relying exclusively on the state to enforce national human rights obligations upon NSAs seems dubious. The paradox is that 'states where human rights protection is most needed are often those least able to enforce them against NSAs, such as TNCs, who possess much desired investment capital or technology'.[208]

Secondly, there is an ongoing debate regarding the classification of victims of human rights violations by states vis-à-vis NSAs. If the state violates an individual's rights, they can be considered a 'lucky' victim under international law as they would have standing to bring an action for remedies directly against the state nationally or before regional or international human rights bodies.[209] In contrast, an individual whose rights were abused by a NSA is not considered to be a victim of a human rights violation and may only have a claim against the NSA under domestic law, which may or may not be successful or enforceable.[210] Importantly, from the perspective of the victim, it is immaterial whether the state or a NSA committed the violation of their rights. Negating the victims of NSAs in this way 'seems cynical and loses sight of the individuals concerned and their experiences'.[211] Traditionalists argue that international human rights law is state-based and should stay that way, while others advocate more progressive approaches to international law that endeavour to better meet the needs of all victims.[212]

On this basis, some contend that direct international human rights obligations on NSAs are necessary to supplement the current indirect ones. This is presented as a potential solution to the lack of state enforcement nationally against NSAs and the resulting accountability gap. Some suggest that international human rights law should be interpreted as currently obliging NSAs, or that international law be specifically amended to create direct obligations on NSAs as well as enforcement

---

[208] Ssenyonjo (n. 6), pp. 121–2; Nowak and Januszewski (n. 30), p. 117.
[209] Carrillo Santarelli (n. 55), p. 2.
[210] Ibid.
[211] Nowak and Januszewski (n. 30), p. 127. See also Eva Brems, *Human Rights: Universality and Diversity* (Nijhoff, 2001), pp. 310–11.
[212] Rodley (n. 9), p. 523.

mechanisms. Santarelli identifies the 'ethical and logical need' to hold NSAs internationally responsible as 'the only way to truly protect human rights'.[213] McBeth submits that international obligations on NSAs are a practical necessity and can be deduced by 'logical implication from the expression of rights as an entitlement to be respected by all'.[214] Some argue that in today's world, 'the orthodoxly narrow' view of states as the only human rights duty-bearers is no longer appropriate.[215] They point to globalisation, TNCs, terrorism and powerful NGOs as indicators that the state-centric system of human rights is increasingly unfit for purpose and must adapt to maintain its relevance.[216]

While these concerns may apply to some types of NSAs like armed groups and TNCs, they are less applicable to social institutions providing healthcare services to their communities. Here again, problems with the catch-all categorisation of NSAs are apparent. A traditional healer or a family group providing healthcare are less threatening to the system of international human rights protection than TNCs. Compared to other NSAs, social institutions are well suited to indirect obligations via state regulation and enforcement without necessitating recourse to the international level. Given that they are closely connected to local culture, values and tradition, the state is better placed to regulate social institutions such as kinship groups, women's associations and traditional healers. However, problems may arise where the state is weak or has not yet established a regulatory framework for NSAs. In such situations the state will be liable internationally for its failings, but leaving limited protection for victims nationally. Where the state is unable to adequately regulate NSAs like social institutions, a better solution than direct international human rights obligations would be to utilise international cooperation to assist those states in creating and implementing regulatory frameworks via knowledge and technology transfer and by providing support to regulatory bodies.

Directly applying international human rights obligations on actors like some social institutions could be seen as unnecessarily diminishing the role of the state in human rights protection, shifting focus and diluting

---

[213] Carrillo Santarelli (n. 55), pp. 3, 6, 8.
[214] McBeth (n. 140), p. 144.
[215] Nowak and Januszewski (n. 30), p. 118; Alston (n. 4), p. 4.
[216] Nowak and Januszewski (n. 30), p. 124; Ssenyonjo (n. 6), p. 134; Alston (n. 4), p. 19; Clapham (n. 4), p. 32; Radhika Coomaraswamy, The Contemporary Challenges to International Human Rights, in Scott Sheeran and Sir Nigel Rodley (eds.), *Routledge Handbook of International Human Rights Law* (Routledge, 2013), p. 139.

authority. One of the central arguments against direct obligations for NSAs is that states may then defer to NSAs, diminishing the pre-existing state obligations and accountability mechanisms.[217] However, where states' national 'regulatory solutions do not deliver, international law may well be the default option'.[218] Now more than ever, momentum is growing for creating international obligations on NSAs, mainly in the sphere of business and human rights. Proposals include extending international criminal law to cover corporate criminal liability, expanding universal jurisdiction before domestic courts, and creating a new treaty or World Court of Human Rights with jurisdiction over states and other entities. Proposals that will improve the practical enjoyment of human rights around the world and effectively repair victims should be welcomed. For Rodley, human rights were special concepts in the relationship between the governed and the Government. However, it is submitted that what makes human rights special is not this relationship, but rather their foundation on human dignity and inalienable character for everyone simply by being human.

4.4.4 Privatising Rights Implementation: A Delicate Balance

The private provision of human rights related services such as healthcare and other 'state functions' has occurred around the world for centuries and continues today. In some situations there may be a long history of social institutions providing such services, with the state traditionally not playing a role. In other situations, private actors such as companies may have more recently taken over service provision as part of neoliberal privatisation. Both situations demonstrate the important and ongoing role of NSAs in implementing the right to health. Through their work, NSAs can improve the efficacy of services and contribute to the quality, accessibility, availability and acceptability of healthcare. Private actors may be involved to varying degrees and for a variety of reasons, including for profit, to care for family members, to promote or pursue religious aims, or charitable purposes. While there are vociferous debates regarding the merits of privatisation, consensus exists that states are permitted under international law to employ NSAs in the domestic implemention of human rights. Not only are states permitted to involve

---

[217] Ssenyonjo (n. 6), p. 110.
[218] Ryngaert (n. 6), p. 193.

4.4 PRIVATISING HUMAN RIGHTS IMPLEMENTATION

NSAs, they are in fact obliged to facilitate their participation, particularly in relation to the right to health. In this way, NSAs can play a role in human rights implementation, despite the state-centric nature of international human rights law.

Notwithstanding the role of NSAs in implementing healthcare, states maintain their obligations under international law and do not outsource or transfer them to NSAs. In this way, 'the buck continues to stop with the state'.[219] This is the case under international human rights law regardless of whether a public or private actor is implementing the human rights domestically. However, where private actors are delivering healthcare, the focus of the state's international obligations shifts from fulfilling rights to protecting against violations by NSAs. These due diligence obligations require states to regulate, monitor and supervise the work of NSAs, as well as to investigate, punish and provide remedies for any violations. Given the vague formulations and lack of enforcement mechanisms for NSAs' international responsibilities, national obligations are important supplements. However, these can be onerous obligations for states, requiring significant resources and expertise. Nevertheless, states will be held responsible internationally for the failure to regulate and hold NSAs accountable. While the treaty bodies have already begun adapting their focus to address the role and regulation of NSAs, more could be done to articulate the international obligations and expectations on states as well as the responsibilities of NSAs.

While the private provision of human rights related services such as healthcare clearly raises a number of legal issues, it is also a matter of policy. Some contend that while states are permitted to use NSAs to implement rights, they should not do so as it may undermine human rights as well as the state's own responsibility. For example, while private initiatives supporting rights are to be welcomed, the state should not hide behind or defer to private actors.[220] The present study makes clear that the state retains a strong role and extensive duties when NSAs are providing rights related services. While states have discretion to rely upon NSAs in this way, their involvement does not displace or relieve the state of any of its obligations. The state cannot *hide* behind NSAs, but rather must *stand* behind them, facilitating and regulating their actions, as well as filling any gaps. Ultimately, the question of whether or how

---

[219] McBeth (n. 140), p. 152.
[220] Clapham (n. 4), p. 73.

much a state involves NSAs is a normative or political question, and, given the pros and cons, a smart mix of both may be preferable.[221] Mixes such as public–private partnerships can bring human rights closer to the public, engaging various actors in society in meaningful ways, and promoting bottom-up support for rights. As such, even if states can implement human rights independently, they should collaborate with NSAs like social institutions in order to reap the social benefits.

4.5 Conclusions: Public and Private Actors in Domestic Implementation

Despite the state-centricity of international law, human rights are influenced by and dependent upon a multiplicity of actors far beyond the state. These NSAs play a compelling and multifaceted role in human rights, both historically and increasingly in today's polycentric world. Indeed, there is a much 'closer relationship between international law and the actions of non-State actors than the traditional dichotomy of national and international law suggests'.[222] Better recognising the actual practice and interaction of NSAs with human rights involves challenging the 'one-dimensional, state-centric paradigm of international human rights law' and revealing states' omnipotence as a mere theoretical construction.[223] In fact, as originally conceived of in the UDHR, human rights were never intended to be the sole domain of states, but rather every organ of society. The UDHR envisaged rights being implemented and upheld both between people horizontally as well as vertically by governing bodies. This initial broad stance was narrowed in the subsequent international human rights treaties, which cast the state as central protagonist. Since then, NSAs have not been formally recognised as duty-bearers in international law, which directly obliges states but only indirectly NSAs. An-Na'im accuses the treaties of having 'hijacked' human rights by rendering them state-centric.[224]

---

[221] Ryngaert (n. 6), pp. 191, 193.
[222] Elizabeth Kirk, Kirsty Sherlock and Alison Reeves, SUDS Law: Non-State Actors and the Haphazard Route to Implementation of International Obligations (2004) *Non-State Actors and International Law* 4, pp. 108–9.
[223] Nowak and Januszewski (n. 30), p. 137.
[224] Abdullahi Ahmed An-Na'im, The Spirit of Laws Is Not Universal: Alternatives to the Enforcement Paradigm for Human Rights (2016) *Tilburg Law Review* 21, p. 274.

Despite the treaties' nominal attention to NSAs, the treaty bodies have taken a progressive approach and elaborated upon their role, responsibilities, and also participatory rights. In their practical work with states and stakeholders in supervising domestic implementation, the treaty bodies were arguably confronted by the irrefutable role and impact of NSAs. As such, they recognised a deficiency of the human rights treaties in essentially erasing NSAs, and sought to ameliorate it by articulating responsibilities. While NSAs have responsibilities under international human rights law, they are not the same as the direct treaty obligations upon states parties. Notwithstanding repeated confirmation by the United Nations and the treaty bodies of the human rights responsibilities on NSAs, they are comparatively ill-defined, of ambiguous sources and lacking in enforcement mechanisms. As such, it is unclear what is expected of NSAs regarding human rights, what actions may be considered a breach of their responsibilities, and any consequences thereof. It is equally unclear what international obligations states have to engage with and facilitate NSAs in fulfilling their responsibilities, or to reprimand them for any failures.

It is, however, clear that states parties may use NSAs to domestically implement their international human rights obligations. While this is not uncontentious and is highly debated from a policy perspective, states may outsource implementation measures as part of their discretion under international law. While states are permitted to outsource implementation to NSAs, they cannot outsource their obligations, which they retain under international law. The duty of due diligence obliges states to establish regulatory frameworks to monitor and supervise the activities of NSAs, as well as to investigate and punish any rights violations. Such regulatory frameworks can be complex and burdensome for states, and failure in this due diligence duty can give rise to a state's international liability. While there is valid concern regarding the role of some NSAs, most of the concerns and critiques regarding privatisation and accountability gaps are less relevant to social institutions, which are typically well-suited and susceptible to state regulation. Where NSAs' involvement promotes the accessibility, acceptability, availability, and quality of healthcare, they should be welcomed.

For example, family groups, traditional healers and religious organisations have long provided healthcare in communities all around the world. These actors enjoy legitimacy and relative authority, sometimes in ways and areas where the state does not, which can make them effective in implementation and building bottom-up support for rights. Harnessing human rights to such domestic forces will help ensure their realisation.[225] As established in Chapter 3, the treaties and treaty bodies all require the effectiveness of implementation measures, so where NSAs like some social institutions can be effective, states should engage them. In fact, states are obliged to foster civil society and other actors, to consult with the public and ensure their participation in decision-making, and to facilitate NSAs' discharge of their responsibilities. The fact that states experience difficulties in regulating NSAs should not mean that their potential contribution to human rights implementation should be foregone. The aim should be both to facilitate the role of NSAs in implementation, as well as developing and enhancing states' ability to regulate that role.

The UN treaty bodies have already begun to focus on this issue in their supervision of states' domestic implementation of the treaties. This could, however, be enhanced by providing guidance to states parties on engaging with NSAs to fulfil their human rights responsibilities, and not just focusing on NSAs as potential violators and states as enforcers. The treaty bodies could contribute to articulating the international rights and responsibilities on 'every organ of society', as well as clarifying the corresponding obligations on states. This could be done by the treaty bodies, for example, in a General Comment addressing the role and responsibility of various NSAs within the scope of their mandates. Of course, the articulation of NSAs' rights and responsibilities in a General Comment would not be binding and the treaty bodies would not be able to enforce them directly against NSAs. Rather, the purpose would be to assist states in their engagement with, and facilitation and regulation of, NSAs in implementing their human rights obligations, and to guide NSAs in the fulfilment of their responsibilities. This could also be taken up by the treaty bodies in their Concluding Observations to states parties.

Finally, while the binds that keep international law moored to the state may be loosening, the present proposition challenges state-centricity in human rights implementation, but not necessarily the state-centricity of international law. While NSAs like social institutions can be involved in implementing states' human rights obligations and fulfilling their own responsibilities, the state stands behind them and remains ultimately accountable for them. As such, no law reform measures are required in order to enable social institutions to participate in human rights

---

[225] Heyns and Viljoen (n. 2), p. 488.

implementation. Current international law is sufficient in both permitting as well as promoting the involvement of social institutions in implementation. The purpose of this chapter was to contribute to the non-state counter-narrative in human rights by demonstrating this pre-existing scope in international law for the role of social institutions in implementing rights. While theoretically possible and permissible under international law, it remains to be seen how the role of social institutions in domestic implementation may function practically. Therefore, the following chapter examines this issue in a qualitative case study.

5

Role of Islamic Law and Institutions in Implementing Women's Right to Family Planning in Indonesia

5.1 Introduction

As demonstrated, culture is a key element in human rights conceptualisation and realisation via implementation. Rather than requiring uniformity, international human rights law accommodates cultural diversity in various ways, including in domestic implementation. The treaties empower states parties to use a host of 'other measures' to implement human rights obligations and to involve non-state actors therein. Non-state actors and norms, including many social institutions, can be instrumentalised to implement rights domestically alongside or in place of measures by state institutions. While the analysis up to this point in the book has been largely theoretical and focused on the legal framework, this chapter presents a case study to analyse the way in which social institutions can contribute to human rights implementation in practice. Such an empirical case study is necessary in order to assess culturally sensitive approaches to human rights implementation in context. While only articulated generally at the international level, international law 'accomplishes its ends under particular conditions'.[1] The aim of the study is therefore to reveal the complexities of human rights implementation in context and the role of social institutions therein.

As explained in the book's introduction, the selected case study explores how women's right to family planning in Indonesia can be implemented via the social institutions of Islamic laws and institutions.[2]

---

[1] Gregory Shaffer and Tom Ginsburg, The Empirical Turn in International Legal Scholarship (2012) *American Journal of International Law* 106:1, p. 1.

[2] Select parts of this case study were published as Julie Fraser, In Search of New Narratives: The Role of Cultural Norms and Actors in Addressing Human Rights Contestation, in Rosemarie Buikema, Antoine Buyse and Antonius Robben (eds.), *Cultures, Citizenship and Human Rights* (Routledge, 2019); Julie Fraser, Challenging State-Centricity and Legalism: Promoting the Role of Social Institutions in the Domestic Implementation of International Human Rights Law (2019) *International Journal of Human Rights* 23:6.

5.1 INTRODUCTION

Islam was deemed an important social institution to focus on as it is the fastest growing religion today, due soon to overtake Christianity as the world's largest. In fact, many states are experiencing a sort of religious revival, with studies showing a relative increase of religiosity among populations.[3] One scholar has claimed that the pertinent 'question of the twenty-first century may very well be religion, particularly Islam'.[4] Indonesia is the fourth largest country in the world, and has the largest Muslim population. It also has strong Islamic institutions that boast huge memberships, with operations impacting upon numerous human rights. Women's rights continue to be some of the most contentious human rights, and are commonly invoked as the quintessential example of the conflict between rights and culture – including Islam. Within the category of women's rights, reproductive rights are simultaneously some of the most sensitive and most important for a woman to be able to enjoy all of her human rights. While all rights are interdependent and indivisible,[5] reproductive rights are particularly crucial as, without reproductive choice, all other rights 'have only limited power to advance the well-being of women'.[6] Despite reproductive rights including issues like child marriage, domestic violence and polygamy, family planning was chosen for the case study due to the focus given to it in Indonesia by local, national and international organisations.

---

[3] Pew Research Centre, Michael Lipka and David Mcclendon, Why People with No Religion Are Projected to Decline as a Share of the World's Population (7 April 2017), www.pewresearch.org/fact-tank/2017/04/07/why-people-with-no-religion-are-projected-to-decline-as-a-share-of-the-worlds-population/ (accessed 27 August 2018); Pew Research Centre, The Future of World Religions: Population Growth Projections, 2010–2050 (2 April 2015), www.pewforum.org/2015/04/02/religious-projections-2010-2050/ (accessed 1 February 2019).

[4] Mohammad H. Fadel, Public Reason as a Strategy for Principled Reconciliation: The Case of Islamic Law and International Human Rights Law (2007) *Chicago Journal of International Law* 8:1, p. 1.

[5] Reproductive rights relate to other human rights, such as the right to life, education, work, sanitation and water, marry and found a family, privacy, security of person, freedom from torture, cruel and inhuman or degrading treatment, and non-discrimination. UN ESCR Committee, General Comment No. 22 on the Right to Sexual and Reproductive Health, E/C.12/GC/22 (2 May 2016), paras. 9–10; Rebecca Cook and Mahmoud Fathalla, Advancing Reproductive Rights beyond Cairo and Beijing (September 1996) *International Family Planning Perspectives* 22:3, p. 116.

[6] Carmel Shalev, Rights to Sexual and Reproductive Health: The ICPD and the Convention on the Elimination of All Forms of Discrimination against Women (2000) *Health and Human Rights* 4:2, p. 59; UN ESCR Committee, General Comment No. 14: The Right to the Highest Attainable Standard of Health, E/C.12/2000/4 (11 August 2000), para. 25.

The Indonesian Government's campaigns regarding family planning and reproductive health more broadly have a long history. While Indonesia has ratified several international human rights treaties that guarantee the right to reproductive health, including the *International Covenant on Economic, Social and Cultural Rights* (ICESCR) and the *Convention on the Elimination of All Forms of Discrimination against Women* (CEDAW),[7] its engagement with the topic pre-dates these treaties. The Government has long sought to promote reproductive health, having instituted a national family planning programme and now providing universal healthcare coverage. These measures were taken over a fifty-year period in order to address the serious reproductive health issues in Indonesia. For example, Indonesia's maternal mortality rate is one of the highest in the Association of Southeast Asian Nations (ASEAN) region and has been slow to improve.[8] Women and girls in Indonesia face numerous obstacles to reproductive health including taboos around sex, marriage and reproduction, as well as gendered stereotypes and decision-making norms. On the basis of persistent issues over several decades, the Government has made women's reproductive health one of its top priorities, and President Widodo recently called to revive the national family planning programme.[9]

Despite these intentions, the Indonesian Government (like many) suffers certain limitations in its ability to implement reproductive rights in practice. Due to factors including governmental decentralisation, diverse cultural norms and strong religious beliefs, the Indonesian state is not necessarily the locus of authority and is curtailed in its reach and

---

[7] *International Covenant on Economic, Social and Cultural Rights* (adopted 16 December 1966, entered into force 3 January 1967), 993 UNTS 3; *Convention on the Elimination of All Forms of Discrimination against Women* (adopted 18 December 1979, entered into force 3 September 1981), 1249 UNTS 13.

[8] UN CEDAW Committee, Consideration of reports submitted by States parties under article 18 of the Convention on the Elimination of All Forms of Discrimination against Women, Combined sixth and seventh periodic reports of States parties: Indonesia, CEDAW/C/IDN/6-7 (7 January 2011), para. 136; UN Human Rights Council, Report of the Special Rapporteur on the right of everyone to the enjoyment of the highest attainable standard of physical and mental health on his mission to Indonesia, A/HRC/38/36/Add.1 (5 April 2018), para. 68.

[9] UN ESCR Committee, Consideration of reports: reports submitted by states parties in accordance with articles 16 and 17 of the Covenant, List of issues in relation to the initial report of Indonesia, Addendum, Replies of Indonesia to the list of issues, E/C.12/IDN/Q/1/Add.1 (17 April 2014), para. 158; UN Human Rights Council, National report submitted in accordance with para. 5 of the annex to Human Rights Council res. 16/21: Indonesia, A/HRC/WG.6/27/IDN/1 (20 February 2017), paras. 57-8.

influence. This is especially the case when state laws or policies are seen by those to whom they are to apply as contrary to Islam. In such circumstances, the state can be perceived as an illegitimate outsider to be rejected rather than as a respected authority to be followed. For example, despite the Government's promotion and provision of family planning, Muslims have typically not accepted contraceptives unless they are endorsed by local Islamic leaders. Given this strong normative role, Islam can be seen as highly influential and a key factor in implementing reproductive rights in Indonesia. This influence can both promote or preclude women's enjoyment of their reproductive rights and access to family planning. This chapter explores Islam's normative influence in Indonesia and the role of Muslim actors in the national family planning programme.

5.1.1 Research Design and Structure

The purpose of the case study is to understand to what extent Islamic law and institutions act as a social resource for implementing the right to family planning in Indonesia. The method employed was traditional legal research complemented by qualitative social science methodology. The desk research comprised document analysis of international law, national Indonesian law, Islamic law and literature. This included the state reports submitted by Indonesia to the UN treaty bodies, as well as the treaty bodies' Concluding Observations in response, Universal Periodic Review reports and reports by UN agencies including the UN Population Fund (UNFPA) and the World Health Organization (WHO). The research was multidisciplinary in that, in addition to law, the research consulted literature from political science, gender and religious studies, anthropology, demographics and health. Semi-structured interviews were conducted in Indonesia to complement the desk research and triangulate the findings. Such socio-legal methodological approaches help to unveil 'how, where and under what conditions norm change takes place'.[10] Interviewees included Indonesian Government officials, civil society representatives, Islamic scholars, leaders and members of Islamic institutions, representatives of international organisations, and academics.

---

[10] Sally Engle Merry, International Law and Sociolegal Scholarship: Toward a Spatial Global Legal Pluralism, in Michael A. Helfand (ed.), *Negotiating State and Non-State Law: The Challenge of Global and Local Legal Pluralism* (Cambridge University Press, 2016), p. 66.

The chapter proceeds in three main parts following this introduction. The second section sets out Indonesia's international human rights law obligations regarding the right to health and specifically reproductive rights. It draws from various international as well as regional instruments ratified by Indonesia. It then sets out how these provisions have been implemented in Indonesian law, policy and practice, with a focus on the socio-cultural determinants impacting upon the realisation of reproductive health. The third part examines Islamic law and institutions in Indonesia and the various roles that they have played in the national family planning programme over the last fifty years. In terms of promoting women's rights, Muslim actors have issued religious rulings (*fatwas*) on reproductive health, advocated reform to promote women's rights, and provided reproductive healthcare services to the public. The fourth section of the chapter considers to what extent this approach to implementing family planning aligns with the framework of international human rights law. This assessment involves a critical examination of how the UN treaty bodies have addressed the role of Islamic law and institutions in Indonesia. The chapter concludes by reflecting more broadly on the role of social institutions in implementing states parties' human rights treaty obligations.

5.2 Right to Reproductive Health under International Law and in Indonesia

The right to health encompasses many aspects and is one of the most complex of international human rights.[11] The right was first articulated internationally by the WHO in 1946, with its Constitution providing that the 'enjoyment of the highest attainable standard of health is one of the fundamental rights of every human being'.[12] It was subsequently included in the 1948 *Universal Declaration of Human Rights* and is legally protected in several international instruments, including

---

[11] UN Human Rights Council, Report of the Special Rapporteur on the right of everyone to the enjoyment of the highest attainable standard of physical and mental health, Paul Hunt, A/HRC/4/28 (17 January 2007), para. 24.

[12] Preamble to the *Constitution of the World Health Organization* (WHO) as adopted by the International Health Conference, New York, 19 June–22 July 1946 (adopted on 22 July 1946 and entered into force 7 April 1948).

article 12 ICESCR, article 12 CEDAW and article 24 *Convention on the Rights of the Child* (CRC).[13] The right is also protected regionally: for example, article 29(1) of the 2012 *ASEAN Human Rights Declaration* guarantees the right of every person 'to the enjoyment of the highest attainable standard of physical, mental and reproductive health, to basic and affordable health-care services, and to have access to medical facilities'.[14] While the ASEAN Declaration specifically references reproductive rights, such rights have been interpreted as being protected as part of the right to health in ICESCR. However, CEDAW and the CRC, respectively adopted thirteen and twenty-three years after the ICESCR, also explicitly protect reproductive rights.

The right to health has been elaborated upon by the UN treaty bodies, Special Rapporteurs, as well as specialised agencies including the WHO and UNFPA. Reproductive health was the focus of the 1994 International Conference on Population and Development (ICPD) in Cairo, and the follow-up 1995 conference in Beijing, which greatly advanced the understanding and scope of reproductive rights. Part of the complexity of the right to health arises from the numerous and interconnected underlying determinants. These include factors like access to adequate food, to clean water and sanitation, but also broader economic and socio-cultural

---

[13] Universal Declaration of Human Rights (adopted 10 December 1948), UNGA Res. 217 A(III) (UDHR), art. 25(1); *Convention on the Rights of the Child* (adopted 20 November 1989, entered into force 2 September 1990), 1577 UNTS 3. See also *Convention on the Elimination of All Forms of Racial Discrimination* (adopted 21 December 1965, entered into force 4 January 1969), 660 UNTS 195 (CERD), art. 5(e)(iv); *Convention on the Rights of Persons with Disabilities* (adopted 13 December 2006, entered into force 3 May 2008), 2515 UNTS 3 (CPRD), art. 25. The right to health is protected in several other international and regional documents; see further UN Office of the High Commissioner for Human Rights, International Standards Right to Health, www.ohchr.org/EN/Issues/Health/Pages/InternationalStandards.aspx (accessed 1 November 2017). Clapham and Rubio consider whether the right to health has become part of customary international law: Andrew Clapham and Mariano Garcia Rubio, The Obligations of States with Regard to Non-State Actors in the Context of the Right to Health (2002) *Health and Human Rights Working Paper Series* No. 3, pp. 22–30.

[14] Association of Southeast Asian Nations (ASEAN) Human Rights Declaration (18 November 2012), art. 29(1). Other regional instruments also protect right to health: *African Charter on Human and Peoples' Rights* (Banjul Charter) (adopted 27 June 1981, entered into force 21 October 1986), 1520 UNTS 217, art. 16; *European Social Charter* (adopted 3 May 1996, entered into force 1 July 1999), ETS No. 163, art. 11; *Additional Protocol to the American Convention on Human Rights in the Area of Economic, Social, and Cultural Rights* (Protocol of San Salvador) (adopted 17 November 1988, entered into force 16 November 1999), OAS Treaty Series No. 69, art. 10.

factors, like gender and poverty.[15] These socio-cultural determinants of health have typically received less attention than the other health determinants. After setting out the international obligations regarding reproductive rights, this section examines how they have been implemented in Indonesia. It focuses on Indonesia's family planning programme, exploring its history, successes and contemporary challenges. The analysis addresses particularly the socio-cultural determinants of reproductive health in Indonesia, such as how Islam and women's position in society impact upon access to family planning goods and services.[16]

5.2.1 Reproductive Health and the Right to Family Planning under International Law

According to article 12(1) ICESCR, the right to health is the right of everyone to the enjoyment of the highest attainable standard of physical and mental health. Rather than a right to be healthy, the ESCR Committee interpreted it 'as a right to the enjoyment of a variety of facilities, goods, services and conditions necessary for the realization of the highest attainable standard of health'.[17] As such, the right to health comprises several interconnected and complex aspects, and can be understood as the right to a health system that creates the conditions for everyone to enjoy the highest attainable standard of health.[18] This acknowledges that ensuring the right to health is more than just providing health services, and that a wide variety of socio-economic factors impact health.[19]

---

[15] Brigit Toebes, *The Right to Health as a Human Right in International Law* (Intersentia, 1999), p. 260; UN ESCR Committee, General Comment No. 22 on the Right to Sexual and Reproductive Health, E/C.12/GC/22 (2 May 2016), paras. 2, 7 and 8.

[16] It is beyond the scope of this chapter to give a full analysis of the right to health. For detailed analysis, see Ben Saul, David Kinley and Jacqueline Mowbray, *The International Covenant on Economic, Social and Cultural Rights: Commentary, Cases, and Materials* (Oxford University Press, 2014), pp. 977–1083.

[17] UN ESCR Committee, General Comment No. 14: The Right to the Highest Attainable Standard of Health, E/C.12/2000/4 (11 August 2000), para. 9.

[18] See ICESCR, art. 12.2(d); UN ESCR Committee, General Comment No. 14 (n. 17), para. 8; UN Human Rights Commission, Report of the Special Rapporteur on the right of everyone to the enjoyment of the highest attainable standard of physical and mental health, Paul Hunt, E/CN.4/2006/48 (3 March 2006), para. 4.

[19] Saul, Kinley and Mowbray (n. 16), p. 985. See also UN General Assembly, Report of the Special Rapporteur on Health, A/62/214 (8 August 2007), paras. 45–8; UN CRC Committee, General Comment No. 15 on the Right of the Child to the Enjoyment of the Highest Attainable Standard of Health (art. 24), CRC/C/GC/15 (17 April 2013), paras. 16–18.

5.2 RIGHT TO REPRODUCTIVE HEALTH IN INDONESIA

To meet their obligations under article 2(1) ICESCR, states parties must employ 'all appropriate means' to realise the right to health. This includes the obligation to respect, by refraining from interfering directly or indirectly with the right to health, and the obligation to protect, including regulating third parties to prevent them violating the right of others.[20] The obligation to fulfil requires states 'adopt appropriate legislative, administrative, budgetary, judicial, promotional, and other measures towards the full realization of the right to health'.[21]

The ICESCR obliges states parties to implement the right to health via various complementary approaches, including laws, community consultation, action plans and international cooperation.[22] While the ECSR Committee has a preference for legislative implementation as seen in Chapter 3,[23] it also recognises the importance of other measures, including educational and social measures.[24] Furthermore, the right is subject to progressive realisation, which means that different standards will apply over time. While some aspects of the right to health – its core content – are immediate obligations, in relation to other aspects states must rather show that they are continuously making all efforts, within the available resources, to better realise the right.[25] Making and measuring progress should be part of a state's

---

[20] UN ESCR Committee, General Comment No. 14 (n. 17), paras. 33-7, 50-2; UN ESCR Committee, General Comment No. 22 (n. 15), paras. 40-4, 56-60.

[21] UN ESCR Committee, General Comment No. 14 (n. 17), paras. 33, 36-7, 52; UN ESCR Committee, General Comment No. 22 (n. 15), paras. 45-8, 61-3; UN CEDAW Committee, General Recommendation No. 24, Women and Health (article 12) A/54/38/Rev.1, chap. I (1999), para. 17.

[22] UN ESCR Committee, General Comment No. 14 (n. 17), para. 1.

[23] As has the Special Rapporteur on the right to health, see UN GA Human Rights Council, Report of the Special Rapporteur on the right of everyone to the enjoyment of the highest attainable standard of physical and mental health, Paul Hunt, A/HRC/7/11 (31 January 2008), para. 105: 'First, the right to the highest attainable standard of health should be recognized in national law. This is very important because such recognition gives rise to legal accountability for those with responsibilities for health systems ... It should be recognized in the national law of all States'.

[24] UN ESCR Committee, General Comment No. 14 (n. 17), para. 33; UN ESCR Committee, General Comment No. 3: The Nature of States Parties Obligations, E/1991/23 (14 December 1990), paras. 4, 7.

[25] However, the Special Rapporteur has noted that 'progressive realization does not mean that a State is free to choose whatever measures it wishes to take so long as they reflect some degree of progress. A State has a duty to adopt those measures that are most effective, while taking into account resource availability and other human rights considerations'. UN GA Human Rights Council, Report of the Special Rapporteur, Paul Hunt, A/HRC/7/11 (n. 23), para. 50.

health plan, which should contain benchmarks and indicators to measure progress and hold states accountable.[26] The ESCR Committee has set out the minimum core obligations on states parties regarding the right to health.[27] These immediate obligations include that states' health systems have a comprehensive national plan, a minimum 'basket' of health-related services and facilities, and ensure public participation and cultural appropriateness.[28] Core health obligations on states parties include reproductive health.[29]

Reproductive health was defined at the 1994 ICPD in Cairo as 'a state of complete physical, mental and social well-being and not merely the absence of disease or infirmity, in all matters relating to the reproductive system and to its functions and processes'.[30] Belonging to both men and women, reproductive rights cover a wide range of issues including the right to be informed about 'and to have access to safe, effective, affordable and acceptable methods of family planning of their choice'.[31] Family planning is not a new phenomenon, with traditional methods of contraception including withdrawal (*coitus interruptus*), fertility awareness and timing (rhythm method), and traditional medicines. Modern contraceptives include medical sterilisation, hormonal pills or implants, intrauterine devices (IUDs), diaphragms and condoms. Importantly, however, the 'Cairo Paradigm' shifted the focus of population programmes away from fertility regulation and towards a concept of reproductive rights.[32]

---

[26] UN ESCR Committee, General Comment No. 14 (n. 17), paras. 57–8; Paul Hunt and Gillian MacNaughton, A Human Rights-Based Approach to Health Indicators, in Mashood Baderin and Robert McCorquodale (eds.), *Economic, Social and Cultural Rights in Action* (Oxford University Press, 2007), p. 308.

[27] UN ESCR Committee, General Comment No. 14 (n. 17), paras. 43–5; UN ESCR Committee, General Comment No. 22 (n. 15), para. 49.

[28] UN GA Human Rights Council, Report of the Special Rapporteur, Paul Hunt, A/HRC/7/11 (n. 23), para. 66; UN ESCR Committee, General Comment No. 14 (n. 17), paras. 43–5.

[29] UN ESCR Committee, General Comment No. 14 (n. 17), para. 44(a).

[30] Programme of Action, adopted at the International Conference on Population and Development, Cairo (5–13 September 1994), www.unfpa.org/sites/default/files/event-pdf/PoA_en.pdf (para. 7.2) (accessed 2 November 2017) (Cairo Programme of Action); Beijing Declaration and Platform for Action, adopted at the Fourth World Conference on Women (4–15 September 1995), www.un.org/womenwatch/daw/beijing/pdf/Beijing%20full%20report%20E.pdf (para. 94) (accessed 2 November 2017) (Beijing Declaration and Platform for Action).

[31] Ibid.

[32] Mindy Jane Roseman and Laura Reichenbach, Global Reproduction Health and Rights: Reflecting on ICPD, in Mindy Jane Roseman and Laura Reichenbach (eds.), *Reproductive Health and Human Rights: The Way Forward* (University of Pennsylvania Press, 2009), p. 4. See also Beijing Declaration and Platform for Action (n. 31), para. 17.

5.2 RIGHT TO REPRODUCTIVE HEALTH IN INDONESIA 173

The right to information as well as choice of contraceptive methods are important aspects of the right to reproductive health. Generally, reproductive rights:

> rest on the recognition of the basic right of all couples and individuals to decide freely and responsibly the number, spacing and timing of their children and to have the information and means to do so, and the right to attain the highest standard of sexual and reproductive health.[33]

While article 24 CRC protects children's right to health, including family planning education and services,[34] CEDAW most comprehensively sets out the right to reproductive health. Rather than simply duplicating the right to health as enshrined in ICESCR, CEDAW's protections are more elaborate and relate specifically to women's particular needs in reproductive healthcare and to addressing discrimination. First, article 10(h) provides that states must ensure women's equal rights with men regarding education and ensure '[a]ccess to specific educational information to help to ensure the health and well-being of families, including information and advice on family planning'.[35] Article 12(1) obliges states to 'take all appropriate measures to eliminate discrimination against women in the field of health care in order to ensure, on a basis of equality of men and women, access to health care services, including those related to family planning'. Article 14(2)(b) requires states to specifically protect the reproductive rights of rural women. Finally, article 16(1)(e) provides that states must ensure that men and women have '[t]he same rights to decide freely and responsibly on the number and spacing of their children and to have access to the information, education and means to enable them to exercise these rights'.

While both men and women have reproductive rights, such rights are especially important for women due to socio-cultural and biological differences. Studies have shown that women's poor reproductive health is directly correlated to gender discrimination.[36] Empowering women

---

[33] Cairo Programme of Action (n. 30), para. 7.3.
[34] CRC, art. 24(2)(d) and (f). See generally UN CRC Committee, General Comment No. 15 (n. 19).
[35] Similarly, regarding discrimination in employment, CEDAW, art. 11(1)(f) requires states to provide women: '[t]he right to protection of health and to safety in working conditions, including the safeguarding of the function of reproduction', and art. 11(2) goes on to further detail provisions regarding maternity and work, including childcare facilities.
[36] Roseman and Reichenbach (n. 32), p. 10.

and promoting their equal status in society is therefore key to improving reproductive health. CEDAW requires states parties to take 'all appropriate measures' in all fields (including political, economic, social and cultural fields) to ensure women's full development and advancement.[37] Such measures can be complicated and far-reaching. For example, states must 'address the social determinants as manifested in laws, institutional arrangements and social practices that prevent individuals from effectively enjoying in practice their sexual and reproductive health'.[38] States must take measures to rectify 'entrenched social norms and power structures that impair the equal exercise' of reproductive rights, such as gender-based stereotypes positioning men as the head of the household and women in subordinate roles as caregivers and mothers.[39] States must eradicate all social barriers including misconceptions, prejudices and taboos surrounding menstruation, pregnancy, delivery and fertility.[40]

Family Planning: Available, Accessible, Acceptable and Quality

According to the health criteria set out by the ESCR Committee, family planning facilities, goods and services must be available, accessible, acceptable and quality.[41] Quality implies that family planning facilities, goods and services are 'scientifically and medically appropriate and of good quality', which requires *inter alia* skilled medical personnel and up-to-date, scientifically approved medicine and equipment.[42] Such quality facilities, goods and services must be available to the population in sufficient quantity, which is inevitably a question of funding and resources.[43] Family planning facilities, goods and services must be accessible both *de jure* and *de facto* to everyone without discrimination. The ESCR Committee held that accessibility comprises various components. First, accessibility means that clinics need to be geographically accessible,

---

[37] CEDAW, art. 3.
[38] UN ESCR Committee, General Comment No. 22 (n. 15), para. 8. See also paras. 35 and 63.
[39] Ibid., paras. 27, 35.
[40] Ibid., para. 48.
[41] UN ESCR Committee, General Comment No. 14 (n. 17), para. 12; UN ESCR Committee, General Comment No. 22 (n. 15), paras. 12-21; UN CRC Committee, General Comment No. 15 (n. 19), paras. 112-16.
[42] UN ESCR Committee, General Comment No. 14 (n. 17), para. 12(d); UN ESCR Committee, General Comment No. 22 (n. 15), para. 21.
[43] UN ESCR Committee, General Comment No. 14 (n. 17), para. 12(a); Saul, Kinley and Mowbray (n. 16), p. 1002.

5.2 RIGHT TO REPRODUCTIVE HEALTH IN INDONESIA

that is 'within safe physical reach for all sections of the population', especially vulnerable or marginalised groups.[44] Secondly, a key part of accessibility is that health goods and services must be affordable for all.[45] Article 12(2) CEDAW requires that states provide free services relating to pregnancy where necessary, and the CEDAW Committee has encouraged free access to contraceptives.[46] Thirdly, the accessibility of family planning facilities, goods and services 'includes the right to seek, receive and impart information and ideas concerning health issues'.[47] The CRC Committee has held that such services must also be accessible for children and adolescents.[48]

Finally, family planning facilities, goods and services must be acceptable to the relevant population, including that they be acceptable specifically to women and girls, and culturally appropriate. The ESCR Committee interprets 'culturally appropriate' as being 'respectful of the culture of individuals, minorities, peoples and communities'.[49] Special Rapporteur Hunt held that a state's health plan must be 'responsive to national and local priorities' and that the drafting process as well as the ultimate plan must respect cultural difference.[50] States should report on the measures taken to ensure that healthcare services are acceptable to women, meaning that they are delivered in a way that ensures a woman's fully informed consent, respects her dignity, guarantees her

---

[44] UN ESCR Committee, General Comment No. 14 (n. 17), para. 12(b); UN ESCR Committee, General Comment No. 22 (n. 15), para. 16. CEDAW, art. 14(2)(b) specifically relates to the health needs of rural women.

[45] UN ESCR Committee, General Comment No. 14 (n. 17), para. 12(b); UN ESCR Committee, General Comment No. 22 (n. 15), para. 17.

[46] Toebes (n. 15), pp. 146–147. See also UN CRC Committee, General Comment No. 15 (n. 19), para. 94.

[47] UN ESCR Committee, General Comment No. 14 (n. 17), para. 12(b); UN ESCR Committee, General Comment No. 22 (n. 15), paras. 18 and 19.

[48] 'States should ensure that health systems and services are able to meet the specific sexual and reproductive health needs of adolescents, including family planning and safe abortion services.' UN CRC Committee, General Comment No. 15 (n. 19), paras. 56, 69–70.

[49] UN ESCR Committee, General Comment No. 14 (n. 17), para. 12(c). Despite these statements, Donders found no further specification of what 'culturally appropriate' means in practice. Yvonne Donders, Exploring the Cultural Dimension of the Right to the Highest Attainable Standard of Health (2015) *PER* 18:2, p. 197.

[50] UN Human Rights Commission, Report of the Special Rapporteur on the right of everyone to the enjoyment of the highest attainable standard of physical and mental health, Paul Hunt, E/CN.4/2006/48 (3 March 2006), para. 4; UN GA Human Rights Council, Report of the Special Rapporteur on the right of everyone to the enjoyment of the highest attainable standard of physical and mental health, Paul Hunt, A/HRC/7/11 (31 January 2008), para. 44.

confidentiality, and are 'sensitive to her needs and perspectives'.[51] As people have the right to contraceptives of their choice, they should have access to various methods and be able to choose the one acceptable to meet their needs.[52] Reflecting the determinants of health outlined above, these needs may be physical as well as socio-cultural, such as the need to comply with one's religion. When reporting to the CEDAW Committee, states must demonstrate that their:

> health legislation, plans and policies are based on scientific and ethical research and assessment of the health status and needs of women in that country and take into account any ethnic, regional or community variations or practices based on religion, tradition or culture.[53]

As argued in Chapter 2, ensuring cultural sensitivity in the right to health is a matter of principle, but also 'makes sense as a matter of practice'.[54] The cultural appropriateness of healthcare is crucial to its utilisation and effectiveness. While some assume that reproductive health technologies are 'neutral' or 'culture-free' and can be implemented across different societies, this is rarely true.[55] While determinants such as education and economic status are also relevant, a person's socio-cultural background plays a key role in their acceptance and utilisation of healthcare.[56] Whether or not a particular cultural community accepts the family planning methods, procedures and service delivery will impact upon their uptake of contraceptives.[57] As such, health goods and services not tailored to this cultural reality will likely go un- or under-utilised and women's rights unfulfilled. Therefore, health policy and communication should be culturally specific, with interventions reflecting the socio-cultural setting of each location.

---

[51] UN CEDAW Committee, General Recommendation No. 24 (n. 21), para. 22.
[52] UN ESCR Committee, General Comment No. 22 (n. 15), para. 62.
[53] UN CEDAW Committee, General Recommendation No. 24 (n. 21), para. 9.
[54] UN GA Human Rights Council, Report of the Special Rapporteur, Paul Hunt (n. 50), para. 44.
[55] Lisa Wynn, Angel Foster, Aida Rouhana and James Trussell, The Politics of Emergency Contraception in the Arab World: Reflections on Western Assumptions and the Potential Influence of Religious and Social Factors (2005) *Harvard Health Policy Review* 6:1, p. 44.
[56] Dominic Azuh, Oluyemi Fayomi and Lady Ajayi, Socio-Cultural Factors of Gender Roles in Women's Healthcare Utilization in Southwest Nigeria (2015) *Open Journal of Social Sciences* 3, p. 106; UN CRC Committee, General Comment No. 15 (n. 19), para. 30.
[57] BKKBN, UNFPA, USAID, FP2020 Indonesia Country Committee, A rights-based strategy for accelerating access to family planning services to achieve Indonesia's development goals (2015), p. 22.

Assessments of what is culturally appropriate need to be kept up-to-date through public consultation, as such appropriateness may change over time given culture's dynamism.

While states are obliged in this way to accommodate culture, Donders found that most of the comments in the ESCR Committee's Concluding Observations focused primarily – as is typical in human rights discourse – on culture as an *obstacle* to enjoying the right to health.[58] She distinguished between two types of cultural dimensions to the right to health: (1) the need to ensure that health facilities, goods and services are culturally appropriate and (2) the need to protect against cultural beliefs or practices that negatively impact upon the right to health. This latter aspect requires states to eradicate or reform cultural beliefs or practices that are detrimental to health, like FGM/C and early marriage.[59] As advocated in Chapter 2, this reform should be done via a culturally sensitive approach and in close consultation with the relevant community. Seen in this way, the requirement under international human rights law for health facilities, goods and services to be culturally appropriate should not be interpreted as permitting unjustifiable limitations on an individual's right to health.[60] As health determinants, socio-cultural factors can have a significant impact (both positive and negative) on an individual's health, and especially reproductive health as seen below.

Non-State Actors and Reproductive Rights

As seen in Chapter 4, states are accountable as duty-bearers for the right to health under international human rights treaties. However, all members of society have a recognised role to play in implementing and realising the right to health. First, international law provides that the public must be able to participate in all health-related decisions at the

---

[58] Donders (n. 49), pp. 192, 198, 203–4. See generally Sally Engle Merry, Human Rights Law and the Demonization of Culture (and Anthropology Along the Way) (2003) *Political and Legal Anthropology Review* 26:1, pp. 55–76.

[59] Donders, ibid., p. 192. CRC, art. 24(3) provides: 'States Parties shall take all effective and appropriate measures with a view to abolishing traditional practices prejudicial to the health of children'. UN CEDAW Committee and CRC Committee, Joint General Recommendation No. 31 of the Committee on the Elimination of Discrimination against Women/General Comment No. 18 on the Committee on the Rights of the Child on Harmful Practices, CEDAW/C/GC31-CRC/C/GC/18 (14 November 2014); UN ESCR Committee, General Comment No. 22 (n. 15), paras. 49(d), 59.

[60] Merry (n. 58), p. 210; Saul, Kinley and Mowbray (n. 16), pp. 1210–11.

local, national and international levels.[61] Special Rapporteurs have identified active and informed public participation on issues including designing the overall health strategy, policy and its implementation as an entitlement rather than a privilege.[62] CEDAW obliges states to adopt a gender perspective in all policies and programmes impacting women's health and to 'involve women in the planning, implementation and monitoring of such policies and programmes'.[63] Children under the CRC also have the right to be heard and to participate in all health policies and services impacting them.[64] As reiterated by Special Rapporteurs, '[i]nclusive, informed and active community participation' is a vital or essential element of the right to health.[65] Public participation has been called 'the right of rights'[66] and is one of the core minimum, immediate obligations on states parties.[67]

In addition to participatory rights, non-state actors (NSAs) have international responsibilities regarding the right to health as set out in Chapter 4. The ESCR Committee has identified individuals, families, communities, civil society, international organisations and the private sector as bearing such responsibilities.[68] This position is supported by article 29 of the UDHR and the UN GA *Declaration on the Rights and Responsibilities of Individuals, Groups and Organs of Society*, and specifically in relation to health by the *Declaration of Alma-Ata*.[69] In relation to healthcare, NSAs can contribute by providing technical and other

---

[61] UN ESCR Committee, General Comment No. 14 (n. 17), paras. 11, 17, 54; International Conference on Primary Health Care, Declaration of Alma-Ata, Alma-Ata USSR (6–12 September 1978) (Declaration of Alma-Ata), art. 4.
[62] UN GA Human Rights Council, Report of the Special Rapporteur, Paul Hunt (n. 50), para. 41; UN General Assembly, Report of the Special Rapporteur on the right of everyone to the enjoyment of the highest attainable standard of physical and mental health, Anand Grover, A/HRC/17/25 (12 April 2011), para. 51.
[63] UN CEDAW Committee, General Recommendation No. 24 (n. 21), para. 31(a) and (c).
[64] CRC, art. 12; UN CRC Committee, General Comment No. 15 (n. 19), paras. 19 and 101.
[65] UN Human Rights Commission, Report of the Special Rapporteur, Paul Hunt (n. 50), para. 7; UN General Assembly, Report of the Special Rapporteur on the right of everyone to the enjoyment of the highest attainable standard of physical and mental health, Anand Grover, A/69/299 (11 August 2014), para. 33.
[66] Sam Foster Halabi, Participation and the Right to Health: Lessons from Indonesia (2009) *Health and Human Rights* 11:1, p. 49.
[67] UN General Assembly, Report of the Special Rapporteur on the right of everyone to the enjoyment of the highest attainable standard of physical and mental health, Anand Grover, A/HRC/17/25 (12 April 2011), para. 19(b).
[68] UN ESCR Committee, General Comment No. 14 (n. 17), para. 42.
[69] UN General Assembly Resolution 53/144, Declaration on the Right and Responsibility of Individuals, Groups and Organs of Society to Promote and Protect Universally

5.2 RIGHT TO REPRODUCTIVE HEALTH IN INDONESIA 179

expertise, and by communicating the views and interests of the relevant communities.[70] Public–private partnerships in healthcare can be crucial for improving access for patients and ensuring standards of the highest quality.[71] Partnerships involving community and women's groups, civil society and faith-based organisations are essential for improving access (especially for disadvantaged groups) and building community support.[72] Particularly when addressing the social determinants of health, state action must involve civil society, local communities, business and international agencies.[73] Bodies including the WHO, UNICEF, UNDP and World Bank have a role to play,[74] as does the international community.[75] On this basis, states should create institutional arrangements and conditions conducive for all NSAs to discharge their responsibilities vis-à-vis the right to health.[76]

While international human rights law foresees such a role and responsibilities for NSAs, their intervention does not remove states' ultimate accountability under the treaties as seen in Chapter 4. While states are encouraged (and sometimes required) to employ, engage and collaborate with NSAs to protect the right to health, they nonetheless remain accountable to the treaty bodies for violations arising from their acts or omissions. States remain liable for violations by NSAs that they failed to

---

Recognized Human Rights and Fundamental Freedoms, A/RES/53/144 (8 March 1999); Declaration of Alma-Ata, art. 4.

[70] UN General Assembly, Report of the Special Rapporteur on the right of everyone to the enjoyment of the highest attainable standard of physical and mental health, Anand Grover, A/69/299 (11 August 2014), para. 33.
[71] BKKBN, UNFPA, USAID, FP2020 (n. 57), p. 22.
[72] Ibid.
[73] World Health Organization, Final Report of the Commission on Social Determinants of Health, Closing the Gap in a Generation: Health Equity through Action on the Social Determinants of Health (2008), p. 27.
[74] UN ESCR Committee, General Comment No. 14 (n. 17), paras. 64, 65; UN ESCR Committee, General Comment No. 22 (n. 15), para. 53.
[75] International assistance and cooperation is an important aspect of the right to health. States should contribute to health facilities, goods and services in other states, provide aid and ensure attention to health in international agreements and organisations. See ICESCR, arts. 2(1), 11(2), 22, and 23; UN Commission on Human Rights, Report of the Special Rapporteur, Paul Hunt, E/CN.4/2003/58 (13 February 2003), para. 28; UN ESCR Committee, General Comment No. 14 (n. 17), paras. 38–9; UN ESCR Committee, General Comment No. 3: The Nature of States Parties Obligations, E/1991/23 (14 December 1990), paras. 13–14.
[76] UN ESCR Committee, General Comment No. 14 (n. 17), para. 42; UN CRC Committee, General Comment No. 15 (n. 19), para. 6. See further Chapter 4.

prevent, investigate or remedy.[77] According to their due diligence duty, states must monitor the private provision of healthcare to ensure equal access and quality of care.[78] The CEDAW Committee requires states parties to report on various aspects of NSAs' involvement, including how 'private healthcare providers meet their duties to respect women's rights to' healthcare.[79] Concerns have been raised about the global trend towards privatisation in healthcare, which can threaten the 'equitable availability and accessibility of health facilities, goods and services, especially for the poor and other vulnerable or marginalized groups'.[80] While NSAs have both rights to participate and responsibilities to fulfil regarding healthcare, states must ensure that their involvement does not reduce, but rather increases access.

5.2.2 Reproductive Health and the Right to Family Planning in Indonesia

As a state party to ICESCR, CEDAW and CRC, Indonesia is bound internationally by the above provisions regarding the right to reproductive health. According to Indonesian law, all international law becomes part of national law and can be invoked by judges.[81] In addition, Indonesia has domestically incorporated international human rights provisions into its 1945 Constitution, national legislation and policies.

---

[77] UN ESCR Committee, General Comment No. 14 (n. 17), para. 51; UN CEDAW Committee, General Recommendation No. 24 (n. 21), paras. 15, 17. See further Chapter 4 at Sections 4.3 and 4.4.
[78] UN CEDAW Committee, General Recommendation No. 24 (n. 21), para. 31(d); UN ESCR Committee, General Comment No. 22 (n. 15), paras. 59–60. See also Clapham and Rubio (n. 13), p. 15.
[79] UN CEDAW Committee, General Recommendation No. 24 (n. 21), para. 14.
[80] UN General Assembly, Interim Report of the Special Rapporteur on the right of everyone to the enjoyment of the highest attainable standard of physical and mental health, Anand Grover, A/67/302 (13 August 2012), para. 3. See further Chapter 4.
[81] Law No. 39 of 1999 on Human Rights, art. 7(2) provides that all international human rights treaties ratified or acceded to by Indonesia become part of national law and can be invoked before the courts. UN ESCR Committee, Consideration of reports: reports submitted by states parties in accordance with articles 16 and 17 of the Covenant, List of issues in relation to the initial report of Indonesia, Addendum, Replies of Indonesia to the list of issues, E/C.12/IDN/Q/1/Add.1 (17 April 2014), para. 1. However, there is debate over whether Indonesia in practice is a monist or a dualist system, with most Indonesian scholars concluding that it is dualist: Simon Butt, The Position of International Law within the Indonesian Legal System (2014) *Emory International Law Review* 28, pp. 1–28.

5.2 RIGHT TO REPRODUCTIVE HEALTH IN INDONESIA

Economic, social and cultural rights are guaranteed in the Constitution and set out in various articles.[82] For example, the Indonesian Constitution guarantees the right to obtain medical care, and further legislation protects the right to health including reproductive health.[83] The Constitution also recognises that the 'family is the most fundamental unit of society' and is entitled to protection by society and the state, and that people have the right to form their own family.[84] Both the Constitution and national law protect gender equality and prohibit (sex) discrimination.[85] According to the Indonesian Government, 'the promotion and protection of the right to health are implemented without discrimination and applicable to all'.[86] To complement these laws, the Government has sought to protect the right to reproductive health including family planning via numerous policies and programmes.

To address its persistently high maternal mortality rate, the Indonesian Government adopted a number of policies and strategies. It launched in the 1980s the Safe Motherhood Initiative and the Village Midwife

---

[82] See, for example, *Indonesian Constitution* (18 August 1945, as amended), arts. 27(2); 28A; 28B; 28C; 28D; 28F; 28H(1) and (3); 28I(2) and (3); 31; 32; 34.

[83] *Indonesian Constitution* (18 August 1945, as amended), Chapter XA on Human Rights, art. 28H(1): 'every person shall have the right to obtain medical care'; and Chapter XIV on Social Welfare, art. 34(3): 'the state shall have the obligation to provide sufficient medical and public service facilities'. The Indonesian Government issued *inter alia*: Law No. 39 of 1999 on Human Rights; Law No. 29 of 2004 on Medical Practice; Law No. 36 of 2009 on Health; Law No. 35 of 2009 on Drugs; Law No. 44 of 2009 on Hospital; Law No. 52 of 2009 on Population Growth and Family Development. See UN ESCR Committee, Implementation of the International Covenant on Economic, Social and Cultural Rights, Initial reports submitted by states parties under articles 16 and 17 of the Covenant: Indonesia, E/C.12/IDN/1 (29 October 2012), paras. 202–3.

[84] *Indonesian Constitution* (18 August 1945 as amended), art. 28B(1) provides that every person has the right to form a family through a legal marriage, as does Law No. 39 of 1999 on Human Rights, art. 10. See UN Human Rights Committee (HRCee), Consideration of Reports submitted by states parties under article 40 of the Covenant, Initial reports of states parties: Indonesia, CCPR/C/IDN/1 (19 March 2012), paras. 300, 303.

[85] Indonesia has ensured non-discrimination through national legislation, including the Constitution (art. 28 and Chapter XA on Human Rights). For example, art. 28I(2) provides 'that every person shall have the right to be free from discriminatory treatment on any grounds whatsoever and shall have the right to protection from such discriminatory treatment'. Non-discrimination is also protected in Law No. 39 of 1999 on Human Rights in art. 3(3). See UN Human Rights Committee (HRCee), Consideration of Reports submitted by states parties under article 40 of the Covenant, Initial reports of states parties: Indonesia, CCPR/C/IDN/1 (19 March 2012), paras. 17–18.

[86] UN ESCR Committee, Implementation of the International Covenant on Economic, Social and Cultural Rights, Initial reports submitted by states parties under articles 16 and 17 of the Covenant: Indonesia, E/C.12/IDN/1 (29 October 2012), para. 204.

programme, the Mother Friendly Movement in 1996, a variety of programmes under the 'SIAGA' brand in 1998, and the Mother and Child Movement in 2010.[87] The highly successful and innovative SIAGA campaigns involved promoting the role of husbands, communities, community and religious leaders, and others in caring for pregnant women.[88] The *Suami SIAGA* (Alert Husband) campaign was 'a multi-media entertainment-education intervention' that engaged husbands on birth preparedness, and trained community leaders and midwives in preventing maternal mortality.[89] The various SIAGA campaigns sought to increase demand for reproductive healthcare services by informing and co-opting members of the community. To support these initiatives, the Government *inter alia* increased budget allocations, trained and placed midwives across the state,[90] and collaborated with local communities, private actors and international donors.[91]

A key aspect of the Government's strategy to improve maternal health was its national family planning programme. The ability for family planning to reduce mortality and improve the health of mothers and children has been well documented. For these reasons, and given Indonesia's large population and its impact upon development,[92] the

---

[87] See, for example, UN CEDAW Committee, Consideration of reports submitted by states parties under article 18 of the Convention on the Elimination of All Forms of Discrimination against Women, Combined fourth and fifth periodic reports of states parties: Indonesia, CEDAW/C/IDN/4-5 (27 July 2005), para. 51(a); Peter Hill, Lieve Goeman, Rahmi Sofiarini and Maddi Djara, 'Desa SIAGA', the 'Alert Village': The Evolution of an Iconic Brand in Indonesian Public Health Strategies (2014) *Health Policy and Planning*, 29, pp. 409-20; UN Human Rights Council, National report submitted by Indonesia in accordance with para. 5 of the annex to HRC Res. 16/21, A/HRC/WG.6/13/IDN/1 (7 March 2012), paras. 76-9.

[88] Hill, Goeman, Sofiarini and Djara, ibid.

[89] Corinne Shefner-Rogers and Suruchi Sood, Involving Husbands in Safe Motherhood: Effects of SUAMI SIAGA Campaign in Indonesia (2004) *Journal of Health Communication* 9, pp. 234, 239-40.

[90] Midwives are the main providers of family planning services in Indonesia; however, they tend to be concentrated in cities. BKKBN, UNFPA, USAID, FP2020 (n. 57), p. 14; UN CRC, Consideration of Reports submitted by States Parties under Article 44 of the Convention, Second periodic reports of states parties due in 1997: Indonesia, CRC/C/65/Add.23 (7 July 2003), para. 311.

[91] UN CEDAW Committee, Consideration of reports submitted by states parties under article 18 of the Convention on the Elimination of All Forms of Discrimination against Women, Combined fourth and fifth periodic reports of states parties: Indonesia, CEDAW/C/IDN/4-5 (27 July 2005), para. 51(a).

[92] Estimates claim that reducing the Indonesian fertility rate by 10 per cent would lead to a corresponding 11 per cent reduction in the poverty rate. David Bloom and David

5.2 RIGHT TO REPRODUCTIVE HEALTH IN INDONESIA

Government has long identified family planning as a key priority. Therefore, in 1970 the Government created the National Family Planning Coordinating Board (*Badan Koordinasi Keluarga Berencana Nasional* – BKKBN) with the aim of addressing population growth, promoting economic progress, and improving health and quality of life.[93] The BKKBN was responsible for implementing the national family planning programme, which over fifty years has succeeded in halving Indonesia's fertility rate. Despite these impressive achievements, in the last decade the fertility rate has plateaued and unmet need persists, contributing to other reproductive health issues. For example, the last decade saw the Indonesian population grow by more than thirty million to a total of 260 million in 2016.[94] Therefore, the Government reiterated their first priority of health development as: 'Improvement of maternal, infant, children and family health, as well as family planning'.[95] The text below explores in greater detail Indonesia's family planning initiatives.

Canning, Population, Poverty Reduction and the Cairo Agenda, in Mindy Jane Roseman and Laura Reichenbach (eds.), *Reproductive Health and Human Rights: The Way Forward* (University of Pennsylvania Press, 2009), p. 54.

[93] BKKBN and UNFPA, Discussion Paper on Family Planning, Human Rights and Development in Indonesia, Complement to the State of the World Population Report 2012 (14 November 2012, Jakarta, Indonesia), p. 1. The pioneer of family planning in Indonesia was an organisation called *Perkumpulan Keluarga Berencana Indonesia* (PKBI), which was formed in the 1950s of doctors and OBGYN specialists concerned about the high maternal mortality rate. Interview with representatives of Indonesian Planned Parenthood Association (PKBI) (26 January 2017, Jakarta, Indonesia); Interview with Ninuk Widyantoro, Women's Health Foundation (YKP) (1 February 2017, Jakarta, Indonesia).

[94] World Bank, Data: Indonesia https://data.worldbank.org/country/indonesia (accessed 24 November 2017).

[95] UN ESCR Committee, Implementation of the International Covenant on Economic, Social and Cultural Rights, Initial reports submitted by states parties under articles 16 and 17 of the Covenant: Indonesia, E/C.12/IDN/1 (29 October 2012), para. 206(a). See also UN ESCR Committee, Consideration of reports: reports submitted by states parties in accordance with articles 16 and 17 of the Covenant, List of issues in relation to the initial report of Indonesia, Addendum, Replies of Indonesia to the list of issues, E/C.12/IDN/Q/1/Add.1 (17 April 2014), para. 158. Recommendations are often made to Indonesia at the Universal Periodic Review on these issues: see UN Human Rights Council, Report of the Working Group on the Universal Periodic Review: Indonesia, A/HRC/21/7 (5 July 2012), recommendations 108.121–124; UN Human Rights Council, Report of the Working Group on the Universal Periodic Review: Indonesia, A/HRC/36/7 (14 July 2018), recommendations 139.91 and 92, 139.108 and 109, and 141.64 and 67.

Indonesia's Family Planning Programme: Past and Present

Indonesia's family planning programme is celebrated as an international success story. The programme succeeded in reducing Indonesia's fertility rate by more than half, from an average in 1965 of 5.6 children per woman, to around 2.3 today.[96] One of the purposes of the family planning programme was to limit the size of families in an effort to reduce poverty and promote development. The programme included an effective communication campaign advocating the small family ideal: 'Two is Enough' (*dua anak cukup*), which was launched to counter the prevailing cultural norm of large families.[97] While multiple children were once viewed as a status symbol and as human resources to support the family, today nearly all Indonesians prefer a small(er) family.[98] Indonesia's family planning programme brought together political will from across various levels of government with community-based services to decrease the fertility rate, as well as to promote women's health and economic participation. The CEDAW Committee noted the success of Indonesia's programme, which they viewed 'as an example of the Government's ability to take highly effective steps to improve the situation of women'.[99] Once considered to be a highly sensitive topic and a forbidden practice, family planning in Indonesia came to be seen as essential.[100]

Family planning services were provided by the BKKBN via the Integrated Services Health Posts (*Posyandu*) in villages across the state. Over the years, the family planning programme employed various campaigns and methods of promoting family planning services. For example, the BKKBN rewarded groups of women who used family planning by providing them with funds to be used as the group determined. It was intended that the women could set up savings and credit groups,

---

[96] The World Bank, Fertility rate, total (births per woman) Indonesia, data.worldbank.org/indicator/SP.DYN.TFRT.IN?locations=ID (accessed 16 September 2019).

[97] BKKBN and UNFPA, Discussion Paper on Family Planning, Human Rights and Development in Indonesia, Complement to the State of the World Population Report 2012 (14 November 2012, Jakarta, Indonesia), p. 1. The slogan was later adapted to be 'Two children is better'.

[98] Iwu Dwisetyani Utomo, Syahmida Arsyad and Eddy Nurul Hasmi, Village Family Planning Volunteers in Indonesia: The Role in the Family Planning Programme (2006) *Reproductive Health Matters* 14:27, p. 74; Interview with Professor Emeritus Sri Moertiningsih Adioetomo PhD, Faculty of Economics and Business Universitas Indonesia (10 February 2017, Depok, Indonesia).

[99] UN CEDAW Committee, Report of CEDAW Committee, 18th and 19th session, A/53/38/Rev.a (14 May 1998), para. 280.

[100] Utomo, Arsyad and Hasmi (n. 98). p. 73.

deciding how to manage the capital, and who was eligible for a loan at what rates.[101] The BKKBN also ran income-generating programmes that created additional funding sources for women. For example, women could use the funds provided to learn a skill and then produce and sell a product such as food or clothing.[102] In another scheme, women who were long-term contraceptive users and had not had a baby in five to sixteen years were publicly rewarded with a medal, certificate and sometimes coconut tree seedlings, which increased their social status.[103] While the Government's programme initially focused on demographics, after the 1994 Cairo Conference it adopted a more rights-based approach. For instance, in the early years, BKKBN set targets and induced or 'peer pressured' women into using contraceptives.[104]

While Government professionals and health experts were involved in the family planning programme, village volunteers also played a significant role in its success.[105] For example, the BKKBN commissioned local family planning groups 'to deploy its mandates at the village level',[106] training over one million volunteers from the villages in topics including nutrition, family planning and immunisation.[107] Prominent women in the community were identified to become volunteers, including wives of government officials, those with higher educational or financial standing, and those well integrated into community social activities.[108] These grass-roots volunteers were trained to make first contact with potential contraceptive users, provide information and motivation for them to use contraception.[109] For example, the BKKBN recruited cadres – usually women – who would go door to door talking to women about family planning and how they can support and empower their families. Among

---

[101] Ibid., p. 75.
[102] Ibid.
[103] Ibid., p. 76.
[104] In the earlier phase of the programme, there were widespread allegations of coercion. Jeremy Menchik, The Co-evolution of Sacred and Secular: Islamic Law and Family Planning in Indonesia (2014) *South East Asia Research* 22:3, p. 368; Interview with Professor Emeritus Sri Moertiningsih Adioetomo PhD, Faculty of Economics and Business Universitas Indonesia (10 February 2017, Depok, Indonesia).
[105] Utomo, Arsyad and Hasmi (n. 98), p. 74.
[106] Harris Solomon, Kathryn Yount and Michael Mbizvo, 'A Shot of His Own': The Acceptability of a Male Hormonal Contraceptive in Indonesia (2007) *Culture, Health & Sexuality* 9:1, p. 5.
[107] Halabi (n. 66), p. 52.
[108] Utomo, Arsyad and Hasmi (n. 98), pp. 76, 78.
[109] Ibid., p. 74.

other things, volunteers organised meetings, collected data, and provided education, counselling and family planning services.[110] A 1997 survey found that women in rural areas regarded women's groups, as well as community, village and religious leaders, to be appropriate sources of information on family planning.[111]

While the family planning programme is internationally recognised as a success and has undoubtedly had a huge impact in Indonesia, contemporary challenges remain. Despite the past progress, Indonesia's contraceptive prevalence rates have plateaued in the last decade. The national contraceptive prevalence rate has been stable (rather than increasing) for two decades, with some provinces experiencing a decrease in use.[112] At the high point, the unmet need for family planning in Indonesia's Papua province was almost 24 per cent.[113] The Government therefore failed to meet its target of a replacement level fertility rate by 2015,[114] and has also not met its Millennium Development Goal 5 on reducing maternal mortality.[115] Not only is family planning 'one of the critical interventions for reducing maternal mortality', but a manageable fertility rate translates per capita into a higher Gross National Product, including higher

---

[110] While the volunteers received social recognition for their work and were empowered within their communities, the women were essentially performing unpaid work for the BKKBN: Utomo, Arsyad and Hasmi (n. 98), pp. 75–80. Bahramitash suggests that the same thing occurred in the Iranian programme where women volunteered and essentially took over the public services responsibilities of the state: Roksana Bahramitash, Family Planning, Islam and Women's Human Rights in Iran (2007) *International Studies Journal* 4:1, p. 36.

[111] Utomo, Arsyad and Hasmi (n. 98), p. 74.

[112] BKKBN, UNFPA, USAID, FP2020 (n. 57), p. 9. See also UN CEDAW Committee, Consideration of reports submitted by states parties under article 18 of the Convention on the Elimination of All Forms of Discrimination against Women, Combined sixth and seventh periodic reports of states parties: Indonesia, CEDAW/C/IDN/6-7 (7 January 2011), para. 141.

[113] BKKBN, UNFPA, USAID, FP2020 (n. 57), p. 12.

[114] UN CEDAW Committee, Combined fourth and fifth periodic reports: Indonesia (n. 91), para. 136.

[115] Millennium Development Goal 5 is on improving maternal health. Indonesia's maternal mortality ratio in 2015 was 126 maternal deaths per 100,000 live births, which is higher than their MDG of 102 per 100,000 life births by 2015. See WHO, UNICEF, UNFPA, World Bank Group and UN Population Division Maternal Mortality Estimation Inter-Agency Group, Maternal Mortality in 1990–2015 Indonesia, www.who.int/gho/maternal_health/countries/idn.pdf (accessed 5 November 2017); UN ESCR Committee, Implementation of the International Covenant on Economic, Social and Cultural Rights, Initial reports submitted by states parties under articles 16 and 17 of the Covenant: Indonesia, E/C.12/IDN/1 (29 October 2012), para. 222.

5.2 RIGHT TO REPRODUCTIVE HEALTH IN INDONESIA

incomes, savings and investments that contribute to poverty eradication.[116] The plateau in the contraceptive prevalence rate and continued unmet need indicates that Indonesians are unable to enjoy their reproductive rights,[117] and that Indonesia is unable to meet some of its development goals.

Indonesia's family planning programme, like others, was affected by the Asian financial crisis in 1997, the fall of Suharto's New Order Government in 1998, and subsequent decentralisation. In 1999, the Government commenced decentralisation, which transformed Indonesia 'from being one of the world's most authoritarian and centralised states to one of its most decentralised and democratic'.[118] While the central government retained authority over foreign policy, security, defence, the judiciary, fiscal policy and religious affairs, all other areas were devolved to regional authorities – including family planning.[119] As such, the Government moved from the direct management of programmes to promoting national standards and initiatives, with local governments playing a major role in designing and managing reproductive health programmes.[120] Some welcomed decentralisation as a way to improve individual and community health by increasing public participation and stakeholder consultation (which is also required under international law).[121] In practice, however, with decentralisation came a large variation

---

[116] BKKBN, UNFPA, USAID, FP2020 (n. 57), p. 16; BKKBN and UNFPA, Discussion Paper on Family Planning, Human Rights and Development in Indonesia, Complement to the State of the World Population Report 2012 (14 November 2012, Jakarta, Indonesia), p. 5.

[117] BKKBN, UNFPA, USAID, FP2020 (n. 57), p. 21.

[118] Simon Butt, Regional Autonomy and Legal Disorder: The Proliferation of Local Laws in Indonesia (2010) *Sydney Law Review* 32, p. 177.

[119] See Law No. 22 of 1999 on Regional Government Administration; Law No. 25 of 1999 on Revenue Sharing of Central and Regional Government; Law No. 32 of 2004 on Regional Administration (repealing Law No. 22 of 1999); Law No. 12 of 2008 on Regional Government. J. A. C. Vel and A. W. Bedner, Decentralisation and Village Governance in Indonesia: The Return to the Nagari and the 2014 Village Law (2015) *Journal of Legal Pluralism and Unofficial Law* 47:3, p. 493; UN ESCR Committee, Implementation of the International Covenant on Economic, Social and Cultural Rights, Initial reports submitted by states parties under articles 16 and 17 of the Covenant: Indonesia, E/C.12/IDN/1 (29 October 2012), paras. 14, 16.

[120] Terence Hull, Eddy Hasmi, Ninuk Widyantoro, 'Peer' Educator Initiatives for Adolescent Reproductive Health Projects in Indonesia (2004) *Reproductive Health Matters* 12:23, p. 37.

[121] Halabi (n. 66), p. 50; Christiana Titaley, Cynthia Hunter, Michael Dibley and Peter Heywood, Why Do Some Women still Prefer Traditional Birth Attendants and Home Delivery? A Qualitative Study on Delivery Care Services in West Java Province, Indonesia (2010) *BMC Pregnancy and Childbirth* 10:43, pp. 11–12.

in family planning services across Indonesia, a decrease in the quality of available healthcare, and an increase in private providers.[122] The district authorities faced various challenges in implementing the family planning programme, including a lack of capacity and trained health workers, and limited funding.[123]

The decrease in funding certainly had an impact on family planning uptake, with some suggesting that Indonesia only decentralised the health system as a cost-saving measure due to financial constraints at the national level.[124] Initially, there was strong international donor support and Government funding for the family planning programme; however, international support fell away and by 2000 most programmes were only funded by the Government.[125] To compensate for this loss, the Government increased 'the necessary and legitimate role of the private sector'[126] in providing family planning services from around 40 per cent in 1997, to 70 per cent in 2012.[127] The UN treaty bodies noted the weakened position of healthcare due to decentralisation and expressed their concern. The CEDAW Committee urged Indonesia to ensure the Convention's implementation, highlighting that decentralisation

---

[122] Several interview participants noted that the districts prioritise family planning differently, with some giving it little emphasis. BKKBN and UNFPA, Discussion Paper on Family Planning, Human Rights and Development in Indonesia, Complement to the State of the World Population Report 2012 (14 November 2012, Jakarta, Indonesia), p. 4; Halabi (n. 66), p. 53.

[123] BKKBN, UNFPA, USAID, FP2020 (n. 57), p. 14.

[124] Halabi (n. 66), p. 51.

[125] Some consider that reproductive rights were largely dropped from the international development agenda in the 2000s – shifting to focus on infectious diseases such as HIV/AIDS. See Laura Reichenbach, The Global Reproductive Health and Rights Agenda: Opportunities and Challenges for the Future, in Mindy Jane Roseman and Laura Reichenbach (eds.), *Reproductive Health and Human Rights: The Way Forward* (University of Pennsylvania Press, 2009), pp. 21–39; Thomas Merrick, Mobilizing Resources for Reproductive Health, in Mindy Jane Roseman and Laura Reichenbach (eds.), *Reproductive Health and Human Rights: The Way Forward* (University of Pennsylvania Press, 2009), p. 60; BKKBN and UNFPA (n. 116), pp. 1–2.

[126] UN CEDAW Committee, Combined fourth and fifth periodic reports: Indonesia (n. 91), para. 120.

[127] BKKBN and UNFPA, Discussion Paper on Family Planning, Human Rights and Development in Indonesia, Complement to the State of the World Population Report 2012 (14 November 2012, Jakarta, Indonesia), pp. 2, 6; BKKBN, UNFPA, USAID, FP2020 (n. 57), p. 12; Katherine Marshall, *Religious Engagement in Family Planning Policies: Experience in Six Muslim-Majority Countries* (World Faiths Development Dialogue, 2015), p. 19.

5.2 RIGHT TO REPRODUCTIVE HEALTH IN INDONESIA

(or indeed privatisation) does not reduce the state's responsibility.[128] The ESCR Committee lamented 'the disparity in the availability and quality of health care services across provinces and regions'.[129] In response, the Government has endeavoured to enhance the BKKBN's stewardship role and the accountability of the relevant institutions.[130]

A positive development has been Indonesia's introduction of universal health insurance, including special coverage for the most disadvantaged. The Government introduced Social Health Insurance (*Jamkesmas*) in 2008, an insurance scheme that covered more than 80 million needy Indonesians for free healthcare including reproductive health.[131] From 2014, the Government transformed and expanded *Jamkesmas* into a National Health Insurance system, which provided health insurance coverage for more than 170 million people.[132] Indonesia's target is to achieve universal health coverage of all Indonesians – around 260 million people. The introduction of this health insurance coverage 'provides an opportunity to deliver equitable and high-quality family planning services, and aim for higher coverage with modern methods of family planning services'.[133] Despite these positive steps, the CEDAW Committee noted the limited percentage allocated to healthcare in the national budget, and the ESCR Committee was concerned that the healthcare system was unable to meet demand for healthcare services after the introduction of the universal health insurance.[134]

---

[128] UN CEDAW Committee, Concluding observations of the Committee on the Elimination of Discrimination against Women: Indonesia, CEDAW/C/IDN/CO/6-7 (7 August 2012), para. 16.

[129] UN ESCR Committee, Concluding observations on the initial report of Indonesia, E/C.12/IDN/CO/1 (19 June 2014), para. 32.

[130] See further Law No. 23 of 2014 on Local Government; BKKBN, UNFPA, USAID, FP2020 (n. 57), p. 16; UN CEDAW Committee, Responses to the list of issues and questions with regard to the consideration of the combined fourth and fifth periodic report: Indonesia, CEDAW/C/IDN/Q/5/Add.1 (17 May 2007), para. 23.

[131] UN ESCR Committee, Implementation of the International Covenant on Economic, Social and Cultural Rights, Initial reports submitted by states parties under articles 16 and 17 of the Covenant: Indonesia, E/C.12/IDN/1 (29 October 2012), paras. 102–4.

[132] UN ESCR Committee, Consideration of reports: reports submitted by states parties in accordance with articles 16 and 17 of the Covenant, List of issues in relation to the initial report of Indonesia, Addendum, Replies of Indonesia to the list of issues, E/C.12/IDN/Q/1/Add.1 (17 April 2014), paras. 111–12; UN Human Rights Council, National report submitted in accordance with para. 5 of the annex to Human Rights Council res. 16/21: Indonesia, A/HRC/WG.6/27/IDN/1 (20 February 2017), paras. 159–60.

[133] BKKBN, UNFPA, USAID, FP2020 (n. 57), p. 16.

[134] UN CEDAW Committee, Concluding observations of the Committee on the Elimination of Discrimination against Women: Indonesia, CEDAW/C/IDN/CO/6-7 (7 August

Given the previous success, current plateau and outstanding development goals, the Indonesian Government has revitalised its national family planning programme.[135] Indonesia created a FP2020 Family Planning Country Committee to instigate collective action by numerous stakeholders (including various levels of Government, private actors and development agencies) to 'achieve universal access to high-quality family planning services, according to the needs of individuals and couples, and to support their reproductive intentions'.[136] The FP2020 plan includes mobilising support for family planning among health workers, religious leaders and women's groups, as well as addressing barriers to access including equity.[137] The aim is to develop 'local-specific materials' with core messaging relating to the cultural and religious barriers to family planning utilisation.[138] As established, culture has a large impact on human rights, and the right to reproductive health in particular. The meaning a culture ascribes to reproduction will impact upon people's 'understandings of their own reproductive health status and will influence their health-care seeking behavior'.[139] This next subsection considers in more detail these socio-cultural factors affecting Indonesia's family planning programme.

Socio-Cultural Determinants of the Right to Family Planning in Indonesia

There are numerous and interacting factors affecting reproductive health and family planning in Indonesia. These include: inadequate or inaccessible healthcare infrastructure, services and facilities; limited education (generally as well as specifically relating to reproductive health); poor nutrition; low-level socio-economic background and socio-cultural

---

2012), para. 41; UN ESCR Committee, Concluding observations on the initial report of Indonesia, E/C.12/IDN/CO/1 (19 June 2014), para. 32.

[135] Terence Hull and Henry Mosley, The Government of Indonesia and the UNFPA, Revitalization of Family Planning in Indonesia (February 2009), www.popline.org/node/649521 (accessed 24 November 2017).

[136] FP2020 is a global initiative established in 2012 to work with governments, civil society, multilateral organisations and the private sector to support the rights of women and girls to decide freely whether, when and how many children they want to have. BKKBN, UNFPA, USAID, FP2020 (n. 57), pp. 5, 17.

[137] Ibid., pp. 23, 29.

[138] Ibid.

[139] Matthew Dudgeon and Marcia Inhorn, Men's Influences on Women's Reproductive Health: Medical Anthropological Perspectives (2004) *Social Science and Medicine* 59, p. 1380.

factors.[140] The socio-cultural factors impacting reproductive health in Indonesia include: (1) the role of the husband as the head of the family with decision-making responsibility; (2) norms regarding marriage and sexuality and (3) gender stereotypes and inequality. All of these factors relate in some way to Islam, as the main non-state normative system in Indonesia with numerous values and traditions regarding reproductive health. Given the pervasive influence of these (and other) norms, understanding and addressing a health issue's socio-cultural determinants can be just as vital as addressing the medical ones.[141] Scholars have even suggested that socio-cultural norms are 'more important determinants of health than health systems themselves'.[142] As such, those designing health systems and providing healthcare should be aware of their patients' values and beliefs in order to understand their worldview and provide appropriate information to guide decision-making.[143] Therefore, the text below examines these socio-cultural norms relating to reproductive health in Indonesia.

Gendered Decision-Making in Reproductive Health A community's beliefs, customs and gendered decision-making systems can promote or constrain positive male engagement in reproductive health.[144] In some (patriarchal) societies, men hold and exercise significant influence over women on a number of topics, including decisions regarding women's health.[145] Despite their sometimes deficient knowledge of the relevant

---

[140] UN ESCR Committee, Implementation of the International Covenant on Economic, Social and Cultural Rights, Initial reports submitted by states parties under articles 16 and 17 of the Covenant: Indonesia, E/C.12/IDN/1 (29 October 2012), para. 223; UN CRC Committee, Consideration of Reports submitted by States Parties under Article 44 of the Convention, Second periodic reports of states parties due in 1997: Indonesia, CRC/C/65/Add.23 (7 July 2003), paras. 266, 295.

[141] Dominic Azuh, Oluyemi Fayomi and Lady Ajayi, Socio-Cultural Factors of Gender Roles in Women's Healthcare Utilization in Southwest Nigeria (2015) *Open Journal of Social Sciences* 3, p. 106.

[142] Ibid., p. 108.

[143] Yenita Agus and Shigeko Horiuchi, Factors influencing the use of antenatal care in rural West Sumatra, Indonesia (2012) *BMC Pregnancy and Childbirth* 12:9, p. 7.

[144] Omokhoa Adedayo Adeleye, Linda Aldoory and Dauda Bayo Parakoyi, Using Local Culture and Gender Roles to Improve Male Involvement in Maternal Health in Southern Nigeria (2011) *Journal of Health Communication: International Perspectives* 16:10, p. 1123.

[145] Azuh, Fayomi and Ajayi (n. 141), p. 108; Frances Ampt, Myo Myo Mon, Kyu Kyu Than, May May Khin, Paul A. Agius, Christopher Morgan, Jessica Davis and Stanley Luchters, Correlates of Male Involvement in Maternal and Newborn Health: A Cross-Sectional

health issue, men can act as 'gatekeepers' to their family's healthcare and present barriers for women and children to access healthcare.[146] For example, according to a religious interpretation in Indonesia, mothers and children who die during childbirth are considered to become martyrs, therefore reducing the impetus to seek medical assistance.[147] Men may also control the economic resources needed to access healthcare, and may directly or indirectly sanction or prohibit certain services and treatments.[148] In such situations it can be difficult for women to access healthcare, including in an emergency.[149] In addition, some *Hadiths* in Islam relating to a wife's obedience to her husband can be misunderstood and prevent timely action to assist women in labour.[150] The strength of this influence in relation to family planning led some to claim that '[c]ontraceptive use and effectiveness depend directly on men's involvement'.[151] In contrast, where women have greater autonomy in decision-making, they are more likely to access healthcare.[152]

While highly diverse and exceptions apply, Indonesia is largely a paternalistic society, 'with the *bapak* (father/husband) as the source of power and benign leadership, and the *ibu* (mother/wife) as his subordinate companion'.[153] In this position, it can be difficult for women to assert their reproductive rights and studies have shown that the most important determinant of contraceptive use was the husband's approval.[154]

Study of Men in a Peri-urban Region of Myanmar (2015) *BMC Pregnancy and Childbirth* 15:122, p. 2; Shefner-Rogers and Sood (n. 89) p. 234.

[146] Ampt, Mon, Than, Khin, Agius, Morgan, Davis and Luchters, ibid., p. 2; Dudgeon and Inhorn (n. 139), p. 1382; Shefner-Rogers and Sood (n. 89), p. 237.

[147] UN CEDAW Committee, Consideration of reports submitted by states parties under article 18 of the Convention on the Elimination of All Forms of Discrimination against Women, Combined sixth and seventh periodic reports of states parties: Indonesia, CEDAW/C/IDN/6-7 (7 January 2011), para. 145.

[148] Dudgeon and Inhorn (n. 139), p. 1383.

[149] Azuh, Fayomi and Ajayi (n. 141), p. 106.

[150] UN CEDAW Committee, Consideration of reports submitted by states parties under article 18 of the Convention on the Elimination of All Forms of Discrimination against Women, Combined sixth and seventh periodic reports of states parties: Indonesia, CEDAW/C/IDN/6-7 (7 January 2011), para. 145.

[151] Dudgeon and Inhorn (n. 139), p. 1383.

[152] Azuh, Fayomi and Ajayi (n. 141), p. 109.

[153] Rosalia Sciortino, The Challenge of Addressing Gender in Reproductive Health Programmes: Examples from Indonesia (1998) *Reproductive Health Matters* 6:11, p. 36.

[154] Some even claimed that given men's overwhelming influence, changes in fertility behaviour were possible even *without* the involvement of women. See ibid.; Interview with Dr Irwan Martua Hidayana, Universitas Indonesia (18 January 2017, Depok, Indonesia).

5.2 RIGHT TO REPRODUCTIVE HEALTH IN INDONESIA 193

For example, despite participating in training that offered 'women-centred interpretations of reproductive rights within the teachings of Islam', some women felt unable to apply this new awareness in their private lives as their husbands had a different view of reproductive rights under Islam.[155] Their husbands reportedly claimed that Islam requires men to take decisions on the number and timing of children, and that 'women merely had to comply'.[156] In order not to disrupt their family lives and suffer an insecure future, some women chose not to confront their husbands and instead accepted compromised reproductive health.[157] Furthermore, given that pregnancy and childbirth are often viewed in Indonesia as 'a woman's natural rite of passage', some believe that women should only have medical assistance if they experience obstetric complications.[158] The Indonesian Government has acknowledged that men's role and responsibility in reproductive health is crucial and must be improved.[159]

The Government implemented the *Suami SIAGA* (ALERT husband) campaign in 1999, which was designed with advice from advertising agencies and funded by the UNFPA. Research for the SIAGA campaigns confirmed the common perception in Indonesia that pregnancy and childbirth were part of a woman's domain and not to be discussed between the sexes.[160] As such, the *Suami SIAGA* campaign had to create a unique approach to stimulate men's involvement, which included TV mini-series and radio broadcasts.[161] Relying upon the SIAGA brand was important as it enjoyed cultural potency due to its 'strong

---

[155] Sciortino (n. 153), p. 35; Rosalia Sciortino, Lies Marcoes-Natsir and Masdar F. Mas'udi, Learning from Islam: Advocacy of Reproductive Rights in Indonesian Pesantren (November 1996) *Reproductive Health Matters* 4:8, p. 93.

[156] Sciortino (n. 153), pp. 35–6. See also Interview with representatives of Indonesian Planned Parenthood Association (PKBI) (26 January 2017, Jakarta, Indonesia).

[157] Sciortino (n. 153), p. 36.

[158] Christiana Titaley, Cynthia Hunter, Peter Heywood and Michael Dibley, Why Don't Some Women Attend Antenatal and Postnatal Care Services? A Qualitative Study of Community Members' Perspectives in Garut, Sukabumi and Ciamis districts of West Java Province, Indonesia (2010) *BMC Pregnancy and Childbirth* 10:61, p. 9; Shefner-Rogers and Sood (n. 89), p. 236.

[159] UN CEDAW Committee, Consideration of reports submitted by states parties under article 18 of the Convention on the Elimination of All Forms of Discrimination against Women, Combined sixth and seventh periodic reports of states parties: Indonesia, CEDAW/C/IDN/6-7 (7 January 2011), para. 145.

[160] Hill, Goeman, Sofiarini and Djara (n. 87), p. 413; Shefner-Rogers and Sood (n. 89), p. 237.

[161] Shefner-Rogers and Sood (n. 89), pp. 239–40.

resonances with traditional Indonesian community support concepts'.[162] Other initiatives also focused on men, such as the NGO Centre for the Development of Pesantren and Society (*Perhimpunan Pengembangan Pesantren dan Masyarakat* – P3M), which hosted discussions for Muslim leaders of both sexes with the aim of promoting 'awareness of gender and reproductive rights from a theological perspective'.[163] The women's branch of Islamic institution Nahdlatul Ulama also undertook community training programmes targeting male audiences.[164] While interventions promoting male involvement in and knowledge of reproductive health should be sensitive to prevailing gender norms,[165] Sciortino highlighted the challenge of involving men in a way that supports women's emancipation, rather than reinforcing unequal gender relationships.[166]

Despite some successes in changing cultural norms regarding reproductive health, male participation in family planning in Indonesia is still low. Typically, contraceptives are seen as something for women, with men referred to as the 'forgotten clients' of contraception.[167] This is due to the strength and pervasiveness of social norms in Indonesia that reinforce women's position in the domestic sphere, engaged in childbearing and childrearing.[168] The UN treaty bodies have lamented the focus of Indonesia's family planning programme on women, emphasising the importance of men's responsibility in family planning.[169] In response, the Government passed new legislation and designed programmes to increase men's participation in family planning in order to realise gender equality.[170] For

---

[162] Hill, Goeman, Sofiarini and Djara (n. 87), p. 418.
[163] Sciortino (n. 153), p. 40; Sciortino, Marcoes-Natsir and F. Mas'udi (n. 155).
[164] Interview with Anggia Ermarini, Chairperson of Fatayat NU (3 February 2017, Jakarta, Indonesia).
[165] Ampt, Mon, Than, Khin, Agius, Morgan, Davis and Luchters (n. 145), p. 2.
[166] Sciortino (n. 153), p. 37.
[167] Solomon, Yount and Mbizvo (n. 106), p. 2.
[168] Utomo, Arsyad and Hasmi (n. 98) pp. 79–80 F. Mas'udi; Sciortino, Marcoes-Natsir and F. Mas'udi (n. 155), p. 90.
[169] The CRC Committee noted the influential role of men and encouraged states to 'integrate education, awareness and dialogue opportunities for boys and men into their policies and plans' on reproductive health. UN CRC Committee, General Comment No. 15 on the Right of the Child to the Enjoyment of the Highest Attainable Standard of Health (art. 24), CRC/C/GC/15 (17 April 2013), para. 57; UN CEDAW Committee, Report of CEDAW Committee, Eighteenth and nineteenth sessions, A/53/38/Rev.a (14 May 1998), para. 280.
[170] UN CEDAW Committee, Consideration of reports submitted by states parties under article 18 of the Convention on the Elimination of All Forms of Discrimination against

example, Law No. 52 of 2009 provides that the husband and wife 'have equal status, rights and obligations in implementing family planning'.[171] In addition, the BKKBN established the Male Participation Directorate in 2000 and promotes family planning not as women's business but as 'family business'.[172] Notwithstanding this, the uptake of male contraceptives in Indonesia remains low, compounded by the negative association of condoms with extramarital sex.[173]

Norms on Marriage and Sexuality The Indonesian Government has long struggled to address extramarital sex and has resisted calls to provide family planning services to sexually active adolescents or unmarried persons. Up to today, the BKKBN only provides goods and services to married couples, as Indonesian law prohibits family planning for unmarried persons.[174] This reluctance to extend information and services is due to the common (religious) perception that sex should not occur outside marriage and that providing information and services to adolescents and single people would encourage them to become sexually active.[175] As such, around half of all adolescents reportedly do not understand their reproductive organs or how one becomes pregnant.[176] The issue is exacerbated by the increasing prevalence of pre-

---

Women, Combined fourth and fifth periodic reports of states parties: Indonesia, CEDAW/C/IDN/4-5 (27 July 2005), para. 137.

[171] Law No. 52 of 2009 on Population Growth and Family Development, art. 25. See UN HRCee, Consideration of Reports submitted by states parties under article 40 of the Covenant, Initial reports of states parties: Indonesia, CCPR/C/IDN/1 (19 March 2012), para. 318.

[172] Utomo, Arsyad and Hasmi (n. 98), p. 79; Interview with BKKBN staff member (2 February 2017, Jakarta, Indonesia).

[173] UN CEDAW Committee, Consideration of reports submitted by states parties under article 18 of the Convention on the Elimination of All Forms of Discrimination against Women, Combined sixth and seventh periodic reports of States parties: Indonesia, CEDAW/C/IDN/6-7 (7 January 2011), para. 145.

[174] UN ESCR Committee, Consideration of reports: reports submitted by states parties in accordance with articles 16 and 17 of the Covenant, List of issues in relation to the initial report of Indonesia, Addendum, Replies of Indonesia to the list of issues, E/C.12/IDN/Q/1/Add.1 (17 April 2014), para. 165. UN Human Rights Council, Compilation on Indonesia: Report of the Office of the United Nations Commissioner for Human Rights, A/HRC/WG.6/27IDN/2 (17 February 2017), para. 74.

[175] Hull, Hasmi and Widyantoro (n. 120), p. 29.

[176] UN CEDAW Committee, Consideration of reports submitted by states parties under article 18 of the Convention on the Elimination of All Forms of Discrimination against Women, Combined sixth and seventh periodic reports of states parties: Indonesia, CEDAW/C/IDN/6-7 (7 January 2011), para. 130.

marital sex, as well as sexually transmitted diseases including HIV/AIDS.[177] Scholars noted that the prevalence and spread of HIV/AIDS in Indonesia indicates that actual sexual behaviour is not always in conformity with religious norms – which is of course typical of many normative systems.[178]

While the BKKBN's family planning programme initially only addressed married couples, after the 1994 Cairo conference it also began to include adolescents in education activities.[179] The first pilot project to reach adolescents in Indonesia was via families, where parents were provided with reproductive health information to discuss with their children. However, this was quickly proven ineffective, as the strong cultural 'taboos and strict rules of propriety and filial respect placed discussion of sexuality out of bound of the nuclear family'.[180] The BKKBN subsequently created a project to inform adolescents about reproductive health via peer educators and counsellors, which enjoyed greater success as it was more culturally appropriate for the community and acceptable to adolescents.[181] As this demonstrates, culture can inform both the message as well as the medium of communication. In addition to government efforts, civil society, the UNFPA and religious groups also initiated or participated in reproductive health programmes targeting adolescents. As a senior religious leader stressed, sexual health education in Indonesia should use religious language and acknowledge religious concerns.[182]

The Indonesian Government and NGOs have collaborated to address adolescent reproductive health issues via programmes run through youth clubs, Islamic boarding schools and teen-girl programmes (*Rematri*).[183]

---

[177] BKKBN and UNFPA (n. 116), p. 4. In 2016, Indonesia had 48,000 new HIV infections. See further UNAIDS, Country: Indonesia (2016), www.unaids.org/en/regionscountries/countries/indonesia (accessed 24 November 2017).
[178] Sciortino, Marcoes-Natsir and F. Mas'udi (n. 155) p. 88. See further Chapter 2.
[179] Hull, Hasmi and Widyantoro (n. 120), p. 30. The Cairo Programme and the Beijing Platform both advocate removing regulatory and social barriers to reproductive health-care and information for adolescents. See Cairo Programme (n. 30), paras. 7.41–7.48; Beijing Declaration and Platform for Action (n. 30), paras. 106–8, 281.
[180] Hull, Hasmi and Widyantoro (n. 120), p. 30.
[181] Ibid., pp. 31–3.
[182] Ibid., p. 37.
[183] UN CEDAW Committee, Consideration of reports submitted by states parties under article 18 of the Convention on the Elimination of All Forms of Discrimination against Women, Combined fourth and fifth periodic reports of states parties: Indonesia, CEDAW/C/IDN/4–5 (27 July 2005), para. 135.

A 'discussion house' involving Islamic boarding school institutions was also created with the mission *inter alia* to talk to teenage girls about reproductive health issues including marriage age, gender equality and protection from sexually transmitted diseases.[184] Despite these efforts, adolescent knowledge of reproductive health in Indonesia remains limited.[185] While sex and reproductive health education is typically lacking in schools, even when it is provided 'the normative views and sexual taboos make such education ineffective in meeting the needs of children and teenagers'.[186] Noting the insufficient sexual and reproductive health education, the CEDAW Committee called upon Indonesia to provide comprehensive and large-scale education for unmarried women and the population in general.[187]

Gender Stereotyping and Inequality Women's position in Indonesian society and stereotyped gender roles for both sexes also impacts upon access to and uptake of family planning services. This is because women's reproductive health 'is determined not only by access to health services but by women's status in society and pervasive gender discrimination'.[188] The Special Rapporteur on health noted that a woman's enjoyment of her reproductive rights is often impaired by her low status in society.[189] Inequality not only impinges upon women's ability to enjoy reproductive rights, but negatively impacts upon their enjoyment of all human rights. While the Indonesian Constitution and various laws and

---

[184] UN CEDAW Committee, Consideration of reports submitted by states parties under article 18 of the Convention on the Elimination of All Forms of Discrimination against Women, Combined sixth and seventh periodic reports of states parties: Indonesia, CEDAW/C/IDN/6-7 (7 January 2011), para. 157.

[185] BKKBN, UNFPA, USAID, FP2020 (n. 57), p. 7.

[186] UN CEDAW Committee, Consideration of reports submitted by states parties under article 18 of the Convention on the Elimination of All Forms of Discrimination against Women, Combined sixth and seventh periodic reports of states parties: Indonesia, CEDAW/C/IDN/6-7 (7 January 2011), para. 76.

[187] UN CEDAW Committee, Concluding observations of the Committee on the Elimination of Discrimination against Women: Indonesia, CEDAW/C/IDN/CO/6-7 (7 August 2012), paras. 41(c), 42(c).

[188] Shalev (n. 6), p. 40. See also Riffat Hassan, Is Family Planning Permitted by Islam? The Issue of a Woman's Right to Contraception, in Gisela Webb (ed.), *Windows of Faith: Muslim Women Scholar-Activists in North America* (Syracuse University Press, 2000), pp. 235-7.

[189] UN Commission on Human Rights, Report of the Special Rapporteur on the right of everyone to the enjoyment of the highest attainable standard of physical and mental health, E/CN.4/2004/49 (16 February 2004), para. 14. See also Shalev (n. 6), p. 59.

policies as set out above guarantee the equality of men and women, their implementation and realisation remains a challenge.[190] The CEDAW Committee noted in 1998 that despite women's *de jure* right to equality, in reality Indonesian 'women remain unequal to men in terms of rights and opportunities because of a combination of traditional and cultural practices and certain laws that are contrary to the spirit, if not the letter, of the principle of equality'.[191] Recognising women's persistent inequality in society, the Indonesian Government reported that 'women's sex roles and stereotyping remain major challenges' to the domestic implementation of CEDAW.[192]

The Government noted that women's low status and lower levels of education resulted from 'traditional stereotyped socio-cultural values and misinterpretation of religious teachings'.[193] For example, problematic socio-cultural factors in Indonesia regarding reproductive health include early and illegal marriage, polygamy and arbitrary divorce.[194] Indonesia noted the difficulties inherent in addressing such cultural practices and their underlying values, particularly when justified on the basis of religious interpretations.[195] In their report to the CEDAW Committee on reproductive health, Indonesia identified that:

> the prevailing culture puts men in charge of decision-making in the family, and women are relegated to the domestic sphere. Many still consider maternity as an exclusively female issue, and not in the greater interest of the nation as it really is. As a result, maternity protection is often deemed less important, and women are seen as responsible for their own reproductive role. The stereotypical role of men as the breadwinner and women as homemakers ... still normatively feature in the day-to-day

---

[190] UN CEDAW Committee, Consideration of reports submitted by states parties under article 18 of the Convention on the Elimination of All Forms of Discrimination against Women, Combined sixth and seventh periodic reports of states parties: Indonesia, CEDAW/C/IDN/6-7 (7 January 2011), para. 9.

[191] UN CEDAW Committee, Report of CEDAW Committee, Eighteenth and nineteenth sessions, A/53/38/Rev.a (14 May 1998), para. 263.

[192] UN CEDAW Committee, Consideration of reports submitted by states parties under article 18 of the Convention on the Elimination of All Forms of Discrimination against Women, Combined fourth and fifth periodic reports of states parties: Indonesia, CEDAW/C/IDN/4-5 (27 July 2005), para. 52(a) and (b).

[193] Ibid., para. 124.

[194] UN CEDAW Committee, Consideration of reports submitted by states parties under article 18 of the Convention on the Elimination of All Forms of Discrimination against Women, Combined sixth and seventh periodic reports of states parties: Indonesia, CEDAW/C/IDN/6-7 (7 January 2011), para. 31.

[195] Ibid.

practice of gender relations ... Women are left behind in all sectors, including health, labour, the economy, and politics.[196]

To overcome these issues, the Government has undertaken a variety of measures, such as advocacy among community leaders (including traditional and religious leaders), the mass media and youth organisations to promote understanding of and support for gender equality.[197] The Government also created the Ministry of Women's Empowerment and Child Protection in 2009, tasked with eliminating discrimination against women and enhancing their role and status.[198] This new Ministry collaborated with the Ministry of Health in issuing a joint agreement to introduce gender mainstreaming throughout the health sector.[199]

Despite these and other measures, the CEDAW Committee continued to express its concern 'at the persistence of adverse cultural norms, practices, traditions, patriarchal attitudes and deep-rooted stereotypes regarding the roles, responsibilities and identities of women and men in the family and in society'.[200] The Committee recalled 'that cultural and religious values cannot be allowed to undermine the universality of women's rights', and that 'culture is not a static concept and that the core values in Indonesian society are not inconsistent with the advancement of women'.[201] The CEDAW Committee lamented that Indonesia 'has not taken sufficient sustained and systematic action to modify or eliminate stereotypes and harmful practices'.[202] As such, gender

---

[196] Ibid., para. 25.
[197] UN CEDAW Committee, Consideration of reports submitted by states parties under article 18 of the Convention on the Elimination of All Forms of Discrimination against Women, Combined fourth and fifth periodic reports of states parties: Indonesia, CEDAW/C/IDN/4-5 (27 July 2005), para. 52(a) and (b).
[198] UN ESCR Committee, Implementation of the International Covenant on Economic, Social and Cultural Rights, Initial reports submitted by states parties under articles 16 and 17 of the Covenant: Indonesia, E/C.12/IDN/1 (29 October 2012), para. 43. See Presidential Regulation No. 47 of 2009 creating the Ministry.
[199] UNHRCee, Consideration of Reports submitted by states parties under article 40 of the Covenant, Initial reports of states parties: Indonesia, CCPR/C/IDN/1 (19 March 2012), para. 49.
[200] UN CEDAW Committee, Concluding observations of the Committee on the Elimination of Discrimination against Women: Indonesia, CEDAW/C/IDN/CO/6-7 (7 August 2012), para. 23.
[201] UN CEDAW Committee, Report of CEDAW Committee, Eighteenth and Nineteenth Sessions, A/53/38/Rev.a (14 May 1998), para. 282.
[202] UN CEDAW Committee, Concluding observations of the Committee on the Elimination of Discrimination against Women: Indonesia, CEDAW/C/IDN/CO/6-7 (7 August 2012), para. 23.

inequality and discrimination against women persist and, as a health determinant, impact upon women's reproductive health and access to family planning. To redress this situation and comply with articles 2(f) and 5(a) CEDAW, the Committee recommended Indonesia implement a comprehensive, results-oriented strategy to eliminate stereotypes, harmful practices and discrimination against women.[203]

Islam's Influence in Indonesia

As can be drawn out from these three factors, Islam is highly relevant to reproductive health and family planning in Indonesia. This is because Islam (like other religions) has 'highly developed codes of behaviour related to sexuality and reproduction that are proscriptive in regulating marriage, sexuality, gender relations and roles, and procreation within the faith group'.[204] Given the scope of Islamic norms, religion pervades almost any discussion in Indonesian society of family life, gender issues or morality.[205] Not only does religion have a profound influence on people's decisions about sexuality and reproduction,[206] but religious organisations both in Indonesia and around the world are major providers of healthcare and information.[207] As such, Islam is a vital sociocultural health determinant in Indonesia. Because of the highly influential role of Islam in most of Indonesian society, the Government acknowledged from the beginning that it was necessary to include religious leaders in its reproductive health programmes – including family planning.[208] The religious beliefs of the Muslim community and its leaders therefore greatly influenced the design and implementation of Indonesia's reproductive health goods, policies and services.[209]

---

[203] Ibid., para. 24.
[204] Frances Kissling, Examining Religion and Reproductive Health: Constructive Engagement for the Future, in Mindy Jane Roseman and Laura Reichenbach (eds.), *Reproductive Health and Human Rights: The Way Forward* (University of Pennsylvania Press, 2009), p. 212.
[205] Suzanne Brenner, Private Moralities in the Public Sphere: Democratization, Islam, and Gender in Indonesia (2011) *American Anthropologist* 113:3, p. 481.
[206] Rebecca Firestone, Laura Reichenbach and Mindy Jane Roseman, Conclusion: Conceptual Successes and Operational Challenges to ICPD: Global Reproductive Health and Rights Moving Forward, in Mindy Jane Roseman and Laura Reichenbach (eds.), *Reproductive Health and Human Rights: The Way Forward* (University of Pennsylvania Press, 2009), p. 230.
[207] Kissling (n. 204), p. 216.
[208] Marshall (n. 127), p. 14.
[209] Sciortino, Marcoes-Natsir and F. Mas'udi (n. 155), p. 87.

5.2 RIGHT TO REPRODUCTIVE HEALTH IN INDONESIA

Part of Islam's influence in Indonesia stems from the fact that it exists as a plural legal system that can have more purchase within a Muslim community than national or international law. For example, according to Riffat Hassan, it is more effective to assure Muslim women that the *Qur'an* supports their reproductive rights than it is to tell them that a UN document will set them free.[210] She claims that Muslim women have become enlivened upon the realisation of the immense possibilities for development that exist within the belief system that defines their worldview.[211] This exemplifies that while human rights can have moral and legal force, they function in a space alongside competing normative claims that must be considered and weighed. Hassan's assertion reflects Merry's call outlined in Chapter 2 for international human rights norms to be vernacularised into the local context. In this process, the substance of human rights is translated into terms and concepts meaningful for the local population (in this case Islam) in order to be effectively promoted and protected. As such, the language of international human rights law may not need to be employed at all in some contexts where recourse to local norms is more effective.

While plural normative systems like Islam and human rights can align (albeit based on different argumentation), they can also compete and conflict. For example, FGM/C is widely practised in Indonesia as 'a long-held tradition and belief which has been passed down through generations'.[212] The Indonesian Government withdrew its prohibition on medically performed FGM/C (*sunat perempuan*) due to religious rulings (*fatwas*) against the prohibition by Islamic leaders (*ulamas*).[213] This

---

[210] Riffat Hassan, Challenging Stereotypes of Fundamentalism: An Islamic Feminist Perspective (Spring 2001) *The Muslim World* 91, p. 66; Riffat Hassan, Is Islam a Help or Hindrance to Women's Development?, in Johan Meuleman (ed.), *Islam in the Era of Globalization: Muslim Attitudes towards Modernity and Identity* (Routledge, 2002), p. 207. Hassan was particularly influential in Indonesia due to her travels there in the 1990s and as her work was translated into Bahasa Indonesia.

[211] Hassan (2001), ibid., p. 66.

[212] UN Human Rights Council, National report submitted in accordance with para. 5 of the annex to Human Rights Council res. 16/21: Indonesia, A/HRC/WG.6/27/IDN/1 (20 February 2017), paras. 59–61.

[213] Council of Indonesian Ulama (*Majelis Ulama Indonesia*) fatwa No. 9A (2008) concerning FGM/C. See UN CEDAW Committee, Consideration of reports submitted by states parties under article 18 of the Convention on the Elimination of All Forms of Discrimination against Women, Combined sixth and seventh periodic reports of states parties: Indonesia, CEDAW/C/IDN/6–7 (7 January 2011), paras. 132, 152; UN CEDAW Committee, Concluding observations of the Committee on the Elimination of Discrimination against Women: Indonesia, CEDAW/C/IDN/CO/6–7 (7 August 2012), paras. 21–2; UN

reversal by the Government illustrates the strong influence of Islam in Indonesia, even in the face of contradicting state and international law. This is also despite the fact that Indonesia is not *per se* an Islamic state.[214] Such examples demonstrate Islam's compelling normative influence in Indonesia, especially in relation to reproductive health. Given this reality, it is crucial that Islamic leaders are engaged and involved in family planning programming in Indonesia. As seen in other Muslim-majority states, Islamic 'beliefs, communities, and leaders at the individual, family, and societal levels can be very significant, encouraging positive attitudes and actions or discouraging various forms of contraception altogether'.[215]

5.2.3 Reproductive Rights in International Law and Indonesia: A Community Concern

This first part of the case study set out Indonesia's international law obligations regarding reproductive health and the socio-cultural context in which these rights have to be realised. As a party to ICESCR, CEDAW and CRC, Indonesia is legally bound to progressively realise the right to health and reproductive health as a core part of that right. While international law requires states to take a variety of measures to implement the right, each state enjoys discretion to determine the measures best suited to its national context that will be effective. As part of the requirement for health facilities, goods and services to be available, accessible, acceptable and quality, states must ensure that reproductive healthcare is culturally appropriate and acceptable to women. This recognises the substantive role of culture in human rights and especially reproductive rights, which shapes the way people conceive of their health as well as health interventions. Arguably for this reason, states must

---

HRCee, Concluding observations on the initial report of Indonesia, CCPR/C/IDN/CO/1 (21 August 2013), para. 12.

[214] The Indonesian state is 'based upon the belief in the One and Only God', that 'guarantees all persons the freedom of worship, each according to his/her own religion or belief'. See Constitution preamble and art. 29. The preamble enshrines Sukarno's philosophy of *Pancasila* (Five Principles), which, while it does not stipulate Islam, includes belief in the 'One and only God'. See further discussion Ratno Lukito, State and Religion Continuum in Indonesia: The Trajectory of Religious Establishment and Religious Freedom in the Constitution, *Indonesian Journal of International and Comparative Law* (2017), pp. 645–81; Myengkyo Seo, Toward Neither an Islam nor a secular state (2012) *Citizenship Studies* 16:8.

[215] Katherine Marshall, Preface, in Marshall (n. 127), p. 3.

ensure the participation of and consultation with the public and other NSAs in the design and implementation of healthcare systems. The ESCR Committee has further acknowledged that NSAs also have international responsibilities regarding the right to health. While states remain accountable under international law, they must both facilitate and monitor the role of NSAs in fulfilling the right to reproductive health.

Indonesia has protected both the right to health and non-discrimination in its Constitution as well as in law and policy. Given the high maternal mortality and fertility rates in the mid-twentieth century, Indonesia instigated an ambitious reproductive healthcare plan. The national family planning programme run by the BKKBN has been operating now for five decades and is recognised internationally for its success. However, fulfilling the right to reproductive health is not simply a matter of enacting legislation and providing health clinics. The Government also had to collaborate with numerous NSAs who expanded demand for as well as access to family planning services, including community and religious groups, NGOs, schools, the media and women's groups. Once rejected, family planning is now widely utilised in Indonesia and the small family norm has replaced the old ideal of multiple children. Despite these long-running programmes and much progress in reducing the fertility rate, family planning and reproductive health generally remain a pressing contemporary issue in Indonesia. This is due to factors including funding limitations, government decentralisation and socio-cultural determinants. On this basis, the Government has reiterated its top health priorities as improving access to reproductive healthcare services, including the family planning programme.

In order for Indonesia to meet its international health obligations, it is necessary to consider this socio-cultural context as well as the actors that operate within it. This is because scholars have noted that the social and psychological distance between a community and its health professionals can be an obstacle,[216] and that health interventions can fail if not culturally appropriate. As seen in this section, the sex education project for adolescents delivered by parents was unsuccessful, as was the family planning programming that only focused on women (and not men). Another example was the failed state ban on medically performed FGM/C in the face of Islamic opposition. Conversely, other initiatives deemed culturally appropriate were well received by the public and

---

[216] Titaley, Hunter, Dibley and Heywood (n. 121), p. 10.

effective in practice. This includes the *SIAGA* campaigns, the empowerment of local women as volunteers to promote family planning, and reproductive health education and advocacy based on Islamic norms. As this illustrates, simply providing healthcare is insufficient, as it is also necessary for the state to build knowledge of and demand for healthcare within a community.

States are required under international human rights law to ensure that health facilities, goods and services are acceptable to particular cultural communities – including religious ones. However, states are not obliged to accommodate cultural norms or practices that are harmful or discriminatory to women, which should rather be reformed or modified. This can include norms like those above relating to gendered decision-making, stereotypes, marriage and sexuality, and practices like FGM/C. As stressed by the treaty bodies and in the literature, eliminating discrimination against women and redressing their low social status is crucial for improving their ability to access reproductive healthcare. However, the state alone cannot eliminate adverse cultural norms and practices to ensure women's equality where they do not have authority over them. This applies to the situation in Indonesia where the state is not an authority on Islam. Therefore, the state lacks the capacity as well as legitimacy to effectively reform such normative systems. This places the state in a difficult position, as it is nonetheless ultimately accountable under international law for something it does not have direct authority over. This exposes a misalignment of interests, capacity and obligation. However, it also highlights the crucial role of NSAs in human rights implementation.

The Indonesian Government had to involve NSAs in its family planning programme for three reasons. First, it was obliged to consult with the public in planning and implementation and to fulfil their right to participation. Secondly, Indonesia was internationally obliged to facilitate private actors in discharging their international responsibilities regarding the right to health. Finally, it was necessary to involve NSAs in order to effectively address the socio-cultural determinants that impact the right to reproductive health. As set out above, many of the socio-cultural determinants relate directly to Islam, arguably, the most important non-state normative system in Indonesia. Therefore, the state had to involve NSAs such as religious leaders, organisations and communities who hold authority and exercise influence over these norms impacting reproductive rights. As powerful social institutions, Islamic law and institutions can increase community acceptance of and access to family planning – and vice versa. For these reasons, Islamic law and institutions were instrumental in the implementation of the right to family planning in Indonesia.

5.3 Family Planning, Islamic Law and Institutions in Indonesia

Like most states in the world, particularly former colonial states, Indonesia is legally plural, with coexisting state and non-state normative orders. The Indonesian legal system is an amalgamation of state law (from the central down to the district laws), religious law (including Islamic law) and Adat (customary) law, each with their own sources, principles and authorities. Legal pluralism has deep roots in Indonesia, as each system of law has a long history and well-established norms.[217] For example, Islam has a long and complex history in Indonesia, beginning in around the fourteenth century with the arrival of Islam via traders. Adat law is even older than Islam and much older than Western law, which was the newest arrival with the Dutch East India Company in the seventeenth century. Rather than being siloed systems of law, there are many overlaps and interactions, with the systems mutually influencing one another and evolving. For example, all three systems of law in Indonesia have normative rules regarding inheritance.[218] This is typical as legally plural situations can support multiple 'coexisting conceptions of permissible action, valid transactions, and ideas and procedures for dealing with conflict' in the same social field.[219] While the state made reforms following Indonesia's independence in 1945 to reduce this pluralism, and since then to resolve conflicts, in practice, substantive pluralism remains intact.[220]

---

[217] For a discussion of the status, history and relationship of these three legal systems in Indonesia, see: Mohammad Daud Ali, *Islamic Law: Introduction to Islamic Jurisprudence and the Legal System in Indonesia* (PT RajaGrafindo Persada, 2016), ch. 4; Ratno Lukito, *Legal Pluralism in Indonesia: Bridging the Unbridgeable* (Routledge, 2013).

[218] See further Yeni Salma Barlinti, Inheritance Legal System in Indonesia: A Legal Justice for People (2013) *Indonesia Law Review* 3:1, pp. 23–41.

[219] Sally Engle Merry, Legal Pluralism and Legal Culture: Mapping the Terrain, in Brian Tamanaha, Caroline Sage and Michael Woolcock (eds.), *Legal Pluralism and Development: Scholars and Practitioners in Dialogue* (Cambridge University Press, 2012), p. 67.

[220] See Adriaan Bedner and Stijn van Huis, Plurality of Marriage Law and Marriage Registration for Muslims in Indonesia: A Plea for Pragmatism (June 2010) *Utrecht Law Review* 6:2, p. 178; Ratno Lukito, Mapping the Relationship of Competing Legal

The focus of this third section of the case study is specifically on the role of Islamic law and its related institutions in the implementation of the right to family planning in Indonesia. First, it briefly introduces Islamic law[221] and then the key Islamic institutions in Indonesia, providing a general overview of their actions relating to Government's family planning programme. Rather than detailing their involvement throughout the programme's five decades, this section provides an illustrative sample of their *fatwas*, advocacy and healthcare services. As seen below, the women's branches of the Islamic institutions played a particularly important role in interpreting Islamic law, advocating family planning and providing reproductive healthcare services to the public. While Islamic institutions in Indonesia have been increasingly addressed in the literature, less attention has typically been given to the numerous women's branches.[222] As such, this section pays particular attention to these institutions and to the female Muslim scholars who reinterpreted Islamic norms to promote women's reproductive rights and equality more generally.

5.3.1 Abridged Introduction to Islamic Law

The word 'Islam' means peace, well-being, surrender or salvation, and the purpose of Islamic law is generally defined as the happiness of all humans in this world and the afterlife.[223] The sources of Islam include the *Qur'an*, *Hadith*, *fiqh*, *Sunnah* and *Shari'ah*. The *Qur'an* is the primary and most authoritative source of Islam as the word of God revealed to the Prophet. The *Hadith* are the Prophet's statements or sayings, and the *Sunnah* is the practice, custom or tradition of the Prophet as contained in the *Hadith*. Meaning 'understanding', *fiqh* is the science of jurisprudence, 'the process of human endeavor to discern and extract legal rules from

---

Traditions in the Era of Transnationalism in Indonesia, in Gary Bell (ed.), *Pluralism, Transnationalism and Culture in Asian Law* (2017), pp. 91–7.

[221] Islamic law is a vast and complex body of law with multiple sources, authorities and interpretations. It is not the intention to set out Islamic law here in detail, nor is it necessary for the present study, which looks at the instrumentalisation of Islamic law, rather than engaging in Islamic exegesis or debate. As such, this section presents only an illustrative (and incomplete) overview, based on a reading of secondary sources.

[222] Van Doorn-Harders book in 2006 was one of the first comprehensive studies on the topic in English: Pieternella van Doorn-Harder, *Women Shaping Islam: Reading The Qur'an in Indonesia* (University of Illinois Press, 2006).

[223] Daud Ali (n. 217), p. 39.

5.3 FAMILY PLANNING, LAW AND INSTITUTIONS

the sacred sources of Islam'.[224] Finally, *Shari'ah*, meaning the path or way, is a complete code of conduct based on the rules and regulations revealed to the Prophet in the *Qur'an* and contained in the *Hadith*.[225] Together, these sources contribute to what is referred to as 'the Islamic tradition'; however, they do not represent 'a coherent or consistent body of teachings or precepts from which a universally agreed upon set of Islamic norms can be derived'.[226] Given the numerous inconsistencies and variances among the sources and their interpretation, 'it is scarcely possible to speak of "Islam" or "the Islamic tradition" as if it were unitary'.[227] This is despite the fact that Islam is typically represented in the West as a monolith in some popular and academic discources.

Contrary to religious groups like Catholics, there is no set religious hierarchy in Sunni Islam (predominant in Indonesia) or ultimate leader like the Pope. In such an environment, there is a great scope for a diversity of views and beliefs within Islam. For example, there are four main schools of Islamic thought (*madhabs*) and Muslims may choose which to follow: *Hanafi*, *Maliki*, *Shafi'i* (predominant in Indonesia) and *Hanbali*. Furthermore, there is a divergence of views within each of these schools and among their followers. These differences are considered to represent 'different manifestations of the same divine will' and are considered as 'diversity within unity'.[228] Islam's intra-plurality is also facilitated by its openness to interpretation. In particular, Islam in Indonesia takes a highly interpretive approach emphasising *fiqh* and jurisprudence, resulting in 'radically diverse' Islamic thought and practice.[229] This interpretive tradition has given rise to multiple understandings of Islamic law not just in Indonesia but around the world. As such, generalisations or representations of Islam as fixed and literal are typically

---

[224] Ziba Mir Hosseini, Muslim Women's Quest for Equality: Between Islamic Law and Feminism (Summer 2006) *Critical Inquiry* 32, p. 632; Daud Ali (n. 217), p. 31.

[225] Given their translation from Arabic, there are different ways to spell Islamic terms like *Shari'ah*, including *Sharia* and *Syariah*. This applies to all of the terms, which lack agreed or formal transcriptions.

[226] Hassan (2000) (n. 188), p. 226.

[227] Ibid., pp. 226–7.

[228] Mohamed Elewa Badar, Islamic Law (*Shari'a*) and the Jurisdiction of the International Criminal Law (2011) *Leiden Journal of International Law* 24, p. 431, citing M. H. Kamali, *Principles of Islamic Jurisprudence* (1991), p. 169.

[229] Rachel Rinaldo, Envisioning the Nation: Women Activists, Religion and the Public Sphere in Indonesia (June 2008) *Social Forces* 86:4, p. 1790; Simon Butt, Islam, The State and the Constitutional Court in Indonesia (2010) *Pacific Rim Law & Policy Journal Association* 19:2, p. 281.

neither accurate nor useful.[230] While some texts such as those regarding faith, prayer, fasting, charity and the pilgrimage (the five pillars of Islam) are fixed and common to the whole Muslim community, others relating to human relations with one another have numerous iterations and variations.[231]

This diversity and contestation within Islam is possible as while the *Qur'an* is sacred and immutable as the word of God, its interpretation is not.[232] Scholars agree that *fiqh*, as a work of human reasoning, is dynamic and subject to change from time to time and place to place.[233] In conjunction with the lack of a clear hierarchy, anyone can interpret Islamic texts if they have the requisite knowledge and skills: knowledge of Arabic, the *Qur'an* and *Hadith*, understanding of the science of Islam and *fiqh*, and honesty.[234] Like jurisprudence in other legal systems, *fiqh* involves the creative processes of reasoning and argumentation. In the absence of consensus, alternative views on a topic are considered equally valid.[235] Additionally, there is no individual or group who censors the results of Islamic scholars' independent reasoning (*ijtihad*). Rather, what is compelling is whether the principles or rules of interpretation and legal theory (*usul al-fiqh*) have been applied. In fact, reasoning is key in Islam and highly valued, with Daud Ali claiming that: 'Among the things that God gives to human beings, the most valuable one is human reason'.[236] For example, in a *Hadith* regarding the judge Mu'adh lbn Jabal, the

---

[230] John Hursh, Advancing Women's Rights through Islamic Law: The Example of Morocco (2012) *Berkeley Journal of Gender, Law & Justice* 27, p. 299.

[231] Two categories have been identified as relating to worship (fixed) and *muamalah* (open). In relation to the latter, regarding relations between people and objects, the *Qur'an* gives only general provisions (only around three per cent of the *Qur'anic* verses), so authorities can manage and formulate them in time and place, so long as they do not conflict with the *Qur'an* and spirit of *Shari'ah*. Daud Ali (n. 217), pp. 21–3, 56, 103; Sciortino, Marcoes-Natsir and F. Mas'udi (n. 155), p. 87.

[232] Hursh (n. 230), p. 291.

[233] Daud Ali (n. 217), pp. 32–4; Hosseini (n. 224), p. 632.

[234] Daud Ali (n. 217), p. 74. For discussion of women gaining these skills and becoming *ulama* in Indonesia, see Nor Ismah, Destabilising Male Domination: Building Community-Based Authority among Indonesian Female Ulama (2016) *Asian Studies Review* 40:4, pp. 491–509.

[235] Onder Bakircioglu, The Principal Sources of Islamic Law, in Tallyn Gray (ed.), *Islam and International Criminal Law and Justice* (Torkel Opsahl Academic Epublisher, 2018), p. 38.

[236] 'Reasoning is created by Allah for humans to develop and make something perfect. No progress can be made without human thought.' Daud Ali (n. 217), pp. 14, 71.

5.3 FAMILY PLANNING, LAW AND INSTITUTIONS

Prophet praised his reliance in decision-making upon the *Qur'an* and *Sunnah*, as well as the use of his own reasoning and judgment.[237]

According to the traditional method of *Qur'anic* exegesis, if a text is definite and absolute with no other meaning or interpretation, then it is considered fixed – *qath'i*. However, if the meaning is unclear or not detailed, then it is *zanni* and open to interpretation. *Ijtihad* is an interpretive technique or methodology whereby, on the basis of concerted effort and reasoning, a qualified person makes a determination according to the time and place of a matter unclear (*zanni*) or not regulated in Islamic law.[238] Through reasoning, analogy (*qiyas*), and interpretation, Islamic law can be applied and adapted to contemporary situations while upholding Islamic doctrine. As such, *itjihad* is a mechanism for developing Islamic law, which functions to accommodate the changes and demands of society over time.[239] A debate arose regarding *ijtihad* and to what extent it can still be practised, or whether the 'gate of *ijtihad*' has closed.[240] Rejecting this, Hallaq argued that accepting that the gates of *ijtihad* were closed would mean that Islam becomes inadequate and unable to apply *Shari'ah* to newly arising problems.[241] In Indonesia today, there are many new issues insufficiently addressed in the *Qur'an* or *Hadith* that require *ijtihad*.[242] The fact that certain aspects can (and do) evolve based on new information and contemporary circumstances reflects the vitality and dynamism within Islamic law.

As such, different Islamic scholars (*ulama*) can make an interpretation after studying the religious texts and *fiqh* and arrive at different outcomes. This internal contestation can and does happen, with, for

---

[237] Akbar Ahmed, *Discovering Islam: Making Sense of Muslim History and Society* (Routledge, 2002), p. 24.

[238] This legal determination cannot conflict with the spirit of Islamic teachings or contradict the *Shari'ah*. Daud Ali (n. 217), pp. 14, 23, 34, 71. See also Sus Eko Ernada, Issues of Compatibility of Human Rights and Islam: The Experience of Egypt and Indonesia (June 2007) *Journal of Indonesian Islam* 1:1, p. 119.

[239] Daud Ali (n. 217), pp. 73, 79.

[240] In this debate some had argued that Islam was sufficiently elaborated with all essential questions addressed, and therefore there was no need for further *ijtihad* – and that the gate had closed. While this position was accepted by many, it was contested and dismissed by others. Wael Hallaq, On the Origins of the Controversy about the Existence of Mujtahids and the Gate of Ijtihad (1986) *Studia Islamica* 63, pp. 130-2.

[241] Ibid. See also Shaykh Taha Jabir Al-Alwani, *Issues in Contemporary Islamic Thought* (International Institute of Islamic Thought, 2005), pp. 65-8.

[242] Interview with Prof. Dr Huzaemah Tahido Yanggo, Rector of Institute of *Qur'an* Studies, Islamic University of Indonesia, and member of MUI *fatwa* Commission (1 February 2017, Jakarta, Indonesia).

example, Indonesian Islamic institutions like Nahdlatul Ulama (NU) and Muhammadiyah taking different positions in *fatwas* on the same issue. A *fatwa* is a religious ruling or statement made by an individual or institution trained in Islamic jurisprudence in response to a request for clarification on an issue of religious principle or dogma.[243] *Fatwas* are a crucial mechanism for transmitting Islamic rules and values from scholars to the general public, and, as 'responsive to political and social pressure', they typically change more rapidly than the bulwark of Islamic jurisprudence.[244] For example, Muhammadiyah recently declared smoking *haram*[245] on the basis of new information regarding its negative health impacts, while others like NU continue to view smoking as permissible (*makrouh*).[246] In this situation there is a difference of opinion (*ikhtilaf*) and it is then for each Muslim to decide for themselves which position to follow, because *fatwas* are not legally binding or enforceable. This interpretive scope and the (sometimes significant) plurality within Islam provides space for dialogue and debate within Muslim communities. This creates an environment that can support reasoned discussions, exchanges of views, as well as a diversity of views, reflecting a saying in Islam that 'differences are a blessing'.[247]

5.3.2 Islamic Law and Institutions in Indonesia

As established, Islam is a comprehensive system regulating not only the spiritual but also the civic aspects of individual and communal life.[248] While not an Islamic state, the Indonesian Constitution provides that the

---

[243] Menchik (n. 104), p. 364; Wael Hallaq, *An Introduction to Islamic Law* (Cambridge University Press, 2009), pp. 9–10.
[244] Menchik, (n. 104), p. 364.
[245] In Islam, all human actions are classified into one of five categories on a spectrum: obligatory (*Wajib*), recommended (*Mustahabb*), permitted (*Masmouh*), disapproved but not forbidden (*Makrouh*), or absolutely forbidden (*Haram*). Daud Ali (n. 217), p. 28
[246] Muhammadiyah *fatwa* No. 6/SM/MTT/III/2010. See further Dessy Sagita and Anita Rachman, Indonesian Clerics Join Smoking Fatwa Row, *Jakarta Globe* (15 March 2010), http://jakartaglobe.id/archive/indonesian-clerics-join-smoking-fatwa-row/ (accessed 3 January 2018).
[247] Interview with Dr Maria Ulfah Anshor, Commissioner with the Indonesian Child Protection Commission (*Komisi Perlindungan Anak Indonesia*) (7 February 2017 Jakarta, Indonesia).
[248] Fadia Hasna, Islam, Social Traditions and Family Planning (April 2003) *Social Policy & Administration* 37:2, p. 182. Daud Ali recalls that 'Islam teaches a holistic way of life, which does not exclude anything'. Daud Ali (n. 217), p. 15.

nation is based on the belief in one God.[249] Islamic law is therefore one of the sources of Indonesian law, applying both normatively and juridically. The normative aspects applied in Indonesia typically relate to the spiritual relationship between God and humans. The Muslim community's adherence to these aspects 'depends on their own sense of faith' and 'on the conscience of each individual Muslim'.[250] The juridical aspects of Islamic law in Indonesia relate to the relationship between humans, and between humans and objects, such as regarding marriage, inheritance and criminal law (in places). The Government introduced the Compilation of Islamic Law (*Kompilasi Hukum Islam di Indonesia*) in 1991, which is a restatement of Islamic law regarding marriage, inheritance and charity, as compiled by prominent *ulama* in a process guided by the Minister and local Offices of Religious Affairs (*Kantor Urusan Agama – KUA*).[251] This Ministry is part of the central Government and administers all religion in Indonesia, though most of its work focuses on Islam.[252]

In addition to the general state courts, Indonesia also has religious state courts (*peradilan agama*) to enforce the juridical aspects of Islamic law, which only apply to Muslims. While such courts may have existed informally since the arrival of Islam to what is now Indonesia, they were formalised by the Dutch during the colonial period.[253] The judges in these contemporary courts are religious scholars and the courts have jurisdiction over matters including marriage, inheritance, charity and Islamic finance.[254] Matters from the religious courts can be appealed to general state courts, including (some matters) to the Constitutional Court and the Supreme Court, Indonesia's highest court, which have the final determination.[255] The religious courts' jurisprudence contributes to the development of Islamic norms and principles in Indonesia. In addition to Islamic law at the central state level, as part of decentralisation the districts may also enact *Shari'ah* inspired by-laws, and the

---

[249] See Constitution preamble and art. 29.
[250] Daud Ali (n. 217), pp. 4, 6.
[251] Bedner and van Huis (n. 220), p. 180; Daud Ali (n. 217), pp. 192–205; Butt (n. 229) p. 289.
[252] Butt (n. 229), pp. 283–4.
[253] Mark Cammack and Michael Feener, The Islamic Legal System in Indonesia (2012) *Pacific Rim Law & Policy Journal* 21:1, pp. 14–15.
[254] Law No. 7 of 1989 on the Religious Courts, art. 49(1). Daud Ali (n. 217), pp. 155, 158–160, 181, 187; Butt (n. 251), p. 284.
[255] Daud Ali (n. 217), p. 185.

province of Aceh has in fact adopted Islamic law, including criminal law, as state law.[256]

As mentioned, in addition to Islamic law being adopted by the state at various levels, Islamic law also applies normatively in Indonesia. Islamic leaders have authority over interpretations of such norms and hold much influence in their communities. For example, '[t]he average Muslim believer seldom contradicts' religious leaders,[257] and 'they see the *"ulama"* – not the state – as the guardians of Islamic law and regard their authority as absolute'.[258] Several interview participants noted that Muslims will typically 'obey' religious leaders. To illustrate, most Muslims consider a marriage valid not depending upon state recognition, but whether it has been concluded according to Islamic law as perceived locally.[259] On this basis, and as seen in the FGM/C example above, despite the state prohibiting something, if permitted by Islamic authorities, the state law may go unenforced. Clearly, it is the *ulama* and other religious leaders – and not the state – who hold authority regarding Islam. Professor Huzaemah (a senior female *ulama* and member of MUI's *fatwa* commission) highlighted this, noting that when the *ulama* speak people are more willing to comply than when only the Government speaks.

As the largest Muslim country in the world, Indonesia is also home to the largest Islamic institutions in the world: Nahdlatul Ulama and Muhammadiyah. These institutions provide a range of services, including spiritual, educational and health, with many members looking to them for guidance and following their teaching. Muhammadiyah was established in 1912 in Yogyakarta by reformists inspired by Egypt's modernists. Muhammadiyah aims to restore purity to Islam by teaching according to the *Qur'an* and the *Hadith,* and removing other religious or cultural influences in Indonesia. Muhammadiyah was formed by mainly urban, more educated Muslims, and is particularly focused on health and education. Muhammadiyah is highly influential

---

[256] See Law No. 44 of 1999 on the Special Status of the Province of Aceh Special Region. Cammack and Feener (n. 253), pp. 38–42; Pieternella van Doorn-Harder, Controlling the Body: Muslim Feminists Debating Women's Rights in Indonesia (2008) *Religion Compass* 2:6, p. 1024.

[257] Van Doorn-Harder, ibid., p. 1028.

[258] Euis Nurlaelawati, Muslim Women in Indonesian Religious Courts: Reform, Strategies, and Pronouncement of Divorce (2013) *Islamic Law and Society* 20:3, p. 271.

[259] Bedner and van Huis (n. 220), p. 187. Compilation of Islamic Law, art. 4 provides that a marriage is valid if done in accordance with Islamic law.

due to 'its national network of schools and hospitals and its access to mass media'.[260] Muhammadiyah's *fatwas* are produced by a commission comprising both male and female *ulama*. As an organisation with around 40 million members, the full spectrum of views is present within Muhammadiyah, ranging from the very traditional to the very progressive. Muhammadiyah has two women's branches: Aisyiyah and Nasyiatul 'Aisyiyah. Established in 1917, Aisyiyah represents women within Muhammadiyah, whereas the subsequent Nasyiatul 'Aisyiyah represents the younger women. A number of Muslim feminist thinkers hail from Muhammadiyah, including Lies Marcoes-Natsir and Siti Ruhaini.

Nahdlatul Ulama (NU) was created after Muhammadiyah in 1926, and is the largest Islamic organisation in the world with over 50 million members. Like Muhammadiyah, NU performs many functions but have Islam as their foundation. However, NU was originally a more traditionalist organisation that included local cultural rituals and beliefs, with members mainly drawn from the rural areas of Java and Madura and the more than 7,000 *pesantren* (Islamic boarding schools). Despite being traditionalist, NU has taken progressive stances on some controversial issues. For example, NU's former leader and President of Indonesia from 1999 to 2001, Abdurrahman Wahid stimulated and protected critical thought, expression and the search for more progressive interpretations of Islamic texts.[261] While previously more involved in politics, NU shifted its focus in the early 1980s to welfare oriented activities, such as education, economic development and modern science.[262] In this period, NU sought to grow and develop civil society in Indonesia and opposed Suharto's regime in various ways.[263] Muslim feminist thinkers hailing from NU include Maria Ulfah Anshor and Siti Musdah Mulia.

Like Muhammadiyah, NU also has two women's branches: Muslimat represents women in NU above the age of approximately forty, while the younger women are represented in Fatayat. It took concerted effort to create Muslimat in 1946, including to gain permission for women to

---

[260] Sciortino, Marcoes-Natsir and F. Mas'udi (n. 155), p. 87.
[261] Ibid.; Arskal Salim, Between ICMI and NU: The Contested Representation of Muslim Civil Society in Indonesia, 1990–2001 (2011) *Al-Jāmi'ah* 49:2, pp. 314–21.
[262] 'Many of the young reformers at that time were convinced that dialogue rather than confrontation was needed with the *umma* and with non-Muslims'. Monika Arnez, Empowering Women through Islam: Fatayat NU between Tradition and Change (2010) *Journal of Islamic Studies* 21:1, p. 70.
[263] Salim (n. 261), pp. 314–21.

speak at NU conferences.[264] Fatayat was subsequently established in 1950 and became an autonomous body in 1962. Today Fatayat has over eight million members, with 480 chapters at the district level, around 2,000 at the sub-district level, and 21,000 at the village level.[265] Fatayat's objectives include to foster young women devoted 'to almighty Allah, to be moral, skilful, responsible, and beneficial to religion and nation; to create a society with gender equality; to create devotion towards the principles, beliefs, and objectives of NU in building Islamic *Shariah*'.[266] Like NU and Muhammadiyah, Fatayat collaborates with other partners including the Government, and undertakes activities for its members including education, literacy and entrepreneurial projects.[267]

Another important Islamic institution is the Indonesian Council of Ulama (*Majelis Ulama Indonesia* – MUI), an independent advisory or consultative body for the Government, which declares *fatwas* on relevant issues. Even when the Government has legislated on a particular topic, such as deforestation or immunisation, they may additionally request a *fatwa* from MUI for an authoritative religious statement on the matter.[268] The MUI is funded by the Government and comprises prominent *ulama* as well as civil servants from the Ministry of Religious Affairs appointed by the Government.[269] MUI's *fatwa* commission has sixty-five members (men and women), comprising members from Islamic organisations across Indonesia including Muhammadiyah and NU. While Muhammadiyah and NU were created independently and

---

[264] Susan Blackburn, Indonesian Women and Political Islam (February 2008) *Journal of Southeast Asian Studies* 39:1, pp. 88 and fn. 18.
[265] Interview with Anggia Ermarini, Chairperson of Fatayat NU (3 February 2017, Jakarta, Indonesia).
[266] Rinaldo (n. 229) p. 1786.
[267] For example, it has offered Bahasa Indonesia as well as English language courses, organised sewing and cooking courses, and run numerous health related projects on topics including HIV/AIDS and domestic violence. Fatayat has a very collaborative approach, working with Komnas Perempuan, the Ministry of Women's Empowerment and Child Protection, the Government, private sector, as well as international organisations like UNICEF. Arnez (n. 262), p. 67. Interview with Anggia Ermarini, Chairperson of Fatayat NU (3 February 2017, Jakarta, Indonesia).
[268] Members of the public may also make a request for a *fatwa*. Interview with Prof. Dr Huzaemah Tahido Yanggo, Rector of Institute of Qur'an Studies, Islamic University of Indonesia, and member of MUI *fatwa* commission (1 February 2017, Jakarta, Indonesia).
[269] Cammack and Feener (n. 253), p. 34; Sciortino, Marcoes-Natsir and F. Mas'udi (n. 155), p. 87.

have huge grassroots membership, the Government under Suharto formed MUI in 1975 as a top-down measure with no membership network.[270] This was done as a way for the Suharto Government to legitimate and support its policies from an Islamic perspective, as well as to involve Islamic leaders in an institutional fashion.[271] For example, Marcoes suggested that MUI's role in the family planning programme was to support government policy from the theological perspective.[272] These three Islamic institutions, and other smaller faith-based organisations, were all engaged in Indonesia's family planning programme.

5.3.3 Role of Islamic Law and Institutions in Indonesia's Family Planning Programme

The Indonesian Government, having recognised the need to include Islamic leaders and groups in the national family planning programme, reached out to Muhammadiyah, NU and MUI to gain their support for the programme and partnered with them on its implementation. The former Director of Collaboration on Population Education at BKKBN, Dr Eddy Hasmi, stated that religious leaders are 'a crucial factor in the development of family planning in Indonesia'.[273] The Government spent time and money engaging with the *ulama*, including taking them abroad to learn best practices in family planning from other states with predominantly Muslim populations like Egypt. This interaction and investment paid off, as '[u]ntil the New Order skilfully negotiated with Islamic leaders, they held that contraception was a sin'.[274] The Government also collaborated with Islamic institutions in the programme's design and delivery. This proactive Government collaboration with religious groups and leaders has been a distinctive feature of Indonesia's family planning programme.[275]

---

[270] Cammack and Feener (n. 253), pp. 33–5. See generally Luthfi Assyaukanie, Fatwa and Violence in Indonesia (2009) *Journal of Religion and Society* 11, pp. 4–6.
[271] Interview with Prof. Dr Nina Nurmila, Commissioner at Komnas Perempuan (25 January 2017, Jakarta, Indonesia); Interview with Dr Siti Ruhaini Dzuhayatin, State Islamic University UIN Sunan Kalijaga (21 February 2017, Yogyakarta, Indonesia).
[272] Interview with Lies Marcoes-Natsir, Rumah Kita Bersama Foundation (4 February 2017, Bogor, Indonesia).
[273] Marshall (n. 127), p. 18.
[274] Blackburn (n. 264), p. 97.
[275] Marshall (n. 127), p. 16.

Family planning is not specifically addressed in either the *Qur'an* or the Indonesian Compilation of Islamic Law. However, *Qur'anic* teachings grant insights as to how the issue may be dealt with or understood within Islam's normative framework.[276] This lack of clarity leaves space for interpretation of the relevant Islamic texts and differing views on the permissibility of family planning. Indonesia's three most prominent Islamic institutions have taken different stances on family planning over the last five decades, and 'radically changed their interpretations of Islamic law in favour of increased access to birth control'.[277] While Muhammadiyah and NU initially regarded family planning as a private matter and were reluctant to endorse the Government's programme, MUI as well as Islamic leaders at the Ministry of Religious Affairs endorsed the programme since its launch in the 1970s.[278] As a creation of the Government and part of the Government respectively, this position from MUI and the Ministry of Religious Affairs is not surprising. While Muhammadiyah and NU came to support the family planning programme, 'they were internally divided about what forms of family planning were permissible and even whether the program itself is sanctioned under Islamic law'.[279] This can be seen through their *fatwas* on the topic as well as their activities and advocacy, which are discussed below in turn.

Fatwas on Family Planning in Indonesia

Up until the 1960s and 70s, most Muslims in Indonesia as well as both NU and Muhammadiyah considered family planning to be forbidden.[280] For example, NU originally rejected family planning, which they considered to oppose God's will.[281] This position was based on an interpretation of Islamic law and several *Qur'anic* verses and *Hadith* that were seen to promote childbearing and an obligation to grow the Muslim community. Some relied upon *Qur'anic* statements referring to children as great assets or a blessing from God (such as *al-Nahl*, Sura 16:72), or to

---

[276] Hassan notes that '[t]he fact that the Qur'an does not say anything against the idea of birth control does not, likewise, necessarily imply that it supports family planning'. Hassan (2000) (n. 188), p. 230.
[277] Menchik (n. 104), p. 359; Sciortino, Marcoes-Natsir and F. Mas'udi (n. 155), p. 87.
[278] Sciortino, Marcoes-Natsir and F. Mas'udi (n. 155), p. 88.
[279] Marshall (n. 127), pp. 16–17.
[280] 'Opposition to or hesitation about family planning is shared across many traditionally conservative societies, with different religious traditions.' Ibid., p. 7.
[281] Arnez (n. 262), p. 69.

5.3 FAMILY PLANNING, LAW AND INSTITUTIONS 217

when the Prophet encouraged his followers to marry and procreate, thus enlarging the community of Muslims and their power.[282] Some Muslims opposed to family planning regard it as infanticide,[283] while others have claimed that family planning is a Western conspiracy to reduce the number of Muslims worldwide.[284] While some Muslims still hold these views today, the position in Indonesia began to change slowly with growing acceptance and contemporary support for family planning.

This change was based on progressive interpretations of Islamic texts and the emphasis or reliance upon certain *Qur'anic* verses or *Hadiths* over others, as well as external and internal advocacy. For example, advocates of family planning typically emphasise Islam's focus on the quality of children, the health of the mother, and the welfare of the family. They argue that rather than originating in the West, family planning commenced fourteen centuries ago among Muslims based on the fact that *coitus interruptus* (or *azl* in Arabic) was practised at the Prophet's time.[285] These advocates rely on two *Hadith* regarding *azl* to claim that the Prophet sanctioned family planning and that all of the major schools of Islamic thought permitted it.[286] Others reiterated that while Islam promotes expanding the *umma* (Muslim nation/community), the emphasis is on the righteousness (*taqwa*) of Muslims – their quality rather than quantity.[287] Despite attributing great value to children, Islam focuses on their quality and on the parental responsibility for rearing and educating them.[288] Neither marriage nor procreation are considered mandatory in Islam, and the *Hadith* in fact highlight 'the harms resulting from having a large progeny when resources are scarce'.[289]

Both Muhammadiyah and NU based their support for family planning on Islam's promotion of family well-being, stressing the importance of the mother's health, the spacing of births and that the family size should not significantly impinge upon the quality of their lives.[290] NU's 1969

---

[282] Hassan (n. 276), p. 232; Hasna (n. 248), p. 183.
[283] Sciortino, Marcoes-Natsir and F. Mas'udi (n. 155), p. 88.
[284] Hasna (n. 282), p. 183. This view was potentially fuelled also by the fact that much of the funding for the BKKBN's programme came from the USAID and UNFPA. See also Wynn, Foster, Rouhana and Trussell (n. 55), p. 44.
[285] Hasna (n. 282), p. 183.
[286] Hassan (n. 276), pp. 232–3.
[287] Hasna (n. 282), p. 183; Hassan (n. 276), p. 233.
[288] Hasna (n. 282), p. 184.
[289] Hassan (n. 276), p. 233; Hasna (n. 282), p. 184.
[290] Marshall (n. 127), p. 16.

fatwa proclaimed that family planning was permissible for the purpose of *keluarga maslahah* – family welfare.[291] This represented a significant shift as NU's earlier 1938 *fatwa* had opposed contraceptives on the basis that pregnancy was considered to be a natural part of women's lives.[292] Similarly, Muhammadiyah shifted its position, moving 'from passive opposition to passive acceptance of family planning, but continued to consider the prevention of pregnancy to be against the teaching of Islam'.[293] Muhammadiyah's 1968 *fatwa* effectively permitted Muslims to use contraceptives that would not entirely prevent pregnancy – that is, sterilisation.[294] Given that all three Islamic institutions at one time opposed permanent contraceptive methods like sterilisation, the BKKBN dropped sterilisation from its programme – notwithstanding the obvious cost and efficiency benefits.[295] This demonstrates the influence of these institutions on state policy. Subsequently, both NU and MUI changed their position and supported sterilisation, arguing that it is consistent with Islam given that there are now techniques available to reverse it.[296]

Another point of contention that was overcome related to intrauterine devices (IUDs). Originally, Islamic leaders rejected IUDs based on the belief that they were a form of abortion, and because they required a woman to expose herself to a male doctor to have the device inserted.[297] Given that the BKKBN viewed IUDs as central to their family planning programme, they arranged meetings with Islamic leaders to discuss their opposition.[298] Marshall claims that this was typical of BKKBN, who reached out to the Islamic institutions when faced with pushback to their policies, and

---

[291] The *fatwa* had eight parts: permitting family planning to space children; prohibiting abortion; family planning must be voluntary; planning should stress health and welfare of the family; prohibiting permanent damage to reproductive organs; consent of husband and wife necessary; planning should be practised according with Islamic law; and that it should not aid immoral acts. Menchik (n. 104), p. 368.

[292] Marshall (n. 127), p. 16.

[293] Muhammadiyah accepted family planning for the purposes of managing or spacing births, but not for limiting them. Sciortino, Marcoes-Natsir and F. Mas'udi (n. 155), p. 87; van Doorn-Harder (2006) (n. 222), p. 115.

[294] Menchik (n. 104), p. 367.

[295] Ibid., pp. 368–9.

[296] Sciortino, Marcoes-Natsir and F. Mas'udi (n. 155), p. 88; Menchik (n. 104), p. 370. Interview with Prof. Dr Huzaemah Tahido Yanggo, Rector of Institute of *Qur'an* Studies, Islamic University of Indonesia, and member of MUI *fatwa* commission (1 February 2017, Jakarta, Indonesia).

[297] NU's 1972 *fatwa* stated that IUDs were not permitted. See Marshall (n. 127), p. 17.

[298] Ibid.

5.3 FAMILY PLANNING, LAW AND INSTITUTIONS

countered by providing incentives to those who promoted family planning.[299] In 1983, MUI and Islamic leaders in the Ministry of Religious Affairs approved IUDs, on the condition that they be inserted either by a female nurse or doctor, or by a male but in the presence of the woman's husband or other witness.[300] Fulfilling these conditions resolved their objection to IUDs, which BKKBN then widely promoted.[301] However, for NU and Muhammadiyah, the use of IUDs remained contested until around the 1990s.[302] Menchik notes that around this time their *fatwas* were

> marked by increased attention to state policy, national development and a conspicuous awareness of the family planning programme. Rather than simply relying on religious authorities, secular authorities came to play an increasingly prominent role in their interpretations of the shari'a. This evolution of the shari'a evolved over time as an outcome of continued, iterated negotiations with the state.[303]

Menchik argues that these institutions altered their interpretation of Islamic law as a result of contemporary scientific knowledge as well as social pressure and state authority.[304] While of course studying Islamic texts, they also consulted secular sources such as medical authorities, government officials, the WHO and other international organisations.[305] In this way, secular authority and forms of knowledge influenced Islamic authority and knowledge on family planning in Indonesia.[306] This can be seen as an interaction of norms, where the systems engage and influence one another, navigating conflicts on overlapping subject matter. Menchik suggests that rather than being diametrically opposed, 'the sacred and the secular are mutually constitutive and co-evolve over time'.[307] This can also be seen in other *fatwas*, such as MUI's more recent ones on the protection of endangered species and deforestation.[308] Regarding family

---

[299] Menchik notes that 'the regime provided both material and political incentives for religious leaders to change their interpretations of the shari'a': Menchik (n. 104), p. 366; Marshall (n. 127), p. 17.
[300] See MUI *fatwa* 16/1983. Sciortino, Marcoes-Natsir and F. Mas'udi (n. 155), p. 88.
[301] Ibid., p. 88, fn. 6.
[302] Menchik (n. 104), p. 369.
[303] Ibid., p. 370.
[304] Ibid., p. 360.
[305] Ibid., p. 375. See also van Doorn-Harder (2006) (n. 222), pp. 8, 17.
[306] Menchik (n. 104), p. 360.
[307] Ibid., p. 362.
[308] MUI, *Fatwa* on protection of endangered species to maintain the balanced ecosystem No. 4–2014 (11 March 2014), https://mui-lplhsda.org/fatwa-mui-on-protection-of-endangered-species-to-maintain-the-balanced-ecosystems-no-4–2014-part-3-english-

planning, Menchik notes that while they utilised some secular sources, none of the institutions relied upon the language of women's rights or equality in justifying their amended interpretations of Islamic law.[309] He concluded that 'theories of secularization, modernization and the global expansion of liberal human rights' apply poorly to such Islamic institutions, which are instead 'driven by non-liberal conceptions of agency'.[310]

Ultimately, NU, Muhammadiyah and MUI's support for family planning was pivotal to the success of the Government's programme. Their *fatwas* in favour of contraceptives informed the Muslim community that family planning was permissible and appropriate.[311] They 'proved to be highly influential partners for the government', given Indonesia's large Muslim population and the fact that around 75 per cent of Indonesians identify with either Muhammadiyah or NU.[312] For this reason, other organisations also seek to work with them to secure *fatwas* in support of health issues such as sanitation.[313] However, '[w]hile NU, Muhammadiyah and the state's reshaping of the shari'a was innovative, it was not unique to Indonesia'.[314] Scholars have noted that Islamic law has the inherent flexibility to adapt in different contexts, and that it has proven similarly dynamic in other periods and places.[315] Today in Indonesia, as in other parts of the Muslim world, contraceptives are widely available and seen as permissible within Islam. However, there is not necessarily a uniform approach and debates persist, typically relating to the tensions between Islamic texts promoting the growth of the Muslim community and those emphasising its quality.[316]

---

version/ (accessed 8 November 2017); MUI, *Fatwa* on Burning Forest (14 November 2006), https://mui-lplhsda.org/islamic-ruling-fatwa-on-burning-forest-interfaith-dialog-cop-22/ (accessed 8 November 2017).

[309] Menchik (n. 104), p. 375.
[310] Ibid.
[311] Marshall (n. 127), p. 18.
[312] Ibid.
[313] Aldan Cronin, UNICEF Indonesia, Sanitation as a matter of religious importance (8 July 2016), http://unicefindonesia.blogspot.nl/2016/07/sanitation-as-matter-of-religious.html (accessed 8 November 2017).
[314] Menchik (n. 104), p. 367.
[315] Concepts justifying flexibility include emergency conditions (*darurat*), custom ('*urf*), and public interest (*maslaha*). See, for example, Menchik (n. 104), p. 367; Hursh (n. 230).
[316] Marshall (n. 127), p. 7; Interview with Director of Rahima (30 January 2017, Jakarta, Indonesia).

Advocacy Programmes and Family Planning Service Provision

In addition to engaging with the state regarding the interpretation of Islamic law, Muhammadiyah and NU also undertook advocacy campaigns to promote family planning and provided healthcare services to the public. Muhammadiyah and Aisyiyah in particular run many health facilities (over 800 between them), which provide family planning services according to Muhammadiyah's *fatwas*.[317] Both Muhammadiyah and NU collaborated with the BKKBN, as the Government encouraged partnerships to promote family planning, utilising 'the schools, mosques, prayer circles, hospitals and social networks of Islamic organizations to implement the programme'.[318] In the field, BKKBN workers would often partner with local religious leaders to provide additional guidance when approaching a potential contraceptive user.[319] Due to their extensive network of *pesantren* '[w]ith thousands of schools and leaders in every province, regency, district and neighbourhood, NU's support accelerated the public's acceptance of family planning'.[320] Fatayat, for example, deliver messages throughout their network of chapters down to the village level. In addition, Muhammadiyah and NU have large communication facilities including TV channels, social media networks and other platforms, and religious leaders could promote family planning in the mosques and during prayers.

NU's 1969 *fatwa* on family planning was the important first step that enabled Muslimat and Fatayat to become heavily involved in promoting 'family welfare'.[321] In fact, Muslimat and Fatayat had supported family planning even before this *fatwa*, and Muslimat in particular had 'pressured NU's central board to change its views on family planning by contesting their interpretation of Islamic law'.[322] NU's subsequent

---

[317] Interview with Dr Emma Rachmawati, Muhammadiyah Prof Dr Hamka University (7 February 2017, Depok, Indonesia); Emma Rachmawati, Dominika Jajkowicz, Lintang Purwara Dewanti and Mouhamad Bigwanto, Mapping Faith-Based Responses to Sexual and Reproductive Health and Rights in Indonesia: A Snapshot from 10 Muslim, Christian, Hindu, Buddhist and Confucian Faith-Based Organizations (2017) *UICIHSS* 45, http://uicihss.uhamka.ac.id/wp-content/uploads/2017/05/4-MAPPING-FAITH-BASED-RESPONSES-TO-SEXUAL.pdf (accessed 3 January 2018).
[318] BKKBN worked with other religious organisations too, including Christians. Marshall (n. 127), pp. 17, 18.
[319] Marshall (n. 127), p. 16.
[320] Menchik (n. 104), p. 368.
[321] Arnez (n. 262), p. 69; Interview with Lies Marcoes-Natsir, Rumah Kita Bersama Foundation (4 February 2017, Bogor, Indonesia).
[322] Marshall (n. 127), p. 17; Menchik (n. 104), pp. 365, 368.

decision to make family planning a mass programme in 1972 'was made upon the request of Muslimat and Fatayat to conduct family planning activities in line with Islamic teachings'.[323] Muslimat and Fatayat have traditionally run most of NU's maternity hospitals, birthing centres and clinics, with Muslimat's clinic in Jombong being 'one of the first to provide women with access to contraception'.[324] Among their initiatives, Muslimat created the Family Welfare Institute (*Lembaga Kemaslahatan Keluarga*) to promote welfare through family planning.[325] Through this programme they 'conducted training for health care workers, partnered with international organizations to educate NU members, and ran over two dozen hospitals and health clinics'.[326]

Fatayat was also highly involved, providing advice and information on family planning and creating Reproductive Health Information Centres (PIKER) in eleven provinces to inform communities about reproductive health and women's rights.[327] Increasingly, Fatayat took a gender-based approach and openly pursued women's empowerment. In fact, it began to focus on reproductive health in the 1980s partly to supplement the Government's family planning programme, which it saw as insufficiently focused on educating and empowering women.[328] Fatayat utilises Islamic sources as a strategy to legitimate its goal of women's empowerment; advocating women's equality by 'referring to Qur'anic verses that emphasize their equal status' with men.[329] On the basis of equality, women are shown, for example, that they do not need to wait for their husband's permission before seeking urgent medical care during a pregnancy.[330] This relates to the socio-cultural determinants of reproductive health highlighted in the section above. Boosted by support from international

---

[323] Arnez (n. 262), p. 69.
[324] Ibid., p. 72; Menchik (n. 104), p. 365.
[325] Arnez (n. 262), p. 69.
[326] Menchik (n. 104), p. 368; Christopher Candland and Siti Nurjanah, Women's Empowerment through Islamic Organisations: The Role of the Indonesia's 'Nahdlatul Ulama' in Transforming the Government's Birth Control Programme into a Family Welfare Programme (February 2004), http://academics.wellesley.edu/Polisci/Candland/KBIndonesia.pdf (accessed 27 November 2017).
[327] Arnez (n. 262), pp. 69, 72; Interview with Dr Maria Ulfah Anshor, Commissioner with the Indonesian Child Protection Commission (*Komisi Perlindungan Anak Indonesia*) (7 February 2017, Jakarta, Indonesia).
[328] Arnez (n. 262), p. 71.
[329] Ibid., pp. 74, 87; Rinaldo (n. 229) p. 1786.
[330] Interview with Dr Maria Ulfah Anshor, Commissioner with the Indonesian Child Protection Commission (*Komisi Perlindungan Anak Indonesia*) (7 February 2017, Jakarta, Indonesia).

5.3 FAMILY PLANNING, LAW AND INSTITUTIONS 223

donors starting in the 1980s, Fatayat became an effective advocacy organisation, training its members to mobilise and wield influence in national debates.[331] As such, Fatayat helped transform the Government's instrumental (and sometimes coercive) approach to family planning to a more voluntary and principled one.[332]

Another faith-based organisation[333] that played an important role was the NGO Centre for the Development of Pesantren and Society (*Perhimpunan Pengembangan Pesantren dan Masyarakat* – P3M) set up in 1983. While long concerned with social justice, it was not until women joined the staff that the organisation took a gender perspective and commenced a reproductive health programme.[334] Prominent Muslim gender activists including Lies Marcoes-Natsir were part of this programme that focused on advancing women's rights through a progressive Islamic framework.[335] Marcoes-Natsir commenced work on the project *Fiqh An-Nisa* (*fiqh* on women), acting 'as a bridge from the secular to Muslim feminists'.[336] Based on the method of reinterpreting Islamic texts, P3M advocated gender equality, which it saw as a prerequisite for respecting reproductive rights.[337] P3M developed an Islamic framework supporting reproductive health, identifying relevant aspects such as respect for life, the right to physical well-being and the right to social welfare.[338] Contrary to dominant Islamic interpretations that position men as decision-makers, P3M argued that women have the right to make decisions because, in Islam, 'each person – man or woman – is responsible and accountable for his or her own individual actions'.[339] This

---

[331] Rinaldo (n. 229), pp. 1797, 1793; Arnez (n. 262), p. 71.
[332] Candland and Nurjanah (n. 326).
[333] Numerous faith-based organisations contributed to the family planning programming; however, it is beyond the scope of this case study to detail them all. Similarly, numerous secular organisations also contributed to the programme, such as the PKBI, the Women's Health Foundation (YKP) and UN agencies, which also partner with Muhammadiyah, NU and BKKBN on family planning projects.
[334] Sciortino, Marcoes-Natsir and F. Mas'udi (n. 155), p. 89.
[335] Brenner (n. 205), p. 483.
[336] Interview with Lies Marcoes-Natsir, Rumah Kita Bersama Foundation (4 February 2017, Bogor, Indonesia).
[337] 'Women, they argue, are equal to men in the sight of God, since they have the same spiritual nature and are both recipients of the Divine breath.' Sciortino, Marcoes-Natsir and F. Mas'udi (n. 155), p. 89.
[338] Ibid., pp. 89–90.
[339] 'P3M is of the opinion that this right of women has been disregarded because of male domination of the religious community and of the interpretation of sacred texts.' Ibid., p. 90.

relates to the socio-cultural determinants of health identified above. P3M held workshops countering normative teachings that childrearing is exclusively women's work, and displayed posters depicting men caring for their children.[340] P3M's work was emancipatory as it offered Muslim women 'a much needed theological basis for improving their place in society'.[341]

Another important faith-based organisation is Rahima, the Centre for Education and Information on Islam and Women's Rights Issues.[342] This organisation was created in 2000 by several members formerly part of P3M. Like P3M, Rahima also works with the *pesantren* community and provides training on women's rights issues through an Islamic perspective.[343] It seeks to find solutions through Islam to contemporary women's rights issues including reproductive health and marriage. Rahima promotes its critical reinterpretations through its training with *pesantren* teachers and administrators, and its journal *Swara Rahima*.[344] In addition, it works with the Government as well as both Muhammadiyah and NU to promote its progressive Islamic perspectives.[345] Key to its success is its use of partners, networks and contacts to gain access to the *pesantren* in various districts in order to deliver its training. As such, its work is premised on enjoying good reputations and relationships with *kyai* and other religious leaders. Several interview participants who engage with *pesantren* on women's rights and health issues noted how the *pesantren* leaders are typically very receptive to them and their messages.

As this demonstrates, Islamic institutions and Muslim women in particular played a vital role in promoting the permissibility of family planning as well as providing reproductive healthcare services in Indonesia. A key aspect of this was the reliance upon and reinterpretation of Islamic texts and norms relating to family welfare and women's equality. Muslim women in Muhammadiyah and NU mobilised support within the women's branches to exert influence upon the main institutions to reform their *fatwas* and enable widespread education campaigns and service provision. These initiatives of Muslim women and Islamic

---

[340] Ibid.
[341] Ibid., p. 93.
[342] See for further information (in Bahasa Indonesia), www.rahima.or.id (accessed 27 November 2017).
[343] Ismah (n. 234), p. 494.
[344] Rachel Rinaldo, Pious and Critical: Muslim Women Activists and the Question of Agency (2014) *Gender & Society* 28:6, p. 840.
[345] Interview with Director of Rahima (30 January 2017, Jakarta, Indonesia).

institutions combined with Government advocacy and incentives to create top-down and bottom-up pressure that succeeded in changing the dominant Islamic norms in favour of family planning. The results are visible in the numerous *fatwas* today supporting women's access to family planning as well as other reproductive healthcare services. The following looks in greater detail at how Muslims, and in particular self-labelled 'Muslim feminists', have engaged with and reinterpreted Islamic texts to effectively promote women's reproductive health and rights more generally in Indonesia.

5.3.4 Pursuing Reproductive and Other Women's Rights through Islam

While Indonesian women have typically enjoyed greater public space than some women in other parts of the world,[346] they increased their share further in the 1980s and 1990s. This was due to, *inter alia*, economic development under Suharto and the rise of the middle class, which provided greater access to education and employment opportunities. Simultaneously, the women's movement globally was gaining ground and made in-roads in Indonesia.[347] Muslim feminism came to Indonesia 'at the right time', as many Muslim women were better educated, having benefited from 'changing attitudes toward marriage and women's education'.[348] The advance of the women's movement in Indonesia also coincided with the Islamic revival and *reformasi*, which contributed to Suharto's downfall in 1998. *Reformasi* was a reaction to Suharto's thirty-year-long authoritarian rule and was 'inspired by the ideals of constitutionalism, democracy, and human rights'.[349] After Suharto stepped down, the democratic space opened up, with a growth in civil society, political parties, dissent and debate. As part of this, the Islamic movement also grew, increasing the influence of Islam in both

---

[346] Mark Cammack, Adriaan Bedner and Stijn van Huis, Democracy, Human Rights and Islamic Family Law in Post-Soeharto Indonesia (2015) *New Middle Eastern Studies* 5:2, p. 2; Blackburn (n. 264), p. 96; Ernado (n. 238), pp. 120–1.

[347] The works of many Muslim feminists around the world were translated into Bahasa Indonesia from the early 1990s. For a detailed discussion of Muslim feminist scholarship and its influences in Indonesia, see Nina Nurmila, The Influence of Global Muslim Feminism on Indonesian Muslim Feminist Discourse (2011) *Al-Jāmi'ah* 49:1, pp. 33–64.

[348] Ibid., pp. 36, 42.

[349] Cammack, Bedner and van Huis (n. 346), p. 1. See also Brenner (n. 205), p. 478.

the public and private spheres, with 'rippling effects in virtually all spheres of social and political life'.[350] The Government decentralisation that followed also created space for (political) Islam to be more influential at the various district levels.[351]

This confluence of events led to the emergence of a cohort of politically aware Muslim women, typically educated in Islamic *pesantren* and universities, with access to greater career options, ties to NGOs and funding from international donors.[352] This young generation of Muslim activists insisted on addressing women's issues and social justice more broadly within an Islamic framework.[353] They 'believed that social reform in Indonesia could be implemented effectively through an Islamic medium because Islam itself is based on an ethic of social justice'.[354] Given that any Muslim with the requisite skills and knowledge can interpret Islamic texts, once women achieved the necessary education they were able to participate in debates on Islamic law.[355] Some Muslim women reinterpreted Islamic law and, adopting woman-friendly perspectives, contested the traditional, conservative views on women.[356] Mir-Hosseini notes the development in the 1980s of a new gender discourse around the Muslim world 'that was and is feminist in its aspirations and demands, yet Islamic in its language and sources of legitimacy'.[357] This sentiment also took root in Indonesia, where Muslim women based their activism or

---

[350] Brenner (n. 205), p. 478. An Islamic revival was experienced across parts of the Muslim world since the 1970s.
[351] Blackburn (n. 264), p. 98.
[352] Rinaldo (n. 344), p. 833; Blackburn, ibid., p. 95; Arnez (n. 262), p. 71.
[353] Brenner (n. 205), p. 481; Cammack, Bedner and van Huis (n. 346), p. 12.
[354] Brenner (n. 205), p. 483.
[355] Arnez (n. 262), p. 79. According to Marcoes, so long as women can prove their quality and capacity for interpretation, they can be accepted and respected. This is difficult, however, as boys are taught a different curriculum in the *pesantren* than girls, who focus more on daily life and women's role. Due to this disadvantage, only exceptional women can rise to the level of men regarding interpretation, and a lot of the current female Islamic scholars are in fact the daughters of *kyais*. Interview with Lies Marcoes-Natsir, Rumah Kita Bersama Foundation (4 February 2017, Bogor, Indonesia). As such, discrimination must be viewed intersectionally. On this topic, see Lorena Sosa, *Intersectionality in the Human Rights Legal Framework on Violence against Women – At the Centre or the Margins?* (Cambridge University Press, 2017).
[356] Blackburn (n. 264), p. 95.
[357] Hosseini (n. 224), p. 640. See also fn. 19 for details of the growing literature on Islamic feminism. While they have similar goals and sometimes methods, '[i]n contrast to secular feminists, Muslim feminists use Islamic sources such as the Qur'an and *hadith* in their struggle for gender equality': Nurmila (n. 347), p. 36.

feminism on the *Qur'an* with the aim of changing 'the lives and mindsets of both women and men'.[358]

These Muslim scholars and activists founded an array of Islamic women's NGOs, in addition to the pre-existing institutions of Fatayat, Muslimat, Aisyiyah and Nasyiatul 'Aisyiyah. These organisations served as 'incubators for women's political discourse and activism', making their activism both effective and transformative.[359] Such civil society and associational life was not new in Indonesia, which has a strong culture of community and volunteerism. This was what BKKBN relied upon when recruiting women to assist in delivering part of their family planning programme in villages across Indonesia. Also in contemporary times, Indonesia reports that '[a]t the informal level, there are a lot of women who are actively involved in organizations and non-governmental organization in the public and political fields'.[360] Far from monolithic, and covering both ends of the political spectrum, these diverse individuals and groups publicly advocate and pursue their visions for the future of Muslim women and all Indonesians.[361]

Muslim Feminist Reinterpretations of Islamic Law

A growing number of Muslim women around the world as well as in Indonesia 'came to see no inherent or logical link between Islamic ideals and patriarchy, no contradiction between Islamic faith and feminism'.[362] These women (and also some men) claim that Islam's basis of justice and equality was obscured over the centuries by the repetition of dominant patriarchal interpretations.[363] These scholars contend that the wisdom of the *Qur'an* and the spirit of the Prophet's teachings have been 'corrupted by generations of interpreters whose cultural biases had led them to assert male superiority'.[364] According to Nurmila, as interpretation is necessarily informed by the interest, values and background of the

---

[358] Van Doorn-Harder (2008) (n. 256), p. 1024.
[359] Rinaldo (n. 229), p. 1784; van Doorn-Harder (2008) (n. 256), p. 1025.
[360] UN HRCee, Consideration of Reports submitted by states parties under article 40 of the Covenant, Initial reports of states parties: Indonesia, CCPR/C/IDN/1 (19 March 2012), para. 40.
[361] Van Doorn-Harder (2008) (n. 256), p. 1024; Brenner (n. 205), p. 487; Rinaldo (n. 229), pp. 1799–800.
[362] Hosseini (n. 224), p. 639. See also Brenner (n. 205), pp. 481–2.
[363] Rinaldo (n. 344), p. 833; Brenner (n. 205), p. 481.
[364] Brenner, ibid.

interpreter, 'no Qur'ānic interpretation is objective'.[365] Mir-Hosseini agrees, noting that as *fiqh* texts are mere human – rather than divine – understandings of Islam, they are fallible and should be challenged as 'patriarchal in both spirit and form'.[366] Such challenges are facilitated by the inherent contestation and interpretability of Islamic texts as noted above. Muslim feminist scholars seek to demonstrate how unequal gender constructions 'contradict the very essence of divine justice as revealed in the Koran'.[367] They believe that as God is just, it is impossible for God to proclaim a position in support of injustice.[368] According to Daud Ali, justice is in fact the principle of all principles in Islam, being the third most mentioned word in the *Qur'an*.[369]

A central tenet of this critique is that rather than installing patriarchy, Islam instead arose within patriarchal social networks pre-existing in seventh-century Arabia.[370] As such, scholars argue that patriarchy does not stem from the religion itself, but that those with authority in Islam have made patriarchal interpretations of it. While 'Islam *is not* patriarchy', nor is it particularly patriarchal, it has been used as a vehicle to perpetuate and entrench patriarchy.[371] Some highlight that Arabic, the language of the *Qur'an*, is not neutral but assigns a gender for nouns and pronouns, and that this linguistic feature has impacted the (biased) interpretation of Islam.[372] Mir-Hosseini claims that women will continue to be second-class citizens 'as long as patriarchy is justified and upheld in the name of Islam'.[373] Therefore, Islamic texts need to be re-examined in order to expose 'the cultural baggage ... smuggled in the name of

---

[365] Nina Nurmila, Feminist Reinterpretations of The Qur'ān (2013) *Journal of Qur'ān and Hadith Studies* 2:2, p. 158.
[366] Hosseini (n. 224), pp. 632–3. See also Shadi Mokhtari, The Search for Human Rights within an Islamic Framework in Iran (October 2004) *The Muslim World* 94, p. 473.
[367] Hosseini (n. 224), p. 642.
[368] According to Mulia the *Qur'an's* 'commitment to the values of equality and freedom is total and unqualified'. Siti Musdah Mulia, Muslim Family Law Reform in Indonesia: A Progressive Interpretation of The Qur'an (August 2015) *Al-Mawarid Journal of Islamic Law* XV:1, p. 9. See also Hassan (2001) (n. 210), pp. 62–3; Nurmila (n. 365), p. 157.
[369] Following God and science. Daud Ali (n. 217), p. 81.
[370] Hasna (n. 282), p. 183; Rinaldo (n. 299), p. 1790.
[371] Hasna (n. 282), p. 190, citing Marcia Inhorn, *Infertility and Patriarchy: The Cultural Politics of Gender and Family Life in Egypt* (University Pennsylvania Press, 1996), p. 33.
[372] Interview with the Director of Rahima (30 January 2017, Jakarta, Indonesia); Interview with Dr Siti Ruhaini Dzuhayatin, State Islamic University UIN Sunan Kalijaga (21 February 2017, Yogyakarta, Indonesia).
[373] Hosseini (n. 224), p. 629.

religion'.[374] For example, when analysing Islamic texts, P3M would distinguish from Islamic principles the elements of Arab culture that are not valid today in Indonesia.[375] In fact, some claim that rather than requiring patriarchy, Islam brought remedies against the pre-existing patriarchal culture.

Numerous scholars highlight the fact that Islam's arrival in Arabia improved women's status and granted them numerous legal rights.[376] For example, Islam provided for women to inherit, prohibited female infanticide and introduced limitations on polygamy.[377] Mulia argues that while women inherited less than men and polygamy was still permitted, the *Qur'an* commenced upon a path of gradually realising gender equality as a strategic measure. She claims that practical considerations (such as the need to avoid social upheaval) made immediate implementation impossible, necessitating a gradual approach to women's emancipation.[378] As such, the mission of women's equality commenced with, but was not completed by, the *Qur'an*.[379] Other Muslim scholars share the view that the *Qur'an* supports women's equality and argue that women's rights are 'compatible with the Islamic spirit of liberation for the oppressed'.[380] In fact, on the basis of his teachings and treatment of women, some claim that the Prophet Muhammad can even be regarded 'as a feminist'.[381] Simply put, 'Muslim feminists believe that the *Qur'an* liberates women'.[382]

---

[374] Brenner (n. 205), p. 481. See also Hassan (n. 368), p. 63; van Doorn-Harder (2006) (n. 222), p. 38.
[375] Sciortino, Marcoes-Natsir and F. Mas'udi (n. 155), p. 91.
[376] Hasna (n. 282), p. 183; Mulia (n. 368), p. 2; Nurmila (n. 347), p. 42; Nina Nurmila, Indonesian Muslim's Discourse of Husband–Wife Relationship (2013) *Al-Jāmi'ah* 51:1, p. 68.
[377] Nurmila (2011), ibid., p. 42; Daud Ali (n. 217), pp. 88–9; Interview with Dr Siti Ruhaini Dzuhayatin, State Islamic University UIN Sunan Kalijaga (21 February 2017, Yogyakarta, Indonesia); Interview with Dr Maria Ulfah Anshor, Commissioner with the Indonesian Child Protection Commission (*Komisi Perlindungan Anak Indonesia*) (7 February 2017, Jakarta, Indonesia). See Daud Ali (n. 217), also for discussion of custom on the Arabian peninsula before Islam was introduced, pp. 98–9.
[378] Musdah Mulia (n. 376), pp. 9–11.
[379] Musdah Mulia (n. 376), p. 10. See also Fadel (n. 2) p. 14.
[380] Nurmila (2011) (n. 347), p. 54.
[381] Ibid., p. 42. See also Brenner (n. 205), p. 481; Interview with Director of Rahima (30 January 2017, Jakarta, Indonesia).
[382] Nurmila (2011) (n. 347), p. 36. See also Nusrat Choudhury, Constrained Spaces for Islamic Feminism: Women's Rights and the 2004 Constitution of Afghanistan (2007) *Yale Journal of Law & Feminism* 19, p. 187.

Indonesian and other Muslim feminists embarked upon an undertaking to dispel the patriarchal cultural aspects and reiterate Islam's support for gender equality. The key method employed was contextual reinterpretation of Islamic texts from a gender perspective. Marcoes explains such a methodology as distinguishing in each verse between the principle (which applies universally) and the particular (which is contextual).[383] A contextual and historical analysis of the sources helps to differentiate the tenets of Islam from 'the cultural norms of early Muslim societies'.[384] This includes an emphasis on the spirit of the *Qur'an*, rather than simply focusing on the letter of the text.[385] According to Mulia, the view in Islam that women are inferior to men is the result of 'an interpretive methodology that is excessively literal and insufficiently attentive to historical context'.[386] She claims that the contextual interpretive methodology is best able to discern Islam's 'universal moral message' as it 'is sensitive to the background and social circumstances in which the text was revealed'.[387] Rather than being revealed onto a blank slate and maintained intact, the pre-existing cultural norms of Arabia coloured Islamic principles. By focusing on the historical context and re-reading Islam's textual sources, scholars are proving that gender inequality embedded in the *fiqh* are not 'manifestations of divine will' but mere human constructions.[388]

Nurmila contends that feminist reinterpretations of Islamic texts offer flexible roles for both men and women. For example, Islamic law, and as applied in the Indonesian Compilation, defines the husband's role as 'the head of the family' and the wife as the 'homemaker' who is to respect and obey her husband.[389] Muslim feminists have challenged this construction on the basis of alternative readings of the *Qur'an* and *Hadith*. Nurmila notes 'that superiority, such as in the level of education and income, is not biologically determined for male only, but can be achieved by either male or female'.[390] As such, a man or a woman with the requisite

---

[383] This method is based on the scholarship of, *inter alia*, Riffat Hassan and Amina Wahud. Interview with Lies Marcoes-Natsir, Rumah Kita Bersama Foundation (4 February 2017, Bogor, Indonesia). This method has also been employed by reformists worldwide. Rinaldo (n. 229), p. 1791.
[384] Hosseini (n. 224), p. 642; Rinaldo, ibid.
[385] Brenner (n. 205), p. 481.
[386] Musdah Mulia (n. 376), p. 7.
[387] Ibid., p. 11.
[388] Hosseini (n. 224), p. 642.
[389] *Qur'anic* verse An-Nisa 4.34. Musdah Mulia (n. 376), p. 12; Nurmila (n. 376), p. 63.
[390] Nurmila (n. 365), p. 165.

5.3 FAMILY PLANNING, LAW AND INSTITUTIONS   231

qualifications can lead the family.[391] She argues that rather than prescribing what the norm should be, some *Qur'anic* verses – such as *An-Nisa* 4:34 – simply describe the situation at the time of revelation.[392] A female *ulama* of MUI argued that while the *Qur'an* provides that women's testimony is only worth half that of men, given the advances in women's education, it appears justified that their testimonies now be accorded equal value.[393] A (male) scholar wrote a book referring to sixty *Hadiths* on gender equality to support arguments in favour of women's rights and to counter those *Hadiths* typically used as justification for women's subordination and domestication.[394]

As noted above, Fatayat also takes an Islamic and gender equality approach in its work. Fatayat undertakes its own progressive interpretations of Islamic texts and engages in consultation and dialogue with other religious scholars and leaders.[395] Fatayat members are apt to do this, as they have typically been schooled in the NU tradition of interpretation, which places heavy emphasis on *fiqh*.[396] Their approach is to present problems and the supporting data to Muslim leaders, and together discuss the issues and their resolution.[397] Research and evidence is necessary to show that the reality of the lived situation is harmful, and therefore requires reform by the *ulama*.[398] Fatayat members emphasise the need to interpret Islamic sources along with male *ulama* from NU,

---

[391] Nurmila (n. 376), p. 77.
[392] Nurmila (n. 365), p. 163; Nurmila (n. 376), p. 70.
[393] Interview with Prof. Dr Huzaemah Tahido Yanggo, Rector of Institute of *Qur'an* Studies, Islamic University of Indonesia, and member of MUI *fatwa* commission (1 February 2017, Jakarta, Indonesia). Similar argumentation has been used regarding other traditional positions, such as the view that women should not lead public institutions. Muhammadiyah argued that while at the time of the *Qur'an's* revelation women were not educated, they are now and as such are fully capable of assuming public responsibility. See Ernada (n. 238), pp. 122–3.
[394] See the work of Faqihuddin Abdul Kodir at the Fahmina Institute as cited in Nurmila (n. 376), p. 74.
[395] Interview with Anggia Ermarini, Chairperson of Fatayat NU (3 February 2017, Jakarta, Indonesia); Interview with member of Fatayat NU and Commissioner with Komnas Perempuan (3 February 2017, Jakarta, Indonesia).
[396] 'N.U.'s emphasis on *Fikh* law helps to open up the possibility for such an interpretive project. This interpretive approach does not rule out profound attention to the text itself.' Rinaldo (n. 229), p. 1791. See also Arnez (n. 262), p. 79.
[397] Interview with Anggia Ermarini, Chairperson of Fatayat NU (3 February 2017, Jakarta, Indonesia); Interview with member of Fatayat NU and Commissioner with Komnas Perempuan (3 February 2017, Jakarta, Indonesia).
[398] Interview with Lies Marcoes-Natsir, Rumah Kita Bersama Foundation (4 February 2017, Bogor, Indonesia).

recognising that 'it is still impossible for them to reinterpret Islamic sources without' male support.[399] The young Muslim women's strategy is to maintain moderation by pursuing progressive approaches without overstepping the boundaries of what is socially acceptable.[400] As this demonstrates, Muslim women are aware of socio-cultural and religious norms in their community, and devise methods that function within those parameters. Rinaldo claims that 'Muslim women's activism in Indonesia provides a vital perspective on the question of agency among women in Muslim contexts'.[401]

Muslim Women's Agency in/through Islam

Despite stereotypes in the West of Muslim women as passive victims, this research and numerous other studies show otherwise. The tacit assumption often made is that religious women in general are oppressed or operate with 'a false consciousness'.[402] Scholarship on agency has, however, disproven the stereotype of religious women as victims of patriarchy, rejecting the dichotomy of women as either empowered/liberated (secular) or victimised/subordinated (religious).[403] Scholars have unpacked the concept of agency, which 'is typically defined as people's capacity to make choices and take action in the world'.[404] On the basis of this scholarship and the present case study, it is clear that Muslim women can be empowered agents in different ways both within and due to their religion. By challenging patriarchal interpretations and advancing their own views from a gender perspective, female Muslim scholars demonstrate their agency by working within Islam to secure their rights. Not only do Muslim women have agency in the way they navigate Islam, but they are also agentive in articulating what Islam is. As cultures – broadly interpreted to include religion – are constructed, the members of cultural communities can and do participate in that construction.

---

[399] Arnez (n. 262), p. 85. See also van Doorn-Harder (2006) (n. 222), p. 12.
[400] Interview with Anggia Ermarini, Chairperson of Fatayat NU (3 February 2017, Jakarta, Indonesia); Interview with member of Fatayat NU and Commissioner with Komnas Perempuan (3 February 2017, Jakarta, Indonesia).
[401] Rinaldo (2014) (n. 344), p. 842.
[402] Orit Avishai, 'Doing Religion' in a Secular World: Women in Conservative Religions and the Question of Agency (August 2008) *Gender & Society* 22:4, p. 411; Kelsy Burke, Women's Agency in Gender-Traditional Religions: A Review of Four Approaches (2012) *Sociology Compass* 6:2, p. 130; Saba Mahmood, *Politics of Piety: The Islamic Revival and the Feminist Subject* (Princeton University Press, 2005), p. 2.
[403] Rinaldo (2014) (n. 344), p. 826; Mahmood, ibid., pp. 1–2, 6–7; Burke, ibid., p. 123.
[404] Rinaldo (n. 344), p. 826.

5.3 FAMILY PLANNING, LAW AND INSTITUTIONS

Rather than narrowing the public space for Muslim women, Indonesia's Islamic revival that commenced in the 1980s presented opportunities that Muslim women capitalised upon. This should not be surprising as '[s]ocial scientists have long viewed religion as a force for mobilization, and have seen religious institutions as the foundation for many social movements'.[405] Islam's growing role in public life expanded the range of legitimate actors and provided Muslim women with a platform to engage on many issues.[406] In this way, women from Islamic organisations across the political spectrum (including the more progressive Fatayat and the more conservative *Partai Keadilan Sejahtera*) were able to take part in re-imagining the Indonesian nation.[407] With women enjoying a louder voice in national discourses and becoming more numerous and active in NGOs, religious institutions and the media, Indonesia experienced a sort of feminisation of the public sphere.[408] In this way, Muslim women were exercising their agency by entering public dialogues, occupying public space and advocating their views on Islam – whether progressive or conservative.

Numerous scholars have engaged critically with this form of women's agency within religion, suggesting 'that Muslim women are agentive in ways that differ from conventional Western notions of agency'.[409] In line with what Menchik noted above, van Doorn-Harder argues that Muslim women's agency need not be defined by or 'follow western-oriented patterns of liberation policies, individualism, and democracy, but has to be analysed within its local, cultural, and historical context'.[410] Mahmood urges a consideration of women's agency beyond secular, liberal, feminist frameworks, towards viewing agency as the capacity for action that is contextually bound and formulated within power structures rather than outside them.[411] This approach recognises that women's agency is impacted by their religion, which can simultaneously constrain as well as empower them.[412] As such, religion can be 'powerful cultural schemas

---

[405] Rinaldo (n. 229), p. 1784, citing José Casanova, *Public Religions in the Modern World* (University of Chicago Press, 1994).
[406] Rinaldo (n. 229), p. 1784.
[407] Ibid., p. 1798.
[408] Ibid.
[409] Rinaldo (2014) (n. 344), p. 825.
[410] Van Doorn-Harder (2008) (n. 256), p. 1023.
[411] Mahmood (n. 402), pp. 17–18.
[412] Rinaldo (2014) (n. 344), p. 827. Noting, of course, that agency and choice can also be impacted by other factors including poverty, education, and custom or culture. In this way, '[c]hoice is seldom free and individual'. Van Doorn-Harder (2008) (n. 256), p. 1022.

that shape how individuals understand themselves, while simultaneously providing a range of resources that allow people to take action in different ways'.[413] For example, as seen in the present case study, Muslim women even justified their agency on the basis of Islam.

Rinaldo argues that some Indonesian Muslim feminists manifest 'pious critical agency', which she defines 'as the capacity to engage critically and publically with religious texts'.[414] She gives the example of Fatayat and Rahima's work in reinterpreting Islamic sources from a gender perspective and publicly advocating those views. According to Rinaldo, this demonstrates that not only can Islam be a resource for women's agency, but that agency is informed by its historical and cultural context.[415] Importantly, pious critical agency reconciles 'being a good Muslim' with being critical of certain Islamic interpretations or practices.[416] In fact, it shows how the rise of a more public Islam (i.e. the Islamic revival in Indonesia) can facilitate novel manifestations of agency compatible with challenging gender hierarchies and building a more equal society.[417] In the same way that culture is often assumed to be an obstacle rather than an asset in human rights literature, (white, Western) gender theories usually conceptualise religion as a constraint on women, rather than considering its potential to be complicit in challenging patriarchy.[418] Women do not necessarily experience religion as a constraint, and pious critical agency demonstrates how the devout can mobilise religion to advance critical discourses on gender and promote women's rights.[419] As such, feminism and religious piety can intersect in unexpected ways.[420]

Some scholars reject the prevailing notion that agency somehow equals resistance, noting that an individual's endeavour to comply with religious norms can also be seen as agentive.[421] This recognises the agency in

---

[413] Rinaldo (2014) (n. 344), p. 829.
[414] Ibid., p. 825.
[415] Ibid., p. 842.
[416] Ibid.
[417] Ibid., p. 843.
[418] Ibid. The Special Rapporteur in the field of cultural rights notes that: 'The tendency to view culture as largely an impediment to women's human rights is both oversimplistic and problematic.' UN General Assembly, Report of the Special Rapporteur in the field of cultural rights, A/67/287 (10 August 2012), para. 3.
[419] Rinaldo (2014) (n. 344), p. 843.
[420] Ibid., p. 825.
[421] Ibid., p. 829; Mahmood (n. 402), pp. 8–10. According to Mahmood, the liberal feminist assumption that agency requires resistance reflects 'a deeper tension within feminism attributable to its dual character as both an *analytical* and a *political prescriptive* project.'

adopting or promoting conservative Islam, as well as in resisting or advocating progressive reforms to it. For example, this approach would recognise as an expression of agency a Muslim woman's decision to wear the veil, as well as to not wear the veil. Mahmood urges the decoupling of agency from progressive politics, in order to acknowledge the agency in resisting as well as inhabiting norms.[422] Equating agency with resistance precludes women who conform to gender-traditional religions from being considered as actors.[423] According to Burke, 'compliant agency' recognises that women can be agentive in the various ways they choose to conform to religious norms, and that women do not all comply in the same way.[424] Avishai would agree, claiming that agency extends to the ways in which members of conservative religions choose to perform their religion.[425] However, this expanded definition may grow to incorporate all actions by religious women, rendering useless the concept of agency.[426] As such, the debate is ongoing regarding what constitutes agency for different individuals in different social contexts.[427]

Finally, it is crucial to recognise agency outside the black and white resist/conform binary, and to consider the various degrees. As stated, Islamic law often gives rise to multiple (conflicting) interpretations and can be applied or deviated from in various ways. As in all Muslim societies, Indonesian Muslim women act or at times are treated in contravention of Islamic teachings.[428] For example, some service providers do not enquire as to whether a patient is married before providing contraceptives, and some women use them despite their husband's prohibition. Scholars remind us that religion can be far from deterministic and will not necessarily dictate an individual's beliefs and practices.[429] As these examples show, '[a]gency is located in the strategic use and navigation of religious traditions and practices to meet the demands of contemporary life'.[430] However, these strategic uses or deviances create gaps between the norms in theory and women's lived

---

[422] Mahmood (n. 402), pp. 14–15, 34.
[423] Burke (n. 402), p. 125.
[424] Ibid., pp. 127–8.
[425] Avishai (n. 402), p. 429.
[426] Burke (n. 402), pp. 128–9.
[427] Ibid., p. 130.
[428] Blackburn (n. 264), p. 104.
[429] Wynn, Foster, Rouhana and Trussell (n. 55), p. 43.
[430] Avishai (n. 402), p. 411.

reality in practice.[431] This is not unique to Indonesia or Islam, as such gaps or hybrid realities occur across different normative systems. These gaps/hybrids present a challenge to leaders who are confronted with maintaining the norm as it is, or reassessing it in light of present circumstances.[432] Based on the dynamism of culture and that people can be agents of change, Nyamu sees these gaps as vital openings for dialogue and advocating reform in line with women's rights.[433] Given that 'practice erodes ideology', women are slowly reforming patriarchal attitudes through social practice.[434]

A Work in Progress: Reform Attempts by Indonesian Muslim Feminists

Muslim feminists and those seeking women's rights within an Islamic framework in Indonesia have been successful in shifting some norms regarding reproductive rights. They have advocated reform on several related topics including abortion[435] and child marriage.[436] However, not all of their aims have been achieved, and their methods and reinterpretations of Islamic texts have upset some in the community – conservatives as well as moderates.[437] While challenging any well-entrenched

---

[431] Blackburn (2008) (n. 264), p. 104.
[432] Ibid.
[433] Celestine Nyamu-Musembi, Are Local Norms and Practices Fences or Pathways? The Example of Women's Property Rights? in A. A. An-Na`im (ed.), *Cultural Transformation and Human Rights in Africa* (Zed Books Ltd, 2002), p. 134. See further discussion in Chapter 2, Section 2.4.
[434] Elizabeth Fernea, The Challenges for Middle Eastern Women in the 21st Century (Spring 2000) *Middle East Journal* 54:2, pp. 186, 192. See also van Doorn-Harder (2006) (n. 222), p. 81.
[435] After a long process, MUI made a *fatwa* on the circumstances where abortion is permitted and the Indonesian health law and regulations were amended to now provide for limited abortion. Interview with Dr Maria Ulfah Anshor, Commissioner with the Indonesian Child Protection Commission (*Komisi Perlindungan Anak Indonesia*) (7 February 2017, Jakarta, Indonesia); Interview with Ninuk Widyantoro, Women's Health Foundation (YKP) (1 February 2017, Jakarta, Indonesia). See also UN Human Rights Council, Report of the Special Rapporteur on the right of everyone to the enjoyment of the highest attainable standard of physical and mental health on his mission to Indonesia, A/HRC/38/36/Add.1 (5 April 2018), paras. 69–70, 72.
[436] Child marriage is widely practised in Indonesia with the Marriage Law No. 1 of 1974, art. 7 setting the age limit for girls at sixteen years. Muhammadiyah, NU and MUI have continued to support child marriage based on the *Qur'an* and *Hadith*. However, in 2018, the Constitutional Court found the law to be discriminatory and ordered its amendment: Decision Number 22/PUU-XV/2017 (13 December 2018).
[437] Arnez (n. 262), p. 88; Nurmila (2011) (n. 347), p. 33; Bedner and van Huis (n. 220), p. 182.

patriarchal norm will elicit a backlash, challenges to the more intimate aspects of socio-cultural life, like reproduction, often trigger the strongest responses.[438] Such a backlash can come from both men and women. While the women's movement has grown in Indonesia, in the period since the *reformasi* conservative Islam has also gained social and political power.[439] In fact, some Muslims were alarmed by the rising influence of conservative and fundamentalist views on women, and were thus inspired to counter them with progressive theological approaches.[440] Two areas of current contention in Indonesia where Muslim feminists have not been successful are FGM/C and polygamy.

FGM/C (*sunat perempuan*) is widespread in Indonesia, typically performed on babies shortly after birth and comprises pricking or symbolic cutting of girls' genitalia.[441] There is a divergence of views on FGM/C, with some opposing the practice and rejecting its link to Islam, while others support it as well as its significance for Islam. The latter includes MUI and NU, which support FGM/C as a traditional practice part of Islam.[442] On this basis, opposition to FGM/C is tantamount to opposition to Islam. Therefore, when the Indonesian Government endeavoured to prohibit the practice, it came into conflict with numerous Islamic groups. However, those opposed to FGM/C include the National Commission on Violence against Women (*Komisi Nasional anti Kekerasan terhadap Perempuan – Komnas Perempuan*)[443] and Fatayat. Based on its analysis and interpretation of

---

[438] Hursh (n, 230), p. 260.
[439] Brenner (n. 205), p. 479.
[440] Ibid., p. 481.
[441] Around half of girls under twelve years old have been cut. UNICEF, Division of Data, Research, and Policy, Statistical Profile on Female Genital Mutilation/Cutting: Indonesia (February 2016), https://data.unicef.org/wp-content/uploads/country_profiles/Indonesia/FGMC_IDN.pdf (accessed 9 November 2017); Indonesian National Commission on Violence against Women (Komnas Perempuan), National Human Rights Institution Independent Report Regarding the Implementation of the Convention on the Elimination of All Forms of Discrimination against Women in Indonesia, 2012–2016, Submitted to the CEDAW Committee (30 December 2016), para. 39.
[442] Regarding MUI, NU and Muhammadiyah's position, see Lanny Octavia, Circumcision and Muslim Women's Identity in Indonesia (2014) *Indonesian Journal for Islamic Studies* 21:3, pp. 419–57.
[443] Indonesian National Commission on Violence against Women (Komnas Perempuan), National Human Rights Institution Independent Report Regarding the Implementation of the Convention on the Elimination of All Forms of Discrimination against Women in Indonesia, 2007–2011, Submitted to the CEDAW Committee (8 October 2011), paras. 28–30.

Islamic texts, Fatayat concluded that FGM/C is not required or condoned in Islam. As per their methods, Fatayat members discussed FGM/C with NU in order to come to an agreed position, but NU rejected their interpretation and continue to support the practice. Nonetheless, Fatayat members have not changed their position in opposition to FGM/C, demonstrating both their agency and independence.[444]

While Fatayat has not succeeded in convincing NU that FGM/C should be prohibited in Islam, the Indonesian Government and the UN treaty bodies have also not succeeded in shifting public sentiment on the practice. This is not unexpected for, as mentioned above, the Government is not considered an authority on Islamic law, and national or international legal measures contrary to well-entrenched local norms are bound to be unsuccessful. As discussed in Chapter 2, top-down prohibitions typically fail to comprehend the nature of the practice and its role within a community, and are susceptible to rejection as outside attempts to control or destroy. Newland argues that the UN's zero tolerance position on FGM/C and critique of Indonesia in this regard 'may complicate and aggravate socio-political relationships with unintended consequences'.[445] One consequence may be reinforcing the image of international law as a form of neocolonialism, making the Indonesian Government hesitant to fulfil its obligations thereunder for fear of being perceived as anti-Islamic in the state with the world's largest Muslim population.[446] As such, more pragmatic culturally sensitive approaches based on dialogue are likely to be more accepted due to their principled respect for cultural diversity.

Another example is the unsuccessful attempt to reform Indonesian marriage law relating to polygamy. First, Suharto's regime attempted to reform marriage law in the 1970s to, *inter alia*, prohibit polygamy.[447] In response, riots broke out with Islamic groups protesting stridently and successfully protecting polygamy's place in national law.[448] Subsequent

---

[444] Fatayat members recognise that this position may be a 'bit naughty', but as they are autonomous of NU, they 'don't need to really comply with our Father'. Interview with Anggia Ermarini, Chairperson of Fatayat NU (3 February 2017, Jakarta, Indonesia); Interview with member of Fatayat NU and Commissioner with Komnas Perempuan (3 February 2017, Jakarta, Indonesia).
[445] Lynda Newland, Female Circumcision: Muslim Identities and Zero Tolerance Policies in Rural West Java (2006) *Women's Studies International Forum* 29, p. 396.
[446] Ibid., pp. 402–3.
[447] Butt (n. 229), pp. 287–8; Musdah Mulia (n. 376), pp. 3–4.
[448] Brenner (n. 205), p. 480.

5.3 FAMILY PLANNING, LAW AND INSTITUTIONS

reform proposals have also failed. For example, another attempt was made in 2004 with the Counter-Legal Draft (CLD) proposed by women's rights activists and the Ministry of Religious Affairs.[449] The CLD was uncompromising in its commitment to men and women's equality in marriage, and based its provisions on reinterpretations of Islamic texts.[450] For instance, the CLD banned polygamy and proposed a single divorce procedure for both men and women.[451] Musdah Mulia, who coordinated the CLD, claimed that it was an exercise of *ijtihad* that sought to empower women and give them their full protection as explained in not only the *Qur'an* and *Sunnah*, but also the Indonesian Constitution.[452] Various groups supported the CLD, notably Fatayat, Muslimat, Komnas Perempuan and numerous other NGOs.[453]

Despite this support and attempts to base the CLD's reforms in Islam, 'the scope of the reforms proved unacceptable to even moderate Muslim organizations'.[454] The CLD was strongly criticised by Islamic organisations including MUI, NU and the conservative group Hizbut Tahrir Indonesia, with suggestions made that it was supported by foreign funders keen to undermine Islam in Indonesia.[455] Professor Huzaemah of MUI and others were critical of the CLD and its interpretive methodology, noting that the interpretations were overly reliant on the purported context and principles of Islam and ignored the text itself.[456] She welcomes interpretations of Islam promoting gender equality so long as they follow the traditional rules of interpretation. Due to the 'immediate storm of controversy', the CLD was revoked by the Ministry of Religious

---

[449] The CLD resulted from two years of research and analysis by the Islamic Law Reform Team created by the Religious Affairs Ministry's Gender Mainstreaming Working Group (PUG), coordinated by Siti Musdah Mulia. Musdah Mulia (n. 376), p. 6, fn. 5.
[450] Cammack, Bedner and van Huis (n. 346), p. 23. Musdah Mulia (n. 376), p. 12.
[451] Musdah Mulia (n. 376), p. 14; Brenner (n. 205), p. 485.
[452] Musdah Mulia (n. 376), p. 17.
[453] Siti Musdah Mulia with Mark Cammack, Toward a Just Marriage Law: Empowering Indonesian Women through a Counter Legal Draft to the Indonesian Compilation of Islamic Law, in R. Michael Feener and Mark E. Cammack (eds.), *Islamic Law in Contemporary Indonesia: Ideas and Institutions* (Harvard University Press, 2007), p. 144.
[454] Cammack, Bedner and van Huis (n. 346), p. 23.
[455] Musdah Mulia with Cammack (n. 453), pp. 142–4; Cammack, Bedner and van Huis (n. 346), p. 21.
[456] Interview with Prof. Dr Huzaemah Tahido Yanggo, Rector of Institute of *Qur'an* Studies, Islamic University of Indonesia, and member of MUI *fatwa* commission (1 February 2017, Jakarta, Indonesia). Another criticism of the method was that the CLD attempted to reinterpret *qath'i* texts – those determined to be certain and not subject to interpretation. Musdah Mulia with Cammack (n. 453), pp. 143–4.

Affairs and withdrawn from Parliament's consideration.[457] The fact that it was proposed as legislation was another problem for the CLD. While Islam supports intra-plurality, once law is codified it becomes fixed and in effect nullifies other views and limits Muslims' ability to choose their interpretation of Islam; rather than plural it becomes uniform. The fact that the CLD was proposed as state law is therefore also a reason for the increased public attention and critique, which may not have been as severe in the absence of codification as state law.

The CLD's failure demonstrates the slow pace of change, the need to be seen to comply with Islamic norms and methods, and the need to ensure critical support for reforms. Since its beginning, the Muslim women's movement has 'always had to strike a delicate balance between the women's aspirations, expectations of the surrounding cultures, male Muslim authority, and the influence of the state'.[458] As such, those advocating women's rights and equality must strategically navigate the reform path. This again reflects their agency. Some suggested that the CLD's drafters made the strategic error of proposing dramatic rather than incremental reforms, and that the process was confrontational rather than based on intense dialogue with other Muslim scholars.[459] Anshor stresses that change is a process, noting that her book on *fiqh* and abortion was initially met with criticism, however, ten years later it is now relied upon by both the Government and NU when referring to abortion.[460] While the CLD was unsuccessful, from a longer-term perspective, women's position in Islamic family law can be seen as gradually improving.[461] Despite polygamy being legal in Indonesia and FGM/C still enjoying support from Islamic leaders, Muslim feminists are continuing their advocacy with the debates ongoing.

The two examples above illustrate how powerful Islam is as a social institution in Indonesia, and how difficult it can be for Muslim feminists to advance their views both within Islamic institutions like NU and among the wider community. Of course, feminists around the world will

---

[457] Musdah Mulia (n. 376), p. 7.
[458] Van Doorn-Harder (2008) (n. 256), p. 1024; van Doorn-Harder (2006) (n. 222), p. 127.
[459] See Brenner (n. 205), p. 485.
[460] Interview with Dr Maria Ulfah Anshor, Commissioner with the Indonesian Child Protection Commission (*Komisi Perlindungan Anak Indonesia*) (7 February 2017, Jakarta, Indonesia).
[461] Cammack, Bedner and van Huis (n. 346), p. 24. Some Indonesian women advocate 'evolution, not revolution': see van Doorn-Harder (2006) (n. 222), p. 83.

recognise many of these difficulties. The examples also show the power of Islamic groups vis-à-vis the Indonesian Government, and how it cannot simply push through legislation implementing its human rights obligations and gender equality. The Government must negotiate and compromise based on the interests of Islamic groups, which also have representation in Government and the legislature as political parties. Therefore, (building) support from within these Islamic groups is imperative to the success of any changes seeking to implement women's rights and equality. There is a multiplicity of actors and fora involved in this larger law reform process, including individual Muslims and their communities, NGOs, Islamic institutions and their various branches, the Government and its ministries, legislature, and political parties, as well as international human rights bodies. As such, securing human rights reform in Indonesia will often require social and political action as well as a solid basis in Islamic law.[462]

Legitimacy and Efficacy of Employing Islam in Human Rights

One particular obstacle to the adoption of progressive reinterpretations of Islam in Indonesia is the Western origin of the terms 'feminism' and 'gender'. This also applies more generally to international law and the language of human rights. For example, the group Hizbut Tahrir Indonesia argued that as a Western product, Muslims do not need feminism as Islam provides the solution to all problems faced by Muslim women.[463] Some claim that feminism in fact exacerbates women's problems as their lives become more difficult due to the repeal of laws granting them special treatment and protection.[464] The fact that women's NGOs in Indonesia often receive funding from international donors like the Ford Foundation fuels 'conservatives' allegations that they serve Western rather than Islamic interests'.[465] For example, after the publication of her book on *fiqh* and abortion, Anshor was accused of having written the book on the orders of an agent or donor

---

[462] Hursh (n. 230), p. 293.
[463] Nurmila (2011) (n. 347), pp. 56–7. This group is controversial in Indonesia for its conservative positions and desire to create an Islamic caliphate, and was in fact banned by the Government in mid 2017. Safrin La Batu, Jokowi Signs Regulation Banning Hizbut Tahrir, *The Jakarta Post* (11 July 2017), www.thejakartapost.com/news/2017/07/11/jokowi-signs-regulation-banning-hizbut-tahrir.html (accessed 10 November 2017).
[464] Nurmila (2011) (n. 347), p. 57.
[465] Brenner (n. 205), p. 484.

institute.[466] This is not just a phenomenon in Indonesia, but occurs also in other Muslim countries such as Morocco, where conservatives have rejected reforms seeking to strengthen women's rights by characterising them as Western.[467] Conservatives in Pakistan and Iran built opposition to family planning by arguing that they were inspired or enforced by the West.[468]

Nurmila, who self-identifies as a Muslim feminist, notes that despite the concepts of feminism and gender being substantially in line with Islamic values of justice and equality, their association with the West (and therefore colonialism) raises suspicion.[469] In response, some Muslim feminists deliberately use the terms in order to address and dispel the issue, while others strategically avoid them. For example, participants of P3M's workshops perceived terms like 'gender' and 'reproductive rights' as foreign to their religious and lived experience.[470] To make its messages more acceptable and avoid accusations of Western influence, P3M instead used language and idioms from Islam.[471] Rather than referring to 'women's rights' in secular terms, it used the concept but translated it into an Islamic equivalent – *huquq al ummahat*.[472] This matching of concepts across normative orders can be seen as an example of Merry's vernacularisation discussed in Chapter 2. Lukito recommends using local languages to the extent possible, stressing the use of Islamic terminology as an effective method for implementing human rights norms by transforming them into local legal postulates.[473] The strength of Islamic law in Indonesia, he notes, is that the tradition is rooted in the heart of the people – it is part of their life.

---

[466] Interview with Dr Maria Ulfah Anshor, Commissioner with the Indonesian Child Protection Commission (*Komisi Perlindungan Anak Indonesia*) (7 February 2017, Jakarta, Indonesia).
[467] Hursh (n. 230), p. 261.
[468] Marshall (n. 127), p. 40; Hasna (n. 282), p. 195.
[469] Nurmila (2011) (n. 347), p. 59.
[470] Sciortino, Marcoes-Natsir and F. Mas'udi (n. 155), p. 90.
[471] Ibid.
[472] Ibid., p. 91; Interview with Lies Marcoes-Natsir, Rumah Kita Bersama Foundation (4 February 2017, Bogor, Indonesia). Fatayat similarly employs the language of Islam in its advocacy of women's empowerment. Interview with Dr Maria Ulfah Anshor, Commissioner with the Indonesian Child Protection Commission (*Komisi Perlindungan Anak Indonesia*) (7 February 2017, Jakarta, Indonesia).
[473] Interview with Prof. Dr Ratno Lukito, State Islamic University UIN Sunan Kalijaga (21 February 2017, Yogyakarta, Indonesia).

5.3 FAMILY PLANNING, LAW AND INSTITUTIONS

Marcoes deliberately uses the term gender, being one of the first to introduce it into Indonesia in the 1990s when it met with potent resistance particularly from religious groups.[474] However, she acted as an interpreter by identifying the relevant Arabic terms and *Qur'anic* principles, which tended to be more acceptable.[475] By acting as a bridge and translating foreign or international concepts for local Muslim audiences, Marcoes functions as a vernaculariser. Similarly, despite sometimes being criticised as a 'Western agent', the NGO Rahima specifically uses the language of human rights in conjunction with Islamic terms.[476] Given Indonesia's participation in the international human rights system, Rahima takes the view that it is important to teach Indonesians about this system and their commitment as a member of the international community. Rahima teaches that human rights are in fact sourced in Islam and were introduced when the *Qur'an* was revealed fourteen centuries ago.[477] Along with other interview participants, Rahima claims that the human rights principles of dignity, equality and justice derive from the *Qur'an* which, together with the *Hadith*, refers to universal values against violence, discrimination and intolerance. Rahima also self-identifies with 'Third World feminists', however, it does not always use this term, sometimes claiming to simply employ a 'new perspective'.[478] In this way, language is used strategically depending on the message, purpose and audience in order to achieve effective and meaningful advocacy.

Similarly, Dzuhayatin deliberately uses the term 'gender', teaching its origin, meaning in Arabic and relevance for Islam.[479] Like Rahima, she takes a formal approach to human rights in the attempt to mainstream them in Muslim society. However, she is also trained in Arabic as well as Islamic scholarship and jurisprudence, and wears a *hijab*. She claims that in order to be persuasive and considered credible, it is necessary to have the background qualifications to support one's position. Both

---

[474] Marcoes claims that the resistance largely resulted from a lack of understanding. Interview with Lies Marcoes-Natsir, Rumah Kita Bersama Foundation (4 February 2017, Bogor, Indonesia); van Doorn-Harder (2006) (n. 222), p. 35.
[475] Nurmila (2011) (n. 347), p. 50; Interview with Lies Marcoes-Natsir, Rumah Kita Bersama Foundation (4 February 2017, Bogor, Indonesia).
[476] Interview with the Director of Rahima (30 January 2017, Jakarta, Indonesia).
[477] Daud Ali also notes that Islam protects human rights, with the main distinction that 'Western' rights are anthropocentric, while Islamic rights are theocentric. Daud Ali (n. 217), p. 38.
[478] Interview with Director of Rahima (30 January 2017, Jakarta, Indonesia).
[479] Interview with Dr Siti Ruhaini Dzuhayatin, State Islamic University UIN Sunan Kalijaga (21 February 2017, Yogyakarta, Indonesia).

Dzuhayatin and Nurmila have attracted criticism for being Westernised or 'contaminated' by the West, given that they studied abroad at Western universities. Nurmila refutes these accusations by recalling her education credentials from an Islamic boarding school and Islamic university, and by wearing a *hijab* and Islamic dress, which she feels makes her progressive ideas more acceptable.[480] It is crucial that Muslim feminists have not only the requisite skills and training to engage in Islamic interpretation, but they must also be authentic in doing so, as 'a blatant means-to-an-end misreading of Shari'a will not aid legal reform efforts'.[481] In this way, Muslim feminists and reformers are not just using religion 'instrumentally, as being a good Muslim is also important'.[482]

On this basis, it is more expedient in Muslim societies to pursue human rights goals such as gender equality through an Islamic rather than an international framework. Despite their obvious relevance, international instruments like CEDAW 'seem to have little currency' in these contexts and, as seen above, may even provoke resistance.[483] Some Indonesians continue to view international law as the 'enemy', a colonising or occupying force,[484] and almost all interview participants agreed that human rights tend to be perceived as Western and therefore foreign. As such, claims for gender equality based on international human rights law or other 'Western' sources are less likely to be accepted by Indonesian Muslims. In contrast, by working within the Islamic framework, using Arabic terms, and engaging Muslim scholars in traditional interpretation, Muslim feminists are less readily dismissed as Western and illegitimate.[485] Two senior female Islamic scholars interviewed noted that in a competition between international and God's law, God's law comes first. This underlines the importance of pragmatic approaches that focus on achieving Islamic reforms in line with human rights, but not necessarily in the language or framework of international human rights law.

The case study illustrates that not only can the content of human rights be pursued via Islam, but that those same goals may be thwarted if

---

[480] Interview with Prof. Dr Nina Nurmila, Commissioner at Komnas Perempuan (25 January 2017, Jakarta, Indonesia).
[481] Hursh (n. 230), p. 302.
[482] Rinaldo (2014) (n. 344), p. 839. See also Hosseini (n. 224), p. 643.
[483] Bedner and van Huis (n. 220), p. 181; Hursh (n. 230), p. 303.
[484] See, for example, Lukito (2017) (n. 220), p. 98.
[485] Hursh (n. 230), p. 294.

the language of international human rights law is explicitly employed. While Muslim feminists and others in Indonesia may draw inspiration from international human rights law and the global women's movement, they typically plead their case domestically on the basis of Islam.[486] In fact, those promoting women's rights based on secular feminism or human rights have to an extent been sidelined. This reinforces culturally sensitive approaches to human rights and the need for rights to have local resonance. By basing their arguments in Islam and using traditional methods of interpretation, Muslim feminists are more likely to be perceived by their communities as trusted, legitimate actors, with pertinent claims. Such an approach is influential as it challenges patriarchal interpretations of Islam, but not Islam itself.[487] This is an essential distinction. By using Islam's terminology, sources and tools, Muslim feminists are able to criticise the gender bias in Islamic traditions in ways that would otherwise not be entertained.[488] Mir-Hosseini argues:

> By advocating a brand of feminism that takes Islam as the source of its legitimacy, these feminist voices are effectively challenging the hegemony of patriarch interpretations of the sharia and the legitimacy of the views of those who until now have spoken in the name of Islam.[489]

In this way, the plurality and interpretive scope inherent in Islam provides space for dialogue within Muslim communities on women's rights. It provides an avenue to develop and advocate ideas, as well as grow support for women's equality. While such processes may take time, they can contribute to effective human rights implementation by creating the conditions for sustainable and meaningful change in the relevant normative order. This path of dialogue and persuasion may be less direct when compared with the Government legislating human rights, but it can be more effective in achieving rights compliance. Scholars argue that the efficacy of such internal reform processes compensates for their potentially 'cumbersome and frustrating' appearance to secular reformers.[490]

---

[486] Bedner and van Huis (n. 220), p. 190.
[487] Hursh (n. 230), pp. 257, 292.
[488] Hosseini (n. 224), p. 640.
[489] Ibid., pp. 643-4.
[490] Hursh (n. 230), p. 295. Sezgin notes the efficacy of such 'gradual' measures of 'revolution' or 'reform' from within that are ultimately 'more likely to be readily adopted' – as opposed to top-down measures by the state. Yüksel Sezgin, How to Integrate Universal Human Rights into Customary and Religious Legal Systems (2010) *Journal of Legal Pluralism and Unofficial Law* 60:5, pp. 29-30. See also Helen Quane, Legal Pluralism and

This view is supported by the scholarship discussed in Chapter 2 that, on the basis of principle, pragmatism or both, reiterates the need for local homegrown reform over external top-down measures. Using measures other than state law to protect human rights may not deliver instant results, but that is also typically the case even when legislation is enacted. All law reform processes suffer limitations in their ability to transform society. This reinforces the need for domestic constituents working within their communities to secure human rights, regardless of the implementation approach taken.

5.3.5 Family Planning in Indonesia: Islam As a Master Key?

For decades, Islamic law and institutions have played a crucial role in the success of Indonesia's national family planning programme. The programme has been hailed as a model of family planning and specifically recognised for its effective partnerships with religious leaders and institutions. In fact, interview participants were in agreement that but for the involvement of Islam, the programme would have failed. While the Government astutely engaged with pre-existing institutions like Muhammadiyah and NU, it also created MUI as a way to institutionalise its relationship with Islamic leaders. All three institutions were involved in and contributed to the national family planning programme in various ways. In particular, the women's branches of Muhammadiyah and NU were material in securing and sustaining their institution's support for family planning. Their internal, bottom-up advocacy, coupled with the Government's top-down measures and incentives, contributed to Muhammadiyah and NU's shift from opposing to supporting family planning. While other factors like economics and education certainly played a role, Hassan urges that in the Muslim world, 'Islam (in all its complexity) is not just one of the factors involved in development issues but the matrix in which all other factors are grounded'.[491]

The success of Indonesia's family planning programme illustrates the importance of addressing not just the medical aspects of contraceptives but the socio-cultural determinants. In addition to the Government

---

International Human Rights Law: Inherently Incompatible, Mutually Reinforcing or Something in Between? (2013) *Oxford Journal of Legal Studies* 33:4, p. 702.

[491] Hassan (2000) (n. 188), p. 237; Hassan (2000) (n. 210), p. 68.

making family planning services available and accessible to the public, it was necessary to engage Islamic norms and actors to build demand for such goods and services and overcome cultural barriers to access. The support of sympathetic Muslim leaders was essential for reinterpretating the relevant Islamic norms and responding to Muslims' moral concerns about contraceptives.[492] This was done by Muhammadiyah, NU and MUI pronouncing their support for family planning in *fatwas*, and by the advocacy and other programmes run, in particular, by the women's branches. It was crucial for the Government to work with these Islamic actors in order to address socio-cultural issues such as norms regarding marriage and sexuality, stereotypes and gendered decision-making norms. The work of Muslim feminists in advocating gender equality more broadly was a necessary contribution to the family planning programme given the link between women's low social status and their inability to access healthcare.

Given the great overlap in subject matter, Islam can be engaged to further human rights goals. As the present example shows, Islamic norms and institutions can play an important role in accepting or opposing human rights, including reproductive rights. Where Islamic norms and values align with human rights – such the case with family planning – much can be achieved. However, when there is a conflict, human rights are often disadvantaged, as seen in the failed attempts to reform polygamy laws. This is because Islam, as a plural legal system in Indonesia, can have more resonance with the Muslim community than both state and international law. This is not unusual in the Muslim world.[493] Therefore, to be effective, it is necessary to build support for human rights from within an Islamic system. In the present Indonesian example, these domestic constituents were Muslim feminists (with or without the label) and others pursuing gender equality through an Islamic framework. While outside actors can play a role in internal reform processes, as set out in Chapter 2, it should be a supporting and not a leading role.

Those seeking gender equality used the interpretative scope inherent in Islam to challenge prior understandings, spark discussion and gain supporters. It was historically new for Muslim women to undertake and

---

[492] Kissling (n. 204), pp. 219–20.
[493] Abdullahi Ahmed An Na'im, Why should Muslims abandon *Jihad*? Human Rights and the Future of International Law? in Richard Falk, Balakrishnan Rajagopal and Jacqueline Stevens (eds.), *International Law and the Third World: Reshaping Justice* (Routledge, 2008), p. 87; Hursh (n. 230), p. 286.

advocate progressive reinterpretations of Islam that challenged what they considered to be patriarchal perspectives.[494] They did this by appealing to the core values in Islam of justice and equality to counter discriminatory interpretations. This approach has also been used outside religion in the sphere of custom. Nyamu advocates internal reform processes to normative systems like customary law by relying upon the system's higher principles to shift discriminatory norms and practices. As explained in Chapter 2, she advises reiterating 'the general principles of fairness and justice in a community's value system' in order to secure the flexible application of what appears to be rigid rules.[495] As seen in the present Indonesian example, this can be an effective strategy as it relies upon internal (versus external) justifications that already enjoy cultural legitimacy. Therefore, changes made can be seen as remedies in line with (or even required by) the normative system, rather than adaptations introduced or imposed from the outside that compromise or dilute the system.

This strategic use of terms, concepts and methodologies illustrates the agency of these Muslim women. Therefore, this research adds to the scholarship debunking stereotypes of Muslim women as passive subordinates. It shows how (some) Muslim women in Indonesia have capitalised upon Islam's growing influence in the public sphere, the global women's movement and Islam's inherent dynamism to pursue gender equality. Rather than necessarily being a constraining factor, these women depended upon Islam, which provided the resources (Islamic texts), tools (interpretation) and pathway (dialogue) for achieving emancipatory reforms. In doing so, their agency was informed and empowered by their religious context. However, this context was not necessarily deterministic, as the women acted as agents of cultural transformation, capable of influencing and shifting Islamic norms. Rather than simply being subject to Islamic norms, they were able to participate in the determination of such norms. The shift of norms from opposing to supporting family planning and other aspects of reproductive health reflect the dynamism of Islam and of culture in general. Being agentive in this way brought with it inherent benefits due to the established legitimacy and authority of Islam within the community. The same goals

---

[494] Rinaldo (n. 344), p. 842.
[495] Celestine Nyamu, How Should Human Rights and Development Respond to Cultural Legitimization of Gender Hierarchy in Developing Countries? (2000) *Harvard International Law Journal* 41:2, p. 413.

5.3 FAMILY PLANNING, LAW AND INSTITUTIONS

pursued via state or international norms would not have been entertained in the same way, but rather *prima facie* rejected.

Naturally, power plays a role and will impact the amount and scope of agency of certain groups and individuals within a given cultural community. While the Muslim women in the present example enjoyed sufficient power, agency, wealth and opportunity to educate themselves, organise and advocate their views, others may not be able to do so. They may lack power, or sufficient power, to agitate for human rights compliant change. While states can influence power dynamics in various ways (i.e. by providing scholarships and funding the activities of progressive women's groups), the feasibility of internal reform on a given issue in a given context must be factored into state decisions on how to most effectively implement their human rights obligations. Clearly, if there are no local receptors or concepts to rely upon that align with the substance of human rights, the state will have to use a different approach to implementation. Equally, if there are no (powerful) internal reform actors within a cultural community to advocate normative change, the state will also have to use a different approach. There are, of course, no silver bullets, and there are limitations to all approaches to human rights implementation, including the use of social institutions.

Whereas passing legislation is (in theory) 'one-size-fits-all', states relying upon social institutions have the burden of tailoring human rights solutions for each cultural community in their jurisdiction. Given culture's dynamism, states will also have to remain vigilant to ensure practice continues to comply with human rights standards. In such processes, practical or ethical trade-offs may have to be made rendering human rights protection less than perfect. In the present Indonesian example, this manifested in the fact that contraceptives are legal for married couples only, and not for unmarried persons. This negatively impacts young people in particular. Despite state and Islamic law to the contrary, secular NGOs in Indonesia currently provide contraceptives to unmarried persons. While this practical solution may fulfil some rights in the interim, denying all people access to family planning is a violation of their human rights under international law. However, simply amending the legislation to permit unmarried persons access to contraceptives will not necessarily be effective if it remains proscribed by Islam. Therefore, the Government will need to continue engaging both secular NGOs and Islamic actors to bridge this gap, and simultaneously provide a safety-net for those who fall between the cracks.

5.4 Reproductive Rights, Islam, Indonesia and the UN Human Rights Treaty Bodies

As this case study has demonstrated, Islam is a social institution highly relevant to human rights in Indonesia. The example of reproductive health and family planning has shown that Islam can be effectively mobilised by both the state and internal actors to help implement the right to health. Section 5.4 considers whether Indonesia's reliance upon Islamic norms and institutions is in line with its international obligations regarding the right to health as set out in Section 5.2. While a thorough and detailed assessment of Indonesia's compliance is beyond the scope and purpose of this section, it addresses the main requirements raised in Section 5.2. Section 5.4 then critically analyses how the various UN treaty bodies have dealt with Islam as a plural legal system and Muslim actors, by examining their Concluding Observations and recommendations to Indonesia regarding its protection of reproductive rights. The section concludes by reflecting on the practice of the UN treaty bodies and how they can improve their monitoring of states parties' domestic human rights implementation.

5.4.1 Indonesia's Use of Social Institutions: Compliant with International Law?

As set out in Section 5.2, as a party to ICESCR, CEDAW and CRC, Indonesia is obliged to progressively realise the right to health and family planning as a part of that right. Indonesia must do so effectively by taking all necessary steps, including the adoption of legal and other measures. In addition to the overall requirement of effectiveness, family planning goods, services and facilities must also be available, accessible, acceptable and quality. This includes being culturally appropriate to the relevant community and acceptable to women. In the design and implementation of its health systems, Indonesia must ensure the participation of and consultation with the public, as well as facilitate NSAs in discharging their international responsibilities. As established in Chapter 3, Indonesia (like all states parties) enjoys discretion to determine those implementation measures best suited to its national context to be effective. As elaborated upon above in Sections 5.2 and 5.3, Indonesia domestically implemented the right to family planning by, *inter alia*, passing legislation, implementing plans and strategies, and engaging with Islamic law and institutions.

Indonesia has taken legislative measures at the different levels of Government, and has implemented various health systems, policies and programmes, including the national family planning programme and the BKKBN. To complement these measures, as seen in Section 5.3, the Government engaged and collaborated with Islamic leaders and groups to promote the permissibility of family planning, increase demand and provide services. In this way, the Government met its international obligation to include members of the public in the design and implementation of its reproductive health policies and programmes, and ensured their cultural appropriateness. For example, when sterilisation was not supported by Islamic institutions, the Government withdrew it from its programme. In addition to developing relationships with Muhammadiyah and NU, the Government innovatively created MUI, which became one of the strongest supporters of the national family planning programme. The Government engaged Islamic leaders and institutions, providing incentives and opportunities for them to contribute to and cooperate with the BKKBN's family planning programme, including taking them abroad to learn best family planning practices from other Muslim majority states.

Complementing these top-down state measures was the work of Muslims within Islamic institutions and NGOs like P3M and Rahima. Institutions like Muhammadiyah and NU issued *fatwas* and also provided reproductive health services directly to the public. While the Indonesian Government cannot claim credit or responsibility for these bottom-up initiatives, the Government did seek and encourage partnerships, provide resources and contribute to an environment conducive for their work. This can be seen as being in line with the state's international obligation to facilitate NSAs fulfilling their own international responsibilities regarding the right to health. This combination of top-down and bottom-up initiatives succeeded in shifting the dominant Islamic norms in favour of family planning. While some issues remain (such as access for unmarried persons) and unmet need persists in places, the right to family planning can be seen as being progressively realised in Indonesia. This is reflected in the present fertility rate of around 2.3 children per woman, and the contraceptive prevalence rate of over 61 per cent.[496] Indonesia's recent adoption of universal health insurance should further

---

[496] The World Bank, Contraceptive prevalence, any method (% of women ages 15–49) Indonesia, available at data.worldbank.org/indicator/SP.DYN.CONU.ZS?locations=ID (accessed 16 September 2019).

realise enjoyment of this right. This success is what has made Indonesia's family planning programme a model for other states around the world.

This variety of measures to implement the right to family planning can be seen as necessary given Indonesia's context and the relevant sociocultural determinants. State legislation alone would not have been effective, and other measures in social, cultural and religious fields were necessary to ensure the right to family planning in practice. This example therefore speaks to the limits of state law to transform society and uphold human rights. The case study demonstrates the benefits of adopting other measures to implement human rights, including a legal pluralist approach employing non-state law. Also important in the Indonesian context was the role played not just by non-state norms but by NSAs, such as Muhammadiyah, NU and Muslim feminists. While states remain accountable under international human rights law as set out in Chapter 4, as long as a right is meaningfully protected in practice, it may be fulfilled by the state or a NSA. States are, of course, required by their due diligence obligations to monitor and regulate NSAs, for example by supervising the quality and accessibility of Muhammadiyah's health clinics.

Rather than states being the sole actors and the rest of society passively receiving rights, community members (and not just their leaders) have agency and the ability to shape cultural norms and implement human rights. Indonesia's mix of complementary measures including legal and other measures by a variety of public and private actors proved effective in implementing the right to family planning. And, as many commentators noted, without involving religious groups and leaders, the family planning programme would have failed. Therefore, the efficacy of Indonesia's programme required the involvement of these social institutions. Given that effectiveness is the UN treaty bodies' key criterion in assessing implementation measures as established in Chapter 3, Indonesia's measures can be seen to be in line with its international human rights obligations. In fact, it can be argued that international human rights law obliges states parties to work with social institutions when this would be effective for implementing the right in question.

In fact, some have suggested that the current plateau in family planning programming could be due to the reduced involvement of NSAs. As seen in this example, based on their relationships of trust with grassroots communities, civil society actors including Islamic institutions and NGOs can have access where the Government does not, especially on sensitive topics and with marginalised groups. While BKKBN previously worked well with various partners, interviewees reported that since around 2000 they have tended to work more independently, engaging in consultation more as a formality than genuine collaboration. Equally, some interview participants suggested that Islamic leaders and institutions today are no longer interested in family planning and could do more in this regard. Given that they have established the Islamic framework supporting family planning, some are of the view that Muhammadiyah and NU believe that their work is done and that it is now up to the Government.[497] As such, the BKKBN may need to work to re-engage Islamic leaders and institutions on the topic of family planning, providing incentives and funding as in the past – but adapted to the contemporary context.

Given that it is permissible and potentially even obligatory within the framework of international human rights law for Indonesia to have utilised and relied upon Islamic law and institutions to implement the right to family planning, the next issue to explore is how the UN treaty bodies have dealt with such measures. Therefore, the following text looks at the UN treaty bodies' recommendations to Indonesia regarding its protection of reproductive rights.

5.4.2 UN Treaty Body Recommendations to Indonesia on Reproductive Rights

As seen in Chapters 3 and 4, the UN treaty bodies have a tendency to focus on the state and state law when supervising the implementation of human rights treaty obligations. Legislative measures are typically their primary recommendation to states, often coupled with other measures such as education and awareness raising. The treaty bodies take this approach generally as well as in relation to human rights issues with strong cultural ties or subject to legal pluralism. Unfortunately, the treaty bodies overwhelmingly focus on the state, often failing in their Concluding Observations to even recognise the existence or influence of social institutions. These findings from earlier chapters also apply to the present case study and to the treaty bodies' recommendations to Indonesia regarding reproductive health. As a party to ICESCR, CEDAW, CRC and the *International Covenant on Civil and Political Rights* (ICCPR),

---

[497] See, for example, Berkley Center for Religion, Peace and World Affairs, Georgetown University, A Discussion with Lies Marcoes, Senior Officer of the Fahmina Institute (14 November 2013), https://berkleycenter.georgetown.edu/interviews/a-discussion-with-lies-marcoes-senior-officer-of-the-fahmina-institute (accessed 12 November 2017).

Indonesia participates in the reporting and treaty-monitoring processes before various treaty bodies. All four of these treaties, and therefore the treaty bodies, address issues related to reproductive health, including discrimination, access to contraceptives, FGM/C, early marriage and polygamy. Their recommendations to Indonesia on these matters are critiqued in turn below.

The UN Human Rights Committee (HRCee), which supervises Indonesia's implementation of the ICCPR, expressed its concern at the prevalence of polygamy and early marriage.[498] As noted above, both polygamy and early marriage are publicly supported in Indonesia by Muslims based on interpretations of Islamic law. Rather than recognising and engaging with Islamic law and actors as relevant social institutions, the HRCee instead focused on state law solutions in its Concluding Observations. The HRCee advised Indonesia 'to ensure that its legislation effectively prohibits polygamy and is effectively implemented, and conduct awareness campaigns among the population', and also to 'review its legislation in order to prohibit early marriages'.[499] Without acknowledging Islamic law, religious leaders or institutions, the HRCee went on to rather vaguely encourage Indonesia to 'strengthen measures to combat early marriage by putting in place mechanisms in the provinces and by pursuing community awareness-raising strategies focusing on the consequences of early marriages'.[500] Despite its vital importance in Indonesia as detailed in this case study, the HRCee does not mention Islam once in these Concluding Observations in relation to reproductive health or any other topic.

The ESCR Committee similarly expressed its concern at the prevalence of early marriage in Indonesia, lamenting 'the lack of information on relevant legal control'.[501] Like the HRCee, without acknowledging the Islamic norms that purport to allow child marriage, the ESCR Committee also focused on state law solutions. The Committee urged Indonesia to 'prevent child marriages, in law and in practice, and to ensure the effectiveness of legal control of child marriage with a view to punishing individuals performing and facilitating child marriages'.[502] It is unclear

---

[498] UN HRCee, Concluding observations on the initial report of Indonesia, CCPR/C/IDN/CO/1 (21 August 2013), para. 29.
[499] Ibid.
[500] Ibid.
[501] UN ESCR Committee, Concluding observations on the initial report of Indonesia, E/C.12/IDN/CO/1 (19 June 2014), para. 22.
[502] Ibid.

5.4 REPRODUCTIVE RIGHTS, ISLAM, INDONESIA & UN

here what role, if any, the Committee envisages non-state law playing to resolve this issue. In relation to the high maternal mortality rate, the ESCR Committee expressed its concern that this was due 'to insufficient sexual and reproductive health services as well as legal and cultural barriers to their access'.[503] The Committee called on Indonesia 'to address disparities in the availability and quality of maternal health care services ... [and] to ensure access to sexual and reproductive health services to unmarried women and teenagers as well as to married women without the consent of spouses'.[504] This latter aspect of access cannot be addressed without engaging the Islamic norms used as the basis for denying certain reproductive health services such as contraceptives to unmarried persons or wives without their husband's consent. Yet, the ESCR Committee does not mention Islam or religion at all in their Concluding Observations to Indonesia.[505]

The CEDAW and CRC Committees also raised the issue of access to contraceptives and teenage pregnancy with Indonesia in their reporting cycles. Both Committees made similar recommendations to those of the ESCR Committee, which did not refer to religious norms relevant to accessing family planning.[506] The CRC Committee further raised the issue of polygamy and made similar recommendations to the HRCee, which urged Indonesia to repeal all discriminatory laws without reference to religious norms, actors or other measures.[507] In relation to discriminatory laws and regulations, the ESCR Committee urged Indonesia to: repeal laws and by-laws that discriminate against women and marginalised groups; raise awareness of Indonesia's obligations under international human rights law; and strengthen mechanisms for reviewing draft laws by decentralised authorities.[508] These recommendations fail to acknowledge any competing non-state normative system like Islam that may influence or inform such discriminatory laws and – as

---

[503] Ibid., para. 33.
[504] Ibid.
[505] With the exception of 'religious communities' when talking about multiple discrimination in para. 13.
[506] UN CRC Committee, Concluding observations on the combined third and fourth periodic reports of Indonesia, CRC/C/IDN/CO/3-4 (10 July 2014), paras. 49–50; UN CEDAW Committee, Concluding comments of the Committee on the Elimination of Discrimination against Women: Indonesia, CEDAW/C/IDN/CO/5 (10 August 2007), para. 37.
[507] UN CRC Committee, Concluding Observations: Indonesia 2014, ibid., paras. 41–2.
[508] UN ESCR Committee, Concluding Observations: Indonesia (n. 501), para. 6.

seen above – relying upon international human rights law as the reason for repealing domestic law may in fact provoke resistance rather than compliance.

In contrast, the CEDAW Committee takes a different approach to discrimination that more often recognises the role of Islam and the need to engage with its norms and actors. For example, to address discriminatory stereotypes and practices the CEDAW Committee recommended Indonesia engage with communities, civil society, school systems, and religious groups and leaders.[509] In relation to discriminatory laws against women, the Committee specifically refers to Islam, urging Indonesia to *inter alia*:

> Raise the awareness of religious groups and leaders about the importance of amending legal provisions; increase support for law reform through partnerships and collaboration with Islamic jurisprudence research organizations, civil society organizations, women's non-governmental organizations and community leaders supportive of the advancement of women's rights; and obtain information on comparative legislation and jurisprudence in which more progressive interpretations of Islamic law have been codified and applied.[510]

These are positive recommendations demonstrating the CEDAW Committee's understanding of culture's inherent relationship with human rights, the role of NSAs, and the interplay of plural legal systems. This is in line with what scholars and activists recommended above in Section 5.3 and in Chapter 2, such as engaging with *fiqh,* building support from within the Muslim community and demonstrating alternative human rights' compliant norms both in theory and in practice. The CEDAW Committee's recommendation for comparative legal studies indicates its understanding of pluralism and how it can be used to develop all of the various normative systems of law. While a welcome addition and strong contrast to the approaches taken by the other Committees, such recommendations still tend to be made by the CEDAW Committee in second place only, with the primary focus remaining on state legislation and enforcement. For example, this recommendation quoted above was

---

[509] See, for example, regarding FGM/C, early marriage and polygamy, UN CEDAW Committee, Concluding observations of the Committee on the Elimination of Discrimination against Women: Indonesia, CEDAW/C/IDN/CO/6-7 (7 August 2012), paras. 23-4.

[510] Ibid., para. 18(c); UN CEDAW Committee, Concluding comments of the Committee on the Elimination of Discrimination against Women: Indonesia, CEDAW/C/IDN/CO/5 (10 August 2007), para. 13.

5.4 REPRODUCTIVE RIGHTS, ISLAM, INDONESIA & UN

the CEDAW Committee's third recommendation to Indonesia. It was preceded by recommendations to ensure that the legislative framework complies with CEDAW by repealing discriminatory laws and amending all discriminatory provincial by-laws.[511]

Another potent example is the UN treaty bodies' responses to Indonesia on the issue of FGM/C. As explained in Section 5.2, due to MUI's *fatwa* in support of FGM/C, Indonesia withdrew its prior ban and permitted FGM/C to be performed by medical practitioners. In response to this, the CEDAW Committee encouraged Indonesia to adopt robust legislation criminalising FGM/C and sanctioning offenders.[512] The Committee added that Indonesia should raise awareness among the public and 'sensitize and collaborate with religious groups and leaders who advocate' FGM/C, encouraging comparative studies with other groups that do not practice it.[513] While an important addition that indicates the CEDAW Committee's focus on religion, it comes only after the initial recommendations on state law and sanctions. The CRC Committee took a similar approach, in that after calling for legislation it urged Indonesia, *inter alia*, to create educational and awareness-raising campaigns with the full participation of civil society and victims of FGM/C, targeting all segments of society including religious leaders.[514] The HRCee also focused first on legislative bans and penalties before advising awareness-raising and educational programmes that target the communities where the practices are widespread 'in order to bring a change in mindset'.[515] Finally, after urging Indonesia to 'effectively enforce the

---

[511] UN CEDAW Committee, Concluding Observations: Indonesia 2012 (n. 509), paras. 18(a) and (b).

[512] Ibid., paras. 21, 22(a); UN CEDAW Committee, Concluding comments of the Committee on the Elimination of Discrimination against Women: Indonesia 2007 (n. 510), para. 21.

[513] UN CEDAW Committee, Concluding Observations: Indonesia 2012 (n. 509), para. 22 (b)–(c). In the Committee's earlier Concluding Observations on this topic, the Committee similarly recommended Indonesia 'develop a plan of action and undertake efforts to eliminate the practice ... including implementing public awareness-raising campaigns to change the cultural perceptions connected with female genital mutilation, and provide education regarding the practice as a violation of the human rights of women and girls that has no basis in religion'. UN CEDAW Committee, Concluding comments of the Committee on the Elimination of Discrimination against Women: Indonesia 2007 (n. 510), para. 21.

[514] UN CRC Committee, Concluding observations on the combined third and fourth periodic reports of Indonesia, CRC/C/IDN/CO/3–4 (10 July 2014), para. 34.

[515] UN HRCee, Concluding observations on the initial report of Indonesia, CCPR/C/IDN/CO/1 (21 August 2013), para. 12.

prohibition of FGM', the ESCR Committee also recommended awareness-raising and 'culturally sensitive education campaigns'.[516]

Here, and as in Chapter 3, the CEDAW Committee's approach can be seen as the most developed and inclusive, referring specifically to engaging with religious groups and leaders, and the utility of comparative legal studies for shifting norms and practices. Despite these more nuanced approaches that refer to religious groups and leaders, all of the UN treaty bodies commenced their recommendations with an insistence upon state law. This reflects the findings in Chapter 3 that the treaty bodies have a legalistic approach to implementation, which prioritises state legislative measures over all 'other measures'. As noted in the critique of legalism, there are several drawbacks to such an approach. As this example of FGM/C shows, Islamic law as determined by institutions like MUI has significant influence in Indonesia and its opposition to a state law can undo those provisions even when they are supported (or obligated) by international law. And even with state legislative prohibitions of FGM/C on the books, it is unlikely that they would be complied with or enforced without widespread public support. As such, it is essential – and not secondary – to recognise and mobilise Islam's plural legal system and actors in order to arrive at a legitimate and sustainable position against FGM/C in Indonesia.

As argued in Chapter 3, it is perhaps to be expected that the CEDAW Committee is the most inclusive of social institutions given that states are mandated by article 5(a) to modify social and cultural patterns incompatible with the Convention. However, as demonstrated in this section, the other treaties (and therefore treaty bodies) also substantively cover rights with cultural dimensions. While the ICCPR does not explicitly stipulate the state obligation of cultural modification, it is nonetheless implicitly required in order to effectively implement many of the rights therein. For example, due to provisions regarding equality and non-discrimination, the HRCee must address issues like polygamy and child marriage. Due to provisions against torture or cruel, inhuman or degrading treatment or punishment, the HRCee must address practices like FGM/C and corporal punishment. The same applies by analogy to the other treaties including the *Convention on the Elimination of Racial Discrimination* and the

---

[516] UN ESCR Committee, Concluding observations on the initial report of Indonesia, E/C.12/IDN/CO/1 (19 June 2014), para. 25.

5.4 REPRODUCTIVE RIGHTS, ISLAM, INDONESIA & UN 259

Convention against Torture.[517] As such, the treaty bodies monitoring the implementation of these treaties should also consider the cultural dimension of rights and the domestic socio-cultural context. While this link between human rights and social and cultural patterns is most clearly established in article 5(a) CEDAW, it is just as applicable in practice to the other treaties and treaty bodies. In this respect, they would be well served to emulate the CEDAW Committee.

It is clear from the above examples that the UN treaty bodies frequently advise awareness-raising and education as ancillary measures to legislation to implement human rights. This pattern was first identifed in Chapter 3. However, like all implementation measures, awareness-raising campaigns and educational measures should also be tailored to the specific target audience and, where possible, vernacularised to local norms, concepts and values. As seen in the Indonesian example, the language of international human rights law can be unfamiliar or, worse, elicit a negative response, whereas rights concepts translated into Islamic terms are more readily accepted. This illustrates that it is not so much the content of rights that is suspect, but its Western packaging. While the language of human rights might be relatively new to some Muslims, the concept is not, as many of these values (i.e. justice and equality) are sourced in the *Qur'an*. Therefore, to ensure that awareness-raising campaigns and educational measures are effective, the treaty bodies should advise states to include social institutions in their design, communication and implementation. They should encourage states parties to foster a dialogue, rather than creating a one-way, top-down learning environment. In this way, national actors can learn about local normative systems and vice versa, together identifying topics of overlap, shared norms, as well as points of contention and possible remedies.

Despite recognition of the human rights responsibilities on all organs of society as set out in Chapter 4, the treaty bodies do not reiterate these international responsibilities in their Concluding Observations. As such, they contribute to the opacity of these theoretical responsibilities, and decline the opportunity to give them (sorely needed) concrete content. Given that their Concluding Observations are supposed to be translated into national languages and widely disseminated, the treaty bodies could

---

[517] *Convention on the Elimination of All Forms of Racial Discrimination* (adopted 21 December 1965, entered into force 4 January 1969), 660 UNTS 195; *Convention against Torture and Other Cruel, Inhuman or Degrading Treatment or Punishment* (adopted 10 December 1984, entered into force 26 June 1987), 1465 UNTS 85.

use them to inform/remind NSAs of their human rights responsibilities generally, and specifically regarding the right to health. The treaty bodies could also use the reporting procedure to follow up with states regarding their obligation to facilitate NSAs discharging their responsibilities, and guide them in doing so in their Concluding Observations. The treaty bodies could assess states' facilitation of the relevant NSAs in context, and engage them on how to improve their relationships and cooperation to most effectively implement human rights. The treaty bodies could also use this opportunity to provide further guidance to states regarding the scope and content of their due diligence obligations when NSAs are fulfilling human rights.

All parties to this dialogue would stand to benefit. For example, via the Concluding Observations, NSAs could learn more about international law and their role/responsibilities in human rights protection. States parties could receive the necessary guidance on managing and collaborating with NSAs. Similarly, through state reports, the UN treaty bodies could gain a better understanding of the relevant social institutions in each state party and make more informed recommendations. Rather than simply addressing state law as in current practice generally, they could embrace legal pluralism as a reality and engage with non-state normative systems such as customary and religious law. This would involve recognising multiple centres of lawmaking above and below the state – debunking the myth that the state has a monopoly on the law.[518] Through this interaction, and via state mediation, international law and non-state law could become conversant, engaging, mutually influencing and shaping one another.[519] This would help facilitate regime interaction and break down the individual silos of international, national and non-state law. It would also be a form of cross-cultural dialogue on human rights advocated by An-Na`im (and discussed in Chapter 2), but taking place in a new forum and on multiple levels.

Finally, taking such an approach would also nuance the treaty bodies' rhetoric regarding culture. As discussed in Chapter 2, there is a tendency in international human rights law to essentialise and other culture. It is

---

[518] Lukito (2017) (n. 220), p. 106.
[519] Quane notes that we are in 'the very early stages in this relationship'. Helen Quane, International Human Rights Law as a Catalyst for the Recognition and Evolution of Non-State Law, in Michael Helfand (ed.), *Negotiating State and Non-State Law: The Challenge of Global and Local Legal Pluralism* (Cambridge University Press, 2016), pp. 113, 128, 132.

5.4 REPRODUCTIVE RIGHTS, ISLAM, INDONESIA & UN

frequently referred to only in relation to 'harmful traditional practices' in the global South like FGM/C and polygamy. In this way, the portrayal of culture as antithetical to human rights is continually reinforced. The treaty bodies could endeavour to reverse this trend by taking a more anthropological perspective of culture, reiterating its ubiquity and the numerous positive roles it plays regarding human rights. Religion specifically warrants a special mention from the treaty bodies regarding its ability to be instrumental in human rights implementation, and Islam in particular given the pervasiveness of Islamophobia today. The treaty bodies could learn here from the UNFPA, which 'has focused more specifically, in more depth, and over a longer period of time on religious roles and actors than any other'.[520] Arguably, the UNFPA appreciates not only the need to be culturally sensitive and to engage with religious norms and groups, but also the proven benefits of doing so. Rather than being unique to Indonesia, including Islamic law and institutions in successful family planning programming has been done in other Muslim majority states, such as Bangladesh, Iran, Senegal, Jordan, Pakistan and Morocco.[521]

5.4.3 UN Treaty Bodies and Social Institutions: A Missed Opportunity

As demonstrated in this case study, involving social institutions like religion can be indispensable to effective human rights implementation. And as seen in Chapter 3, states may use a variety of 'other measures' for implementation with the controlling criterion being effectiveness. Therefore, states may be obliged to involve social institutions in implementing the right to reproductive health where this would be effective. States are additionally obliged to involve social institutions due to obligations to ensure public participation, cultural appropriateness of healthcare goods, facilities and services, and to support private actors fulfilling their own responsibilities. If states can be seen to have an obligation to engage social institutions, then the UN treaty bodies not raising this measure are failing to pursue states fully regarding their obligations. Further, if engaging social institutions is an effective implementation measure for states to take, then the treaty bodies currently not recommending this are doing states a

---

[520] Azza Karam, Foreword, in Marshall (n. 127), p. 2. See UNFPA reports such as: *Culture Matters: Lessons from a Legacy of Engaging Faith-based Organizations* (2008, UNPFA).
[521] Marshall (n. 127); Hasna (n. 282); Ali Mohammad Mir and Gul Rashida Shaikh, Islam and Family Planning: Changing Perceptions of Health Care Providers and Medical Faculty in Pakistan (2013) *Global Health Science and Practice* 1:2; Hursh (n. 230).

disservice. Equally, if state legislative measures are *not* an effective measure in context, then the treaty bodies are also doing states a disservice by focusing predominately on such measures. It is proposed that the treaty bodies would find it beneficial to their mandate to more consistently acknowledge and address social institutions. They could capitalise upon the reporting cycle to engage with states on their specific, tailored implementation measures and the various norms and stakeholders involved.

Alternatively, it could be argued that it is not the place of the treaty bodies to be overly prescriptive in their Concluding Observations out of respect for state sovereignty and discretion in implementation. On this basis, the treaty bodies may be deliberately restrained (and vague) in their recommendations, drawing states' attention to problematic areas without dictating specific remedial measures. While this may have been the traditional position, over the years of operation all of the treaty bodies have developed increasingly sophisticated and detailed recommendations to states. This is done in line with their mandate to supervise states parties' implementation of the treaties and to partake in constructive dialogue with them on the progress made and difficulties encountered. Therefore, engaging states regarding their social institutions could be seen as part of their sophistication promoting enhanced human rights implementation. Rather than an adversarial encounter, the open discussion between states and treaty bodies is well suited to exploring specific issues of implementation. Furthermore, given that the Concluding Observations are not binding, states' sovereignty and discretion is not diminished by more direct or specific recommendations.

Given the complex and diverse environments in which international human rights law has to be implemented around the world, the work of the treaty bodies may be enhanced by broadening and diversifying the implementation measures envisaged and advised to states parties. This would also go some distance in addressing the critiques of state-centricism and legalism levelled at international human rights law. As seen in the present case study, there are limits to the ability of states to transform society. The state is but one of many actors implicated in human rights and responsible for their realisation. Similarly, as recognised in the treaties themselves, state law is one tool to implement human rights, but not the only one. Given that the treaties all recognise other, non-legislative measures of implementation, and that states can engage NSAs to fulfil their obligations, the treaty bodies can avoid state-centric legalism without changing their mandate – just their practice. The treaty body members could shift their focus to be more open to other culturally sensitive approaches to human rights implementation, including engaging social institutions. Such a step would indicate that, despite international human rights law itself being state-centric, the treaty bodies recognise the crucial role of and need for social institutions to effectively implement human rights in practice. Given that Indonesia will continue to report on reproductive rights in coming years,[522] the treaty bodies have further opportunities to address these issues.

5.5 Conclusions: Role of Islamic Law and Institutions in Implementing Women's Right to Family Planning in Indonesia

This chapter presented a case study in order to examine in practice culturally sensitive approaches to human rights implementation and the legal analysis in the preceding chapters. The purpose was to explore why and how social institutions can play a role in the domestic implementation of states' international treaty obligations. The chosen study of Islamic law and institutions in the implementation of women's right to family planning in Indonesia proved a fitting illustration. While international human rights treaties set out vital minimum standards to be enjoyed by all human beings in the abstract, the pressing challenge lies in their domestic implementation within each particular setting. Rather than implementation being a straightforward process, the Indonesian case study exemplified the complexity of human rights in context and the myriad actors and norms involved. Specifically, it highlighted the crucial role that social institutions like Islam can play in effectively implementing human rights given their social embeddedness and local legitimacy. This case study demonstrated the relevance of Islamic norms and actors to family planning, as well as their contributions to its implementation. In doing so, it showed how social institutions can, and at times do, play an important role in human rights implementation.

As the state with the world's largest Muslim population, it is not surprising that Islam is highly influential across Indonesia. And given the numerous Islamic norms relating to reproduction, it is also not surprising that Islamic law and institutions played a large role in

---

[522] Indonesia has several outstanding reports to the UN treaty bodies as of September 2019. For example, it was due to report to the CEDAW Committee in July 2016; to the HRCee in July 2017; to the ESCR Committee in May 2019; and to the CRC Committee in October 2019.

Indonesia's family planning programme. The Government commenced this programme fifty years ago and now it is hailed as an international success for having halved Indonesia's fertility rate. Once considered to be a sensitive topic and forbidden practice, family planning is now widely accepted across Indonesia. While there were other contributing factors, much of the family planning programme's success has been attributed to the Government's involvement of Islamic law and institutions. Indeed, there is consensus around the fact that the family planning programme would have failed *but for* the involvement of Islamic law and institutions. This indicates that the Government's involvement of Islam was not merely preferable but rather central. This is because, in Indonesia's legally plural setting, Islam as a non-state normative system can have more resonance within the Muslim community than both national and international law – particularly international human rights law.

For Indonesia to meet its international health obligations, it was necessary to address Islam as a socio-cultural determinant that strongly influences health-seeking behaviour. Indonesia was also legally obliged to ensure the cultural appropriateness of its reproductive healthcare system and to ensure public participation in its design and delivery. The Indonesian Government did this, engaging Islamic leaders, institutions and communities from the outset of the family planning programme. Rather than simply making family planning services accessible to the public, it was necessary to engage with Islamic norms and actors to build public demand for such services. This was done by Islamic leaders declaring contraceptives permissible via *fatwas*, and by Islamic institutions advocating reproductive rights and providing family planning services to the public. These actors were well placed to be effective in this role, given their established trust and legitimacy within the Muslim community. In this way, the Indonesian Government borrowed the legitimacy and social capital of Islam in order to support and promote its family planning programme. The Government did this by providing incentives and initiating partnerships with Islamic leaders and institutions including NU and Muhammadiyah, and also by creating MUI.

These top-down measures were complemented by the bottom-up work of Muslim women who advocated internal reform from within these institutions. Demonstrating the agency of those within Muslim communities – including Muslim women – these internal advocates relied upon Islam's intra-plurality and in-built processes that facilitate dialogue, dissent and dynamism. As such, both the Government as well as individual Muslims mobilised Islam to support the right to family planning in Indonesia. As the state does not have authority to determine or change Islamic norms, it had to work with the Muslim community to do so. This shows that multiple actors, and not just the state, have a role to play in human rights implementation, and, beyond that, also international responsibilities. Despite being a complex and uncertain process, internal human rights reform initiated from within the Muslim community was both the principled and pragmatic approach to implementing the right to family planning. As this example illustrates, where the values of Islam and Muslim actors are aligned with human rights, much can be achieved. This research therefore calls for further consideration by states parties and the UN treaty bodies of rights implementation possibilities beyond those offered by formal state institutions.

The treaty bodies in particular have much scope to further address the role of social institutions in implementing human rights. Their present focus on the state is an obvious result of the fact that international law binds the state as the party to the treaty. However, there are limitations to this approach. Given their state focus, the treaty bodies do not deal well with social institutions or their incorporation/co-optation into the human rights paradigm.[523] As seen in the Indonesian case study, the state is not well placed to change a religious community's norms that conflict with international human rights standards. Any such state intervention would typically be viewed as foreign and therefore illegitimate. To be effective, measures implementing human rights need to be initiated by or with the relevant cultural community and to enjoy local legitimacy. As noted above, this places states in the difficult position where they are accountable under international law for something they do not have direct authority over. On this basis, the treaty bodies' focus on the state and its law for human rights implementation appears somewhat misplaced. The present legal analysis has demonstrated that without changing their mandate, the treaty bodies could shift their practice to better recognise and engage with social institutions relevant to rights implementation.

The Indonesian case study exemplifies the culturally sensitive approaches to human rights as set out in Chapter 2, demonstrating not just their theoretical benefits but their instrumentality in practice. The findings highlight the importance of contextual approaches to human

---

[523] Valeska David and Julie Fraser, A Legal Plural Approach to the Use of Cultural Perspectives in the Implementation and Adjudication of Human Rights Norms (2017) *Buffalo Human Rights Law Review* 23, pp. 94–5.

rights implementation, which is generalisable to other cases. It is also submitted that the more specific findings in the case study have broader implications. Remaining within the Indonesian context, the findings may also apply to the domestic implementation of other human rights. While the precise argumentation in each case will depend on the relevant Islamic texts, the same method may be employed of engaging with and reinterpreting Islamic law, initiating internal dialogue, and advocating human rights' compliant positions from within the Muslim community. In fact, this process is already underway in Indonesia. For example, *fatwas* have been issued by various *ulama* in an attempt to protect public health and the environment, combat human trafficking, and regarding security and terrorism.

While *fatwas* can be linked to pro-human rights behaviours and positions, they can also oppose them. Assyaukanie examines the connection between *fatwas* and violence in Indonesia, concluding that intolerant *fatwas* have been linked to subsequent violence.[524] For example, a 2015 *fatwa* by MUI called for same-sex or homosexual acts to be punished, including by the death penalty.[525] This ruling can be seen to contradict human rights law, which protects individuals from discrimination and violence based on sex, sexual orientation and gender identity.[526] Despite MUI's *fatwa*, internal contestation exists, with other Muslims like Siti Musdah Mulia arguing that Islam rejects discrimination and hatred of LGBT persons based on its core principles of justice and equality.[527] These examples illustrate how powerful Islamic groups can be as actors in Indonesia and how Islam can be used to both oppose as well as uphold human rights. This last example also illustrates that there are, of course, no silver bullets and there are limitations to all approaches to human rights implementation, including relying upon religion.

---

[524] Assyaukanie (n. 270), pp. 1–21.
[525] Antonia Molloy, Indonesia's Highest Islamic Clerical Body Issues Fatwa Proposing Death Penalty for People Caught Having Gay Sex, *The Independent* (16 March 2015), www.independent.co.uk/news/world/asia/indonesias-highest-islamic-clerical-body-issues-fatwa-proposing-death-penalty-for-people-caught-10111564.html (accessed 3 February 2019).
[526] See, for example, UN Office of the High Commissioner for Human Rights, Born Free and Equal: Sexual Orientation and Gender Identity in International Human Rights Law, HR/PUB/12/06 (2012), www.ohchr.org/Documents/Publications/BornFreeAndEqualLow Res.pdf (accessed 3 February 2019).
[527] See Siti Musdah Mulia, Understanding LGBT Issues in Islam Promoting the Appreciation of Human Dignity (2nd CSBR Sexuality Institute, 11–18 September 2009, Istanbul).

5.5 CONCLUSIONS

Clearly, Islam will not be a panacea for all human rights problems. Religion and Islam itself can be a sensitive topic in Indonesia, and Indonesia's highly diverse society makes it impossible to address all issues through an Islamic framework. It is therefore necessary to acknowledge the limitations not only of the state and its law in implementing human rights, but also those of non-state law. Legal pluralism has been instrumental in challenging the centrality of state law and revealing the more layered and contested reality of normative systems and social life.[528] However, as de Sousa Santos recalls, 'there is nothing inherently good, progressive, or emancipatory about "legal pluralism"'.[529] The same can be said about social institutions in general. While it is important to recognise the variety of tools available in a given context to effectively implement human rights, including formal and informal institutions, how they are used is a question of human agency. This again reiterates the importance of domestic constituents for human rights above and beyond the state. Ultimately, all organs of society have a role to play and responsibilities regarding human rights realisation. As such, human rights implementation should not be solely the purview of formal state institutions, but also of informal social institutions.

---

[528] Merry (n. 219), pp. 66, 70.
[529] Boaventura de Sousa Santos, *Toward a New Legal Common Sense: Law, Globalization, and Emancipation* (2nd ed., Butterworths, 2002), p. 89.

6

Conclusions: Social Institutions and the Future of Domestic Human Rights Implementation

6.1 Introduction

International human rights treaties set out the minimum standards to be enjoyed by all humans on account of their dignity, but they remain empty promises until implemented domestically. However, implementation has proved wanting in states all around the world. In addressing the challenge of implementation, this book presented three main critiques. The first is that human rights are not sufficiently connected to the lives and experiences of people in different cultural communities. In parts of the global South as well as North, people are suspicious of human rights and international law, viewing them as something Western – or simply foreign. This disconnect adversely affects the resonance of rights and their implementation. The second critique is that to date the dominant approach to implementing rights has been legal incorporation. Law has come to monopolise the field of human rights, overshadowing other disciplines and methods of effectively implementing rights. However, legalistic approaches have their disadvantages, with laws going unimplemented, unenforced or even creating a backlash. Finally, the third critique is that of state-centricity. Many non-state actors and norms are implicated in human rights implementation in practice, but are marginalised due to international law's preoccupation with the state.

The situation of implementation is further threatened due to the increasing contestation of rights and even their posited decline. In this environment, 'business as usual' would be the wrong approach for the human rights movement to take. As such, this book does not invite incremental changes, but rather fundamental ones in order to realise the enjoyment of human rights in practice. This book has argued that social institutions can be an effective response to the three critiques presented above. Given their embedded nature and legitimacy within communities, as well as their normative overlap with human rights, social institutions can be vital assets in implementing rights. Involving social institutions can ensure that rights are communicated and implemented in culturally appropriate ways, which not only facilitates their adoption but also pays due respect to cultural diversity. The approach is therefore both pragmatic and principled. As seen in the Indonesian case study, change in line with international human rights law is not only possible but can also be profound when advocated by Muslims according to Islamic law. This reflects the special position of Islam within the Indonesian Muslim community, and the influential role that social institutions like religion play in communities all around the world.

This case study confirmed that human rights can be implemented outside the Western model of state-centric legality. Rather than a prerequisite for rights implementation, it can be seen as a form of imperialism or hegemony to only promote this model. The Indonesian case study also illustrated Muslim women advocating human rights norms via an Islamic framework, exercising agency beyond liberal concepts. The use of Islamic law to promote human rights compliance also demonstrates how normative systems outside state law can be effectively instrumentalised. Religion can be an ally in human rights implementation. Religion, as well as culture generally, should not be ostracised (or worse, demonised) in international human rights discourse. Such discourse is alienating for many people – rights holders – around the world. This point is especially pertinent given the world's growing religiosity, and the rise of Islam as the world's largest religion. Even if state institutions and mechanisms support rights, they may be undone if social institutions are not supportive. Therefore, while formal state institutions should be used to domestically implement human rights, so too should informal social institutions.

This concluding chapter reflects upon the book's contribution to scholarship and practice on the effective domestic implementation of international human rights treaty obligations. From an academic perspective, the book adds to the body of knowledge on rights implementation, which is lacking in multidisciplinary, socio-legal studies employing empirical approaches. By doing so, it contributes to a more comprehensive understanding of the factors effecting human rights implementation in practice. The book problematised the predominant reliance by both states and the UN treaty bodies upon formal institutions such as state law to implement human rights, highlighting other informal social institutions as resources and actors that can be effectively mobilised. The analysis informs not just the practice of states parties in domestic implementation, but also the UN treaty bodies responsible for supervising such implementation. Based on this analysis, this final chapter presents recommendations to states parties as well as to the UN treaty bodies in their supervisory role. Taking a step back, the chapter looks ahead and further afield to consider the broader implications of the book's conclusions, and proposes avenues for further research.

6.2 Connecting Rights to Communities: In Search of Better Narratives

More than seven decades after the Universal Declaration of Human Rights (UDHR),[1] the language of international human rights is unknown to many people around the world, who may view rights as foreign, unfamiliar or even irrelevant. Where there is some knowledge, there can also be misunderstanding regarding the nature and content of rights, generating suspicion, mistrust and opposition. The work of Indonesian Muslim feminists illustrated that it is not so much the content of human rights that is suspect, but rather its Western packaging. While the language of human rights is relatively new, the concept of rights is not alien to Muslims, as many of the same values of justice and equality can be found in the *Qur'an*. This illustrates the foundationally relative nature of rights, and the fact that they can be sourced from the worlds' cultural, philosophical and religious traditions. They can be justified based upon Christianity, Islam, natural law or Confucianism. By the UDHR declining to denote one foundation or to exhaustively acknowledge the foundations, the various societies of the world can justify or derive rights from their own values and beliefs. This was done deliberately by the UDHR drafters, as privileging one system or worldview over another would be unacceptable as hegemonic. Rather, human rights value, respect and accommodate cultural diversity in a variety of ways.

While rights apply universally, they are not culturally neutral or objective. Almost all rights have a cultural dimension due to the fact that culture includes a society's values and norms, which necessarily impacts upon their understanding and expectations of human rights.[2] For example, Islamic norms on sexuality and reproduction are part of the cultural dimension of the right to family planning in Indonesia. As seen in that study, addressing the socio-cultural determinants of the right to

---

[1] Universal Declaration of Human Rights (adopted 10 December 1948), UNGA Res. 217 A(III) (UDHR).
[2] Federico Lenzerini, *The Culturalization of Human Rights Law* (Oxford University Press, 2014), pp. 123, 152, 213.

6.2 CONNECTING RIGHTS TO COMMUNITIES

health can be as important as addressing the medical aspects. Interview participants agreed that *but for* the involvement of Islamic law and institutions, Indonesia's family planning programme would have failed. Voices in the universality and cultural relativism debate have sought to highlight this issue, urging the international human rights system to be more inclusive and respectful of the world's cultural diversity in order to ensure its universality. As seen in Chapter 2, some of the strongest, most persistent and persuasive criticism of the international human rights system is based on cultural arguments. Human rights are often critiqued as Western due to the West's dominant role in drafting the UDHR and the subsequent creation of the international human rights system. Despite the relativism debate becoming less dichotomous, it remains a pressing challenge for human rights to better accommodate cultural diversity and dispel the Western bias.

For example, culture continues to be portrayed in international human rights discourse as something static, backward and ancient. The examples perpetually highlighted in the scholarship and at the United Nations include practices typically from the global South such as FGM/C, child marriage and polygamy. In this way, 'culture' is presented as an obstacle to human rights in the modern state (which is itself a cultural project). This approach essentialises and others culture, denying its heterogeneity, dynamism and ubiquity. A more nuanced, anthropological perspective of culture – including religion – needs to be adopted. This is particularly necessary regarding Islam, given its frequent misrepresentations and the rise of Islamophobia. The fact is that culture and human rights can be and often are mutually supportive. Contextualising or framing human rights in terms of or as compatible with local cultures can aid their adoption. Conversely, rights will lack legitimacy in societies where they are seen as foreign to or conflicting with local cultural values. As seen in Chapter 2, scholarship has connected the legitimacy of norms to their efficacy in practice. In this way, culture can play a positive role in international human rights law and facilitate its domestic implementation – serving as an asset and not an obstacle. Recognising this, scholars have advocated culturally sensitive approaches to implementing human rights, including relying upon social institutions.

Culturally sensitive approaches to human rights implementation involve vernacularising or translating international human rights concepts based on the local context; reducing the role of state law; employing home-grown solutions for human rights problems; and relying on culture's dynamism and contestation to promote rights compliance.

While principled in their respect for cultural diversity, the common reason advanced for the necessity of such approaches is their effectiveness in practice. This is due to the fact that people are more inclined to observe normative positions they believe to be endorsed by their own cultural traditions and not imposed by outsiders.[3] These culturally sensitive approaches to implementing rights rely upon social institutions, drawing upon local cultural resources and agency. For example, social institutions such as traditional medicine, women's associations and religious or customary law can be mobilised as home-grown pathways for effectively implementing rights. Culturally appropriate and embedded entities like social institutions are important in this process due to their established legitimacy in a community, ability to shape behaviour and foster compliance. The Indonesian case study exemplified culturally sensitive approaches to human rights, highlighting not just their theoretical benefits but their instrumentality in practice.

The study demonstrated that in the Indonesian context and based on the example of family planning, Islam as a social institution can and should be engaged by the state. In fact, it was less an example of how the state should involve Islam, but rather that it *must* do so in order to be effective. The study illustrated that multiple actors and norms, and not just those of the state, have a distinct role to play within their sphere of influence. Given its lack of authority regarding Islamic law, the Indonesian Government was dependent upon internal, bottom-up reform from within the Muslim community to implement the right to family planning. This internal reform was in turn dependent upon the inherent dynamism and contestation of Islamic law, making the case study a prime example of how internal actors are agents in negotiating cultural norms. As the reforms were introduced by Muslims and according to Islamic interpretive processes, they were more likely to be viewed by the community as legitimate and applicable. While this process of negotiation and reform was internal, the Government encouraged and facilitated internal actors pursuing human rights compliant interpretations of Islam. This supportive (rather than direct) role of the state as an external actor was also advocated in the literature in Chapter 2. This shows the need for human rights to have domestic constituents, and for states to find and support such actors within their communities.

---

[3] Abdullahi Ahmed An-Na`im, Conclusion, in Abdullahi Ahmed An-Na`im (ed.), *Human Rights in Cross-Cultural Perspectives: A Quest for Consensus* (University of Pennsylvania Press, 1992), p. 431.

Islamic law and institutions were influential in Indonesia as they enjoy widespread resonance within the large Muslim community, more so than both national and international law – particularly international human rights law. In Indonesia, international human rights are often perceived as Western and foreign to local values and beliefs. Many former colonial states like Indonesia approach international law with scepticism given the historical role of international law in justifying as well as facilitating colonialism.[4] Numerous interview participants remarked upon the poor resonance of human rights in Indonesia and the limited understanding of rights in general, which helped fuel suspicion towards them. A representative of the NGO Rahima noted that rights are seen as part of the 'Western agenda' and that those promoting them – including Indonesians – can be labelled as 'Western agents'. However, given their normative overlap, Islam can be engaged to further human rights goals. For example, according to Riffat Hassan, it is easier to assure Muslim women that the *Qur'an* supports their reproductive rights than it is to tell them that a UN document will set them free.[5] As such, it can be more effective to rely upon Islamic norms rather than international ones to increase a Muslim community's acceptance and utilisation of family planning. On this basis, the Indonesian Government engaged extensively with Islamic leaders and institutions to promote its family planning programme.

As seen in the case study, it may not be necessary to use the specific language of human rights at all, deferring rather to equivalent or similar terms and concepts in local value systems like Islam. However, such vernacularisation is not a simple process and requires actors intimately familiar both with the international system and language of human rights as well as the local cultural norms and values. Even in this situation, translation is rarely straightforward and can result in misrepresentations or even a perversion of the idea of human rights. Another problem is that if rights are translated so thoroughly that they completely blend into the existing power relations, then they may lose their potential to create social change.[6] This presents a conundrum as while rights are more

---

[4] Antony Anghie, International Human Rights Law and a Developing World Perspective, in Scott Sheeran and Sir Nigel Rodley (eds.), *Routledge Handbook of International Human Rights Law* (Routledge, 2013), p. 112.

[5] Riffat Hassan, Challenging Stereotypes of Fundamentalism: An Islamic Feminist Perspective (Spring 2001) *The Muslim World* 91, p. 66.

[6] Sally Engel Merry, Legal Transplants and Cultural Translation: Making Human Rights in the Vernacular, in Mark Goodale (ed.), *Human Rights: An Anthropological Reader* (Blackwell Publishing, 2009), p. 266.

easily accepted when used in ways that readily link to local norms and values, in such a form they may pose less of a threat to the *status quo* and hence support or tolerate inequalities contrary to human rights.[7] As such, while it may be pertinent in some situations to rely only upon local translations, in others it may be important to specifically use human rights language where the recognition of rights can be transformational.[8] While most of the Muslim women interviewed in Indonesia relied predominantly upon Islamic terms and concepts in their work, some deliberately used human rights language to teach empowerment and dispel misunderstandings about rights. The relevant question to ask in any situation is therefore what the added value – if any – will be of using the language of human rights, or what will be lost by dispensing with these terms?

Key to culturally sensitive approaches to human rights implementation is that culture is not deterministic: people can be agents of cultural change. This is important because in order to be effective, cultural change needs to be initiated and pursued by those within a cultural community, and not be imposed from above or abroad. As seen in the case study, rather than simply being subject to Islamic norms, Muslim women could participate in the determination of such norms. These findings add to the growing scholarship debunking stereotypes of Islam as patriarchal and Muslim women as passive. It illustrated how in the Indonesian context, some Muslim women were able to capitalise upon certain factors, including Islam's growing influence in the public space and the global women's movement, to pursue gender equality. Rather than being a constraining factor, these women depended upon Islam, which provided the resources (Islamic texts), tools (interpretation) and pathway (dialogue) for achieving emancipatory reforms. In doing so, their agency was informed and empowered by their socio-cultural (religious) context, rather than constrained by it.[9] Muslim scholars and activists were able to introduce a gender critique and engage in dialogue on equality by employing Islam. The same goal pursued via state or international norms would not have

---

[7] Peggy Levitt and Sally Engel Merry, Vernacularization on the Ground: Local Uses of Global Women's Rights in Peru, China, India and the United States (2009) *Global Networks* 9:4, pp. 457–8. See also Stephen Hopgood, Jack Synder and Leslie Winjamuri, Conclusion: Human Rights Futures, in Stephen Hopgood, Jack Synder and Leslie Winjamuri (eds.), *Human Rights Futures* (Cambridge University Press, 2017), p. 313.

[8] Merry (n. 6), p. 297.

[9] Rachel Rinaldo, Pious and Critical: Muslim Women Activists and the Question of Agency (2014) *Gender & Society* 28:6, p. 843.

6.2 CONNECTING RIGHTS TO COMMUNITIES

been entertained in the same way. As this example shows, much can be achieved where the values of Islam and Muslim actors align with human rights.

Despite such successes, there are also limitations to the use of Islam to promote the right to family planning. For example, Islamic norms continue to permit sexual interaction only within the context of marriage, and as a result refuse unmarried persons access to contraceptives. The prohibition of contraceptives for unmarried persons has been codified into national law. This has adverse consequences particularly for young people, and violates their human rights. Under international law, Indonesia remains responsible for protecting this right and is liable for its violation. However, with the Government's apparent knowledge, secular NGOs provide contraceptive services to unmarried persons. While this is a practical solution that may fulfil some rights in the interim, the Government remains legally obliged internationally to ensure that rights are fully implemented. However, simply amending the legislation to permit unmarried persons access to contraceptives will not necessarily be effective if it remains proscribed by Islam. Therefore, the Government will need to continue engaging with NGOs and Islamic norms and actors to bridge this gap. While such law reform processes can take time, be complex and uncertain, they can lead to meaningful change to a community's norms in line with human rights.

These findings support the need for translations or narratives of human rights that better connect to the local context. This is necessary not just in Southern societies that may perceive of rights as Western, but also for Western societies who similarly view rights as foreign. All around the world, there is a lack of understanding about human rights and a related suspicion, including in Indonesia but also in Australia, the USA and the Netherlands. On the basis of its 'exceptionalism', the USA remains reluctant to embrace international human rights law, and is an outlier for its failure to ratify ICESCR, CEDAW and particularly the CRC. Recent research in the Netherlands found that due to limited public knowledge of human rights, some working in human rights fields chose to avoid the term as it was 'perceived as alien, foreign and not relevant to the locality'.[10] As such, they adjusted the terminology based on their audience, choosing instead terms like 'equality for all' or 'every person

---

[10] Barbara Oomen and Esther van den Berg, Human Rights Cities: Urban Actors as Pragmatic Idealistic Human Rights Users (2014) *Human Rights and International Legal Discourse* 8, p. 181.

counts'.[11] Similarly, there is a tendency in Australia to rely on concepts of 'fairness' to represent human rights issues of equality and justice. Domestically, Australia remains suspicious of human rights, with the Government deciding after a public consultation to *not* adopt national human rights legislation.[12]

In communities all around the world, there is a need for better translations of rights and narratives supporting their adoption. The multiple foundations of human rights in the religions and philosophies of the world are an important entry point in this regard. In this way, each community can develop its own narrative showing how international human rights relate to – or stem from – its values and belief systems. This will assist in building a culture of human rights and domestic constituents supporting rights nationally. Today's challenging times may not mean the end of human rights, but rather an opportunity to take stock, re-imagine and re-engage a wider variety of actors on human rights. In addition to the formal state institutions, social institutions like religion are also needed to participate in resolving human rights contestation and forging supporting narratives. This is particularly important in contemporary times where there is increasing religiosity around the globe. Islam especially will become a more prominent player in the future as the world's largest religion. Rather than an obstacle to rights enjoyment, religion and culture can be formidable allies in human rights protection. The international human rights movement would be well served to better recognise this. Ultimately, this will contribute to the development of a more decentred understanding of human rights that takes a global perspective reflecting a plurality of voices.[13]

6.3 All the Tools in the Toolbox: Rejecting Legalism in Implementation

In addition to the need for new narratives supporting rights in local communities, there is a corresponding need for new methods of effectively implementing human rights. While the human rights treaties set out

---

[11] Ibid., p. 183.
[12] See, for example, Australian Human Rights Commission, Media Release: Important steps to better protect human rights but substantial gaps remain (21 April 2010), www.humanrights.gov.au/news/media-releases/2010-media-release-important-steps-better-protect-human-rights-substantial-gaps (accessed 18 November 2017).
[13] Ilias Bantekas and Lutz Oette, *International Human Rights Law and Practice* (Cambridge University Press, 2013), pp. 41–2.

6.3 REJECTING LEGALISM IN IMPLEMENTATION

the minimum standards in law, there is a large gap between these norms and their enjoyment in practice. It was therefore a focus of this book to address the pressing contemporary challenge of effective human rights implementation. As seen in Chapter 3, international human rights treaties oblige states parties to 'take steps' necessary to 'give effect' to the treaty provisions.[14] While the treaty standards are to be enjoyed universally, the methods of domestic implementation are not dictated by the treaties, nor do they need to be uniform. In fact, the methods of implementation employed by various states should not be the same, as the rich diversity across the world rebuts any presumption of uniformity. The cultural dimension of almost all rights demands specialised implementation measures that may not be applicable, let alone replicable, elsewhere. While states parties are obliged to give domestic effect to the treaty provisions, it is their prerogative to determine the manner of implementation.

As such, the international human rights system grants states parties discretion to tailor their implementation methods to their socio-cultural, political and economic context. If not purpose designed to fit the specific context, the implementation measure may be a blunt instrument of limited effect – or even counter-productive. This is crucial, because according to the treaties and the interpretation thereof by the treaty bodies, the controlling criteria for implementation measures is that the rights be *effectively* protected. As such, while the states parties may choose their method of domestic human rights implementation, their discretion is not absolute. It is the intention of the treaties, and therefore central to the work of the treaty bodies, that human rights are meaningfully enjoyed in practice and not just protected in theory. The treaty bodies will assess a state's method of implementation according to its effectiveness in practice, its use in good faith, and its compatibility with the object and purpose of the treaty. Subject to these criteria and the supervision of the treaty bodies, states can employ in their discretion legislative or other measures to implement their human rights treaty obligations.

While the treaties themselves do not proffer many examples of implementation measures, the treaty bodies have expanded upon this in their

---

[14] See, for example, *International Covenant on Civil and Political Rights* (adopted 16 December 1966, entered into force 23 March 1976), 999 UNTS 171 (ICCPR), art. 2(2); *International Covenant on Economic, Social and Cultural Rights* (adopted 16 December 1966, entered into force 3 January 1976), 993 UNTS 3 (ICESCR), art. 2(1).

supervisory role. As seen in Chapter 3, the legal measures envisaged include constitutional amendments, enacting legislation, as well as ancillary regulatory and procedural measures, and adjudication by courts. The types of other non-legislative implementation measures envisaged by the treaties and treaty bodies include the establishment of National Human Rights Institutes (NHRIs) and ombudspersons; adopting national action plans, policies and strategies and the allocation thereto of financial and other resources; temporary special measures and quotas; capacity building, counselling and mentoring programmes; vocational and technical training; information dissemination and awareness-raising campaigns; education; employing the arts, theatre and music; and international cooperation and assistance. The treaty bodies – albeit to different degrees – also envisage states engaging in consultation, dialogue and collaboration with NSAs, such as the media, non-governmental organisations (NGOs), communities and civil society. Such measures are not recommended in isolation but rather in combination, sometimes representing an holistic approach to implementation.

While this menu of implementation measures appears broad and is not exhaustive, in practice, the treaty bodies and scholarship focus only on legislative measures. Chapter 3 demonstrated that despite the treaties not necessarily prescribing domestic legal incorporation, this is the treaty bodies' primary focus and preferred manner of implementation. This reflects the legalisation of human rights and the predisposition to pursuing its objectives through legal mechanisms.[15] This myopic approach fails to acknowledge the limits of the law and the utility of other methods of implementation. While legal measures of implementation have delivered many advances regarding the legal protection and enforcement of rights, the efficacy of this method (especially in isolation) has been oversold. Particularly regarding sensitive cultural issues, state legislative bans can go unenforced, failing to change norms and behaviour, and may even elicit a backlash. Numerous such examples can be drawn from legislative measures to prohibit 'harmful traditional practices' that do not in fact reduce their occurrence. As seen in the Indonesian case study, both legislative and other measures (or a combination thereof) can effectively implement human rights. However, legalism has curtailed the

---

[15] Jack Donnelly, The Virtues of Legalization, in Saladin Meckled-García and Başak Çali (eds.), *The Legalization of Human Rights: Multidisciplinary Perspectives on Human Rights and Human Rights Law* (Routledge, 2006), p. 67.

6.3 REJECTING LEGALISM IN IMPLEMENTATION

imagination and promotion of other methods of implementation, and shunned the germane insights of other disciplines like anthropology or sociology. As such, a multidisciplinary approach going beyond law needs to be taken when fashioning human rights implementation measures.

Legalism also implies a focus on the modern state as the authority responsible for the creation and enforcement of positive state law. It is necessarily state-centric and therefore Western-centric, in that it is based on the European Westphalian model.[16] Casting state law as *the* law recognises only the modern state model, invisibilising other plural legal systems beneath and beyond the state that exist in virtually all societies today. However, such plural legal systems like religious and customary law are social institutions that can provide opportunities for implementing human rights; a fact not sufficiently recognised or capitalised upon by the UN treaty bodies. It would be a mistake to think that state law matters above all else regarding shaping human behaviour.[17] The utility of plural legal systems was demonstrated in the Indonesian case study, which exemplified the instrumentalisation of Islamic law to promote women's access to family planning. Given their local cultural legitimacy, human rights may be better adopted and protected by non-state law than by positive state law, emphasising the need to go beyond state-centric legality. On this basis, the treaty bodies should not merely allow but also encourage states parties to go beyond state law and to explore the variety of tools and resources available in their societies that can be employed to effectively implement human rights. The treaty bodies' practice to date, however, leaves much room for improvement.

Despite the case study illustrating the centrality of Islamic law and institutions in pursuing reproductive health in Indonesia, they are virtually absent in the UN treaty bodies' Concluding Observations. For example, the Human Rights Committee (HRCee) expressed its concern at the prevalence of polygamy and child marriage, which both have implications for women's reproductive health. Polygamy and child marriage are publicly supported in Indonesia based on interpretations of Islamic law. Rather than recommending that Indonesia engage with Islamic law and actors on the topic, the HRCee instead focused on state

---

[16] Abdullahi Ahmed An-Na'im, The Spirit of Laws Is Not Universal: Alternatives to the Enforcement Paradigm for Human Rights (2016) *Tilburg Law Review* 21, p. 273.

[17] Brian Tamanaha, Understanding Legal Pluralism: Past to Present, Local to Global (2008) *Sydney Law Review* 30, p. 410.

law solutions.[18] In fact, the HRCee does not mention Islam at all in its Concluding Observations to Indonesia – nor does the Economic, Social and Cultural Rights (ESCR) Committee. By failing to acknowledge Islamic law and actors, the HRCee and the ESCR Committee forego the opportunity to engage a vital social institution in the implementation of reproductive rights in Indonesia. This suggests a propensity to view culture (including religion) as an obstacle to rights rather than an asset in their implementation. Furthermore, their insistence upon state law as the measure of implementation illustrates their legalistic approach to human rights.

In contrast, the CEDAW Committee in its Concluding Observations recognises Islam and recommends Indonesia engage with its norms and actors. Regarding combating female genital mutilation/cutting (FGM/C), polygamy and child marriage, the Committee recommended Indonesia engage with religious groups and leaders.[19] These recommendations demonstrate that the CEDAW Committee understands culture's inherent relationship to human rights and the interplay of plural legal systems. Its approach can also be seen as consistent with the recommendations in Chapter 2 regarding culturally sensitive approaches to implementation. However, these recommendations are still only made by the CEDAW Committee in second place, with the primary focus remaining on state legislation and enforcement.[20] As this demonstrates, while the CEDAW Committee also takes a more progressive approach than the HRCee and the ESCR Committee, its recommendations to Indonesia regarding matters inherently related to Islam remain state-centric and legalistic.

However, if state legislative measures are *not* an effective measure in context, then the treaty bodies are doing states parties a disservice by focusing predominantly on such measures. Equally, if engaging social institutions like religion *is* an effective implementation measure for a state party to take, as seen in the Indonesian example, then the treaty bodies not recommending this measure are also doing states a disservice. If fact, states may be obliged to involve social institutions in implementing rights, like the right to reproductive health, where this would be

---

[18] UN HRCee, Concluding Observations on the Initial Report of Indonesia, CCPR/C/IDN/CO/1 (21 August 2013), para. 29.

[19] UN CEDAW Committee, Concluding Observations of the Committee on the Elimination of Discrimination against Women: Indonesia, CEDAW/C/IDN/CO/6–7 (7 August 2012), paras. 18(c), 23–4.

[20] Ibid., para. 18(a) and (b).

effective. States are additionally obliged to involve social institutions due to obligations to ensure public participation and the cultural appropriateness of healthcare goods, facilities and services. If states can be seen to have an obligation to engage social institutions, then the UN treaty bodies not raising this measure are failing to pursue states fully regarding their obligations. By virtue of their ability to render or reveal rights as culturally compatible and guide behaviour, social institutions can increase the efficacy of human rights implementation. Based on this linkage with effectiveness, anyone – indeed everyone – dedicated to realising human rights should be interested in such culturally sensitive approaches to implementation.

Given the complex and diverse environments in which human rights have to be implemented, the work of the treaty bodies would be enhanced by diversifying the measures recommended to states parties. As recognised in the treaties themselves, state law is but one tool available to implement human rights. Given that the treaties all recognise other measures of implementation and the involvement of other actors, the treaty bodies can adjust their approach without having to change their mandate. The treaty bodies could shift their focus to be more open to other implementation measures, including engaging social institutions like plural legal systems. Such a shift would better reflect the complex process of domestic implementation, which involves not just states or state law, but indeed every organ of society. The UN treaty bodies should further consider rights implementation beyond the possibilities offered by formal state institutions and to include also social institutions. This is done on a practical basis, to secure better effectiveness of implementation measures, and also a normative one, to better respect states' cultural diversity.

6.4 Going beyond State-Centricity in Human Rights

Finally, another broader discussion that this book contributes to is the general shift away from positioning the state as the key actor in international law. As seen in Chapters 4 and 5, NSAs have long been involved in human rights, often well before the state. For example, social institutions like religious and kinship groups have been fulfilling state-like functions such as providing healthcare and education in many places before the state became involved. Similarly, women's associations and savings clubs have long been providing a form of social security and access to finance through their operations. While the state's central role was cemented in law with the two 1966 Covenants and replicated in subsequent treaties at the international and regional levels, this legal construction was never fully aligned with practice and the real life roles and activities of NSAs regarding human rights. Not only have NSAs continued to be involved, their role has even increased due to a variety of factors including globalisation, privatisation, technological developments, the expansion of multilateral institutions and the growth of civil society. There are numerous examples today of private actors stepping up and fulfilling human rights. This reflects how human rights practice is *already* polycentric, despite the state's virtual monopoly under international law.

In addition to the role of social institutions as examined in this book, businesses have long played a positive role in human rights and they are continuing to do so in new ways. For example, social enterprises are for-profit businesses that use their profit for social purposes including human rights. Social enterprises differ from charities in that they are not reliant upon donations but earn income for their charitable purposes by selling commercial products. Examples include 'thankyou' in Australia, which sells products like soap and baby care items in order to fund safe water, sanitation and child and maternal health services.[21] 'Thinx' in the USA sells women's underwear to fund human rights education for girls focused on sexual and reproductive health.[22] These are two of many such examples in a growing social enterprise sector. Rather than spending charitable donations or public taxes on human rights related goods and services, social enterprises use a business model to do so. As these examples show, private individuals are coming together in different ways to promote and protect human rights. Another example is Canada's programme for private citizens to sponsor refugee resettlement.[23] This programme harnesses private citizens' support for refugees, who fulfil international protection obligations as an alternative to the state. Such practices can be seen as precursors to a new

---

[21] For more information, see 'thankyou', https://thankyou.co (accessed 30 November 2017).

[22] For more information, see 'Thinx', www.thinx.org (accessed 30 November 2017).

[23] Canada introduced the programme in 1978 and allows organisations or a group of citizens or permanent residents to sponsor a refugee, which includes financial support and general assistance to help the person selected settle into the community. See for more information, Government of Canada, Guide to the Private Sponsorship of Refugees Program, www.cic.gc.ca/english/resources/publications/ref-sponsor/index.asp (accessed 30 November 2017).

6.4 GOING BEYOND STATE-CENTRICITY

vision of human rights diverging from state-centrism where individuals also share sovereignty.[24]

While still state actors, sub-national actors have gained attention recently for their role in human rights protection. For example, Human Rights Cities have arisen as a global force, comprising local authorities that base their urban policies on international human rights norms.[25] In Europe alone there are now over 400 recognised Human Rights Cities.[26] Utrecht, the first in the Netherlands, uses human rights as a moral category to create a checklist or benchmark for making and assessing local policies.[27] While a city's human rights policies can support those on the national level, they can also oppose them. For example, San Francisco in the USA has claimed to implement CEDAW, despite the fact that the USA has not ratified the treaty.[28] In the wake of President Trump's announcement that the USA would withdraw from the UN *Framework Convention on Climate Change* (Paris Agreement), numerous US cities – as well as private actors – declared that they would continue to implement the agreement.[29] Cities are crucial sites for human rights as they are

---

[24] Yahyaoui argues that via this programme '[i]ndividuals are able to step into the international arena and fulfil international obligations better and more efficiently than states'. Ekaterina Yahyaoui Krivenko, Hospitality and Sovereignty: What Can We Learn from the Canadian Private Sponsorship of Refugees Program? (2012) *International Journal of Refugee Law* 24:3, pp. 580, 589, 600–1.

[25] Oomen and van den Berg (n. 10), pp. 161, 163.

[26] These states have signed the European Charter for the Safeguarding of Human Rights in the City, Adopted at St Denis (18 May 2000). For further information and a list of signatory cities, see United Cities and Local Government, Committee on Social Inclusion, Participatory Democracy and Human Rights, www.uclg-cisdp.org/en/right-to-the-city/european-charter (accessed 28 September 2017).

[27] Oomen and van den Berg (n 10) pp. 176–8.

[28] In 1998, San Francisco became the first city in the world to adopt an ordinance reflecting the principles of CEDAW. The Cities for CEDAW project was created and numerous other US cities have joined. See, for further information, City and County of San Francisco, Department on the Status of Women, Cities for CEDAW, http://sfgov.org/dosw/cities-cedaw (accessed 30 November 2017). For general information on Cities for CEDAW, see http://citiesforcedaw.org> (accessed 30 November 2017).

[29] UN *Framework Convention on Climate Change* (Paris Agreement) (adopted on 12 December 2015, entered into force 4 November 2016), No. 54113. 'America's Pledge' brings together leaders from both the private and public sectors to ensure that the USA remains a leader in reducing emissions and delivering the state's ambitious climate goals in the Paris Agreement: see www.americaspledgeonclimate.com (accessed 30 November 2017). Furthermore, over 2,500 leaders from across the USA have signed the 'We Are Still In' declaration committing to taking action on climate change: see 'We Are Still In', www.wearestillin.com (accessed 30 November 2017).

closer to communities and arguably best equipped to realise rights.[30] On the other end of the spectrum, there are also inter-state actors stepping up their role in human rights, as seen by the European Union's accession to the *Convention on the Rights of Persons with Disabilities*, and its intention to accede to the *European Convention on Human Rights*.[31] This reflects the fact that human rights regulation is moving both up and down – and out of the state's monopoly.

These examples illustrate how international human rights law's preoccupation with the state is at odds with practice. In response, and as set out in Chapter 4, NSAs have slowly been recognised to hold international human rights responsibilities. First, the UDHR was a people's document envisaging rights being upheld both between people horizontally as well as vertically by states – by every organ of society. This reflects the complex reality of rights and the various conditions, factors and stakeholders impacting upon their enjoyment. The UN General Assembly subsequently recognised the international responsibilities on NSAs, including individuals, groups and organs of society.[32] While the UN treaties overwhelmingly create obligations only for states, the treaty bodies have elaborated upon the responsibilities of NSAs. Cognisant of the gap between the treaties and the reality of human rights implementation in practice, the treaty bodies recognised that NSAs have a responsibility regarding human rights – albeit one they cannot enforce given that their mandate is restricted to states. Despite the confirmation of NSAs' human rights responsibilities, they remain ill-defined, of unclear sources, and lacking in enforcement mechanisms. As such, elucidation is needed regarding what is expected of NSAs regarding human rights,

---

[30] Oomen and van den Berg (n. 10), pp. 166, 183. Regarding the benefits of decentralisation, see Simon Hoffman, The UN Convention on the Rights of the Child, Decentralisation and Legislative Integration: A Case Study from Wales (2019) *International Journal of Human Rights* 23:3.

[31] *Convention on the Rights of Persons with Disabilities* (adopted 13 December 2006, entered into force 3 May 2008), 2515 UNTS 3. The European Union intended to accede to the European Convention until Opinion 2/13 was issued by the Court of Justice of the European Union. See, for example, Steve Peers, The EU's Accession to the ECHR: The Dream becomes a Nightmare, Special Section – Opinion 2/13: The EU and the European Convention on Human Rights (2015) *German Law Journal* 16, pp. 213–22.

[32] See, for example, UN General Assembly, Resolution 53/144, Declaration on the Right and Responsibility of Individuals, Groups and Organs of Society to Promote and Protect Universally Recognized Human Rights and Fundamental Freedoms A/RES/53/144 (8 March 1999).

6.4 GOING BEYOND STATE-CENTRICITY

what actions may be considered a breach of their responsibilities, and any ramifications thereof.

While such clarification is lacking, it is not an obstacle to NSAs like some social institutions implementing human rights under the present system. This is because advocating such a role for NSAs challenges state-centricity in the implementation of human rights, but not necessarily the state-centricity of international law. For example, as seen in Chapter 3, under international law states have discretion in implementation and may use legislative or 'other measures'. All of the treaty bodies envisage a role therein for NSAs, and, to varying degrees, have even granted them participatory rights in addition to responsibilities. They also recognised corresponding obligations upon states to facilitate NSAs discharging their human rights responsibilities. This was well done in the Indonesian case study, with the Government engaging with Islamic actors and institutions, providing them with funding and incentives, as well as partnerships. However, states are falling short in other contemporary situations. For example, the documented state repression of civil society around the world[33] can be seen as a violation of this obligation to faciliate NSAs, as well as other rights to freedom of expression, association and assembly. The curtailing of civic space needs therefore to be addressed as an impediment to NSAs fulfilling their human rights responsibilities and a violation of states' international obligations.

Finally, while states must facilitate NSAs, they must also regulate and monitor them. As seen in Chapter 4, states may delegate or outsource implementation measures to NSAs, but they may not outsource their obligations, which they retain under international human rights law. Where NSAs are performing the implementation measures, the focus of states' international obligations shifts from fulfilling rights to protecting them. The duty of due diligence obliges states to establish regulatory frameworks to monitor and supervise the activities of NSAs, as well as to provide supplementary safeguards as necessary. States must also investigate and punish any rights violations by NSAs and provide remedies to victims. Failure to fulfil their due diligence duty can give rise to a state's international liability. Therefore, even when a NSA performs the implementation measures, the state continues to be liable internationally for effective implementation as well as for any violation. In this way, states

---

[33] See Antoine Buyse, Squeezing Civic Space: Restrictions on Civil Society Organizations and the Linkages with Human Rights (2018) *International Journal of Human Rights* 22:8, pp. 966–88.

cannot absolve themselves of their treaty obligations by delegating them to NSAs. This is particularly important, as under the treaties NSAs abusing rights cannot be held accountable internationally, as they are only subject to indirect treaty obligations to be enforced by states nationally. However, problems arise with this construction where the state is not able to fulfil its due diligence obligations and protect against abuse by third parties.

As a result of the increased focus on NSAs abusing rights, a detailed debate has arisen and circled around the question of whether NSAs can be bound by international human rights law. This usually focuses on armed opposition groups and large or transnational corporations. In this context, many have critiqued the state-centric nature of international law, arguing that it fails to adequately address current issues regarding NSAs and human rights. The greater the power of NSAs – particularly relative to the state – the more necessary it is to develop international human rights law to govern them.[34] In relation to armed groups, this has led to complex argumentation regarding their legal personality and ability to be bound by international law, and also to the development of international criminal law, which applies to individuals (not states). Regarding corporations, this has led to the promotion of corporate social responsibility and given rise to the business and human rights movement. This is now a central issue in human rights and the focus of much scholarship and debate. A highlight was the UN's promulgation of the *Guiding Principles on Business and Human Rights* (Ruggie Principles) and the potential for a new treaty addressing businesses (as well as states).[35]

These developments are part of the evolution of international human rights law, and seek to ensure that it remains fit for purpose and suited to contemporary realities. As argued in Chapter 4, law reform proposals that will improve the practical enjoyment of human rights around the world and effectively repair victims should be welcomed. International human rights law should be victim-centred, which in present conditions will require it to become less state-centric. Opening up direct

---

[34] David Weissbrodt, Roles and Responsibilities of Non-State Actors, in Dinah Shelton (ed.), *The Oxford Handbook of International Human Rights Law* (Oxford University Press, 2013), p. 721.

[35] UN Human Rights Council, Resolution 17/4, Guiding Principles on Business and Human Rights, A/HRC/17/31 (16 June 2011); UN Human Rights Council, Resolution 26/9, Elaboration of an international legally binding instrument on transnational corporations and other business enterprises with respect to human rights, A/HRC/RES/26/9 (26 June 2014).

international legal obligations to actors beyond the state like armed groups and corporations may better protect victims by reflecting the global reality and experience of people in different contexts in different states. Many questions remain regarding how this would be achieved both *de jure* and *de facto*, and are the subject of ongoing discussion and debate in various fora. However, obliging a broader range of actors in relation to human rights is reminiscent of the UDHR's preamble which proclaims that it is incumbent upon every individual and organ of society to secure the universal and effective observance of rights. Here it seems we may have come full circle.

While state-centricity is a persistent legal norm, it is increasingly exposed as a fiction in reality. Polycentric and pluralistic approaches to human rights are growing, with the periphery increasingly actively involved rather than passively receiving. As former UN High Commissioner for Human Rights Mary Robinson noted, 'We are all custodians of human rights'.[36] The present book and other scholars welcome this shift, with An-Na'im, for example, calling for a people-centred approach to human rights. Critical of the current legalistic and state-centric approach, he submits that in order for rights to be protected they need to be radically reinvented with these two characteristics removed.[37] An-Na'im proposes that 'it is citizens acting through a variety of strategies and levels, who can ensure systematic and sustainable protection of human rights'.[38] Similarly, Falk is critical of the 'Westphalian logic' and is optimistic about the reduced dependency upon states and a greater role for a variety of actors 'to legitimate and delegitimise behaviour'.[39] Inclusive participation in human rights implementation can improve simultaneously their legitimacy and efficacy.

6.5 Recommendations (or Where to Next?)

Flowing from these conclusions, several modest recommendations can be made to states as well as the UN treaty bodies. First, when planning

---

[36] UN High Commissioner for Human Rights, Mary Robinson, cited in UN Commission on Human Settlements, Activities of the United Nations Centre for Human Settlements (Habitat): Progress Report of the Executive Director, HS/C/17/INF/6 (30 March 1999).
[37] An-Na'im (n. 16), p. 259.
[38] Ibid., pp. 271–2.
[39] Richard Falk, International Law and the Future, in Richard Falk, Balakrishnan Rajagopal and Jacqueline Stevens (eds.), *International Law and the Third World* (Routledge, 2008), pp. 23–4, 31.

domestic implementation, and to the extent that they do not already, states should undertake broad consultation and seek to identify culturally sensitive approaches available in their national context. This consultation should include both state and NSAs including representatives or members of social institutions. States' NHRIs could be a key part of this process, being well placed to identify relevant local social institutions and potentially serving as vernacularisers. Based on this consultation, states should design tailor-made measures to implement the various rights in the various national contexts. While some states will be more homogeneous, others are highly diverse. The selected implementation measures should represent an holistic approach, employing a combination of measures and actors to be most effective. For example, an holistic approach could include both state and NSAs in implementation, as well as state and non-state normative systems. Additionally, states should facilitate an environment in which NSAs, social institutions and indeed every organ of society can fulfil their human rights responsibilities. States should identify domestic constituents from within local communities and support them to develop a culture of rights from the bottom up.

When reporting to the UN treaty bodies, states parties should provide information on their contextualised implementation measures including any instrumentalisation of social institutions. States should ensure that experts from a variety of academic disciplines provide input to the report, and that a range of NSAs including social institutions are consulted. The NHRI should also report on their relevant activities, and social institutions themselves should be encouraged by the state to submit shadow reports where possible. States should also cooperate and assist one another regarding contextualised implementation measures, sharing knowledge and experience particularly where the relevant social institutions cross borders and have a wider influence. For example, states with Muslim populations could consult one another regarding human rights implementation measures based on Islam. This could also be done via the Human Rights Council's Universal Periodic Review (UPR). When states parties are nominating and voting for candidates to serve on the UN treaty bodies, they should ensure that candidates have a sufficient diversity of expertise to supervise implementation. For example, more attention needs to be given to candidates from non-legal backgrounds to ensure that the Committees benefit from a diverse range of expertise relating to human rights.

In relation to state reporting, the UN treaty bodies could invite states parties to report on how their implementation measures relate to their national cultural context, and whether/how social institutions have been instrumentalised. The treaty bodies could amend the Harmonised Reporting Guidelines to reflect the need for this information in general. The treaty bodies could also request this information specifically from states in the List of Issues submitted in advance of a report. Additionally, the treaty bodies could invite shadow reports from civil society actors including some social institutions, who could provide their own information and assessment of culturally sensitive approaches to implementation in their state. The treaty body members could also discuss this directly with civil society representatives, given that it is the practice of some Committees to meet with them prior to the constructive dialogues with states. Similarly, in the dialogue with states parties, the treaty body members could engage orally with states about their culturally sensitive approaches to implementation and discuss the steps taken to tailor measures to their domestic context and to involve social institutions.

In their Concluding Observations, and to the extent that they do not do so already, the treaty bodies should make recommendations cognisant of the role and impact of social institutions, advising states to engage meaningfully with them in implementation. The treaty bodies should shift their central focus away from state law to include other effective measures and more holistic approaches to implementation. This would require the treaty bodies to modify their discourse on culture and traditional practices to better reflect their heterogeneity, dynamism and ubiquity. The treaty bodies could inform their practice in this regard based on other UN agencies such as the UN Population Fund (UNFPA) and UN Children's Fund (UNICEF), which engage regularly with cultural norms and actors. Specifically, the treaty bodies could stress the role of social institutions in implementing rights, as well as the scope and necessity for states to collaborate with them. As such, the treaty bodies could further contribute to the elaboration of the international human rights responsibilities on NSAs and their relationship to state obligations. This could be done via Concluding Observations or in a General Comment. While such a General Comment would not be binding and the treaty bodies would be unable to apply it directly to NSAs, it could be used to assist states in their engagement with, and facilitation and regulation of NSAs implementing human rights, and to guide NSAs in the fulfilment of their responsibilities.

While the present research addressed international human rights law, focusing on the UN treaty bodies and the right to family planning in Indonesia, the key findings are potentially of broader application. For example, the conclusions regarding effective implementation measures may also be relevant to the UN's Charter-based human rights mechanisms, such as the UPR. This Review relates specifically to the UN human rights treaties analysed in this book. As noted above, the UPR could provide a forum for states to share best practices regarding engaging and regulating social institutions in domestic implementation. NGOs and other stakeholders (including some social institutions) may also participate in this holistic and periodic Review. Given the similarities between the international and regional human rights treaties, the present findings may also apply before regional systems in Africa, the Americas and Europe. The human rights instruments in these three systems also allow other – non-legislative – measures of implementation and a role for NSAs. Further research could be undertaken to determine to what extent culturally sensitive approaches to implementation involving social institutions can be accommodated in these systems. While less developed, there is also scope to analyse such approaches to human rights implementation vis-à-vis the ASEAN and Arab human rights mechanisms.

While the case study focused on Islam in Indonesia, the findings can potentially be extrapolated to other contexts. However, modesty is necessary. Given the great diversity within Islam, it cannot be assumed that the present findings will necessarily apply in other Muslim communities. In her study of family planning in six Muslim majority states, Marshall found that the roles of religious actors and beliefs were very different.[40] However, while each setting is unique and requires a tailored approach, findings from the present study relate to and reinforce similar studies in other states with large Muslim populations,[41] and may apply more broadly. This is possible because 'Islamic law has a universal character' and is applicable to all Muslims regardless of their residence or nationality.[42] Furthermore, Islamic jurisprudence

---

[40] Katherine Marshall, *Religious Engagement in Family Planning Policies: Experience in Six Muslim-Majority Countries* (World Faiths Development Dialogue, 2015), p. 39.

[41] For example, Hursh's study in Morocco and Hasna's in Jordan: John Hursh, Advancing Women's Rights through Islamic Law: The Example of Morocco (2012) *Berkeley Journal of Gender, Law & Justice* 27; Fadia Hasna, Islam, Social Traditions and Family Planning (April 2003) *Social Policy & Administration* 37:2.

[42] Mohammad Daud Ali, *Islamic Law: Introduction to Islamic Jurisprudence and the Legal System in Indonesia* (PT RajaGrafindo Persada, 2016), p. 173.

and thinking transcends borders and influences *ulama* in other countries. As seen in this study, Indonesian *ulama* travelled to Egypt to learn about their family planning programme under Islam, and the Indonesian Muslim feminists were greatly influenced by those from abroad. In this way, Muslim communities are not isolated and what happens in one has the ability to impact another. As such, further research could be undertaken to determine the extent to which the present findings apply in other Islamic settings.

Finally, the present conclusions may also be relevant to states not only in their own domestic processes of implementing their treaty obligations, but also in their foreign policy initiatives promoting human rights in other states. Many states, such as the Netherlands, have a strong human rights focus in their foreign policy and fund human rights projects abroad. Such states may be able to learn from the present research and apply the findings regarding culturally sensitive approaches to implementation both at home and in their foreign policy. In much the same way, the research findings can also be used by NGOs, foundations and development actors working to realise human rights in various culturally diverse contexts. In fact, some development actors are further advanced than human rights actors in employing such culturally sensitive approaches. Over the years, many development organisations, not shackled to the framework of international human rights law, have by-passed the state and invested directly in local organisations – including some social institutions. This was seen in the Indonesian example, where private organisations like the Ford Foundation supported projects run by Muslim women. Here, the international human rights community could also learn best practices from development actors.

Today's challenging times see traditional (albeit qualified) support for human rights from the West waning and the rise of the South, and with it religiosity, contributing to louder (but always present) contestation of rights. These times may not present us with the end of human rights, but rather an opportunity to take stock, re-imagine and re-engage a wider variety of norms and actors on human rights. In addition to formal state institutions, it is necessary for informal social institutions to participate in resolving human rights contestation, forging supportive narratives and protecting rights in practice. Given the multiplicity of challenges facing human rights around the world, a plurality of actors and norms – indeed, every organ of society – is needed to work in support of rights. Human rights cannot flourish if only enforced top-down by a select collection of international and national institutions. This approach serves to reinforce the perception of rights as foreign and imposed. Rather, domestic constitutents or local allies are required to promote rights from the bottom up. These actors and their cultural resources should be embraced as diverse foundations for the universality of human rights. This presents an opportunity to re-engage with the promises of human rights, which remain fundamental yet elusive.

SELECT BIBLIOGRAPHY

Afshari, Reza, Relativity in Universality: Jack Donnelly's Grand Theory in Need of Specific Illustrations (2015) *Human Rights Quarterly* 37:4

Agus, Yenita and Shigeko Horiuchi, Factors Influencing the Use of Antenatal Care in Rural West Sumatra, Indonesia (2012) *BMC Pregnancy and Childbirth* 12:9

Ahmed, Akbar, *Discovering Islam: Making Sense of Muslim History and Society* (Routledge, 2002)

Alston, Philip, The 'Not-a-Cat' Syndrome: Can the International Human Rights Regime Accommodate Non-State Actors? in P. Alston (ed.), *Non-State Actors and Human Rights* (Oxford University Press, 2005)

Ampt, Frances, Myo Myo Mon, Kyu Kyu Than, May May Khin, Paul A. Agius, Christopher Morgan, Jessica Davis and Stanley Luchters, Correlates of Male Involvement in Maternal and Newborn Health: A Cross-sectional Study of Men in a Peri-urban Region of Myanmar (2015) *BMC Pregnancy and Childbirth* 15:122

An-Na'im, Abdullahi Ahmed, Human Rights and Islamic Identity in France and Uzbekistan: Mediation of the Local and Global (2000) *Human Rights Quarterly* 22:4

Islam and Human Rights, in J. Witte Jr and M. C. Green (eds.), *Religion and Human Rights: An Introduction* (Oxford University Press, 2012)

The Spirit of Laws Is not Universal: Alternatives to the Enforcement Paradigm for Human Rights (2016) *Tilburg Law Review* 21:255–274

Toward a Cross-Cultural Approach to Defining International Standards of Human Rights: The Meaning of Cruel, Inhuman, or Degrading Treatment or Punishment, in A. A. An-Na'im (ed.), *Human Rights in Cross-Cultural Perspectives: A Quest for Consensus* (University of Pennsylvania Press, 1992)

Why Should Muslims Abandon *Jihad*? Human Rights and the Future of International Law? in R. Falk, B. Rajagopal and J. Stevens (eds.), *International Law and the Third World: Reshaping Justice* (Routledge, 2008)

Ando, Nisuke, National Implementation and Interpretation, in D. Shelton (ed.), *The Oxford Handbook of International Human Rights Law* (Oxford University Press, 2013)

Anghie, Antony, International Human Rights Law and a Developing World Perspective, in S. Sheeran and N. Rodley (eds.), *Routledge Handbook of International Human Rights Law* (Routledge, 2013)
  The Evolution of International Law: Colonial and Postcolonial Realities, in R. Falk, B. Rajagopal and J. Stevens (eds.), *International Law and the Third World: Reshaping Justice* (Routledge, 2008)
Arnez, Monika, Empowering Women through Islam: Fatayat NU between Tradition and Change (2010) *Journal of Islamic Studies* 21:1
Assim, Usang and Julia Sloth-Nielsen, Islamic Kafalah as an Alternative Care Option for Children Deprived of a Family Environment (2014) *African Human Rights Law Journal* 14:322–345
Assyaukanie, Luthfi, Fatwa and Violence in Indonesia (2009) *Journal of Religion and Society* 11:1–21
Avishai, Orit, 'Doing Religion' in a Secular World: Women in Conservative Religions and the Question of Agency (August 2008) *Gender & Society* 22:4
Azuh, Dominic, Oluyemi Fayomi and Lady Ajayi, Socio-Cultural Factors of Gender Roles in Women's Healthcare Utilization in Southwest Nigeria (2015) *Open Journal of Social Sciences* 3:105–117
Badar, Mohamed Elewa, Islamic Law (*Shari'a*) and the Jurisdiction of the International Criminal Law (2011) *Leiden Journal of International Law* 24:411–433
Bahramitash, Roksana, Family Planning, Islam and Women's Human Rights In Iran (2007) *International Studies Journal* 4:1
Bakircioglu, Onder, The Principal Sources of Islamic Law, in Tallyn Gray (ed.), *Islam and International Criminal Law and Justice* (Torkel Opsahl Academic Epublisher, 2018)
Bantekas, Ilias and Lutz Oette, *International Human Rights Law and Practice* (Cambridge University Press, 2013)
Barbour, Rosaline, *Introducing Qualitative Research: A Student Guide to the Craft of Doing Qualitative Research* (SAGE, 2008)
Barlinti, Yeni Salma, Inheritance Legal System in Indonesia: A Legal Justice for People (2013) *Indonesia Law Review Year* 1:3
Bedner, Adriaan and Stijn van Huis, Plurality of Marriage Law and Marriage Registration for Muslims in Indonesia: A Plea for Pragmatism (June 2010) *Utrecht Law Review* 6:2
Bell, Daniel, The East Asian Challenge to Human Rights: Reflections on an East West Dialogue (1996) *Human Rights Quarterly* 18:641–667
Blackburn, Susan, Indonesian Women and Political Islam (February 2008) *Journal of Southeast Asian Studies* 39:1
Bloche, M. Gregg, Is Privatisation of Health Care a Human Rights Problem, in K. de Feyter and F. Gómez Isa (eds.), *Privatisation and Human Rights in the Age of Globalisation* (Intersentia, 2005)

Bloom, David and David Canning, Population, Poverty Reduction and the Cairo Agenda, in M. J. Roseman and L. Reichenbach (eds.), *Reproductive Health and Human Rights: The Way Forward* (University of Pennsylvania Press, 2009)

Boerefijn, Ineke, International Human Rights in National Law, in C. Krause and M. Scheinin (eds.), *International Protection of Human Rights: A Textbook* (Turku/Åbo: Åbo Akademi University, Institute for Human Rights, 2009)

The Reporting Procedure under the Covenant on Civil and Political Rights (Intersentia, 1999)

Börzel, Tanja and Thomas Risse, Human Rights in Areas of Limited Statehood: The New Agenda, in R. Risse, S. Ropp and K. Sikkink (eds.), *The Persistent Power of Human Rights: From Commitment to Compliance* (Cambridge University Press, 2013)

Bragato, Fernanda, Human Rights and Eurocentrism: An Analysis from the Decolonial Studies Perspective (2013) *The Global Studies Journal* 5:3

Breen, Claire, Rationalising the Work of UN Human Rights Bodies or Reducing the Input of NGOs? The Changing Role of Human Rights NGOs at the United Nations (2005) *Non-State Actors and International Law* 5:101–126

Brems, Eva, Enemies or Allies? Feminism and Cultural Relativism as Dissident Voices in Human Rights Discourse (1997) *Human Rights Quarterly* 19:136–164

Human Rights: Universality and Diversity (Martinus Nijhoff Publishers, 2001)

Reconciling Universality and Diversity in International Human Rights Law, in A. Sajó (ed.), *Human Rights with Modesty: The Problem of Universalism* (Martinus Nijhoff Publishers, 2004)

Reconciling Universality and Diversity in International Human Rights: A Theoretical and Methodological Framework and Its Application in the Context of Islam (April–June 2004) *Human Rights Review* 5:3

Brems, Eva and E. Desmet, Studying Human Rights Law from the Perspective(s) of Its Users (2014) *Human Rights and International Legal Discourse* 8:111–120

Brenner, Suzanne, Private Moralities in the Public Sphere: Democratization, Islam, and Gender in Indonesia (2011) *American Anthropologist* 113:3

Brett, Rachel, Non-Governmental Organizations and Human Rights, in C. Krause and M. Scheinin (eds.), *International Protection of Human Rights: A Textbook* (Turku/Åbo: Åbo Akademi University, Institute for Human Rights, 2009)

Burke, Kelsy, Women's Agency in Gender-Traditional Religions: A Review of Four Approaches (2012) *Sociology Compass* 6:2

Butt, Simon, Islam, the State and the Constitutional Court in Indonesia (2010) *Pacific Rim Law & Policy Journal Association* 19:2

Regional Autonomy and Legal Disorder: The Proliferation of Local Laws in Indonesia (2010) *Sydney Law Review* 32:177–192

Buyse, Antoine, Squeezing Civic Space: Restrictions on Civil Society Organizations and the Linkages with Human Rights (2018) *International Journal of Human Rights* 22:8

Çali, Başak and Saladin Meckled-García, Introduction: Human Rights Legalized – Defining, Interpreting, and Implementing an Ideal, in S. Meckled-García and B. Çali (eds.), *The Legalization of Human Rights: Multidisciplinary Perspectives on Human Rights and Human Rights Law* (Routledge, 2006)

Cammack, Mark and Michael Feener, The Islamic Legal System in Indonesia (2012) *Pacific Rim Law & Policy Journal* 21:13–42

Cammack, Mark, A. Bedner and S. van Huis, Democracy, Human Rights, and Islamic Family law in Post-Soeharto Indonesia (2015) *New Middle Eastern Studies* 5:2

Candland, Christopher and Siti Nurjanah, Women's Empowerment through Islamic Organisations: The Role of the Indonesia's 'Nahdlatul Ulama' in Transforming the Government's Birth Control Programme into a Family Welfare Programme (February 2004)

Carozza, Paolo, Human Dignity, in D. Shelton (ed.), *The Oxford Handbook on International Human Rights Law* (Oxford University Press, 2013)

  Subsidiarity as a Structural Principle of International Human Rights Law (2003) *American Journal of International Law* 97:1

Carrillo Santarelli, Nicolas, Non-State Actors' Human Rights Obligations and Responsibility under International Law (2008) *Revista Electronica de Estudios Internacionales* 15

Cassese, Antonio, *International Law in a Divided World* (Oxford University Press, 1986)

Castellino, Joshua, Application of International Standards of Human Rights Law at Domestic Level, in A. R. Chowdhury and J. H. Bhuiyan (eds.), *An Introduction to International Human Rights Law* (Martinus Nijhoff Publishers, 2012)

Cerna, Christina, East Asian Approaches to Human Rights (1995) *Buffalo Journal of International Law* 2

Chapman, Audrey, The Impact of Reliance on Private Sector Health Services on the Right to Health (June 2014) *Health and Human Rights Journal* 16:1

Charnovitz, Steve, Nongovernmental Organizations and International Law (2006) *American Journal of International Law* 100:348–372

Choudhury, Nusrat, Constrained Spaces for Islamic Feminism: Women's Rights and the 2004 Constitution of Afghanistan (2007) *Yale Journal of Law & Feminism* 19:155–200

Clapham, Andrew, *Human Rights Obligations of Non-State Actors* (Oxford University Press, 2006)

  The Use of International Human Rights Law by Civil Society Organisations, in S. Sheeran and N. Rodley (eds.), *Routledge Handbook of International Human Rights Law* (Routledge, 2013)

Clapham, Andrew and M. Garcia Rubio, The Obligations of States with Regard to Non-State Actors in the Context of the Right to Health (2002) *Health and Human Rights Working Paper Series* No. 3

Cook, Rebecca, Human Rights and Maternal Health: Exploring the Effectiveness of the Alyne Decision (2013) *Journal of Law, Medicine, and Ethics* 41:103–123

Cook, Rebecca and Mahmoud Fathalla, Advancing Reproductive Rights Beyond Cairo and Beijing (September 1996) *International Family Planning Perspectives* 22:3

Coomans, Fons, Fred Grünfeld and Menno Kamminga, Methods of Human Rights Research: A Primer (2010) *Human Rights Quarterly* 32:1

Coomaraswamy, Radhika, Identity Within: Cultural Relativism, Minority Rights and the Empowerment of Women (2002) *The George Washington International Law Review* 34:483–514

    The Contemporary Challenges to International Human Rights, in S. Sheeran and N. Rodley (eds.), *Routledge Handbook of International Human Rights Law* (Routledge, 2013)

Cowan, Jane, Anthropology and Human Rights: Do Anthropologists Have an Ethical Obligation to Promote Human Rights? An Open Exchange, in M. Goodale (ed.), *Human Rights: An Anthropological Reader* (Blackwell, 2009)

Crawshaw, Steve, Neo-Westphalia, So What? in Doutje Lettinga and Lars van Troost (eds.), *Debating the Endtimes of Human Rights: Activism and Institutions in a Neo-Westphalian World* (Amnesty International, 2014)

Dai, Xinyuan, The 'Compliance Gap' and the Efficacy of International Human Rights Institutions, in T. Risse, S. Ropp and K. Sikkink (eds.), *The Persistent Power of Human Rights: From Commitment to Compliance* (Cambridge University Press, 2013)

Daud Ali, Mohammad, *Islamic Law: Introduction to Islamic Jurisprudence and the Legal System in Indonesia* (PT RajaGrafindo Persada, 2016)

David, Valeska, Reparations at the Human Rights Committee: Legal Basis, Practice and Challenges (2014) *Netherlands Quarterly of Human Rights* 32:1

David, Valeska and Julie Fraser, A Legal Pluralist Approach to the Use of Cultural Perspectives in the Implementation and Adjudication of Human Rights Norms (2017) *Buffalo Human Rights Law Review* 23:75–118

de Feyter, Koen, Law Meets Sociology in Human Rights (2011) *Development and Society* 40:1

    Localizing Human Rights, Institute of Development Policy and Management, Discussion Paper (January 2006)

    Treaty Interpretation and the Social Sciences, in F. Coomans, F. Grünfeld, and M. T. Kamminga (eds.), *Methods of Human Rights Research* (Intersentia, 2009)

de Gaay Fortman, Bas, Article 1 UDHR: From Credo to Realisation, in Y. Haeck, B. McGonigle Leyh, C. Burbano-Herrera and D. Contreras-Garduno (eds.),

The Realisation of Human Rights: When Theory Meets Practice: Studies in Honour of Leo Zwaak (Intersentia, 2013)

de Pauw, Marijke, Women's Rights: From Bad to Worse? Assessing the Evolution of Incompatible Reservations to the CEDAW Convention (2013) *Merkourios Utrecht Journal of International and European Law* 29:77

de Sousa Santos, Boaventura, *If God Were a Human Rights Activist* (Standford Studies in Human Rights, 2015)

Toward a New Legal Common Sense: Law, Globalization, and Emancipation (2nd ed., Butterworths, 2002)

de Wolf, Antenor Hallo, Human Rights and the Regulation of Privatized Essential Services (2013) *Netherlands International Law Review* 60:2

de Wolf, Antenor Hallo and B. Toebes, Assessing Private Sector Involvement in Health Care and Universal Health Coverage in Light of the Right to Health (2016) *Health and Human Rights* 18:2

Donders, Yvonne, Cultural Pluralism in International Human Rights Law: The Role of Reservations, in A. Vrdoljak (ed.), *The Cultural Dimension of Human Rights* (Oxford University Press, 2013)

Do Cultural Diversity and Human Rights Make a Good Match? (2010) *International Social Science Journal* 61:199

Exploring the Cultural Dimension of the Right to the Highest Attainable Standard of Health (2015) *PER* 18:180–222

Human Rights and Cultural Diversity: Too Hot to Handle? (2012) *Netherlands Quarterly of Human Rights* 30:4

Human Rights: Eye for Cultural Diversity, Inaugural Lecture Delivered upon the Appointment to the Chair of Professor of International Human Rights and Cultural Diversity at the University of Amsterdam (29 June 2012)

Donders, Yvonne and V. Vleugel, The Receptor Approach: A New Human Rights Kid on the Block or Old Wine in New Bags? (2014) *Human Rights Quarterly* 36:653–662

Donnelly, Jack, Human Rights and Human Dignity: An Analytic Critique of Non-Western Conceptions of Human Rights (1982) *The American Political Science Review* 76:2

The Relative Universality of Human Rights (May 2007) *Human Rights Quarterly* 29:2

The Virtues of Legalization, in S. Meckled-García and B. Çali (eds.), *The Legalization of Human Rights: Multidisciplinary Perspectives on Human Rights and Human Rights Law* (Routledge, 2006)

Universal Human Rights in Theory and Practice (3rd ed., Cornell University, 2013)

Donoho, Douglas, Human Rights Enforcement in Twenty-First Century (2006–7) *Georgia Journal of International and Comparative Law* 35:1

Dudgeon, Matthew and Marcia Inhorn, Men's Influences on Women's Reproductive Health: Medical Anthropological Perspectives (2004) *Social Science and Medicine* 59:1379–1395

Dwisetyani Utomo, I., S. Arsyad and E. Nurul Hasmi, Village Family Planning Volunteers in Indonesia: The Role in the Family Planning Programme (2006) *Reproductive Health Matters* 14:27

Edwards, George, Attributes of Successful Human Rights Non-governmental Organisations (NGOs) – 60 years after the 1948 Universal Declaration of Human Rights, in A. R. Chowdhury and J. H. Bhuiyan (eds.), *An Introduction to International Human Rights Law* (Martinus Nijhoff Publishers, 2012)

Engle, Karen, Culture and Human Rights: The Asian Values Debate in Context (1999–2000) *New York University Journal of International Law and Politics* 32:291–334

From Skepticism to Embrace: Human Rights and the American Anthropological Association from 1947–1999 (2001) *Human Rights Quarterly* 23:536–559

Ernada, Sus Eko, Issues of Compatibility of Human Rights and Islam: The Experience of Egypt and Indonesia (June 2007) *Journal of Indonesian Islam* 1:1

Eslava, Luis and Sundhya Pahuja, Between Resistance and Reform: TWAIL and the Universality of International Law (2011) *Trade, Law and Development* 3:1

Falk, Richard, International Law and the Future, in R. Falk, B. Rajagopal and J. Stevens (eds.), *International Law and the Third World* (Routledge, 2008)

Fernea, Elizabeth, The Challenges for Middle Eastern Women in the 21st Century (Spring 2000) *Middle East Journal* 54:2

Firestone, Rebecca, Laura Reichenbach and Mindy Jane Roseman, Conclusion: Conceptual Successes and Operational Challenges to ICPD: Global Reproductive Health and Rights Moving Forward, in M. J. Roseman and L. Reichenbach (eds.), *Reproductive Health and Human Rights: The Way Forward* (University of Pennsylvania Press, 2009)

Flinterman, Cees, The Universal Declaration of Human Rights (2008) *Netherlands Quarterly of Human Rights* 26:4

Flyvbjerg, Bent, Five Misunderstandings About Case-Study Research (April 2006) *Qualitative Inquiry* 12:2

Forsythe, David, Human Rights Studies: On the Dangers of Legalistic Assumptions, in F. Coomans, F. Grünfeld and M. T. Kamminga (eds.), *Methods of Human Rights Research* (Intersentia, 2009)

Fortin, Katharine, *The Accountability of Armed Groups under Human Rights Law* (Oxford University Press, 2017)

Foster Halabi, Sam, Participation and the Right to Health: Lessons from Indonesia (2009) *Health and Human Rights* 11:1

Fraser, Julie, Challenging State-Centricity and Legalism: Promoting the Role of Social Institutions in the Domestic Implementation of International Human Rights Law (2019) *International Journal of Human Rights* 23:6

In Search of New Narratives: The Role of Cultural Norms and Actors in Addressing Human Rights Contestation, in Rosemarie Buikema, Antoine Buyse and Antonius Robben (eds.), *Cultures, Citizenship and Human Rights* (Routledge, 2019)

Fraser, Julie and Henrike Prudon, Integrating Human Rights with Local Norms: Ebola, Burial Practices, and the Right to Health in West Africa (2017) *Intercultural Human Rights Law Review* 12:71–114

Freeman, Michael, Putting Law in Its Place: An Interdisciplinary Evaluation of National Amnesty Laws, in S. Meckled-García and B. Çali (eds.), *The Legalization of Human Rights: Multidisciplinary Perspectives on Human Rights and Human Rights Law* (Routledge, 2006)

Universalism of Human Rights and Cultural Relativism, in S. Sheeran and N. Rodley (eds.), *Routledge Handbook of International Human Rights Law* (Routledge, 2013)

Galligan, Denis and Deborah Sandler, Implementing Human Rights, in S. Halliday and P. Schmidt (eds.), *Human Rights Brought Home: Socio-Legal Perspectives on Human Rights in the National Context* (Hart Publishing, 2004)

Geertz, Clifford, *The Interpretation of Cultures* (Basic Books, 1973)

George, Erika, Virginity Testing and South Africa's HIV/AIDS Crisis: Beyond Rights Universalism and Cultural Relativism Toward Health Capabilities (2008) *California Law Review* 96:1447–1518

Giddens, Anthony, *The Constitution of Society: Outline of the Theory of Structuration* (Polity Press, 1984)

Glendon, Mary Ann, *A World Made New* (Random House, 2002)

Goodale, Mark, Anthropology and the Grounds of Human Rights, in D. Shelton (ed.), *The Oxford Handbook of International Human Rights Law* (Oxford University Press, 2013)

The Myth of Universality: The UNESCO 'Philosophers' Committee' and the Making of Human Rights (2018) *Law & Social Inquiry* 43:3

Green, Judith and Nicki Thorogood, *Qualitative Methods for Health Research* (SAGE, 2004)

Grünfeld, Fred, The United Nations and Non-State Actors: Legitimacy and Compliance (1997) *SIM Special* No. 19

Hallaq, Wael, *An Introduction to Islamic Law* (Cambridge University Press, 2009)

On the Origins of the Controversy about the Existence of Mujtahids and the Gate of Ijtihad (1986) *Studia Islamica* 63:129–141

Halliday, Simon and Patrick Schmidt (eds.), *Human Rights Brought Home: Socio-Legal Perspectives on Human Rights in the National Context* (Hart Publishing, 2004)

Hasna Fadia, Islam, Social Traditions and Family Planning (April 2003) *Social Policy & Administration* 37:2

Hassan, Riffat, Challenging Stereotypes of Fundamentalism: An Islamic Feminist Perspective (Spring 2001) *The Muslim World* 91:55–70
  Is Family Planning Permitted by Islam? The Issue of a Woman's Right to Contraception, in G. Webb (ed.), *Windows of Faith: Muslim Women Scholar-Activists in North America* (Syracuse University Press, 2000)
Hathaway, Oona, Do Human Rights Treaties Make A Difference? (2002) *Yale Law Journal* 111:1935–2042
  Why Do Countries Commit to Human Rights Treaties? (August 2007) *Journal of Conflict Resolution* 51:4
Henrysson, Elin and Sandra Joireman, On the Edge of the Law: Women's Property Rights and Dispute Resolution in Kisii, Kenya (2009) *Law and Society Review* 43:39–60
Herskovits, Melville, Statement on the Human Rights, submitted to the UN Commission on Human Rights by the American Anthropological Association Executive Board (1947) *American Anthropology* 49:4
Heyns, Christof and Frans Viljoen, The Impact of the United Nations Human Rights Treaties on the Domestic Level (2001) *Human Rights Quarterly* 23:3
  The Impact of the United Nations Human Rights Treaties on the Domestic Level (Kluwer Law International, 2002)
Hill, Peter, Lieve Goeman, Rahmi Sofiarini and Maddi Djara, 'Desa SIAGA', the 'Alert Village': The Evolution of an Iconic Brand in Indonesian Public Health Strategies (2014) *Health Policy and Planning* 29:409–420
Hoffman, Simon, The UN Convention on the Rights of the Child, Decentralisation and Legislative Integration: A Case Study from Wales (2019) *International Journal of Human Rights* 23:3
Hopgood, Stephen, Human Rights on the Road to Nowhere, in Stephen Hopgood, Jack Synder and Leslie Vinjamuri (eds.), *Human Rights Futures* (Cambridge University Press, 2017)
  The Endtimes of Human Rights (Cornell University Press, 2013)
  The Endtimes of Human Rights, in Doutje Lettinga and Lars van Troost (eds.), *Debating the Endtimes of Human Rights: Activism and Institutions in a Neo-Westphalian World* (Amnesty International, 2014)
Howard, Rhoda, Dignity, Community, and Human Rights, in A. A. An-Na'im (ed.), *Human Rights in Cross-Cultural Perspectives: A Quest for Consensus* (University of Pennsylvania Press, 1992)
Hull, Terence, Eddy Hasmi, Ninuk Widyantoro, 'Peer' Educator Initiatives for Adolescent Reproductive Health Projects in Indonesia (2004) *Reproductive Health Matters* 12:23
Hull, Terence and Henry Mosley, The Government of Indonesia and the UNFPA, *Revitalization of Family Planning in Indonesia* (February 2009)

Hunt, Paul and Gillian MacNaughton, A Human Rights-Based Approach to Health Indicators, in M. Baderin and R. McCorquodale (eds.), *Economic, Social and Cultural Rights in Action* (Oxford University Press, 2007)

Hunt, Paul, J. Bueno de Mesquita, J. Y. Lee and S. A. Way, Implementation of Economic, Social and Cultural Rights, in S. Sheeran and N. Rodley (ed.), *Routledge Handbook of International Human Rights Law* (Routledge, 2013)

Hursh, John, Advancing Women's Rights through Islamic Law: The Example of Morocco (2012) *Berkeley Journal of Gender, Law & Justice* 27:252–306

Ibhawoh, Bonny, Between Culture and Constitution: Evaluating the Cultural Legitimacy of Human Rights in the African State (2000) *Human Rights Quarterly* 22:838–860

  Cultural Relativism and Human Rights: Reconsidering the Africanist Discourse (2001) *Netherlands Quarterly of Human Rights* 19:1

Ismah, Nor, Destabilising Male Domination: Building Community-Based Authority among Indonesian Female Ulama (2016) *Asian Studies Review* 40:4

Isser, Deborah, Understanding and Engaging Customary Justice Systems, in D. Isser (ed.), *Customary Justice and the Rule of Law in War-Torn Societies* (United States Institute of Peace, 2011)

Joseph, Sarah and Joanna Kyriakakis, The United Nations and Human Rights, in S. Joseph and A. McBeth (eds.), *Research Handbook on International Human Rights Law* (Edward Elgar, 2010)

Kamminga, Menno, The Evolving Status of NGOs under International Law: A Threat to the Inter-State System?' in P. Alston (ed.), *Non-State Actors and Human Rights* (Oxford University Press, 2005)

Kanetake, Machiko, *María de los Ángeles González Carreño v Ministry of Justice*, Judgment No. 1263/2018 of 17 July 2018 (ROJ: STS 2747/2018) (2019) *American Journal of International Law* 113:3

Kaplan, Seth, *Human Rights in Thick and Thin Societies: The Universal Declaration and Bridging the Gap* (Cambridge University Press, 2018)

Kapur, Ratna, Revisioning the Role of Law in Women's Human Rights Struggles, in S. Meckled-García and B. Çali (eds.), *The Legalization of Human Rights: Multidisciplinary Perspectives on Human Rights and Human Rights Law* (Routledge, 2006)

Kinley, David, Bendable Rules: The Development Implications of Human Rights Pluralism, in B. Tamanaha, C. Sage and M. Woolcock (eds.), *Legal Pluralism and Development: Scholars and Practitioners in Dialogue* (Cambridge University Press, 2012)

Kirk, Elizabeth, Kirsty Sherlock and Alison Reeves, SUDS Law: Non-State Actors and the Haphazard Route to Implementation of International Obligations (2004) *Non-State Actors and International Law* 4:87–109

Kissling, Frances, Examining Religion and Reproductive Health: Constructive Engagement for the Future, in M. J. Roseman and L. Reichenbach (eds.),

Reproductive Health and Human Rights: The Way Forward (University of Pennsylvania Press, 2009)

Kontos, Alexis, 'Private' Security Guards: Privatized Force and State Responsibility under International Human Rights Law (2004) *Non-State Actors and International Law* 4:199–238

Krivenko, Ekaterina Yahyaoui, Hospitality and Sovereignty: What Can We Learn From the Canadian Private Sponsorship of Refugees Program? (2012) *International Journal of Refugee Law* 24:3

Islamic View of Women's Rights: An International Lawyer's Perspective (2009) *Journal of East Asia & International Law* 2:103–128

Landman, Todd, Social Science Methods and Human Rights, in F. Coomans, F. Grünfeld and M. T. Kamminga (eds.), *Methods of Human Rights Research* (Intersentia, 2009)

Lauren, Paul Gordon, The Foundations of Justice and Human Rights in Early Legal Texts and Thought, in D. Shelton (ed.), *The Oxford Handbook of International Human Rights Law* (Oxford University Press, 2013)

Lenzerini, Federico, *The Culturalization of Human Rights Law* (Oxford University Press, 2014)

Levitt, Peggy and Sally Engle Merry, Vernacularization on the Ground: Local Uses of Global Women's Rights in Peru, China, India and the United States (2009) *Global Networks* 9:4

Liu, Lydia H., Shadows of Universalism: The Untold Story of Human Rights around 1948 (Summer 2014) *Critical Inquiry* 40:385–417

Lukito, Ratno, *Legal Pluralism in Indonesia: Bridging the Unbridgeable* (Routledge, 2013)

Mapping the Relationship of Competing Legal Traditions in the Era of Transnationalism in Indonesia, in Gary Bell (ed.), *Pluralism, Transnationalism and Culture in Asian Law* (2017)

State and Religion Continuum in Indonesia: The Trajectory of Religious Establishment and Religious Freedom in the Constitution (2017) *Indonesian Journal of International and Comparative Law* 5:645–682

Mahmood, Saba, *Politics of Piety: The Islamic Revival and the Feminist Subject* (Princeton University Press, 2005)

Marshall, Katherine, *Religious Engagement in Family Planning Policies: Experience in Six Muslim-majority Countries* (World Faiths Development Dialogue, 2015)

Martens, Kerstin, Mission Impossible? Defining Nongovernmental Organizations (2002) *Voluntas: International Journal of Voluntary and Nonprofit Organizations* 13:3

McBeth, Adam, Every Organ of Society: The Responsibility of Non-State Actors for the Realization of Human Rights (2008–9) *Journal of Public Law & Policy* 30:1

Privatising Human Rights: What Happens to the State's Human Rights Duties when Services Are Privatised? (2004) *Melbourne Journal of International Law* 5:133–154

McCorquodale, Robert, Non-State Actors and International Human Rights Law, in S. Joseph and A. McBeth (eds.), *Research Handbook on International Human Rights Law* (Edward Elgar, 2010)

McEvoy, Kieran, Beyond Legalism: Towards a Thicker Understanding of Transitional Justice (December 2007) *Journal of Law and Society* 34:4

McGonigle Leyh, Brianne, Changing Landscapes in Documentation Efforts: Civil Society Documentation of Serious Human Rights Violations (2017) *Utrecht Journal of International and European Law* 33:84

Meckled-García, Saladin and Başak Çali (eds.), *The Legalization of Human Rights: Multidisciplinary Perspectives on Human Rights and Human Rights Law* (Routledge, 2006)

Menchik, Jeremy, The Co-evolution of Sacred and Secular: Islamic Law and Family Planning in Indonesia (2014) *South East Asia Research* 22:3

Merrick, Thomas, Mobilizing Resources for Reproductive Health, in M. J. Roseman and L. Reichenbach (eds.), *Reproductive Health and Human Rights: The Way Forward* (University of Pennsylvania Press, 2009)

Merry, Sally Engle, Human Rights Law and the Demonization of Culture (And Anthropology Along the Way) (May 2003) *PoLAR* 26:1

Legal Pluralism (1988) *Law and Society Review* 22:869–896

Legal Pluralism and Legal Culture: Mapping the Terrain, in B. Tamanaha, C. Sage and M. Woolcock (eds.), *Legal Pluralism and Development: Scholars and Practitioners in Dialogue* (Cambridge University Press, 2012)

Legal Transplants and Cultural Translation: Making Human Rights in the Vernacular, in M. Goodale (ed.), *Human Rights: An Anthropological Reader* (Blackwell Publishing, 2009)

Transnational Human Rights and Local Activism: Mapping the Middle (2006) *American Anthropologist* 108:1

Middelburg, Annemarie, *Empty Promises? Compliance with the Human Rights Framework in Relation to Female Genital Mutilation/Cutting in Senegal* (Middelburg, 2016)

Miller, Seumas, Social Institutions, in E. Zalta (ed.), *The Stanford Encyclopedia of Philosophy* (Winter 2014 Edition, 8 February 2011)

Mir Hosseini, Ziba, Muslim Women's Quest for Equality: Between Islamic Law and Feminism (Summer 2006) *Critical Inquiry* 32:629–649

Mokhtari, Shadi, The Search for Human Rights Within an Islamic Framework in Iran (Oct 2004) *The Muslim World* 94:469–479

Moore, Sally Falk, Law and Social Change: The Semi-Autonomous Social Field as an Appropriate Subject of Study (1973) *Law and Society Review* 7:719–746

Morsink, Johannes, *The Universal Declaration of Human Rights: Origins, Drafting, and Intent* (Pennsylvania Studies in Human Rights, 1999)

Musdah Mulia, Siti, Muslim Family Law Reform in Indonesia: A Progressive Interpretation of The Qur'an (August 2015) *Al-Mawarid Journal of Islamic Law* XV:1

Musdah Mulia, Siti with Mark E. Cammack, Toward a Just Marriage Law: Empowering Indonesian Women through a Counter Legal Draft to the Indonesian Compilation of Islamic Law, in R. M. Feener and M. E. Cammack (eds.), *Islamic Law in Contemporary Indonesia: Ideas and Institutions* (Harvard University Press, 2007)

Mutua, Makau, Book Review (2001) *American Journal of International Law* 95

Human Rights: A Political and Cultural Critique (University of Pennsylvania Press, 2002)

Human Rights International NGOs: A Critical Evaluation, in C. Welch (ed.), *NGOs and Human Rights: Promise and Performance* (University of Pennsylvania Press, 2001)

What Is TWAIL? (2000) *American Society of International Law Proceedings*

Neuman, Gerald, Subsidiarity, in D. Shelton (ed.), *The Oxford Handbook of International Human Rights Law* (Oxford University Press, 2013)

Neumayer, Eric, Do International Human Rights Treaties Improve Respect for Human Rights? (Dec 2005) *Journal of Conflict Resolution* 49:6

Newland, Lynda, Female Circumcision: Muslim Identities and Zero Tolerance Policies in Rural West Java (2006) *Women's Studies International Forum* 29

Niang, Cheikh, The Dimba of Senegal: A Support Group for Women (1994) *Reproductive Health Matters* 2:4

Nowak, Manfred, *Human Rights or Global Capitalism: The Limits of Privatization* (University of Pennsylvania Press, 2017)

Nowak, Manfred and Karolina Miriam Januszewski, Non-State Actors and Human Rights, in M. Noortmaan, A. Reinisch and C. Ryngaert (eds.), *Non-State Actors in International Law* (Hart Publishing, 2015)

Nurlaelawati, Euis, Muslim Women in Indonesian Religious Courts: Reform, Strategies, and Pronouncement of Divorce (2013) *Islamic Law and Society* 20:3

Nurmila, Nina, Feminist Reinterpretations of The Qur'ān (2013) *Journal of Qur'ān and Hadith Studies* 2:2

Indonesian Muslim's Discourse of Husband–Wife Relationship (2013) *Al-Jāmi'ah* 51:1

The Influence of Global Muslim Feminism on Indonesian Muslim Feminist Discourse (2011) *Al-Jāmi'ah* 49:1

Nyamu, Celestine, An Actor-oriented Approach to Rights in Development (2005) *IDS Bulletin* 36:1

Are Local Norms and Practices Fences or Pathways? The Example of Women's Property Rights, in An-A. A. Na`im (ed.), *Cultural Transformation and Human Rights in Africa* (Zed Books Ltd, 2002)

How Should Human Rights and Development Respond to Cultural Legitimization of Gender Hierarchy in Developing Countries? (2000) *Harvard International Law Journal* 41:2

Octavia, Lanny, Circumcision and Muslim Women's Identity in Indonesia (2014) *Indonesian Journal for Islamic Studies* 21:3

Okafor, Obiora Chinedu, Newness, Imperialism, and International Legal Reform in Our Time: A TWAIL Perspective (2005) *Osgoode Hall Law Journal* 43:1&2

Okere, B. Obinna, The Protection of Human Rights in Africa and the African Charter on Human and Peoples' Rights: A Comparative Analysis with the European and American Systems (1984) *Human Rights Quarterly* 6

Oomen, Barbara and Esther van den Berg, Human Rights Cities: Urban Actors as Pragmatic Idealistic Human Rights Users (2014) *Human Rights and International Legal Discourse* 8

Osiatyński, Wiktor, The Historical Development of Human Rights, in S. Sheeran and N. Rodley (eds.), *Routledge Handbook of International Human Rights Law* (Routledge, 2013)

Prag, Ebbe, *Women Making Politics in Rural Senegal: Women's Associations, Female Politicians and Development Brokers* (LAP LAMBERT Academic Publishing, 2010)

Preis, Ann-Belinda, Human Rights as Cultural Practice: An Anthropological Critique (1996) *Human Rights Quarterly* 18:286–315

Quane, Helen, International Human Rights Law as a Catalyst for the Recognition and Evolution of Non-State Law, in M. Helfand (ed.), *Negotiating State and Non-State Law: The Challenge of Global and Local Legal Pluralism* (Cambridge University Press, 2016)

Legal Pluralism and International Human Rights Law: Inherently Incompatible, Mutually Reinforcing or Something in Between? (2013) *Oxford Journal of Legal Studies* 33:675–702

Rachmawati, Emma, Dominika Jajkowicz, Lintang Purwara Dewanti and Mouhamad Bigwanto, Mapping Faith-Based Responses to Sexual and Reproductive Health and Rights in Indonesia: A Snapshot from 10 Muslim, Christian, Hindu, Buddhist and Confucian Faith-Based Organizations (2017) UICIHSS

Rajagopal, Balakrishnan, Counter-hegemonic International Law: Rethinking Human Rights and Development as Third World Strategy, in R. Falk, B. Rajagopal and J. Stevens (eds.), *International Law and the Third World: Reshaping Justice* (Routledge, 2008)

Reichenbach, Laura, The Global Reproductive Health and Rights Agenda: Opportunities and Challenges for the Future, in M. J. Roseman and L. Reichenbach (eds.), *Reproductive Health and Human Rights: The Way Forward* (University of Pennsylvania Press, 2009)

Reinisch, August, The Changing International Legal Framework for Dealing with Non-State Actors, in P. Alston (ed.), *Non-State Actors and Human Rights* (Oxford University Press, 2005)

Renteln, Alison Dundes, Relativism and the Search for Human Rights (1988) *American Anthropologist* 90:56-72

The Human Rights Dimensions of Virginity Restoration Surgery, in Marie-Claire Foblets, Michele Graziadei and Alison Dundes Renteln (eds.), *Personal Autonomy in Plural Societies: A Principle and its Paradoxes* (Routledge, 2018), pp. 206-19

The Unanswered Challenge of Relativism and the Consequences for Human Rights (1985) *Human Rights Quarterly* 7:4

Rinaldo, Rachel, Envisioning the Nation: Women Activists, Religion and the Public Sphere in Indonesia (June 2008) *Social Forces* 86:4

Pious and Critical: Muslim Women Activists and the Question of Agency (2014) *Gender & Society* 28:6

Rishmawi, Mervat, The Revised Arab Charter on Human Rights: A Step Forward? (2005) *Human Rights Law Review* 5:2

Risse, Thomas and Stephen Ropp, Introduction and Overview, in T. Risse, S. Ropp and K. Sikkink (eds.), *The Persistent Power of Human Rights: From Commitment to Compliance* (Cambridge University Press, 2013)

Robinson, Mary, From Rhetoric to Reality: Making Human Rights Work (2003) *European Human Rights Law Review* 1:1-8

Human Rights at the Dawn of the 21st Century (1993) *Human Rights Quarterly* 15:629-639

Rodley, Nigel, Can Armed Opposition Groups Violate Human Rights? in K. Mahoney and P. Mahoney (eds.), *Human Rights in the Twenty-First Century: A Global Challenge* (Martinus Nijhoff Publishers, 1993)

Human Rights NGOs: Rights and Obligations (Present Status and Perspectives) (1997) *SIM Special* 19:41-60.

Non-State Actors and Human Rights, in S. Sheeran and N. Rodley (eds.), *The Routledge Handbook of International Human Rights Law* (Routledge, 2013)

The Role and Impact of Treaty Bodies, in D. Shelton (ed.), *The Oxford Handbook of International Human Rights Law* (Oxford University Press, 2013)

Roseman, Mindy Jane and Laura Reichenbach, Global Reproduction Health and Rights: Reflecting on ICPD, in M. J. Roseman and L. Reichenbach (eds.), *Reproductive Health and Human Rights: The Way Forward* (University of Pennsylvania Press, 2009)

Roy, Olivier and Pasqual Annicchino, Human Rights between Religions, Cultures, and Universality, in A. Vrdoljak (ed.), *The Cultural Dimension of Human Rights* (Oxford University Press, 2013)

Ryngaert, Cedric, Non-State Actors: Carving out a Space in a State-Centred International Legal System (2016) *Netherlands International Law Review* 63:183–195

Ryngaert, Cedric, M. Noortmann and A. Reinisch, Concluding Observations, in M. Noortmann, A. Reinisch and C. Ryngaert (eds.), *Non-State Actors in International Law* (Hart Publishing, 2015)

Sage, Caroline and Michael Woolcock, Introduction, in B. Tamanaha, C. Sage and M. Woolcock (eds.), *Legal Pluralism and Development: Scholars and Practitioners in Dialogue* (Cambridge University Press, 2012)

Salim, Arksal, Between ICMI and NU: The Contested Representation of Muslim Civil Society in Indonesia, 1990–2001 (2011) *Al-Jāmi'ah* 49:2

Sano, Hans-Otto and Hatla Thelle, The Need for Evidence-Based Human Rights Research, in F. Coomans, F. Grünfeld and M. T. Kamminga (eds.), *Methods of Human Rights Research* (Intersentia, 2009)

Saul, Ben, David Kinley and Jacqueline Mowbray, *The International Covenant on Economic, Social and Cultural Rights: Commentary, Cases, and Materials* (Oxford University Press, 2014)

Schabas, William, *The Universal Declaration of Human Rights* (Cambridge University Press, 2013)

Schachter, Oscar, The Obligation of the Parties to Give Effect to the Covenant on Civil and Political Rights (1979) *The American Journal of International Law* 73:3

Scheinin, Martin, International Mechanisms and Procedures for Monitoring, in C. Krause and M. Scheinin (eds.), *International Protection of Human Rights: A Textbook* (Turku/Åbo: Åbo Akademi University, Institute for Human Rights, 2009)

Schmidt, Patrick and Simon Halliday, Introduction: Socio-Legal Perspectives on Human Rights in the National Context, in S. Halliday and P. Schmidt (eds.), *Human Rights Brought Home: Socio-Legal Perspectives on Human Rights in the National Context* (Hart Publishing, 2004)

Schrijver, Nico, Paving the Way towards ... One Worldwide Human Rights Treaty! (2011) *Netherlands Quarterly of Human Rights* 29:3

Sciortino, Rosalia, The Challenge of Addressing Gender in Reproductive Health Programmes: Examples from Indonesia (1998) *Reproductive Health Matters* 6:11

Sciortino, Rosalia, Lies Marcoes-Natsir and Masdar F. Mas'udi, Learning from Islam: Advocacy of Reproductive Rights in Indonesian Pesantren (Nov. 1996) *Reproductive Health Matters* 4:8

Seibert-Fohr, Anja, Domestic Implementation of the International Covenant on Civil and Political Rights Pursuant to Its Article 2 Para. 2, in J. A. Frowein and R. Wolfrum (eds.), *Max Planck Yearbook of United Nations Law* (vol. 5, Kluwer, 2001)

Seo, Myengkyo, Defining 'Religious' in Indonesia: Toward Neither an Islamic nor a Secular State (2012) *Citizenship Studies* 16:8

Sezgin, Yüksel, How to Integrate Universal Human Rights into Customary and Religious Legal Systems (2010) *Journal of Legal Pluralism and Unofficial Law* 60:5

Shaffer, Gregory and Tom Ginsburg, The Empirical Turn in International Legal Scholarship (2012) *American Journal of International Law* 106:1

Shalev, Carmel, Rights to Sexual and Reproductive Health: The ICPD and the Convention on the Elimination of All Forms of Discrimination against Women (2000) *Health and Human Rights* 4:2

Shefner-Rogers, Corinne and Suruchi Sood, Involving Husbands in Safe Motherhood: Effects of SUAMI SIAGA Campaign in Indonesia (2004) *Journal of Health Communication* 9:233–258

Smith, Rhona K. M., *Textbook on International Human Rights* (5th ed., Oxford University Press, 2012)

Solomon, Harris, Kathryn Yount and Michael Mbizvo, 'A Shot of His Own': The Acceptability of a Male Hormonal Contraceptive in Indonesia (2007) *Culture, Health & Sexuality* 9:1

Sosa, Lorena, *Intersectionality in the Human Rights Legal Framework on Violence Against Women – At the Centre or the Margins?* (Cambridge University Press, 2017).

Spiro, Peter, NGOs and Human Rights: Channels of Power, in S. Joseph and A. McBeth (eds.), *Research Handbook on International Human Rights Law* (Edward Elgar, 2010)

Ssenyonjo, Manisuli, Economic, Social and Cultural Rights: An Examination of State Obligations, in S. Joseph and A. McBeth (eds.), *Research Handbook on International Human Rights Law* (Edward Elgar, 2010)

   Non-State Actors and Economic, Social, and Cultural Rights, in M. Baderin and R. McCorquodale (eds.), *Economic, Social, and Cultural Rights in Action* (Oxford University Press, 2007)

Tamanaha, Brian, Understanding Legal Pluralism: Past to Present, Local to Global (2008) *Sydney Law Review* 30:375–411

Thérien, Jean-Philippe and Philippe Joly, 'All Human Rights for All': The United Nations and Human Rights in the Post-Cold War Era (2014) *Human Rights Quarterly* 36:2

Titaley, Christiana, Cynthia Hunter, Peter Heywood, Michael Dibley, Why Don't Some Women Attend Antenatal and Postnatal Care Services? A Qualitative Study of Community Members' Perspectives in Garut, Sukabumi and Ciamis Districts of West Java Province, Indonesia (2010) *BMC Pregnancy and Childbirth* 10:61

Titaley, Christiana, C. Hunter, M. Dibley and P. Heywood, Why Do Some Women Still Prefer Traditional Birth Attendants and Home Delivery? A Qualitative Study on Delivery Care Services in West Java Province, Indonesia (2010) *BMC Pregnancy and Childbirth* 10:43

Toebes, Brigit, *The Right to Health as a Human Right in International Law* (Intersentia, 1999)

The Right to Health and the Privatization of National Health Systems: A Case Study of the Netherlands (2006) *Health and Human Rights* 9:1

Toft, Monica Duffy, False Prophecies in the Service of Good Works, in Doutje Lettinga and Lars van Troost (eds.), *Debating the Endtimes of Human Rights: Activism and Institutions in a Neo-Westphalian World* (Amnesty International, 2014)

Tomuschat, Christian, *Human Rights: Between Idealism and Realism* (2nd ed., Oxford University Press, 2008)

Turner, Jonathan, *The Institutional Order: Economy, Kinship, Religion, Polity, Law, and Education in Evolutionary and Comparative Perspective* (Longman, 1997)

Twining, William, Legal Pluralism 101, in B. Tamanaha, C. Sage and M. Woolcock (eds.), *Legal Pluralism and Development: Scholars and Practitioners in Dialogue* (Cambridge University Press, 2012)

van Doorn-Harder, Pieternella, Controlling the Body: Muslim Feminists Debating Women's Rights in Indonesia (2008) *Religion Compass* 2:6

Women Shaping Islam: Reading The Qur'an in Indonesia (University of Illinois Press, 2006)

Vel, J. A. C. and A. W. Bedner, Decentralisation and Village Governance in Indonesia: The Return to the Nagari and the 2014 Village Law (2015) *Journal of Legal Pluralism and Unofficial Law* 47:3

Vrdoljak, Ana (ed.), *The Cultural Dimension of Human Rights* (Oxford University Press, 2013)

Weissbrodt, David, Roles and Responsibilities of Non-State Actors, in D. Shelton (ed.), *The Oxford Handbook of International Human Rights Law* (Oxford University Press, 2013)

Westendorp, Ingrid, Personal Status Law and Women's Right to Equality in Law and in Practice: The Case of Land Rights of Balinese Hindu Women (2015) *Journal of Human Rights Practice* 7:430–450

Woodford-Berger, Prudence, Associating Women: Female Lineage, Collective Identities and Political Ideology, in E. Evers Rosander (ed.), *Transforming Female Identities: Women's Organizational Forms in West Africa* (Nordiska Afrikainstitutet, 1997)

Woodiwiss, Anthony, The Law Cannot Be Enough: Human Rights and the Limits of Legalism, in S. Meckled-García and B. Çali (eds.), *The Legalization of*

Human Rights: Multidisciplinary Perspectives on Human Rights and Human Rights Law (Routledge, 2006)

Wynn, Lisa, Angel Foster, Aida Rouhana and James Trussell, 'The Politics of Emergency Contraception in the Arab World: Reflections on Western Assumptions and the Potential Influence of Religious and Social Factors' (2005) *Harvard Health Policy Review* 6:1

Zeidenstein, George, The Conundrum of Population and Reproduction Health Programs in the Early Twenty-First Century, in M. J. Roseman and L. Reichenbach (eds.), *Reproductive Health and Human Rights: The Way Forward* (University of Pennsylvania Press, 2009)

Zwart, Tom, Using Local Culture to Further the Implementation of International Human Rights: The Receptor Approach (2012) *Human Rights Quarterly* 34:546–569

INDEX

African Charter on Human and
  Peoples' Rights, 32
Aisyiyah (Indonesia), 213
Akamba tribe (Kenya), 55
Alston, Philip, 116
American Anthropological Association
  (AAA), 26–7
American Declaration on the Rights
  and Duties of Man, 25
Anghie, Antony, 32
An-Na'im, Abdullahi Ahmed, 33, 49,
  56–8, 85, 160, 287
Anshor, Maria Ulfar, 240–1
Arab Charter on Human Rights, 33
ASEAN Human Rights Declaration, 31,
  169
Asian values debate, 17, 29–32, 48
Assyaukanie, Luthfi, 266
Australia, 276, 282
Austria, 95

Bali, 55
Bangkok Declaration, 30
Benin, 95, 97
Brazil, 151
Brems, Eva, 17, 32, 44
Burundi, 45–6, 100, 102

Cairo Declaration on Human Rights in
  Islam, 33
Canada, 282
Cassin, René, 122
CAT (Convention against Torture), 74,
  83, 134–5
CAT Committee (Committee against
  Torture), 70, 82, 87, 134–5

CEDAW, see Convention on the
  Elimination of All Forms of
  Discrimination against Women
CEDAW Committee, see Committee
  on the Elimination of All Forms
  of Discrimination against
  Women
Centre for the Development of
  Pesantren and Society (P3M)
  (Indonesia), 193–4, 229, 242
CERD Committee (on the Elimination
  of Racial Discrimination), 74,
  82, 133–4
CERD (Convention on the Elimination
  of All Forms of Racial
  Discrimination), 74
Chang, PC, 25
children and children's rights, 2, 84–5,
  128, 254
cities, 283–4
Clapham, Andrew, 122, 129
Colombia, 105
colonialism and Western bias, 30–2, 57,
  241–6, 273
Committee against Torture (CAT
  Committee), 70, 82, 87, 134–5
Committee on Economic, Social and
  Cultural Rights (ESCR
  Committee)
  comments and statements on
    cultural appropriateness, 39–40
    health and healthcare, 174–5,
      177–8, 189
    NSAs, 129–33, 150
    privatisation, 146
    State discretion, 68, 70

312

INDEX

Concluding Observations, 99–103, 108–10, 280
methods of treaty implementation, 72–3
Reporting Guidelines, 91–2, *see also* Harmonised Guidelines, *see also* International Covenant on Economic, Social and Cultural Rights (ICESCR)
Committee on the Elimination of All Forms of Discrimination against Women (CEDAW Committee)
 comments and statements on
  health and healthcare, 175, 180, 184, 188–9, 198–200, 255–9
  NSAs, 135, 148–50
 Concluding Observations, 99, 103–10
 methods of treaty implementation, 75–6, 84–8
 Reporting Guidelines, 92–3, *see also* Harmonised Guidelines, *see also* Convention on the Elimination of All Forms of Discrimination against Women (CEDAW)
Committee on the Elimination of Racial Discrimination (CERD Committee), 74, *see also* Convention on the Elimination of All Forms of Racial Discrimination (CERD)
Committee on the Rights of the Child (CRC Committee)
 comments and statements on
  health and healthcare, 255–6
  NSAs, 138–41, 149–50, 155
 methods of treaty implementation, 73–6, 83–8, *see also* Convention on the Rights of the Child (CRC)
compliance gap, 6, 64–5
Convention against Torture (CAT), 74, 82, 134–5
Convention for the Protection of All Persons from Enforced Disappearance, 37

Convention on the Elimination of All Forms of Discrimination against Women (CEDAW)
 cultural modification, 109
 equality, 71–2
 health and healthcare, 175, 178
 methods of implementation, 7, 84
 NSAs, 135
 reporting, 92
 reservations, 18, 33, *see also* Committee on the Elimination of All Forms of Discrimination against Women (CEDAW Committee)
Convention on the Elimination of All Forms of Racial Discrimination (CERD), 74, 82, 133–4
Convention on the Rights of Persons with Disabilities, 37
Convention on the Rights of the Child (CRC), 64, 68, 83, 138–41, 173, 178, *see also* Committee on the Rights of the Child (CRC Committee)
corporations, 119–20, 132, 150, *see also* private sector providers; social enterprises
Covenants, *see* International Covenant on Civil and Political Rights (ICCPR); International Covenant on Economic, Social and Cultural Rights (ICESCR)
CRC (Convention on the Rights of the Child), 64, 68, 83, 138–41, 173, 178
CRC Committee, *see* Committee on the Rights of the Child
cultural relativism, 29–35
culturally sensitive approaches to human rights implementation
 and state law, 44–8, 60, *see also* vernacularisation
 effectiveness, 58–61
 home-grown solutions, 48–53
 in reproductive health, 175–7
 need and scope for, 42–4

culturally sensitive approaches to human rights implementation (cont.)
  opportunities for promoting rights, 54–8
  overview and rationale, 41–2
culture, dynamic nature and relation to human rights, 38–9, 51

Daud Ali, Mohammed, 228
Declaration of Alma-Ata, 178
Declaration on the Right and Responsibility of Individuals, Groups and Organs of Society to Promote and Protect Universally Recognized Human Rights and Fundamental Freedoms, 124
Declaration on the Rights and Responsibilities of Individuals, Groups, and Organs of Society, 178
Declaration on the Rights of Indigenous Peoples, 37
Denmark, 133
dignity, respect for, 23, 27–9
Donders, Yvonne, 47–8, 177
Donnelly, Jack, 25, 28, 44, 112–13
Draft Articles on Responsibility of States for Internationally Wrongful Acts, 126
Dzuhayatin, Siti Ruhaini, 243–4

ESCR Committee, see Committee on Economic, Social and Cultural Rights
European Convention on Human Rights, 69–70
European Court of Human Rights, 69–70

family planning, see reproductive health and family planning
Fatayat (Indonesia), 222–3, 231–2, 234, 239
fatwas, 1–2, 216–20
female genital mutilation/cutting (FGM/C), 11, 84–5, 106, 201, 237–8, 257–8

feminism, see Muslim feminists in Indonesia
Ford Foundation, 241, 291
France, 98
Freeman, Michael, 48–9, 52

gender stereotyping, 104–6, 197–200
George, Erika, 47
Greece, 96, 98, 102
Guiding Principles on Business and Human Rights (Ruggie Principles), 120, 124–5

Harmonised Guidelines, 90–1, 289
Hasmi, Eddy, 215
Hassan, Riffat, 201, 246, 273
health, right to, 168–72, 176–80, *see also* reproductive health and family planning
HIV/AIDS, 11, 47, 50
Hizbut Tahrir Indonesia, 239, 241
Hopgood, Stephen, 13
housing rights, 100–1
Human Rights Cities, 283
Human Rights Committee (HRCee)
  comments and statements on cultural modification, 258–9
  NSAs, 128–9
  State discretion, 67, 69
  Concluding Observations, 8, 75, 94–9, 108–10
  constructive discussions, 88–9
  legalistic approach, 87
  methods of treaty implementation, 71–2, 75, 81
  recommendations to Indonesia, 279–80
  Reporting Guidelines, 92, *see also* Harmonised Guidelines, *see also* International Covenant on Civil and Political Rights
Human Rights Council Universal Periodic Review (UPR), 288, 290
Hunt, Paul, 175
al-Hussein, Zeid Ra'ad, 13
Huzaemah, Tahido Yanggo, 212, 239

INDEX

Ibhawoh, Bonny, 28, 50
ICCPR, see International Covenant on Civil and Political Rights
ICESCR, see International Covenant on Economic, Social and Cultural Rights
imperialism, see colonialism and Western bias
Indonesia, 164–267
  child marriage, 2, 254
  decentralisation of government, 187–8
  family planning programme, 182–90
  female genital mutilation/cutting (FGM/C), 237–8, 257–8
  health insurance, 189
  inheritance rights on Bali, 55
  Islamic law and institutions, 210–15
  legal pluralism, 267
    compliance with international law, 250–61
  Muslim feminists, 225–7
    reinterpretations of Islamic texts, 227–46
  polygamy, 238–40, 254
  reproductive health and family planning
    campaigns, 166–7, 251–2
    law and policy, 180–90
    role of Islam, 200–2, 215–25, 236–41, 246–61, 263–7
    socio-cultural determinants, 190–205
  significance as case study, 17–19
Indonesian Council of Ulama (MUI), 1, 214–16, 237, 239, 246–7
inheritance rights, 51, 55
International Conferences on Population and Development (ICPD), 169, 172
International Covenant on Civil and Political Rights (ICCPR)
  cultural modification, 109, 258
  methods of implementation, 71, 80–1
  NSAs, 128–9
  State discretion, 66–7, see also Human Rights Committee (HRCee)

International Covenant on Economic, Social and Cultural Rights (ICESCR)
  methods of implementation, 72, 81
  NSAs, 128–33
  right to health, 168–72
  State discretion, 68, see also Committee on Economic, Social and Cultural Rights (ESCR Committee)
International Law Commission, 67–8, 70–2
Iraq, 96–7, 101–2
Islam and Islamic law
  compatibility with human rights law, 250–61
  concepts of feminism and gender, 241–6
  diversity and universal character, 290–1
  fatwas, 1–2, 216–20
  importance to human rights implementation, 270–5
  Indonesia
    child marriage, 2, 254
    female genital mutilation/cutting (FGM/C), 237–8, 257–8
    law and institutions, 210–15
    Muslim feminists and feminist reinterpretations of Islamic texts, 225–46
    polygamy, 238–40, 254
    role in reproductive health and family planning, 167, 200–2, 215–25, 236–41, 246–61, 263–7
  Islamic reservations, 33
  overview, 16–17, 165, 206–10
  ulama, 156–7, see also Indonesian Council of Ulama (MUI)
Italy, 101

Kenya, 51, 55
Kisii tribe (Kenya), 51

Lauren, Paul Gordon, 27–8
Lebanon, 104
Lee, Kuan Yew, 30

legal pluralism, 267
  compatibility with international law, 250–61
legalisation and legalism of human rights, 7–10, 76–80, 276–81
Lenzerini, Federico, 27, 38
Liberia, 104, 106
Lukito, Ratno, 242

Macedonia, 96–7
Mahmood, Saba, 233, 235
Marcoes-Natsir, Lies, 213, 215, 223, 230, 243
marriage
  child marriage, 2, 84–5, 254
  polygamy in Indonesia, 238–40, 254
Marshall, Katherine, 218–19, 290
McBeth, Adam, 122, 157
media, 83–4, 134, 139
Menchik, Jeremy, 17–18, 233
Merry, Sally Engle, 39, 51–2, 201, 242
Mir-Hosseini, Ziba, 226, 228
Morsink, Johannes, 25
Muhammadiyah (Indonesia), 215–21, 246–7
MUI, see Indonesian Council of Ulama
Mulia, Siti Musdah, 229–30, 239, 266
Muslim feminists in Indonesia
  background, 225–7
  concepts of feminism and gender, 241–6
  reinterpretations of Islamic texts, 227–46
Muslimat (Indonesia), 213–14, 239
Mutua, Makau, 31, 36

Nahdlatul Ulama (NU) (Indonesia), 194, 212–22, 237, 239, 246–7
Nasyiatul 'Aisyiyah (Indonesia), 213
National Congress of Female Muslim Clerics (Indonesia), 1
National Human Rights Institutes (NHRIs), 95
the Netherlands, 275–6, 283, 291
New Zealand, 103
non-governmental organisations (NGOs), 118–19, 123, 134–5
non-state actors (NSAs), 114–63
  and reproductive rights, 177–80
  corporations, 119–20, 132, 150
  in relation to social institutions, 117
  media, 83–5, 134, 139
  non-governmental organisations (NGOs), 118–19, 123, 134–5
  obligations and responsibilities
    in declarations and instruments, 121–5, 284
    private healthcare providers, 143–60
    under treaties, 125–43
  overview, 114–20
  parents and families, 138–9
  recognition by treaty bodies, 83–4, 102–5, 161–2, 259–63
Norms on the Responsibilities of Transnational Corporations and Other Business Enterprises with Regard to Human Rights, 119–20
Nowak, Manfred, 147
NSAs, see non-state actors
NU, see Nahdlatul Ulama
Nurmila, Nina, 227–8, 230–1, 242, 244
Nyamu-Musembi, Celestine, 46, 48–9, 54, 56–7, 85, 236, 248

P3M, see Centre for the Development of Pesantren and Society
polygamy in Indonesia, 238–40, 254
Portugal, 104
poverty reduction, 58–61
privatisation and private sector providers, 143–60, 180

Rahima (Indonesia), 224, 234
ratification, 4, 64, 88
receptor approach (Zwart), 11–12, 44, 47–50
Renteln, Alison Dundes, 53
reproductive health and family planning, 164–267
  impact of gendered decision-making, 191–2
  in Indonesia
    family planning programme, 182–90

law and policy, 180–90
rationale for case study, 18–19, 165
role of Islam, 200–2, 215–25, 236–41, 246–61, 263–7
socio-cultural determinants, 190–205
rights under international law, 170–6
role of NSAs, 177–80
research methodology, 16
reservations, 18, 33
Rinaldo, Rachel, 17
Robinson, Mary, 27, 287
Rodley, Sir Nigel, 117, 124, 155, 158
Russia, 107

San Marino, 96
Seibert-Fohr, Anja, 95
Senegal, 49
sexual orientation and gender identity, 96, 100
Slovakia, 99, 105
Slovenia, 104–5, 107
social enterprises, 282
social institutions
  definition and relation to NSAs, 14–15, 117, see also Islam and Islamic law; non-state actors (NSAs)
South Africa, 11, 47, 50
State discretion, 5–6, 67–71, 89
State-centricity, 4, 120–1, 160
States, study recommendations, 287–8, 291
Statute of the International Court of Justice, 120–1
Sudan, 102
Suriname, 95–6

Tajikistan, 101–3
Third World Approaches to International Law (TWAIL), 29, 31–2
Timor-Leste, 104
Tomuschat, Christian, 110
treaty bodies
  Concluding Observations, 94
  general approach to NSAs, 160–2, 259–63, 284–5
  Reporting Guidelines, 90–3
  role in implementation, 88–93
  study recommendations, 162, 289, see also Committee on Economic, Social and Cultural Rights (ESCR Committee); Committee on the Elimination of All Forms of Discrimination against Women (CEDAW Committee); Committee on the Elimination of Racial Discrimination (CERD); Committee on the Rights of the Child (CRC Committee); Human Rights Committee (HRCee)
Turkmenistan, 105

UDHR, see Universal Declaration of Human Rights
ulama, 212, see also Indonesian Council of Ulama (MUI)
United Arab Emirates, 104
United Nations Population Fund (UNFPA), 261
United States, 25, 275, 282–3
Universal Declaration of Human Rights (UDHR)
  importance of, 21, 35–7
  in relation to NSAs, 2, 121–3, 128, 160
  right to health, 168, 178
  universality and Western bias, 23–9, 35
universality, 23–37, 41, 43

vernacularisation, 51–3, 242, 273–4
Vienna Convention on the Law of Treaties (VCLT), 69
Vienna Declaration, 36, 123

Wahid, Abdurrahman, 213
women
  concepts of feminism and gender in Islam, 241–6
  female ulama, 231
  representation in decision-making positions, 98

women (cont.)
  violence against, 96–7, *see also* Muslim feminists in Indonesia
women's rights
  inheritance rights and access to land, 51, 55
  reproductive rights, *see* marriage; reproductive health and family planning, *see also* Committee on the Elimination of All Forms of Discrimination against Women; Convention on the Elimination of All Forms of Discrimination against Women (CEDAW)
workers' rights, 131
World Conference on Human Rights, 36, 123
World Health Organization (WHO), 168

Zwart, Tom (receptor approach), 11–12, 44, 47–50